THE GERMAN–JEWISH DIALOGUE

The German–Jewish Dialogue illustrates the presence of Jews within German literature from the mid eighteenth century to the present day. It was in the eighteenth century that sympathetic observers first urged the admission of Jews in Germany and Austria to full civil rights, and that Jews began to speak for themselves as contributors to German literature and philosophy. Around 1800 Jewish women came forward as writers, though at first only in private letters; while the partial lifting of civil disabilities led the generation of Heine, Börne, and Marx into journalism and radical politics. Later in the nineteenth century the appeal of German culture spread to the traditional communities further east, in Poland and Galicia. In 1896 Theodor Herzl published his manifesto of Zionism, which encouraged the young generation of Jewish writers and intellectuals to seek ways of combining their deep loyalty to German and European culture with a new conception of Jewish identity centring on vital energies and religious impulses and conflicts. The National Socialists sought to extinguish the international humanism in which Jews were prominent, by means of expulsion, discrimination, and eventually genocide. Jewish survivors have commemorated the Holocaust in elegiac poetry and in fiction. Younger Jewish writers confront the question whether a Jew can still live in Germany, where both the denial and the admission of guilt impose unbearable strains.

For present-day readers, consciousness of the Holocaust and its aftermath can be an obstacle to appreciating the depth, complexity, and richness of Jews' involvement in German culture from the Enlightenment to the 1930s. This anthology is designed to show how the German–Jewish dialogue gave rise to great and subtle texts that are central to German literature.

RITCHIE ROBERTSON is Reader in German at Oxford University and a Fellow of St John's College. He is the author of *Kafka: Judaism, Politics, and Literature* (OUP, 1985), *Heine* (Peter Halban, 1988), and *The 'Jewish Question' in German Literature, 1749–1939* (OUP, 1999), and has translated several books from German.

OXFORD WORLD'S CLASSICS

*For almost 100 years Oxford World's Classics have brought
readers closer to the world's great literature. Now with over 700
titles—from the 4,000-year-old myths of Mesopotamia to the
twentieth century's greatest novels—the series makes available
lesser-known as well as celebrated writing.*

*The pocket-sized hardbacks of the early years contained
introductions by Virginia Woolf, T. S. Eliot, Graham Greene,
and other literary figures which enriched the experience of reading.
Today the series is recognized for its fine scholarship and
reliability in texts that span world literature, drama and poetry,
religion, philosophy and politics. Each edition includes perceptive
commentary and essential background information to meet the
changing needs of readers.*

OXFORD WORLD'S CLASSICS

The German–Jewish Dialogue

An Anthology of Literary Texts 1749–1993

Edited by
RITCHIE ROBERTSON

OXFORD
UNIVERSITY PRESS

Oxford University Press, Great Clarendon Street, Oxford OX2 6DP

Oxford New York
Athens Auckland Bangkok Bogotá Buenos Aires Calcutta
Cape Town Chennai Dar es Salaam Delhi Florence Hong Kong Istanbul
Karachi Kuala Lumpur Madrid Melbourne Mexico City Mumbai
Nairobi Paris São Paulo Singapore Taipei Tokyo Toronto Warsaw

and associated companies in Berlin Ibadan

Oxford is a registered trade mark of Oxford University Press

Published in the United States
by Oxford University Press Inc., New York

For textual copyright details see pp. 381–2

Editorial matter © Ritchie Robertson 1999

First published as an Oxford World's Classics paperback 1999

British Library Cataloguing in Publication Data
Data available

Library of Congress Cataloging in Publication Data
Data available
ISBN 0-19-283910-1

1 3 5 7 9 10 8 6 4 2

Typeset by RefineCatch Limited, Bungay, Suffolk
Printed in Great Britain by
Cox & Wyman Ltd., Reading, Berkshire

CONTENTS

INTRODUCTION

This anthology is intended to introduce English-speaking readers to an important aspect of German culture and a major body of Jewish writing. Of the twenty-five items, twenty are by Jewish writers on various aspects of Jewish experience, while the remaining five illustrate the responses of Gentile writers to the Jews in their midst. The items, many of which have never been translated before, are chosen not only for their representative character but for their literary merit. Although literature is understood here in a broad sense that includes letters, diaries, and biographies, my aim has been not to rival but to complement the massive anthology by Paul Mendes-Flohr and Jehuda Reinharz, *The Jew in the Modern World*, to which the reader is directed for a wider historical framework. The only passage common to both anthologies is one paragraph from a letter by Rahel Levin.

The title of the anthology corresponds to the self-understanding of German Jews by insisting on their membership of German culture. 'If anyone disputes my German character,' wrote the nineteenth-century liberal Jewish politician Gabriel Riesser, 'I consider him a murderer.' To understand such a statement, we need to think our way back to the period, lasting about a century and a half, when German-speaking culture was most intensely creative. Philosophy from Kant to Wittgenstein, music from Haydn to Schoenberg, science from Alexander von Humboldt to Einstein, and literature from Goethe to Kafka, are only the most obvious of German cultural achievements. The second name in each instance illustrates the crucial role of German Jews in German culture.

German culture, thus understood, was remote from politics. As in the Italian Renaissance, cultural energy accompanied political disunity. In 1800 there was no place called Germany; there were many large and small German states, with a traditional primacy accorded to Austria as the seat of the Holy Roman Emperor. The founding of the German Empire in 1871 excluded Austria and the German-speaking population of the Habsburg Empire's major cities. The narrowly chauvinistic demand for a single nation incorporating all 'Germans' and excluding others runs like an undercurrent through the nineteenth century, becoming particularly audible around 1880. The trauma of defeat in the First World War made many Germans seek a scapegoat and find it in the half-imaginary figure of 'the Jew'. Actual German Jews, still attached to the humane legacy of Kant and Goethe, were unprepared for the violent resentment of the other Germany.

After the Holocaust it was hard to understand the attachment of past generations to a German humanism that seemed belied by Nazism. Hence Gershom Scholem, the historian of Jewish mysticism, thundered in 1964: 'The Jews attempted a dialogue with the Germans, starting from all possible points of view and situations, demandingly, imploringly, and entreatingly, servile and defiant, with a dignity employing all manner of tones and a godforsaken lack of dignity.' To Scholem, a lifelong Zionist who had left Germany for Palestine in 1923, Jewish attachment to Germany seemed a huge and fatal mistake. But if we adopt a more historical perspective, we shall see better how the position of Jews in Germany and Austria before the rise of Hitler was sometimes painfully, but also fruitfully, ambivalent. Admission to German, and hence to European, culture was a liberating and stimulating experience. But their position in German society was insecure. They received full civil rights in Austria only in 1867, in Germany in 1871; and thereafter subtle forms of discrimination continued, while crude anti-Semitic utterances became increasingly hard to ignore. Their acculturation was out of step with their social assimilation. Yet this very imbalance, this uneasy sense of marginality, was itself a spur to creativity.

The German–Jewish dialogue begins in the eighteenth century. Most Jews still lived in self-enclosed rural communities, some in urban ghettos. Their isolation resulted both from the all-embracing demands of the Torah (the Jewish Law) and from the many restrictions imposed on them by governments, limiting their rights of residence, obliging them to specialize in trade by denying them access to most professions, and requiring them to pay special taxes. Theological animus against Jews for their failure to recognize Jesus as the Messiah was already fading, and the Enlightenment's arguments for the toleration of diverse religions on the basis of their shared ethical principles were gaining ground, while enlightened administrators were arguing that states should make full use of their human resources instead of excluding some groups from unrestricted participation in social life. One of the first proponents of Jewish emancipation was the young Gotthold Ephraim Lessing, who, having abandoned the study of theology, was making a living as a free-lance writer, something still unusual in Germany. In 1754 he described his play *The Jews*, written five years earlier, as 'the result of very serious reflection on the disgraceful oppression under which a nation must groan, whom, I should have thought, a Christian cannot contemplate without a kind of reverence'. Later, having become embroiled in controversy with a conservative theologian over the character of the Scriptures as divine revelation, Lessing provided a rejoinder in dramatic form with his play *Nathan the Wise* (1779), where a saintly Jew expresses the ethical values that, being common to the three monotheisms Judaism, Christianity, and Islam, should, in Lessing's view, make it unnecessary to argue over which if any of their doctrines are divinely revealed. Lessing's plays plead most effectively for toleration by presenting vivid and likeable characters and by exposing prejudice as foolish rather than wicked. The warning given by the Traveller in *The Jews* against generalizing about entire nations is a truly enlightened sentiment, especially as it undermines the Baron's absurd confidence that he can recognize a Jew at first sight. These plays form part of a large body of philo-Semitic eighteenth-century dramas and novels that seek to overcome our prejudices by holding up noble Jews for our admiration; the main English example is Richard Cumberland's *The Jew* (1794). The weakness of philo-Semitism, however, is that in presenting exceptional Jews, it seems to confirm prejudice against ordinary Jews. Similar criticisms, as we shall see, were to be levelled against some well-intentioned portrayals of good Jews in German fiction after the Second World War.

German Jews, meanwhile, were seeking actively to improve their own lives. Through commercial contacts with Gentiles, they became aware of the exciting intellectual innovations of the Enlightenment. A traditional education, based on Talmud study and excluding any secular knowledge, seemed unattractive by comparison. In the 1750s Jewish communities witnessed a much-publicized dispute between Jonathan Eybeschütz and Jacob Emden, two eminent rabbis of Altona near Hamburg, in which Emden accused Eybeschütz of supplying pregnant women with protective amulets containing covert references to the magic powers of Sabbatai Zvi, the false Messiah whose appearance had convulsed European Jewry a century earlier. Gentile intellectuals, meanwhile, were responding to Newton's recasting of the physical universe, to Leibniz's philosophical case for providence, to Shaftesbury's arguments for social cohesion based on man's innate sociability, and to Voltaire's popularization of philosophical scepticism.

Jews who wanted to explore this new intellectual world could best do so in Berlin. The capital of Prussia, a sizeable state ruled by an enlightened despot, Frederick the Great, it had a large Jewish population: between 300 and 400 Jewish families, many headed by rich bankers or factory-owners, enjoyed royal protection, while a perhaps equal population of community officials, tradesmen, and domestic servants had their presence tolerated. This situation created exceptional opportunities for social and intellectual intermingling between Gentiles and Jews. The Berlin Enlightenment and its aftermath, from the age of Lessing to that of Hegel, is among the most important settings for the German–Jewish dialogue.

Famous partners in this dialogue were Lessing and Moses Mendelssohn. The son of a scribe in Dessau, Mendelssohn arrived in Berlin in 1743, learnt standard German, French, and Latin, became a friend of Lessing and other Berlin intellectuals, and immersed himself in Enlightenment thought. He not only acquired a high reputation through his publications on metaphysics and aesthetics, but demonstrated by his existence that a Jew could contribute fully to the intellectual life of Europe. Many Enlighteners, notably Voltaire (who lived in Berlin from 1750 to 1753 at the summons of Frederick the Great), thought Judaism a hopelessly superstitious religion. Episodes like the Emden–Eybeschütz dispute seemed to confirm their view. Mendelssohn set himself the task of redefining Judaism. Following the example of the medieval philosopher Maimonides, who in his *Guide for the Perplexed* had sought to show that the Torah was fully compatible with reason, Mendelssohn argued in his treatise *Jerusalem* that Judaism depended on reason alone; it had no doctrines or dogmas that required the authority of revelation; what was revealed to Moses at Sinai was not a set of doctrines but a way of living which was embodied in the Law. Thus Mendelssohn hoped both to show that Judaism was compatible with the rational deism favoured by the Enlightenment, and, by emphasizing its ethical seriousness, to preserve it from the destructive effects of

Voltairean scepticism. He succeeded in the former aim, founding an image of the rational Jew which became central to the self-understanding of German Jews and to their identification with the German culture typified by Lessing and Kant. But his theoretical defence of the Jewish Law could not prevent it from being eroded in practice. As Jews mingled more with Gentiles, they became increasingly reluctant to wear different clothes, eat different food, observe a different weekly routine, and devote time to religious exercises that seemed incompatible with reason. A much-quoted letter from the artist Daniel Chodowiecki reports in 1783 that the upper-class Jews of Berlin eat forbidden foods, buy and sell on the Sabbath, and ignore fast-days. Of Mendelssohn's six children, all but one converted to Christianity after his death. His successor as leader of the Berlin Jewish community, David Friedländer, wrote in 1799 to a well-known liberal theologian, Provost Teller, suggesting that he and other prominent Jews should escape legal restrictions by converting to Christianity, provided they could be assured that the apparent dogmas of their new religion were only metaphorical. Teller, no doubt dismayed at the effects of his liberalism, replied discouragingly. Nevertheless, in the generations after Mendelssohn the choice of religion often seemed a matter of indifference, and nominal conversion an easy way of escaping from tiresome burdens.

Mendelssohn's disciple Salomon Maimon, who testifies in his autobiography to his master's personal benevolence, illustrates this rejection of Judaism. Born in what was then Poland, Maimon escaped from what he considered the two tyrannies of the rabbinate and the aristocracy. He once displayed his defiant temperament when a rabbi, seeking to impress him, showed him a *shofar* (the ram's horn sounded at New Year) and asked: 'Do you know what this is?' to which Maimon replied: 'Yes! It is the horn of a goat,' whereupon the rabbi fell flat on his back with horror at such irreverence. This aggressive rejection of Jewish tradition is present also in Maimon's assertion that he is no longer part of the Jewish community.

While Mendelssohn wrote original philosophical treatises on Enlightenment themes, Maimon came forward as an expositor of the new philosophy of Kant. Kant's *Critique of Pure Reason* (1781), notorious from the outset for its difficulty, found several of its first commentators among Jews, not only Maimon but also the Berlin physician Markus Herz and the essayist Lazarus Bendavid. It has often been pointed out that Jewish writers were particularly active in editing and expounding the great works of German literature. The tradition of Jewish Kantians extends to Hermann Cohen in the early twentieth century. An intense devotion to Goethe is evident from the early letters, translated here, of Rahel Levin, who later promoted a cult of Goethe at a time when the obscurity of his late writings, and his opposition to the then dominant Romantic movement, made him marginal to literary life. The textual study of Goethe was initiated by the convert Michael Bernays (a relative by marriage of Sigmund Freud), and some of the most original twentieth-century approaches to Goethe came from the Jewish critics Georg Simmel, Friedrich Gundolf, and Walter Benjamin.

Rahel Levin, later known as Rahel Varnhagen after her marriage to the Prussian diplomat Varnhagen von Ense, was the hostess of one of the best-known Jewish salons in Berlin. The first of these crystallized around Henriette Herz, wife of Markus Herz. The salon provided a setting for Jews and Gentiles to meet and for intelligent women to escape in some measure from the confinement which Rahel bewails in her letters. Aristocrats and professional men, academics and writers, came together with cultivated women to discuss intellectual topics and often to hear informal lectures; the atmosphere provided relief from the stultifying boredom of conventional upper-class gatherings described so sarcastically by Goethe in *The Sorrows of Young Werther* (1774). From Berlin the salon spread to Vienna, introduced by Fanny von Arnstein: the daughter of a leading Berlin banker, she married the contractor Nathan Arnstein, who was raised to the nobility by the Emperor of Austria in 1798.

Such encounters between Jews and Gentiles also had an influence on legal emancipation. Through Berlin society Mendelssohn became friendly with the civil servant Christian Wilhelm von Dohm and persuaded him to write the treatise advocating Jewish emancipation, *On the Civil Improvement of the Jews* (1781); while a generation later, the frequenters of Rahel's salon included the Berlin civil servant Wilhelm von Humboldt (brother of the explorer and scientist Alexander), who not only founded the University of Berlin (now called the Humboldt University) in 1810 but also drafted proposals for granting civil rights to Jews. Dohm's and Humboldt's proposals represent radically different approaches to Jewish emancipation. Dohm argues that, through no fault of their own, the restrictions imposed on Jews have corrupted their character, and that while being granted civil rights and allowed to continue practising their religion, they should also be induced to change their educational practices and professional occupations so as to improve their character and prove their suitability for citizenship. Humboldt, by contrast, wants the Jews to be given full civil rights without strings attached, as had been done in France by the National Assembly in 1791; they should be emancipated as individuals, not as members of a religious group. While neither set of proposals directly became law, the emancipation of Jews in Germany was eventually carried out in the spirit of Dohm, in that legal provisions applied to Jews as a distinct group and were conceived as an 'emancipation contract': Jews' emancipation was seen as requiring them continually to demonstrate their fitness to be citizens. The long-term result was to reinforce the distinctness of Jews at the same time as allowing them to merge with the rest of the population. On the one hand, the Jews were invited to assimilate; on the other, they were reminded of their singularity.

The legal emancipation of the Jews in the German-speaking world began in 1781 with the Patents of Toleration issued by the reforming Austrian Emperor Joseph II, allowing Jews to practise agriculture, trades, and professions, to set up large businesses, and to attend schools and universities. The German states were slow to follow. The first Jews anywhere in the German-speaking world to enjoy full civil rights were those living in the territories west of the Rhine which were annexed by France and brought under the Napoleonic Code in 1798. The Prussian reform movement pioneered by enlightened bureaucrats obtained civil rights for Jews there in 1812, though not the full equality Humboldt would have liked: Jews were still excluded from state employment, which in Germany comprised all manner of officials from judges to postmen. After the final defeat of Napoleon and the reorganization of Europe by the conservative powers at the Congress of Vienna in 1815, the rights of Jews in different German territories varied widely and were sometimes substantially diminished. Thus, in Prussia in 1822 Jews were excluded from teaching-posts in universities and schools unless they adopted Christianity; this regulation induced Heine, among many others, to make an opportunistic (and shamefaced) conversion in 1825. The revolutions of 1848, in which Jews, especially in Vienna, played a prominent part, introduced citizenship independent of religious confession for all Germans, but these rights were repealed with the suppression of the revolutions. However, their long-term effect was to strengthen liberalism and enhance Jewish self-esteem. In the 1860s Jewish legal disabilities were repealed in many German states; in 1867 Jews throughout the Austro-Hungarian Empire received full civil rights; in 1869 the North German Confederation enacted a similar measure, and with the founding of the German Empire in 1871 all Jews in Germany received full legal emancipation.

Just as progress towards emancipation was only gradual, so was the tendency of Jews to assimilate through conversion and intermarriage. Throughout the nineteenth century, despite considerable social mixing, Jews tended to live in the same neighbourhoods and belong to the same associations, so that historians now describe them as preserving a distinct subculture. Within this subculture they could participate in German culture while being only partially integrated into German society. Moreover, they were rendered visible as Jews by their concentration in certain professions, like medicine and journalism, and by their predominant membership of the middle class.

To the many impulses that tended to keep Jews distinct, another was added with the rise of German nationalism at the beginning of the nineteenth century. Modern nationalism finds its theorist in Johann Gottfried Herder, whose *Ideas on the Philosophy of Human History* (1784–91) interpreted history as an organic sequence of civilizations, each sustained by a particular nation or *Volk*. Every *Volk* had its own gifts and its own spirit (*Volksgeist*) which was expressed through its culture, especially through such forms of creativity as poetry and music. The Persian, the Greek, and the Roman nations had dominated history in turn; now came the Germans, who would be succeeded by the Slavs. The Jews did not quite fit into Herder's scheme. Since they survived as a distinct race 2,000 years after the flourishing of their culture, he once described them by the fateful term 'parasite'. But by linking modern Jews to those of the Old Testament, and celebrating in another work the spirit of Hebrew poetry, Herder unwittingly founded a conception of Jewish nationhood which was to inspire the Zionism of Martin Buber and bear literary fruit in the poetry of Else Lasker-Schüler.

Conceptions of the German *Volk* were enlisted in response to the humiliating defeat of Prussia by Napoleon's troops at the battles of

Jena and Auerstädt in 1806. The depths of the German *Volksgeist* were explored by the philosopher Johann Gottlieb Fichte in his *Lectures to the German Nation* (1807–8), delivered in French-occupied Berlin, and by the brothers Grimm with their research into medieval German culture and their compilation of German folk-tales. The story 'The Jew in the Thorn-Bush' gives the Jew a place in the popular imagination as the demonic other, the adversary who, just because he is a Jew, is sure to be a villain seeking to harm good Germans. In some circles anti-Semitism became respectable, aided by a fashionable reaction against the ideals of the Enlightenment. Some young Romantic writers, especially Clemens Brentano and Achim von Arnim, despite their attendance at Berlin salons, openly denounced Jews; their 'Christian-German Dining Club' was entertained at its first meeting in March 1811 with a would-be humorous speech by Brentano attacking 'Philistines' (conventional middle-class people) and Jews, whom he associated disparagingly with 'humanity and enlightenment'. A couple of academics published pamphlets denying that Jews could be citizens of a Christian German state. And in the summer of 1819 the people of several cities (Würzburg, Heidelberg, Frankfurt, Hamburg), irritated by economic hardship, vented their anger on the Jews as scapegoats. Crowds uttering the old Crusader war-cry 'Hep hep' (*Hierosolyma est perdita*—Jerusalem is lost) attacked and plundered Jewish shops before order was restored by the police and by public-spirited citizens. Was there any connection between these riots and the distasteful follies of young Romantics? Rahel Varnhagen at least thought so, writing an embittered letter to her brother: 'The hypocritical new love for the Christian religion—God forgive me my sin!—for the Middle Ages, with their art, poetry, and faith, stirs up the people to the only atrocity in which it remembers its old liberties—attacking the Jews.' The Hep-Hep riots, as they are known, soon died down. Whether they were the last expression of an old popular anti-Semitism, or the first premonition of a new anti-Semitism artificially promoted by demagogues, they seemed only a minor disturbance in the nineteenth century's progress towards civil equality.

At the same period, a new generation of Jewish intellectuals was entering the public sphere, led by Ludwig Börne, Heinrich Heine, and Karl Marx. They were only loosely, if at all, attached to Judaism, but were intensely interested in the intellectual currents of the modern world, and drawn to radical politics. They adopted the new profession of journalism, cultivated witty and biting styles modelled on Lessing and Voltaire, and associated themselves with varieties of early Socialism and with the political and sexual radicalism of the 'Young German' movement of the 1830s. Other Jewish writers emerged as contributors to nineteenth-century Germany's large body of realist fiction. The leading figures were Berthold Auerbach, famous especially for his *Black Forest Village Tales* (1843–53), and Fanny Lewald, known as 'the German George Sand', for her novels about social problems.

Of these writers, it is Heine who shows the most complex attitude towards Jewishness and Judaism. He was fascinated by the German past that was being explored by philologists like the Grimms. Instead of trying to preserve the Jewish past like Mendelssohn, or rejecting it like Friedländer, he wanted to explore it through historical research. In the early 1820s, while studying at Göttingen and Berlin, Heine belonged to a scholarly society devoted to the 'Wissenschaft des Judentums' (academic study of Judaism). His contribution was to begin writing a historical novel, *The Rabbi of Bacherach*, which evoked the Jews of medieval Germany in the way that Sir Walter Scott had described medieval Britain. Heine's interest in the Jewish past is also apparent in the long poem given here, 'Jehuda ben Halevy', which draws on the scholarly study by Michael Sachs of the Jewish poets of medieval Spain.

Other Jewish writers found new subject-matter in the Eastern European ghetto. In Bohemia, Moravia, Poland, Galicia (the north-easternmost province of the Austrian Empire), and Russia, millions of Jews still led a traditional life in relatively closed communities dominated by religious practice. Many, especially in Galicia and the Ukraine, were 'Hasidim'. Hasidism, a revival movement, which placed inward devotion above external practice, had been founded in the eighteenth century by Israel ben Eliezer, known as the Baal Shem ('Master of the Name'). Hasidic leaders claimed the power to ascend to Heaven and intercede for their followers. They established courts attended by large numbers of clients; Salomon Maimon visited a leading Hasidic centre and gave in his autobiography a satirical description of what he considered its frauds and superstitions. For Western readers, fictional accounts of Eastern Jewish life could seem intriguingly exotic; they could evoke affectionate nostalgia for the lifestyle of one's own great-grandparents; or they could arouse indignation on behalf of people denied access to Western culture by a superstitious rabbinate. The latter was the response that Karl Emil Franzos, the greatest writer of ghetto fiction, wanted to produce. His stories and travel sketches set in 'Half-Asia', the name he coined for the far east of Europe, assail both the intolerance of obscurantist Hasidim and the corruption of Habsburg bureaucrats, while pleading the cause of Jews who seek access to a humane culture typified by Lessing and Schiller.

Alongside fiction about Jews by Jews, we find fiction about Jews by Gentiles, which presents readers nowadays with problems of understanding and evaluation. A succession of major novelists express impeccable liberal sentiments while depicting Jews in their fiction through stereotypes that now seem disturbing. Gustav Freytag's bestseller *Debit and Credit* (1855) presents a range of Jewish types dominated by the unscrupulous villain Veitel Itzig, the sworn enemy of Freytag's virtuous German hero. Wilhelm Raabe in *The Hungry Pastor* (1864) adopts a Dickensian fairy-tale mode to oppose good and evil in the persons of his dreamy German hero and his calculating Jewish villain, who, to make matters worse, changes his identity from Moses Freudenstein to the worldly and sophisticated Dr Theophil Stein. Theodor Fontane's Jewish figures include the seductive Ebba Rosenberg in *Beyond Recall* (1891) and the humorously treated but untrustworthy traders in *The Stechlin* (1898). And Thomas Mann, a declared philo-Semite who married into a family of converted Jews, innocently caused great offence by his depiction of Jewish plutocrats in 'The Blood of the Volsungs' (written in 1905 but not published till 1921). Two considerations are relevant. First: in all these texts the Jew typified social mobility in a society that until recently had been or had at least seemed stable and unchanging; hence he or she became the focus, and sometimes the scapegoat, for the unease and ambivalence generated by social change. Secondly: since German liberalism emancipated Jews as Jews, not as citizens indistinguishable from any others, Jews in fiction tended to appear first and foremost as Jews, not as ordinary people who just happened to be Jewish. Hence we have in German fiction a great gallery of memorable Jewish characters, including Naphta in Mann's *The Magic Mountain* (1924) and Breisacher and Fitelberg in his *Doctor Faustus* (1947).

Saar's story 'Seligmann Hirsch' offers a partial exception to this rule, as the main figure is primarily a character study illustrating social insensitivity combined with a desperate need to be wanted— the kind of person we either guiltily avoid or endure with a sense of martyrdom; but it was natural to make such a character a social parvenu and a Jew among Gentiles. Stefan Zweig's story 'Book-Mendel' is based on the same model—an eccentric character explored by a narrator. In both stories, the narrator's reactions to the title figure are important. While Saar's narrator is intrigued and irritated by Hirsch, and finally sorry for him, Zweig's narrator admires Mendel's feats of memory as an eccentric homage to the life of the mind, but is anxious to distinguish Mendel's mental dexterity from the intuitive and creative operation of his own mind.

Anti-Semitism emerged as a public force in the 1870s. The triumphal nationalism of a newly founded Empire that had won a series of wars was disturbed by financial scandals involving Jews and by Jewish immigration across the Polish frontier. In an essay published in November 1879, the Prussian historian Heinrich von Treitschke described the Jews as an alien and disruptive element in Germany and claimed that many people were chorusing: 'The Jews are our misfortune!' Although his complaints may be seen as the misleading exaggerations of a conservative reluctant to criticize his fellow-Germans, they coincided with the foundation of an Anti-Semitic League in September 1879 by Wilhelm Marr, who coined the term 'anti-Semitism'. More generally, Treitschke's article helped to make anti-Semitism a widely acceptable viewpoint and to promote a steady flow of anti-Semitic polemic that made attentive German Jews continually uneasy. Meanwhile, in Austria the politician Karl Lueger fought his way to the mayoralty of Vienna with the aid of gross anti-Semitic rhetoric. The rapid changes brought to German and Austrian society by belated industrialization, the growth of finance, the decline of agriculture, and the swelling of cities like Berlin and Vienna, caused widespread alarm for which 'the Jews' provided a convenient scapegoat.

At the same period, the prestige of biology was lending an impetus to the pseudo-science of race. Then as now, Darwin's theories of evolution were illegitimately applied to human society. The evolutionary principle of the 'survival of the fittest' was thought to show that 'inferior' races must adapt or perish. Socially conditioned features, like the poor physique of undernourished Jewish immigrants, were interpreted as immutable racial qualities. The claims made by Richard Wagner in his polemic *Jewry in Music* (1850) that Jews could not master German properly were revived and elaborated into an argument that Jews could never be absorbed into German culture and society. In *The Foundations of the Nineteenth Century* (1899), the adoptive German Houston Stewart Chamberlain sketched vague but terrifying visions of islands of civilization inhabited by pure-blooded Aryans, around whom swirled a racial chaos. Such notions were to seize the imagination of Adolf Hitler. The old religious anti-Semitism was now replaced by a combination of economic and racial anti-Semitism which offered thoughtless or half-educated people an alluringly comprehensive explanation for what was wrong with the world.

Admittedly, anti-Semitism could still be dismissed as impotent rhetoric. Although the German Empire under the chancellorship of Bismarck created solidarity by identifying public enemies, these enemies included Catholics (the objects of the 'Kulturkampf' in the mid-1870s) and Socialists (banned from political activities from 1878 to 1890), but not Jews, while the explicitly anti-Semitic political parties were short-lived and insignificant. However, anti-Semitism became an integral part of a right-wing outlook that idealized a pre-industrial, rural Germany; while, despite the efforts of the Socialist leader August Bebel to dispel it, anti-Semitism was common on the left, taking the form of hostility to Jewish capital.

Theodor Herzl, as Paris correspondent of the Vienna *New Free Press*, observed the strength of anti-Semitism in France and feared it could spread to Central Europe, while from 1881 onwards streams of Jewish refugees from pogroms in Tsarist Russia passed through Germany, mostly on their way via Hamburg to Britain and America. Herzl concluded that the Jews needed a state of their own, and produced a blueprint for it in *The Jewish State* (1896). He was not the originator of Jewish nationalism: anticipations can be found in *Rome and Jerusalem* (1862) by the Communist Moses Hess and in *Autoemancipation* (1882) by the Russian Jewish doctor Leo Pinsker; but he initiated Zionism as a concrete political movement.

It was left to others, above all to the philosopher and religious thinker Martin Buber (1878–1965), to think afresh about Jewish identity and to call for a Jewish renaissance. The Jewish state imagined by Herzl is a liberal European state transplanted to another continent, with Viennese-style coffee-houses to make the immigrants feel at home. Buber, however, rejected the café-haunting Jewish journalist, along with his ancestor the ghetto-bound Talmudist, as degenerate types produced by the Diaspora. Brought up by his grandparents in Galicia, Buber early came in contact with traditional Hasidic communities; and when, as a student of philosophy in Vienna, he embraced Zionism, he also thought it necessary to rediscover the authentic Jew. He first followed the lead given by Herder and looked back to biblical times. When they had their own territory and their own language, the Jews were a harmonious people of farmers, warriors, prophets, and poets. But even modern Jews, according to Buber, could discover their true Jewishness by looking within themselves and experiencing a mystical sense of solidarity with their people. Although Buber's early orations, coloured by the racial psychology of his age, now make strange reading, they appealed powerfully to small groups of young, idealistic Zionists. Buber also sought to dismantle the image of the rational Jew propagated by Mendelssohn and display the passionate, mystical character of the authentic Jew. To this end he devoted himself to the study of Hasidism and translated into a rather precious, literary German many inspiring anecdotes about Hasidic holy men. His Hasidic books, beginning with *The Tales of Rabbi Nachman* (1906) and *The Legend of the Baal Shem* (1908), introduced a large and enthusiastic readership to an unfamiliar side of Judaism.

Buber's influence in reshaping the self-understanding of German-Jewish intellectuals cannot be overestimated. It was not uncontroversial. Gershom Scholem was initially inspired by Buber, and by a range of religious and prophetic writers from Nietzsche to Rilke; but when he got to know Walter Benjamin in 1915 he rejected Buber, deriding the notion of the 'Jewish experience', and soon afterwards began devoting himself to a lifelong study of Jewish mysticism understood as an objective system rather than a subjective experience. Scholem pointed out later that Buber's interpretation of Hasidism was based only on the tales and hagiographies, not on the sermons and treatises which were at least as copious a part of Hasidic literature. But his objection, however well-founded, ignores the fact that Buber was not writing an academic study but seeking to arouse his Jewish readers to a new conception of themselves.

Those who responded to Buber included Else Lasker-Schüler, whose *Hebrew Ballads* (1913) depict intense and primitive passions among the 'wild Jews' of the Old Testament. Sharing Buber's disapproval of the effects of the Diaspora on modern Jews, Lasker-Schüler once declared that they should give up the name 'Jews' and call themselves Hebrews instead. Her story 'The Wonder-Working Rabbi of Barcelona' combines diverse Jewish traditions—miracle-working rabbis are a feature of Hasidism, yet the story is set in medieval Spain—in a curious, original style to evoke a kind of mythic consciousness, antithetical to the Enlightenment image of the rational Jew. Franz Kafka, though not impressed by Buber's oratory, sought him out in Berlin in February 1914 and consulted him about the 'unjust judges' of Psalm 82, a text which seems connected to the novel *The Trial* which Kafka wrote later that year; and two of Kafka's stories were published in Buber's Zionist periodical *The Jew*. Later Nelly Sachs, whose early work derives from Christian legends and from Rilke, began exploring Judaism with the aid of Buber's Hasidic stories, supplemented with extracts from the Kabbalah in Scholem's translation.

Buber's new conception of Jewish identity converged with the image being formed independently by the Viennese writer Richard Beer-Hofmann. In September 1898 Beer-Hofmann wrote a lullaby for his newly born eldest child which evokes the continuity of the race as a corrective to the solitude of the individual. It ends:

> Are you sleeping, Miriam, my child?
> We are but banks, and in us there flows
> Blood of the past—to the future it goes,
> Blood of our fathers, proud, restless and wild.
> *All* are within us. Who feels alone?
> You are their life—their life is your own—
> Sleep, my Miriam, my life, my own!

This poem expressed the sense of identity felt by the generation that absorbed Buber's teaching. Beer-Hofmann went on to depict the rediscovery of an ancient Jewish identity, rooted in the Orient, in his impressionist novel *George's Death* (1900), while his metaphysical drama *Jacob's Dream* (1919), intended as the prologue to a series of plays about King David, undertakes a bold inquiry into the special relationship of the Jewish people to God and into the justification of the suffering that He apparently imposes on them. Beer-Hofmann's play, far too little known, has acquired an additional resonance in the aftermath of the Holocaust.

While Buber's redefinition of Jewish identity appealed to a number of writers and intellectuals, German Jewry as a whole continued a gradual process of integration. In 1912 Kafka attended a lecture by the demographer Felix Theilhaber who argued that thanks to conversion and intermarriage German Jews were gradually vanishing into the general population. On the other hand, anti-Semitic prejudice, producing various forms of social exclusion, exerted the opposite pressure. By the 1890s some Jews with little attachment to Judaism were refusing to convert because it would have felt like a betrayal. One of them was Herzl, who wrote in 1893: 'One cannot desert the "faith of one's fathers", even when one no longer has it.' The First World War was an important watershed. Jews were blamed for domestic privations; in 1916 the German army ordered a census of Jews serving in the front line, implying that, as rumour had it, many were shirking their duty. The results of the census were never released. It almost certainly found that Jews were over-represented in front-line warfare. But by its very existence the census made German Jews feel distrusted and rejected. Germany's unexpected defeat after the Allied offensive in September 1918, and the subsequent revolutionary upheavals—the Spartacist uprising in Berlin in January 1919, the Socialist seizure of power in Bavaria followed by the Munich Soviet of April 1919—in which Jewish radicals were conspicuous, further strengthened anti-Semitism. In 1920 there appeared in the West *The Protocols of the Elders of Zion*, a crude forgery originating with the Tsarist secret police. It claimed that the First Zionist Congress organized by Herzl in 1897 had really been an occasion for Jewish conspirators to plan to take over the world by using democracy and the press to turn the Gentile population into a herd of ignorant slaves. Though soon exposed as a fake, the *Protocols* formed part of a body of paranoid and anti-Semitic writing which notably included *Mein Kampf*, dictated by Hitler to a secretary during his brief imprisonment for trying to start an uprising in Munich.

Insecurity and marginality may stimulate creativity. It was especially in Vienna under the anti-Semitic mayor Lueger, and in Germany during the precarious Weimar Republic, that a German–Jewish culture flourished. Some of its representatives responded to marginality by adopting universalist creeds that erased the differences between them and the majority. Thus psychoanalysis, whose early pioneers were predominantly Jews, was presented as a scientific theory based on biology which could not only explain the relation between the intellect and the emotions but account for all cultural phenomena—art, religion, politics—irrespective of historical differences. Socialism, to which many Jews were attracted, offered itself as an ethical politics rising above differences of nationality. The Institute of Social Research, founded at Frankfurt in 1923 and associated especially with Theodor Adorno and Max Horkheimer, went further by seeking to understand modern mass culture as a system of domination, in contrast to the liberating function which art had briefly possessed in the age of Goethe and Schiller. A similar homage to classicism may be seen in the work of the Warburg Institute, opened in 1926 for the study of the classical tradition in European art. And the humanism of the German Enlightenment underlies the neo-Kantian idealism of Hermann Cohen and the phenomenology of Edmund Husserl.

In diverse ways, German Jews affirmed a cultural tradition while exploring, questioning, and innovating. Although anti-Semites claimed that Jews were destructive in corroding old certainties, their innovations show a strong element of intelligent conservatism which has not been sufficiently stressed. A violent break with the past can be found in the vitalist novels of Hans Henry Jahnn, in the taboo-smashing poetry and plays of the young Brecht, and in the experiments of Dadaism, but rarely in the work of Jewish writers. Arthur Schnitzler anticipated Joyce by using stream-of-consciousness technique in *Lieutenant Gustl* (1901) and *Fräulein Else* (1924), without sacrificing the pleasures of realist narrative; Joseph Roth's polished and subtle fiction similarly retains the virtues of narrative coherence and empathy with its characters while increasingly invoking the mythic and symbolic overtones present not only in 'The Leviathan' but also in his most explicitly Jewish novel, *Job: The Story of a Simple Man* (1930). The Zionist Arnold Zweig made a realist story into a universal parable of justice in *The Dispute over Sergeant Grischa* (1927), while Stefan Zweig continued the nineteenth-century tradition of the Novelle and Lion Feuchtwanger and Jakob Wassermann reached a wide public with novels whose popularity has led them to be unfairly disparaged by academic critics. Kafka, who might seem an extreme modernist, was in fact conservative in his literary tastes, numbering among his 'literary blood-brothers' classic writers like Kleist and Grillparzer and masters of nineteenth-century realism like Flaubert and Dostoevsky. The most outspoken conservative among Jewish writers was Karl Kraus, who attacked the journalistic corruption of language and imagination with an intricate prose style and appeals to the cultural authority of Goethe and Shakespeare, yet retained a discriminating appreciation of new writing which enabled him to praise Lasker-Schüler and Brecht.

This deeply civilized German-Jewish culture, exceptional in its devotion to the life of the mind, was destroyed or dispersed by the National Socialists. About half of Germany's 600,000 Jews managed to escape the Holocaust by emigrating. The Warburg Institute moved to London, the Frankfurt School transferred their operations to New York. Husserl, to his grief, found himself supplanted by his disloyal pupil Heidegger. German psychoanalysis came under the leadership of Jung, who welcomed National Socialist neo-paganism as a revival of the German national psyche (though after the war he wrote a shrewd analysis of the German character entitled 'After the Catastrophe'). Books by Jewish authors and those sympathetic to them, like Thomas Mann, were ceremonially burned by German students and professors. Émigré scientists, scholars, and artists provided enormous enrichment to the cultural life of Britain and America, while their departure depleted German culture to an extent which Bernt Engelmann has tried to quantify in *Germany Without Jews* (1984). He points out that the contribution of German Jews to medicine, chemistry, physics, and mathematics, as well as to artistic creation and production, far exceeded their share of the population. The National Socialist aspiration for a homogeneous racial state inflicted damage on German culture which has not been and cannot be made good.

That, of course, is only a minor aspect of the moral catastrophe represented by the Holocaust. The resources of technology and bureaucracy were applied to exterminate the Jews of Europe, along with gypsies and homosexuals; meanwhile, the conquered Poles were intended to become illiterate slaves, and the campaign in Russia was pursued, as we now know, with deliberate brutality. If the Holocaust looks like bureaucracy gone mad, a little of its obsessively orderly character is indicated in Jurek Becker's story 'The Wall', set in the

Lodz Ghetto, where the inmates begin each day with a roll-call. This illustrates the senseless discipline imposed by Germans in ghettos and camps. 'The prohibitions are innumerable,' records Primo Levi in his recollections of Auschwitz, *If This is a Man* (1947): 'to approach nearer to the barbed wire than two yards; to sleep with one's jacket, or without one's pants, or with one's cap on one's head; to use certain washrooms or latrines. . .' In Becker's story this discipline is enforced by the Jewish ghetto police. It is they who terrorize the boy after catching him in the wrong hut. Such people were often ex-criminals, feared by other Jews for their brutality. Jews' acquiescence in their oppression, whether by active assistance or by passive obedience, has occasioned much controversy. Was it defensible as an attempt to protect their community? Or does it, as the psychoanalyst Bruno Bettelheim argued, illustrate a submissiveness to authority acquired over generations in the Eastern European ghetto? Becker's ghetto fiction provides, if not answers, at least material for this debate. Although he does not mention the acts of quiet, dangerous resistance that did go on in the ghetto, like the compilation and preservation of a secret chronicle, he does show a spirit of courage and enterprise alive in the two boys at the centre of the story.

Complicity in the Holocaust was widespread. Thomas Mann responded to the opening up of the death-camps after the war with the words: 'Everything German, everyone who speaks, writes, loves in German, is affected by this shameful revelation. Those inhuman deeds were committed not by a handful of criminals but by hundreds of thousands of a so-called German elite, men, boys, and dehumanized women.' This case for collective guilt was reinforced by the psychoanalytic argument proposed by Alexander and Margarete Mitscherlich that post-war Germany suffered from a collective inability to mourn. To avoid confronting the loss of their ego-ideal Hitler and being reminded of their complicity in the crimes he superintended, the West Germans threw themselves into the task of rebuilding their cities and their industries. In East Germany the past could be even more effectively ignored as the benighted era before the advent of Communism. On the other hand, the reconstruction of Germany was an urgent task, made more so by the necessity to absorb some 7 million Germans expelled from Eastern Europe. Perhaps, as the Mitscherlichs seem to imply, some collective act of contrition could have cleared the air; but it was hardly a realistic prospect.

At any rate, post-war Germany seemed to have no place for Jews. When Nelly Sachs and later Paul Celan sought to mourn the Holocaust in poetry, they were living outside Germany, in Sweden and France respectively. However, post-war Germany has in fact a number of writers, including some of the most lively figures on the literary scene, who are Jews or of Jewish descent. They include the controversial literary critic Marcel Reich-Ranicki and the poet and singer Wolf Biermann, who was expelled from the GDR in 1976 for his critical attitude to its regime and in 1989 was equally critical of many fellow-writers' naive response to its collapse. With their often aggressive individualism, such writers challenge not only the conformism of their critics but also the conventions for portraying Jews in post-war fiction. Well-intentioned philo-Semitic writers often portray Jews as passive victims who need the help of benevolent Gentiles: for example, Judith, the Berlin Jewish woman who is smuggled across the Baltic in Alfred Andersch's *Zanzibar* (1957), or Sigismund Markus in Günter Grass's *The Tin Drum* (1959), who is helplessly devoted to a Gentile woman. Just as Lessing and his contemporaries wanted Jews to be noble, so, it has been argued, post-war writers want Jews to be good, sad, passive figures whom one can pity without ambivalence. But real people are not like that, and real Jews insist on disturbing the simple moral schemes of their well-wishers.

Moral simplicities have a hard time in the fiction of Jurek Becker, the greatest Jewish writer to live in post-war Germany. Becker spent part of his early childhood in the Lodz Ghetto, the setting for 'The Wall' and for his first novel, *Jacob the Liar* (1969), which presents a deep moral dilemma with gentle humour despite the threat of destruction hanging over the inmates. This masterpiece offended some critics: how could anyone, let alone a Jew, write a funny novel about the Holocaust? Having broken this taboo, Becker broke another in his novel *Bronstein's Children* (1986), where three Jewish concentration-camp survivors take revenge on one of their guards by capturing and torturing him. Instead of being virtuous and forgiving, the Jew here shows a very human vindictiveness. 'If you poison us, do we not die? And if you wrong us, shall we not revenge?'

Other Jewish writers have challenged taboos in essays and short stories. Several of the most stimulating recent writers have insisted on facing up to the past by rejecting the well-meant platitudes of philo-Semitism and exposing the resentments which, they feel, still separate Jews from Germans. Henryk M. Broder, a pungent essayist who has now left Germany for Israel, asserts in his book *The Eternal Antisemite* (1986): 'The Germans will never forgive the Jews for Auschwitz.' Many ordinary Jews living in Germany have testified to their unease at living in a country where, although they feel linguistically and culturally at home, they may be rubbing shoulders with the children of war criminals. They cannot identify with Germany, but do not necessarily want to identify with a beleaguered and militant Israel. Yet they also show awareness that the memory of the Holocaust can bulk too large. For Jews who are cut off from Jewish tradition and religious practice, yet refuse to deny their Jewishness in a post-Holocaust world, there is the danger of basing their Jewish identity only on a consciousness of victimhood and on a morbid preoccupation with the horrors recorded now in many Holocaust museums. Katja Behrens's story 'Everything Normal' illustrates the unease of Jews in Germany who understandably feel unable to pass off an anti-Semitic remark as a casual indiscretion. The narrator's willingness to generalize about Germans, however, is disturbingly reminiscent of anti-Semites' generalizations about Jews. It needs to be held against the standpoint of the Traveller in Lessing's *The Jews*: 'I am no friend to general judgements on entire nations.' Other writers, notably Maxim Biller and Rafael Seligmann—whose best book, *Rubinstein's Auction* (1989), had to be published at the author's own expense and aroused an outcry from the Jewish community— draw on American models (Philip Roth, Joseph Heller) for a fast-moving and hard-hitting irony that rejects any single or simple attitude to the situation of Jews in Germany. Refusing to make their fiction comfortable or easily consumable, they simultaneously allure and attack the reader.

Can we speak of a revival of German–Jewish culture? There are hopeful signs. Several Reform synagogues have recently been opened in Berlin; the Jewish Museums in Frankfurt and Vienna are important cultural centres; there are lively periodicals devoted to Jewish matters. On the other hand, the bulk of Germany's present-day Jewish population consists of Russian Jews benefiting from the collapse of the Soviet Union, to whom German cultural traditions are foreign. And the fiction by Biller, Behrens, and Seligmann that thematizes Jewishness seems restricted to a narrow range of admittedly intense themes. However, in the often arid literary landscape of present-day Germany we should be thankful for books that have the power to entertain, arrest, and shock. And we should not underestimate the scope for cultural renewal and reinvention, especially in a Germany which, at least in its major cities, is beginning to share the multicultural character of other Western countries.

In preparing this anthology I have been helped by Catherine Clarke of Oxford University Press, who first broached the idea, and most of all by my editor Judith Luna, who supported the project enthusiastically, read the entire text, and made many valuable suggestions. The translations are my own unless otherwise stated. I am most grateful to John Felstiner for contributing his Celan translations, to Karen Leeder for commenting on my translation of Beer-Hofmann, and to Edward Timms for his advice on the near-impossible task of translating Kraus.

NOTE ON THE TEXTS

Unless otherwise indicated, the texts have been translated by the editor. The following editions have been used:

Gotthold Ephraim Lessing, *Werke*, ed. Herbert G. Göpfert *et al.*, 8 vols. (Munich: Hanser, 1970–9).

Moses Mendelssohn, *Gesammelte Schriften*, vol. 7: *Schriften zum Judentum I*, ed. Simon Rawidowicz (Berlin: Akademie-Verlag, 1930).

Salomon Maimons Lebensgeschichte, ed. Jakob Fromer (Munich: Müller, 1911).

Rahel Varnhagen, *Briefwechsel*, ed. Friedhelm Kemp, 4 vols. (Munich: Kösel, 1966–7).

Brüder Grimm, *Kinder- und Hausmärchen*, ed. Heinz Rölleke (Stuttgart: Reclam, 1980).

Ludwig Börne, *Sämtliche Schriften*, ed. Peter and Inge Rippmann, 5 vols. (Dreieich: Melzer, 1977).

Heinrich Heine, *Sämtliche Schriften*, ed. Klaus Briegleb, 6 vols. (Munich: Hanser, 1968–76).

The Complete Poems of Heinrich Heine: a modern English version by Hal Draper (Oxford: OUP, 1982).

Karl Emil Franzos, *Erzählungen aus Galizien und der Bukowina*, ed. Joseph Peter Strelka (Berlin: Nicolai, 1988).

Ferdinand von Saar, *Seligmann Hirsch*, ed. Detlef Haberland (Tübingen: Niemeyer, 1987).

Theodor Herzl, 'An Autobiography', *Jewish Chronicle*, 14 January 1898 (revised).

Thomas Mann, *Gesammelte Werke*, 13 vols. (Frankfurt: Fischer, 1974).

Your Diamond Dreams Cut open My Arteries: Poems by Else Lasker-Schüler, tr. Robert P. Newton (Chapel Hill, NC: University of North Carolina Press, 1982).

Gershom Scholem, *Tagebücher. 1. Halbband, 1913–1917*, ed. Karlfried Gründer and Friedrich Niewöhner (Frankfurt: Jüdischer Verlag, 1995).

Franz Kafka, *The Transformation and Other Stories*, tr. Malcolm Pasley (London: Penguin, 1992).

Richard Beer-Hofmann, *Gesammelte Werke* (Frankfurt: Fischer, 1963).

Else Lasker-Schüler, *Gesammelte Werke*, ed. Friedhelm Kemp, 3 vols. (Munich: Kösel, 1962).

Stefan Zweig, *Novellen*, 2 vols. (Berlin and Weimar: Aufbau, 1980).

Karl Kraus, *Schriften*, ed. Christian Wagenknecht, 20 vols. (Frankfurt: Suhrkamp, 1989–94).

Joseph Roth, *Werke*, ed. Klaus Westermann and Fritz Hackert, 6 vols. (Cologne: Kiepenheuer & Witsch, 1989–91).

Nelly Sachs, *Selected Poems*, tr. Michael Hamburger *et al.* (New York: Farrar, Straus & Giroux, 1967; London: Cape, 1968).

John Felstiner, *Paul Celan: Poet, Survivor, Jew* (New Haven and London: Yale University Press, 1995) (revised and enlarged).

Franz Fühmann, *Das Judenauto* (Zürich: Diogenes, 1968).

Jurek Becker, *Nach der ersten Zukunft: Erzählungen* (Frankfurt: Suhrkamp, 1980).

Maxim Biller, *Wenn ich einmal reich und tot bin: Erzählungen* (Munich: dtv, 1993).

Katja Behrens, *Salomo und die anderen* (Frankfurt: Fischer, 1993).

SELECT BIBLIOGRAPHY

GENERAL

Aschheim, Steven E., *Brothers and Strangers: The East European Jew in German and German Jewish Consciousness, 1800–1923* (Madison, Wis., 1982).

Beller, Steven, *Vienna and the Jews, 1867–1938: A Cultural History* (Cambridge, 1989).

Berghahn, Klaus L., *The German–Jewish Dialogue Reconsidered: A Symposium in Honor of George L. Mosse* (New York, 1996).

Gay, Peter, *Freud, Jews and Other Germans* (New York, 1978).

Gay, Ruth, *The Jews of Germany: A Historical Portrait* (New Haven and London, 1992).

Gilman, Sander L., *Jewish Self-Hatred: Anti-Semitism and the Hidden Language of the Jews* (Baltimore and London, 1986).

—— and Remmler, Karen (eds.), *Reemerging Jewish Culture in Germany: Life and Literature Since 1989* (New York and London, 1994).

—— and Zipes, Jack (eds.), *The Yale Companion to Jewish Writing and Thought in German Culture, 1096–1996* (New Haven and London, 1997).

Kaplan, Marion A., *The Making of the Jewish Middle Class: Women, Family, and Identity in Imperial Germany* (New York and Oxford, 1991).

Low, Alfred D., *Jews in the Eyes of the Germans: From the Enlightenment to Imperial Germany* (Philadelphia, 1979).

Marrus, Michael R., *The Holocaust in History* (London, 1988).

Mendes-Flohr, Paul, and Reinharz, Jehuda (eds.), *The Jew in the Modern World: A Documentary History*, 2nd edn. (New York and Oxford, 1995).

Meyer, Michael A., *The Origins of the Modern Jew: Jewish Identity and European Culture in Germany, 1749–1824* (Detroit, 1967).

—— (ed.), *German–Jewish History in Modern Times*, 4 vols. (New York, 1996–8).

Mosse, George L., *German Jews Beyond Judaism* (Bloomington and Cincinnati, 1985).

Pulzer, Peter, *The Rise of Political Anti-Semitism in Germany and Austria*, 2nd edn. (London, 1988).

Reinharz, Jehuda, and Schatzberg, Walter (eds.), *The Jewish Response to German Culture from the Enlightenment to the Second World War* (Hanover, NH, and London, 1985).

Robertson, Ritchie, *The 'Jewish Question' in German Literature, 1749–1939* (Oxford, 1999).

Sorkin, David, *The Transformation of German Jewry, 1780–1840* (New York and Oxford, 1987).

Wistrich, Robert S., *The Jews of Vienna in the Age of Franz Joseph* (Oxford, 1989).

LESSING

Lessing, G. E., *Laocoon, Nathan the Wise, Minna von Barnhelm*, Everyman's Library (London, 1930).

Lamport, F. J., *Lessing and the Drama* (Oxford, 1981).

Lea, Charlene A., 'Tolerance Unlimited: "The Noble Jew" on the German and Austrian Stage (1750–1805)', *German Quarterly*, 64 (1991), 166–77.

Robertson, Ritchie, ' "Dies hohe Lied der Duldung"? The Ambiguities of Toleration in Lessing's *Die Juden* and *Nathan der Weise*', *Modern Language Review*, 93 (1998), 105–20.

MENDELSSOHN

Mendelssohn, Moses, *Jerusalem, or On Religious Power and Judaism*, trans. Allan Arkush (Hanover, NH, and London, 1983).

Altmann, Alexander, *Moses Mendelssohn: A Biographical Study* (London, 1973).

—— 'Moses Mendelssohn as the Archetypal German Jew', in Jehuda Reinharz and Walter Schatzberg (eds.), *The Jewish Response to German Culture from the Enlightenment to the Second World War* (Hanover, NH, and London, 1985), 17–31.

Sorkin, David, *Moses Mendelssohn and the Religious Enlightenment* (London, 1996).

MAIMON

Maimon, Solomon, *An Autobiography*, trans. J. Clark Murray (Paisley and London, 1888).

Robertson, Ritchie, 'From the Ghetto to Modern Culture: The Autobiographies of Salomon Maimon and Jakob Fromer', *Polin: A Yearbook of Polish–Jewish Studies*, 7 (1992), 12–30.

LEVIN

Arendt, Hannah, *Rahel Varnhagen: The Life of a Jewess*, trans. Richard and Clara Winston (London, 1957).

Hertz, Deborah, *Jewish High Society in Old Regime Berlin* (New Haven and London, 1988).

Spiel, Hilde, *Fanny von Arnstein: Daughter of the Enlightenment 1758–1818*, trans. Christine Shuttleworth (Oxford and New York, 1991).

GRIMM

Grimm, Jacob and Wilhelm, *Selected Tales*, trans. David Luke and others (Harmondsworth, 1982).

Ellis, John M., *One Fairy Story Too Many: The Brothers Grimm and their Tales* (Chicago, 1983).

Michaelis-Jena, Ruth, *The Brothers Grimm* (London, 1970).

Tatar, Maria, *The Hard Facts of the Grimms' Fairy Tales* (Princeton, 1987).

BÖRNE

Figes, Orlando, 'Ludwig Börne and the Formation of a Radical Critique of Judaism', *Leo Baeck Institute Yearbook*, 29 (1984), 351–82.

Gross, John, *Shylock: Four Hundred Years in the Life of a Legend* (London, 1992).

HEINE

The Complete Poems of Heinrich Heine: A Modern English Version, trans. Hal Draper (New York and Oxford, 1982).

Heine, Heinrich, *Selected Prose*, trans. Ritchie Robertson (London, 1993).

Prawer, S. S., *Heine's Jewish Comedy: A Study of his Portraits of Jews and Judaism* (Oxford, 1983).

—— *Frankenstein's Island: England and the English in the Writings of Heinrich Heine* (Cambridge, 1986).

Reeves, Nigel, *Heinrich Heine: Poetry and Politics* (Oxford, 1974).

Robertson, Ritchie, *Heine* (London, 1988).

Sammons, Jeffrey L., *Heinrich Heine: A Modern Biography* (Princeton, 1979).

FRANZOS

Sommer, Fred, *'Halb-Asien': German Nationalism and the Eastern European Works of Karl Emil Franzos* (Stuttgart, 1984).

Steiner, Carl, *Karl Emil Franzos, 1848–1904: Emancipator and Assimilationist* (New York, 1990).

SAAR

Howe, Patricia, 'The Image of the Past in Ferdinand von Saar's Novellen', in Karl Konrad Polheim (ed.), *Ferdinand von Saar: Ein Wegbereiter der literarischen Moderne* (Bonn, 1985), 137–49.

Paulin, Roger, *The Brief Compass: The Nineteenth-Century German Novelle* (Oxford, 1985).

HERZL

Herzl, Theodor, *Altneuland/Old–New Land*, trans. Paula Kellner (Haifa, 1960).

—— *The Jewish State: An Attempt at a Modern Solution of the Jewish Question*, trans. Sylvie D'Avigdor (London, 1967).

Beller, Steven, *Herzl* (London, 1991).

Kornberg, Jacques, *Theodor Herzl: From Assimilation to Zionism* (Bloomington and Indianapolis, 1993).

Robertson, Ritchie, and Timms, Edward (eds.), *Theodor Herzl and the Origins of Zionism* (= *Austrian Studies*, 8) (Edinburgh, 1997).

Wheatcroft, Geoffrey, *The Controversy of Zion: How Zionism Tried to Resolve the Jewish Question* (London, 1996).

MANN

Anderson, Mark M., ' "Jewish" Mimesis? Imitation and Assimilation in Thomas Mann's "Wälsungenblut" and Ludwig Jacobowski's *Werther, der Jude*', *German Life and Letters*, 49 (1996), 193–204.

Hayman, Ronald, *Thomas Mann: A Biography* (London, 1995).

Heilbut, Anthony, *Thomas Mann: Eros and Literature* (London, 1996).

LASKER–SCHÜLER

Your Diamond Dreams Cut Open My Arteries: Poems by Else Lasker-Schüler, translated by Robert Newton (Chapel Hill, NC, 1980).

Cohn, Hans W., *Else Lasker-Schüler: The Broken World* (Cambridge, 1974).

Schwertfeger, Ruth, *Else Lasker-Schüler: Expressionist, Woman, Jew, and Exile* (Oxford, 1991).

Yudkin, Leon I., *Else Lasker-Schüler: A Study in German Jewish Literature* (Northwood, 1991).

SCHOLEM

Scholem, Gershom, *From Berlin to Jerusalem*, trans. Harry Zohn (New York, 1980).

—— *On Jews and Judaism in Crisis: Selected Essays of Gershom Scholem*, ed. Werner J. Dannhauser (New York, 1976).

Biale, David, *Gershom Scholem: Kabbalah and Counter-History* (Cambridge, Mass., 1979).

KAFKA

Kafka, Franz, *The Transformation and Other Stories*, trans. Malcolm Pasley (London, 1992).

Alter, Robert, *Necessary Angels: Tradition and Modernity in Kafka, Benjamin and Scholem* (Cambridge, Mass., 1991).

Pawel, Ernst, *The Nightmare of Reason: A Life of Franz Kafka* (New York, 1984).

Robertson, Ritchie, *Kafka: Judaism, Politics, and Literature* (Oxford, 1985).

BEER-HOFMANN

Elstun, Esther N., *Richard Beer-Hofmann: His Life and Work* (University Park, Pa., and London, 1983).

Le Rider, Jacques, 'The "Cultural Zionism" of Richard Beer-Hofmann', in *Modernity and Crises of Identity: Culture and Society in Fin-de-Siècle Vienna*, trans. Rosemary Morris (Cambridge, 1993), 270–93.

ZWEIG

Zweig, Stefan, *The Buried Candelabrum*, trans. Eden and Cedar Paul (London, 1937).

—— *The World of Yesterday* (London, 1943).

—— *The Royal Game and Other Stories*, trans. Jill Sutcliffe (London, 1981).

Prater, D. A., *European of Yesterday: A Biography of Stefan Zweig* (Oxford, 1972).

Turner, David, *Moral Values and the Human Zoo: The 'Novellen' of Stefan Zweig* (Hull, 1988).

KRAUS

Kraus, Karl, *In These Great Times: A Karl Kraus Reader*, ed. and trans. Harry Zohn (Manchester, 1984).

—— *Half-Truths and One-and-a-Half-Truths: Selected Aphorisms*, trans. Harry Zohn (Manchester, 1986).

Theobald, John, *The Paper Ghetto—Karl Kraus and Anti-Semitism* (Frankfurt, 1996).

Timms, Edward, *Karl Kraus, Apocalyptic Satirist* (New Haven and London, 1986).

—— 'Kraus's Shakespearean Politics', in Kenneth Segar and John Warren (eds.), *Austria in the Thirties: Culture and Politics* (Riverside, Calif., 1991), 345–58.

ROTH

Roth, Joseph, *Weights and Measures*, trans. David Le Vay (London, 1982).

—— *Job: The Story of a Simple Man*, trans. Dorothy Thompson (London, 1983).

Roth, Joseph, *Hotel Savoy; Fallmerayer the Stationmaster; The Bust of the Emperor*, trans. John Hoare (London, 1986).
—— *The Radetzky March*, trans. Joachim Neugroschel (London, 1995).
Chambers, Helen (ed.), *Co-Existent Contradictions: Joseph Roth in Retrospect* (Riverside, Calif., 1991).

SACHS

Sachs, Nelly, *Selected Poems*, trans. Michael Hamburger *et al.* (New York, 1967; London, 1968).
Rudnick, Ursula, *Post-Shoa Religious Metaphors: The Image of God in the Poetry of Nelly Sachs* (Frankfurt and New York, 1995).

CELAN

Celan, Paul, *Poems*, trans. Michael Hamburger (Manchester and New York, 1980).
Chalfen, Israel, *Paul Celan: A Biography of his Youth*, trans. Maximilian Bleyleben (New York, 1991).
Colin, Amy, *Paul Celan: Holograms of Darkness* (Bloomington and Indianapolis, 1991).
Felstiner, John, *Paul Celan: Poet, Survivor, Jew* (New Haven and London, 1995).

FÜHMANN

Dundes, Alan (ed.), *The Blood Libel Legend: A Casebook in Anti-Semitic Folklore* (Madison, Wis., 1991).
Fox, Thomas C., *Border Crossings: An Introduction to East German Prose* (Ann Arbor, 1993).
Tate, Dennis, *The East German Novel* (Bath, 1984).

BECKER

Becker, Jurek, *Jacob the Liar*, trans. Melvin Kornfeld (New York, 1975).
—— *Five Stories*, ed. David Rock, Manchester German Texts (Manchester and New York, 1993).
Dobroszycki, Lucjan, *The Chronicle of the Lodz Ghetto, 1941–1944*, trans. Richard Lourie and others (New Haven and London, 1984).
Johnson, Susan M., *The Works of Jurek Becker: A Thematic Analysis* (Chapel Hill, NC, 1986).

FURTHER READING IN OXFORD WORLD'S CLASSICS

Georg Büchner, *Danton's Death, Leonce and Lena, Wozzeck*, trans. and ed. Victor Price.

Annette von Droste-Hülshoff, 'The Jew's Beech', in Andrew J. Webber (ed.), *Eight German Novellas*, trans. Michael Fleming.

J. W. von Goethe, *Faust, Parts One and Two*, trans. and ed. F. D. Luke.

Friedrich Nietzsche, *Beyond Good and Evil*, trans. and ed. Marion Faber, with an introduction by Robert C. Holub.

—— *On the Genealogy of Morals*, trans. and ed. Douglas Smith.

—— *Twilight of the Idols*, trans. and ed. Duncan Large.

CHRONOLOGY

1665   Sabbatai Zvi proclaims himself the Messiah and sets off apocalyptic excitement among Jews throughout Europe; in 1666 he renounces his claim and converts to Islam.

1743   Moses Mendelssohn arrives in Berlin.

1752   The Baal Shem, founder of Hasidism, circulates the 'Holy Epistle' describing his ascent to Heaven.

1781   Joseph II's Patents of Toleration begin emancipation of Jews in Austria–Hungary. Publication of Dohm's *On the Civil Improvement of the Jews*.

1786   Death of Mendelssohn.

1791   Civil rights granted to Jews in revolutionary France.

1806   France defeats Prussia at battles of Jena and Auerstädt.

1806–13   French legislation on Jewish rights applies to French-occupied parts of western Germany.

1808   Napoleon's decree (annulled in 1818) temporarily restricts French Jews' rights to practise trade and professions.

1811   Jews in Frankfurt are no longer obliged to live in a ghetto.

1812   Jews in Prussia (though only those enjoying official protection) are granted civil rights, though still ineligible for state employment.

1815   Congress of Vienna confirms civil rights currently held by Jews, but *not* the complete equality briefly permitted by French occupiers.

1819   Anti-Semitic riots (the 'Hep Heps') in many South German towns.

1831   Heine emigrates to Paris.

1843   Marx, whose radical Rhineland newspaper has been suppressed by the Prussian government, arrives in Paris and meets Heine.

1848   Revolutions in Vienna, Berlin, and other European cities.

1850   Richard Wagner publishes his anti-Semitic *Jewry in Music*.

1867   Establishment of 'Compromise' between Austria and Hungary, united under the Habsburg dynasty, with full civil rights for all Jews in both territories.

1871   Founding of the German Empire; extension of full civil rights to all Jews in its territories.

1873   Stock market crash in Germany and Austria.

1879   Heinrich von Treitschke's article 'Our Prospects' initiates public controversy over anti-Semitism. Wilhelm Marr founds the League of Anti-Semites.

1881   Outbreak of anti-Semitic violence in Russia; beginning of mass Jewish emigration.

1896   Theodor Herzl publishes *The Jewish State*.

1897   Karl Lueger becomes mayor of Vienna. August: First Zionist Congress held in Basle.

1899   November: Freud publishes *The Interpretation of Dreams* (dated 1900).

1914   Most German and Austrian Jews join in enthusiastic support for war.

1916   German War Office orders census of Jews serving at the front.

1917   British troops enter Jerusalem (conquered from Turkey, which was allied with Germany and Austria in the war); the Balfour Declaration promises to establish a national home for the Jews.

1918   November: in wake of German defeat, Kaiser Wilhelm II abdicates and a republic is proclaimed. Kurt Eisner's left-wing government takes power in Bavaria.

1919   January: Spartacist uprising in Berlin. April: Munich Soviet proclaimed; suppressed by central government troops. August: constitution of the Weimar Republic proclaimed.

1924   Hitler, tried for high treason in attempting a revolution, is sentenced to five years' imprisonment but serves only eight months, during which he dictates *Mein Kampf*.

1933   30 January: Hitler appointed Reich Chancellor. 28 February: 'Reichstag Fire Decree' suspends civil rights. 1 April: nationwide boycott of Jewish shops.

1935   September: Nuremberg Laws deny citizenship to German Jews.

1936–9   Arab uprising against Jewish settlement in Palestine.

1938   March: German annexation of Austria. 9 November: 'Kristallnacht', nationwide pogroms in which 91 Jews are killed, many others injured, 191 synagogues burnt, and thousands of Jewish shops looted.

1939 September: Germany attacks Poland; Britain and France declare war.

1941 1 September: German Jews compelled to wear the yellow star. December: mass gassing of Jews begins at Chelmno in Poland.

1942 January: Wannsee Conference in Berlin to plan 'final solution to Jewish question'. June: systematic gassing of Jews begins at Auschwitz-Birkenau.

1945 January: Auschwitz liberated by Soviet Army. May: Germany surrenders. July–August: the Potsdam Conference (Churchill, later Attlee; Truman; Stalin; and their foreign ministers) agrees to partition Germany.

1948 14 May: State of Israel proclaimed.

1949 Establishment of the Federal Republic of Germany in the former British, French and American zones of occupation. October: German Democratic Republic proclaimed in the former Soviet zone.

1961 August: building of the Berlin Wall.

1966 Nobel Prize for Literature awarded to Nelly Sachs and S. Y. Agnon.

1976 Wolf Biermann expelled from GDR for his critical writing; many writers protest.

1989 9 November: opening of the Berlin Wall.

1990 3 October: unification of Germany.

THE GERMAN–JEWISH
DIALOGUE

G. E. LESSING

The Jews

Gotthold Ephraim Lessing (1729–81) was Germany's first freelance man of letters. At the behest of his authoritarian father, a Protestant pastor, he initially studied theology at Leipzig University, but abandoned it for medicine and then adopted a precarious career as a journalist. His early works include comedies, poems, epigrams, reviews, and controversial essays mostly in defence of reputedly heretical theologians. His sentimental play *Miss Sara Sampson* (1755) was a pioneering domestic tragedy, transferring intense emotions from the heroic stage to a middle-class setting; but the comedy *Minna von Barnhelm or The Soldier's Fortune* (1767) succeeds far better in combining realistic characterization and language with a comic plot and a contemporary setting (Berlin in 1763, just after the Seven Years War), while another domestic tragedy, *Emilia Galotti* (1772), shows a vast advance over *Sara* in taut plotting, economical dialogue, and emotional range. Of the many literary and theological controversies Lessing engaged in, especially when employed by the Duke of Brunswick as librarian at Wolfenbüttel, the most serious followed his publication of the *Wolfenbüttel Fragments* (1777) by his late friend Hermann Samuel Reimarus, a sceptical inquiry into the historicity of the biblical accounts of Moses and Jesus. For sharing Reimarus's doubts about revelation, miracles, and resurrection, Lessing was attacked by Pastor Goeze of Hamburg, and replied sharply until the Duke ordered him to stop. To express his views, Lessing returned to the theatre with his blank-verse play *Nathan the Wise* (1779), featuring a Jewish merchant in the Jerusalem of the Second Crusade. A complicated plot of mistaken identities enables Lessing to polemicize against Christianity and express through Nathan a plea for toleration based on scepticism towards religious dogma and exaltation of ethical conduct as the core of religion.

Both Lessing's dramatic technique and his concern for toleration are well shown in his early comedy *The Jews*, written in 1749 and published in 1754. It undermines common prejudices against Jews, showing how easily they can be used as scapegoats for Gentile vices and crimes, and discourages rash generalizations about entire nationalities. Lessing's sympathy for 'an oppressed part of the human race', as he calls the Jews in a 1753 review, preceded his friendship with Moses Mendelssohn, whom he met early in 1754 through Aaron Gumpertz (1723–69), a Berlin Jewish scholar who had recommended Mendelssohn as a good chess partner. *The Jews* is not simply a didactic play: its central figure, the Traveller, invites a smile by his pedantic distinction between gratitude and friendship and by his extreme reluctance to identify the criminal; and the lively dialogue among the servants shows Lessing's gift for comedy, while the frustrated romance between the serious Traveller and the vivacious Young Lady anticipates the precarious but successful relationship between Tellheim and Minna in Lessing's later comic masterpiece.

———

DRAMATIS PERSONAE

A Traveller
Christoph, his servant
The Baron
A Young Lady, his daughter
Lisette, her maid
Martin Krumm, the Baron's steward
Michel Stich

Scene 1
MICHEL STICH, MARTIN KRUMM

MARTIN KRUMM. You stupid Michel Stich!

MICHEL STICH. You stupid Martin Krumm!

MARTIN KRUMM. Let's face it, we've been a pair of bloody fools. It wouldn't have mattered tuppence if we'd killed one more person!

MICHEL STICH. But how could we have made a better job of it? Weren't we well masked? Wasn't the coachman on our side? How could we help it if luck was against us? I've said hundreds of times that without that confounded luck, one can't even be a good villain.

MARTIN KRUMM. Well, thinking it over, we've just staved off the gallows for another few days at most.

MICHEL STICH. Oh, never mind the gallows! There would have to be a lot more of them if all thieves were hanged. You hardly see one gallows every two leagues; and most of them are empty. I think the high-and-mighty judges will abolish them out of sheer politeness. What are they good for, anyway, except to make people like us shut our eyes when we go past?

MARTIN KRUMM. Oh! I don't even do that. My father and my grandfather died on the gallows, and I don't ask anything better. I'm not ashamed of my parents.

MICHEL STICH. But these honest folk will be ashamed of you. You haven't done nearly enough to be considered their lawful son.

MARTIN KRUMM. Oh, don't worry; I'm not going to let our master off lightly. And what's more, I want my revenge on that wretched stranger who robbed us of such a juicy morsel. He'll have to part with his watch—Aha! Look, here he comes. Off you go! I'm about to perform my masterpiece.

MICHEL STICH. Yes, but share and share alike!

Scene 2
MARTIN KRUMM, THE TRAVELLER

MARTIN KRUMM. I'll pretend I'm stupid.—Your very humble servant, sir; my name's Martin Krumm, and I make so bold as to be the appointed steward on this here estate.

THE TRAVELLER. I believe you, my friend. But haven't you seen my servant anywhere?

MARTIN KRUMM. At your service, no I haven't; but I've had the honour to hear many good things about your worthy self. And so I'm very pleased to have the honour to enjoy the honour of your acquaintance. I'm told that last night, when my master was on his way here, you saved him from a very perilous peril. And since I can't help being delighted at my master's good fortune, I'm delighted—

THE TRAVELLER. I understand your meaning; you mean to thank me for supporting your master—

MARTIN KRUMM. Yes, exactly; that's just it!

THE TRAVELLER. You are an honest man—

MARTIN KRUMM. I am indeed! Honesty can get one a long way.

THE TRAVELLER. It is no small pleasure for me to have gained the affection of so many upright people by such a slight act of kindness. Your gratitude is superfluous as a reward for what I did. I was obliged to do it by the universal love of humanity. It was my duty; and I should have been content to have it regarded as no more than that. You are much too kind, you good people, in thanking me for doing what you would doubtless have done for me just as readily, if I had found myself in a similar plight. Can I be of service to you in any other way, my friend?

MARTIN KRUMM. Oh, I won't trouble you with service, sir. I've got a lad who serves me when I need something. But—I'd be curious to know what actually happened. Where was it? Were there many villains? Were they going to kill our good master, or did they just want his money? The one would have been better than the other.

THE TRAVELLER. I'll tell you the whole story in a few words. It was perhaps an hour's journey from here, where the road passes between two high banks, that the robbers attacked your master. I was on the same road, and his terrified cries for help made me ride up to him as fast as I could, along with my servant.

MARTIN KRUMM. You don't say!

THE TRAVELLER. I found him in an open carriage—

MARTIN KRUMM. You don't say!

THE TRAVELLER. Two fellows in masks—

MARTIN KRUMM. Masks, eh? You don't say!

THE TRAVELLER. I do not know whether they wanted to kill him, or simply to tie him up, in order to rob him more safely.

MARTIN KRUMM. You don't say! Of course they must have wanted to kill him, the godless creatures!

THE TRAVELLER. I should not like to say that, in order not to speak worse of them than they deserve.

MARTIN KRUMM. Oh yes, believe you me, they wanted to kill him all right. I know for a fact—

THE TRAVELLER. How can you know that? But never mind. As soon as the robbers caught sight of me, they abandoned their prey, and ran as hard as they could to the nearby thickets. I fired my pistol at one of them. But it was already so dark, and he was so far away, that I doubt whether I hit him.

MARTIN KRUMM. No, you didn't hit him—

THE TRAVELLER. Do you know that?

MARTIN KRUMM. I just meant, because it was already dark; and they say you can't take good aim in the dark.

THE TRAVELLER. I cannot describe the gratitude that your master showed to me. He declared a hundred times that I had saved his life, and urged me to go back to his estate with him. I wish my circumstances would let me spend more time with this agreeable man; but as it is, I must continue my journey today. And that is why I am looking for my servant.

MARTIN KRUMM. Oh, then I mustn't keep you. But excuse me a moment—now what was I going to ask? The robbers—tell me now—what did they look like? How did they walk? They were disguised, but how?

THE TRAVELLER. Your master is firmly convinced that they were Jews. They had beards, that's true; but they talked like ordinary peasants hereabouts. If they were wearing masks, as I'm sure they were, the twilight must have helped them. For I cannot understand how Jews should cause trouble on the highway, since so few of them are tolerated in this country.

MARTIN KRUMM. Yes, yes, I'm quite certain they were Jews. Perhaps you don't know the godless scum. They're all swindlers, thieves, and highwaymen, every man jack of them. That's why the good Lord God cursed their nation. It's lucky for them I'm not king, because I wouldn't leave a single one of them alive. Ah, may God protect all honest Christians from these people! If the good Lord doesn't hate them, then why is it that in the disaster in Breslau a while back there were nearly as many of them killed as there were Christians? Our vicar mentioned that very wisely in his last sermon. You'd think they must have been listening, and wanted to take revenge straight away on our good master. Oh, my dear sir, if you want to have good fortune and prosperity in this world, beware of the Jews, worse than the plague.

THE TRAVELLER. Would to God it was only the rabble that spoke in this fashion!

MARTIN KRUMM. For example, sir, I once went to the fair—yes, when I remember the fair, I'd like to poison all the damned Jews at once, if only I could. The crowd was so thick, they nicked one man's handkerchief, another man's snuff-box, someone else's watch, and I don't know what all else. They're as quick as greased lightning when it comes to stealing, and they're that skilful, our schoolmaster's organ-playing is nothing to it. For example, sir, they first of all press right close up against you, like I'm doing with you—

THE TRAVELLER. Mind your manners, my friend!

MARTIN KRUMM. Oh, I'm just showing you. When they stand like this—look—quick as a flash they've got their hand in your fob-pocket. [*Instead of reaching for his watch, he puts his hand in his coat pocket and pulls out his snuff-box.*] But they do it all so skilfully, you'd swear they were putting their hand *this* way when it's going *that* way. If they talk about your snuff-box, you can be sure they're after your watch, and if they talk about your watch, they've got their eye on your snuff-box.

[*He reaches for the watch, but is caught*]

THE TRAVELLER. Gently now! What's your hand doing here?

MARTIN KRUMM. You can see, sir, I wouldn't be any good as a villain. If a Jew put his hand in there, you'd never see your good watch again. But I see I'm making a nuisance of myself, so I'll make so bold as to take my leave of you, and beg to remain, in gratitude for showing me such kindness, my honourable master's most obedient servant, Martin Krumm, appointed steward on this noble estate.

THE TRAVELLER. Be off with you!

MARTIN KRUMM. Remember what I told you about the Jews. They're a godless, thieving lot.

Scene 3
THE TRAVELLER

THE TRAVELLER. However stupid that fellow is, or pretends to be, he may be a more malicious rascal than any Jew ever was. When a Jew practises deceit, nine times out of ten a Christian has given him seven excuses to do it. I doubt if many Christians can boast of dealing honestly with a Jew; and they are surprised when he repays like for like? If two nations are to live together faithfully and uprightly, each must contribute an equal share. But what if one of them considers it a matter of religion, and practically a work of merit, to persecute the other? Still—

Scene 4
THE TRAVELLER, CHRISTOPH

THE TRAVELLER. Why do I have to spend an hour looking for you whenever I want you?

CHRISTOPH. You must be joking, sir. I can't be in more than one place at once, can I? So is it my fault that you don't go to that place? You can always find me where I am.

THE TRAVELLER. Indeed? and you're unsteady on your feet? Now I understand why you are so ingenious. Do you have to get drunk first thing in the morning?

CHRISTOPH. Drunk, did you say? I've hardly started drinking. Apart from a few bottles of good local wine, a few glasses of brandy, and a roll of bread, I haven't touched a thing, as sure as I'm an honest man. I'm completely sober.

THE TRAVELLER. You look it. And my advice as a friend is to double your portions.

CHRISTOPH. Excellent advice! I shan't fail to regard it as an order, as my duty requires. I'm off, and you'll see how obedient I can be.

THE TRAVELLER. Be sensible! Instead, you can go and saddle and load the horses. I want to leave this very morning.

CHRISTOPH. If you were joking when you advised me to have a double breakfast, how can I suppose that you're being serious now? You seem anxious to make fun of me today. Are you so cheerful on account of the young lady? Oh, she's a delightful little thing. But she should be a little older, just a little bit older. Don't you agree, sir? If a woman hasn't reached a certain ripeness—

THE TRAVELLER. Go and do what I told you.

CHRISTOPH. You're getting serious. All the same, I'll wait until you tell me a third time. The matter is too important! You might be in too much of a hurry. And I've always been in the habit of giving my master plenty of time to reflect. Do think what you're doing in leaving a place so quickly where we're so well looked after. We only arrived yesterday. We've gained the master's unlimited gratitude, yet we've had no more than dinner and breakfast with him.

THE TRAVELLER. Your bad manners are insufferable. Anyone who decides to be a servant should learn to make less fuss.

CHRISTOPH. Very good, sir! You're beginning to moralize; in other words, you're getting angry. Calm down; I'm on my way—

THE TRAVELLER. You are clearly not in the habit of thinking very hard. The kindness we showed this gentleman ceases to be a good deed as soon as we seem to expect the slightest gratitude for it. I shouldn't even have let him urge me to come here. The pleasure of having helped an unknown person without hope of reward is so great in itself! And he himself would have wished blessings on us far in excess of the exaggerated gratitude he now displays. Anyone whom we oblige to thank us at great length and at considerable expense does us a service that may be more disagreeable to him than our good deed was to us. Most people are so corrupt that they find the presence of a benefactor extremely burdensome. It seems to offend their pride—

CHRISTOPH. Your philosophy, sir, takes my breath away. Good! You shall see that I'm just as noble-hearted as you are. I'm off; in a quarter of an hour you can mount your horse.

Scene 5
THE TRAVELLER, THE YOUNG LADY

THE TRAVELLER. I have not lowered myself to this person's level, but his behaviour towards me is very low.

THE YOUNG LADY. Why have you left us, sir? Why are you here by yourself? Have you grown tired of our company during the few hours you have spent at our house? I hope not. I try to please everyone; and you are the last person I should want to displease.

THE TRAVELLER. I beg your pardon, miss. I only wanted to give my servant orders to prepare for our departure.

THE YOUNG LADY. What are you talking about? Your departure? When did you arrive, for heaven's sake? Perhaps a melancholy mood has put this thought in your head. But can't you stand us even for one whole day? That's terrible. I assure you, if you even think of leaving, I'll be cross.

THE TRAVELLER. That is the most painful threat you could have uttered.

THE YOUNG LADY. No? Seriously? Would you feel pain if I were cross with you?

THE TRAVELLER. Who could be unmoved by the anger of a charming woman?

THE YOUNG LADY. What you say does sound rather as if you were teasing me; but I'll take it seriously, at the risk of being mistaken. Well then, sir—people do tell me I'm rather charming—and I tell you again, I shall be dreadfully, dreadfully angry if you think of leaving between now and New Year.

THE TRAVELLER. The date is kindly chosen. So you would show me the door in the middle of winter, in the most unpleasant weather—

THE YOUNG LADY. Why, who said any such thing? I only said that at that time, for the sake of civility, you may begin to think about leaving. But that doesn't mean we'll let you go; we'll beg you—

THE TRAVELLER. For the sake of civility, perhaps?

THE YOUNG LADY. Why, who'd ever have thought that such an honest face could be such a tease? Oh, here comes Papa. I must be off! Don't say I was here. He's always telling me I'm too fond of gentlemen's company.

Scene 6
THE BARON, THE TRAVELLER

THE BARON. Hasn't my daughter been to see you? Why is the wild thing in such a hurry?

THE TRAVELLER. It is an immeasurable good fortune to have such a pleasant, cheerful daughter. The delightful innocence and the unaffected wit with which she talks are enchanting.

THE BARON. You are too generous to her. She has not spent much time among people of her rank, and the art of pleasing, which can scarcely be learnt in the country, and which can often accomplish more even than beauty, is one she has never mastered. Everything about her is nature left to itself.

THE TRAVELLER. And that is all the more appealing, the less one meets with it in the towns. There, everything is false, forced, artificial. Indeed, people are so far gone as to consider 'nature' synonymous with stupidity and coarseness.

THE BARON. What could please me more than to see how precisely our ideas and judgements coincide? Oh, I wish I had had a friend like you long ago!

THE TRAVELLER. You are being unjust to your other friends.

THE BARON. My other friends, did you say? I'm fifty years old: I have had acquaintances, but never a friend. And friendship has never appeared so charming as in the few hours during which I have sought yours. How can I earn it?

THE TRAVELLER. My friendship means so little that merely to ask for it suffices to obtain it. Your request is far more valuable than what you are asking for.

THE BARON. Oh, sir, the friendship of my benefactor—

THE TRAVELLER. Allow me—that is not friendship. If you see me in this false guise, I cannot be your friend. Say for the sake of argument that I am your benefactor: must I not fear that your friendship is merely the effect of gratitude?

THE BARON. Cannot the two be combined?

THE TRAVELLER. Hardly! A noble heart considers gratitude a duty; but friendship is based on arbitrary emotions.

THE BARON. But how am I to—I'm quite bewildered by your delicate taste.

THE TRAVELLER. Do not esteem me more highly than I deserve. At the most I am a man who has done his duty with pleasure. Duty in itself does not merit gratitude. For doing it with pleasure, I am sufficiently rewarded by your friendship.

THE BARON. I'm still more bewildered by your nobility of heart. But perhaps I'm too bold. I have not yet ventured to ask your name or your rank. Perhaps I am offering my friendship to one who—who would despise—

THE TRAVELLER. Forgive me, sir! You—you are—you think far too highly of me.

THE BARON [*aside*]. Should I ask him? He might take my curiosity amiss.

THE TRAVELLER [*aside*]. If he asks, what am I going to tell him?

THE BARON [*aside*]. If I don't ask him, he might think it rude.

THE TRAVELLER [*aside*]. Shall I tell him the truth?

THE BARON [*aside*]. No, I'll take the safest course. I'll have his servant questioned.

THE TRAVELLER [*aside*]. If only I could escape from this uncertainty!

THE BARON. Why so pensive?

THE TRAVELLER. I was about to ask you the same question, sir—

THE BARON. I know; sometimes one forgets oneself. Let's talk about something else. Do you know, the people who attacked me *were* Jews, after all? The mayor of the village has just told me that a few days ago he met three of them on the highway. As he described them to me, they looked more like villains than like honest people. And why should I doubt it? A nation that is so keen on profit does not care whether it gets it by right or wrong means, by cunning or violence. And it seems made for commerce, or, in plain English, for swindling. Polite, pliable, enterprising, and discreet: these qualities would make the Jews admirable if they did not use them for our misfortune. [*He pauses*] The Jews have caused me plenty of harm and annoyance before now. When I was still serving in the army, I let myself be talked into signing a bill of exchange for an acquaintance; and the Jew to whom it was made out not only forced me to pay, but even made me pay twice over. Oh, they are the vilest, most malicious people! What do you think? You seem quite downcast.

THE TRAVELLER. What am I to say? I must say I have often heard this complaint—

THE BARON. And isn't it true that there's something in their faces that puts us against them? You only have to look in their eyes to see how spiteful, unscrupulous, selfish, deceitful, and perjured they are. But why are you turning away from me?

THE TRAVELLER. I gather, sir, that you are an expert on physiognomy: and I am afraid that my face—

THE BARON. Oh, I'm very sorry. How could you think of such a thing? Without being an expert on physiognomy, I must tell you that I have never found such an honest, noble-hearted, and kindly expression as yours.

THE TRAVELLER. To tell you the truth, I am no friend to general judgements on entire nations. Don't take my frankness amiss. I rather think that in all nations there may be good and bad souls. And among the Jews—

Scene 7

THE YOUNG LADY, THE TRAVELLER, THE BARON

THE YOUNG LADY. Oh dear! Papa—

THE BARON. Now, now; what a wild thing! A moment ago you ran away from me: what was that all about?

THE YOUNG LADY. I wasn't running away from you, papa, but only from your scolding.

THE BARON. A very subtle distinction. But what was it that deserved my scolding?

THE YOUNG LADY. Oh, you know already. You saw me! I was talking to this gentleman—

THE BARON. Well?

THE YOUNG LADY. And the gentleman is a male person, and you told me not to have too much to do with male persons.

THE BARON. This gentleman is an exception, as you should have noticed. I wish he could endure you. I shall be pleased to see you constantly in his company.

THE YOUNG LADY. Oh dear! It will be for the first and last time, I'm afraid. His servant is already packing—and that's what I wanted to tell you.

THE BARON. What? Who? His servant?

THE TRAVELLER. Yes, sir, I gave him orders. My arrangements, and my fear of being a nuisance—

THE BARON. Whatever am I to think of this? Am I to be denied the good fortune of proving that you have gained the devotion of a grateful heart? I beg you, add to your first kindness a second, which I shall value as highly as the saving of my life; stay with me for some time—at least for a few days; I should never forgive myself for letting a man like you go away, unknown, unhonoured, unrewarded, if I could do anything to keep you. I have invited some of my relatives today, so that I can share my pleasure with them and give them the good fortune of meeting my guardian angel.

THE TRAVELLER. Sir, I have no choice but to—

THE YOUNG LADY. Stay here, sir, stay here! I'll run and tell your servant to unpack again. But here he is.

Scene 8

CHRISTOPH *booted and spurred, with two cloak-bags under his arms; the foregoing characters*

CHRISTOPH. Right, sir, everything's ready. Let's be off! Shorten your farewells a bit. Why do so much talking if we can't stay here?

THE BARON. What prevents you from staying here?

CHRISTOPH. Certain considerations, sir, based on my master's obstinacy, with his noble-heartedness as pretext.

THE TRAVELLER. My servant is often foolish: forgive him. I see that your requests are indeed more than mere compliments. I yield, so that the fear of being rude may not lead me into rudeness.

THE BARON. Oh, what thanks I owe you!

THE TRAVELLER. You can go and unpack again. We'll stay until tomorrow.

THE YOUNG LADY. Come on, are you deaf? What are you hanging about for? You're to go and unpack again.

CHRISTOPH. I've a right to be cross. I feel as if I were going to be angry; but since it only means that we're staying here, and will get food and drink, and be well looked after, so be it! I don't usually like being put to trouble for nothing; do you know that?

THE TRAVELLER. Silence! You are too impudent.

CHRISTOPH. Because I'm telling the truth.

THE YOUNG LADY. Oh, it's wonderful that you're staying. Now I'll be twice as nice to you. Come along, I'll show you our garden; you'll like it.

THE TRAVELLER. If you like it, miss, it's certain I will.

THE YOUNG LADY. Come along; but it'll soon be lunchtime. Papa, you don't mind?

THE BARON. Of course not; I'll come with you.

THE YOUNG LADY. No, no, we couldn't ask you to do that. You must have work to do.

THE BARON. At present I have nothing more important to do than to see to my guest's enjoyment.

THE YOUNG LADY. He won't mind if you leave us; will you, sir? [*Whispers to him*] Do say no. I'd like to be alone with you.

THE TRAVELLER. I shall repent of having been so readily induced to stay, the moment I see myself giving you the slightest inconvenience. I beg you—

THE BARON. Oh, don't take any notice of what the child says.

THE YOUNG LADY. Child? Papa! Don't embarrass me like that! The gentleman will think I've just got out of my pram! Don't worry; I'm old enough to go for a walk with you—come along! But look: your servant is still standing there with the cloak-bags under his arms.

CHRISTOPH. I thought that concerned only the person who found it disagreeable?

THE TRAVELLER. Silence! You are shown too much honour—

Scene 9
LISETTE, *the foregoing characters*

THE BARON [*seeing Lisette approaching*]. If you don't mind accompanying my daughter into the garden, sir, I'll follow you right away.

THE YOUNG LADY. Oh, stay as long as you like. We'll pass the time somehow. Come along!

[*Exeunt the Young Lady and the Traveller*

THE BARON. Lisette, I want a word with you!

LISETTE. Well?

THE BARON [*whispers to her*]. I still don't know who our guest is. There are reasons why I would rather not ask him. Couldn't you get his servant—

LISETTE. I know what you're after. My curiosity made me think of it for myself, and that's why I came.

THE BARON. Do your best, then, and inform me. It will be worth your while.

LISETTE. Just go.

CHRISTOPH. So you won't take it amiss, sir, if we have a good time in your house. But please don't put yourself out on my account; I'm happy with what you have.

THE BARON. Lisette, I entrust him to your care. Don't let him go short of anything. [*Exit*

CHRISTOPH. I respectfully place myself in your kindly care, miss, knowing you won't let me go short of anything. [*About to go*

Scene 10
LISETTE, CHRISTOPH

LISETTE [*detaining him*]. No, sir, I couldn't possibly let you be so impolite! Aren't I enough of a woman to be worthy of a short conversation?

CHRISTOPH. Well I never! You're very sharp, miss. Whether you're enough of a woman, or too much of one, I can't say. Judging from your lively tongue, I'd be inclined to say the latter. But be that as it may, allow me to take my leave; you can see I've got my hands full, and my arms as well. I'll be with you the moment I feel hungry or thirsty.

LISETTE. That's what our Ostler does.

CHRISTOPH. I'll be hanged! He must be a smart man; he does what I do!

LISETTE. Would you like to meet him? He's chained up in the back yard.

CHRISTOPH. Damn it all! I think you mean the dog. Ah, so you must have thought I meant bodily hunger and thirst. I didn't, though; I meant the hunger and thirst of love. *That* kind, miss! Do you like my explanation?

LISETTE. More than I like the thing you were explaining.

CHRISTOPH. You don't say! Just between you and me: maybe you'd like it if I made you a declaration of love?

LISETTE. Perhaps! Are you going to? Seriously?

CHRISTOPH. Perhaps!

LISETTE. Ugh, what an answer! 'Perhaps'!

CHRISTOPH. But it was exactly the same as your own.

LISETTE. But on my lips it means something entirely different. 'Perhaps' is a woman's greatest security. For however badly we may play our cards, we must never show our hand.

CHRISTOPH. Now if that's your meaning, I fancy we're coming to the point. [*He drops both cloak-bags on the ground*] Why do I work my hands to the bone? Lie there!—I love you, miss.

LISETTE. That's what I call saying a lot in a few words. Let's analyse it.

CHRISTOPH. No, let's not bother. But so that we can exchange ideas in peace, be so good as to sit down! I'm tired of standing. Don't stand on ceremony! [*He presses her to sit on one of the cloak-bags.*] I love you, miss.

LISETTE. But I'm sitting on something terribly hard. I think there are books in here.

CHRISTOPH. Yes, tender and witty ones; and yet they're a hard seat for you? It's my master's travelling library. There are comedies that make you cry, and tragedies that make you laugh; tender heroic poems; profound drinking-songs; and other such new-fangled trifles. But let's change places. You sit on mine—don't stand on ceremony!—mine is softer.

LISETTE. Pardon me! I couldn't be so rude—

CHRISTOPH. Don't stand on ceremony! No compliments! Won't you? Then I'll carry you over.

LISETTE. Since you order me to—

> [*She stands up and is about to sit on the other cloak-bag.*

CHRISTOPH. Order you? God forbid! No, 'order' is saying a lot. If you take it that way, you'd better stay where you are.

> [*Sits down on his cloak-bag again*

LISETTE [*aside*]. The rude thing! But I must put up with it—

CHRISTOPH. Where were we? Oh yes—love. You see, miss, I love you. Je vous aime, I'd say, if you were a French marquise.

LISETTE. Well I never! Are you a Frenchman?

CHRISTOPH. No, I must confess my shame: I'm only a German. But I've had the good fortune to have dealings with several Frenchmen, and so I've learnt pretty well what a proper fellow needs. You can tell as soon as you look at me.

LISETTE. Does that mean you and your master have just come from France?

CHRISTOPH. Oh no!

LISETTE. Well then, where have you come from?

CHRISTOPH. The place we come from is a few leagues beyond France.

LISETTE. You're not from Italy, are you?

CHRISTOPH. You're getting warm.

LISETTE. From England, then?

CHRISTOPH. Almost; England is one of its provinces. Our home is more than fifty leagues from here—But, good God! My horses! The poor beasts are still standing with their saddles on. Forgive me, miss! Quick! Up you get! [*He takes the cloak-bags under his arms*] Despite my ardent love, I have to go and do what's needful. We've still got the whole day, and, better still, the whole night. We'll soon become one. I'll know where to find you.

Scene 11
MARTIN KRUMM, LISETTE

LISETTE. I won't get much out of him. He's either too stupid or too smart; and there's no fathoming either of these.

MARTIN KRUMM. Well, Miss Lisette? That's the fellow who wants to cut me out!

LISETTE. He doesn't need to.

MARTIN KRUMM. Doesn't he? I thought I was your sweetheart.

LISETTE. That's what you think, Master Steward. People like you have the right to think nasty thoughts. So I'm not annoyed with you because you thought that, but because you said it. What business have you with my heart, I'd like to know? What kindnesses or presents have given you any right to it? People don't give their hearts away for nothing. Do you imagine I don't know what to do with mine? I'll find an honest man to give it to, sooner than cast it before the swine.

MARTIN KRUMM. You've got the devil of a temper! I must have a pinch of snuff. Perhaps that will help me sneeze.
    [*He takes out the stolen snuff-box, toys with it for a while, and
    finally takes a pinch of snuff in an absurdly conceited fashion*

LISETTE [*looking askance at him*]. Damn! Where did the fellow get that box from?

MARTIN KRUMM. Could you fancy a little pinch of snuff?

LISETTE. Oh, your most humble serving-maid, Master Steward!
                                                    [*Takes a pinch*

MARTIN KRUMM. Amazing what a silver snuff-box can do! Could an earwig be more insinuating?

LISETTE. Is it a silver snuff-box?

MARTIN KRUMM. If it weren't silver, Martin Krumm wouldn't have it.

LISETTE. Will you permit me to look at it?

MARTIN KRUMM. Yes, but only in my hands.

LISETTE. The chasing is wonderful.

MARTIN KRUMM. Yes, it weighs nearly three ounces.

LISETTE. I'd like a box like that, just for the sake of the chasing.

MARTIN KRUMM. When I have it melted down, the chasing is yours.

LISETTE. How kind! It must be a present?

MARTIN KRUMM. Yes—it didn't cost me a penny.

LISETTE. Really, a present like that could quite bedazzle a woman! You can make your fortune with it, Master Steward. At least, if I were assailed with silver boxes, I wouldn't know how to defend myself. With a box like that, a lover could have his way with me.

MARTIN KRUMM. I see what you're driving at!

LISETTE. Since it cost you nothing, I'd advise you, Master Steward, to win a young lady with it—

MARTIN KRUMM. I see what you're driving at!

LISETTE [*ingratiatingly*]. I wonder if you'd make me a present of it?

MARTIN KRUMM. Sorry! People don't give their silver snuff-boxes away for nothing. And do you imagine, Miss Lisette, that I don't know what to do with mine? I'll find an honest man to give it to, sooner than cast it before the swine.

LISETTE. I've never known anything so stupid and rude! Fancy setting as much store by a snuff-box as a heart!

MARTIN KRUMM. Yes, a silver snuff-box and a heart of stone—

LISETTE. It might stop being of stone if—but what's the use of talking? He isn't worthy of my love. What a soft-hearted fool I am! [*Beginning to cry*] I really thought the steward was one of the honest people who mean what they say—

MARTIN KRUMM. And what a soft-hearted fool I am, to think a woman means what she says! There, Lizzie, don't cry! [*He gives her the box.*] Am I worthy of your love now? All I ask to begin with is a little kiss on your lovely hand! [*He kisses her.*] Ah, that tastes good!

Scene 12
THE YOUNG LADY, LISETTE, MARTIN KRUMM

THE YOUNG LADY [*enters stealthily and knocks* MARTIN KRUMM'S *head down onto* LISETTE's *hand*]. Why, Master Steward, kiss my hand as well!

LISETTE. What the—!

MARTIN KRUMM. Gladly, miss—   [*about to kiss her hand*

THE YOUNG LADY [*smacks him on the cheek*]. You lout, don't you understand a joke?

MARTIN KRUMM. The Devil take a joke like that!

LISETTE. Ha, ha, ha! [*laughing at him*] Oh, how sorry I am for you, dear steward—ha, ha, ha!

MARTIN KRUMM. Oh? You're laughing too? Is that all the thanks I get? Very well, very well! [*Exit*

LISETTE. Ha, ha, ha!

Scene 13
LISETTE, THE YOUNG LADY

THE YOUNG LADY. If I hadn't seen it with my own eyes, I'd never have believed it. You let a man kiss you? And the steward, of all people?

LISETTE. What right have you to spy on him? I thought you were going for a walk in the garden with the stranger.

THE YOUNG LADY. Yes, and I'd still be with him if Papa hadn't joined us. But I can't say a sensible word to him. Papa is too serious for anything—

LISETTE. Why, what do you mean by a sensible word? What have you to talk about with him that Papa isn't supposed to hear?

THE YOUNG LADY. All sorts of things! But if you ask me any more, you'll make me cross. I like the strange gentleman, and that's that. You don't mind my admitting that?

LISETTE. You'd have a terrible row with Papa, wouldn't you, if he provided you with a man like that as a bridegroom? Seriously though, who knows what he might do. Pity you're not a few years older, and then it might happen quite quickly.

THE YOUNG LADY. Oh, if my age is the problem, Papa can say I'm a few years older than I am. I certainly won't contradict him.

LISETTE. No, I've got a better idea. I'll give you some of my years, and that will help us both. I won't be too old, and you won't be too young.

THE YOUNG LADY. That's right; what a good idea!

LISETTE. Here comes the stranger's servant; I must have a word with him. It's all for your good. Leave me alone with him. Off you go.

THE YOUNG LADY. But don't forget about the years—do you hear, Lisette?

Scene 14
LISETTE, CHRISTOPH

LISETTE. You must be hungry or thirsty, sir, as you're back so soon.

CHRISTOPH. Yes, indeed! But hungry and thirsty in the sense that I explained. To tell you the truth, my dear young lady, I had my eye on you as soon as I dismounted yesterday. But as I only expected to stay a few hours, I thought it wasn't worth my while to make your acquaintance. What could we have done in such a short time? We'd have had to start our romance at the end. But it's a risky thing, too, to pull the cat out of the stove by the tail.

LISETTE. That's true! But now we can do things properly. I can tell you my doubts; you can resolve them. We can think what we're doing at each step of the way, and we mustn't buy a pig in a poke. If you had made your declaration of love to me yesterday, I'd have accepted. But just think of the risk I'd have run if I hadn't had time to ask about your rank, fortune, country, previous employment, and so forth!

CHRISTOPH. For goodness sake! Would that have been necessary? What a fuss! If we got married, you might make things even worse!

LISETTE. Oh, if we were talking about a mere marriage, it would be absurd for me to be so careful. But a love-affair is quite another matter! Here the slightest detail becomes important. So don't imagine you'll get the least favour from me unless you satisfy my curiosity about everything.

CHRISTOPH. Well, how far does that go?

LISETTE. Since the best guide to a servant is his master, I especially want to know—

CHRISTOPH. Who my master is? Ha, ha! That's a good one. You're asking me something that I'd be glad to ask you, if I thought you knew any more than I do.

LISETTE. You needn't think you'll get away with that stale excuse. Come on, I must know who your master is, or our whole friendship is over.

CHRISTOPH. I have known my master for no more than four weeks. That's when he took me into his service in Hamburg. Since then I've travelled with him, but never taken the trouble to ask about his rank or name. This much is certain, he must be rich; for neither he nor I went short of anything on the journey. What more do I need to bother about?

LISETTE. What can I expect of your love, if you won't trust even such a tiny thing to my discretion? I'd never be like that to you. For example, I've got a beautiful silver snuff-box here—

CHRISTOPH. Well?

LISETTE. If you'd just ask me nicely, I'd tell you who I got it from—

CHRISTOPH. Oh, I don't care about that. I'd rather know who's going to get it from you.

LISETTE. I haven't made up my mind about that yet. But if you don't get it, blame yourself and nobody else. I wouldn't leave your honesty unrewarded.

CHRISTOPH. Or rather my loose mouth! But as true as I'm an honest fellow, if I'm discreet this time, it's because I've got to be. For I've got nothing to reveal. Damn it! I'd love to give away my secrets if I had any.

LISETTE. Goodbye! I won't assault your virtue any longer. I only hope your virtue soon provides you with a silver box and a sweetheart, since it's just deprived you of both.   [*About to go*

CHRISTOPH. Where are you going? Patience! [*Aside*] I see I'm compelled to tell lies. After all, I'm not going to let a present like that escape me. Anyway, what's the harm?

LISETTE. Well, are you going to tell? But I can see you don't want to. All right; I don't want to know—

CHRISTOPH. Yes, yes, I'll tell you everything! [*Aside*] I wish I were good at lying!—Just listen! My master is—he's a nobleman. He comes—we've both come—from—from Holland. He had—certain difficulties—a trifle—a murder—so he had to flee—

LISETTE. What? Because he murdered someone?

CHRISTOPH. Yes—but it was a respectable murder—he had to flee because of a duel—and now—he's on the run—

LISETTE. And what about you, my friend?

CHRISTOPH. I—I'm on the run too. The dead man—I mean, the friends of the dead man—sent people to pursue us; and because of this pursuit—well, you can work out the rest for yourself. What else can a man do, damn it? Think for yourself: a cheeky young puppy insults us. My master knocks him down. There's only one thing for it! If anyone insults me, I do the same, or—or punch him in the face. An honest fellow can't let people walk all over him.

LISETTE. Well said! I like people like that; because I'm a bit intolerant too. But just look, here comes your master! You'd never think to look at him that he was so short-tempered and cruel!

CHRISTOPH. Come along! Let's keep out of his way. He might see, just by looking at me, that I've betrayed his secret.

LISETTE. That's fine—

CHRISTOPH. But the silver box—

LISETTE. Come along. [*Aside*] I must first see what my master will give me for the secret I've discovered; if it's worth my while, he can have the box.

Scene 15
THE TRAVELLER

THE TRAVELLER. I can't find my snuff-box. It's a trifle; all the same, I regret its loss. I wonder if the steward—But I may have lost it; I may have dropped it out of carelessness. One mustn't insult anyone, even with suspicions. All the same, he pressed close to me; he reached for my watch; I caught him in the act; may he not have reached for the box, without being caught?

Scene 16
MARTIN KRUMM, THE TRAVELLER

MARTIN KRUMM [*catching sight of the Traveller and about to turn back*]. Oh, oh!

THE TRAVELLER. Now, just come closer, my friend! [*Aside*] He's as shy as if he knew what I was thinking!—Well? come closer!

MARTIN KRUMM [*aggressively*]. Oh, I haven't the time! I know you want to chat with me. I've got more important things to do. I don't want to hear about your heroic deeds ten times over. Tell them to someone who doesn't know about them already.

THE TRAVELLER. What's this? A short time ago the steward was simple-minded and polite, now he's impudent and rude. Which is your true mask?

MARTIN KRUMM. You've got a right cheek calling my face a mask. I don't want to quarrel with you, or else—   [*about to go away*

THE TRAVELLER. His impudent behaviour strengthens me in my suspicion.—No, no, patience! There's something I need to ask you—

MARTIN KRUMM. And I won't answer, however much you need to ask. So don't bother.

THE TRAVELLER. I'll risk it—but how sorry I'd be if I did him an injustice.—My friend, have you seen my snuff-box? I can't find it.

MARTIN KRUMM. What sort of question is that? I can't help it if someone stole it, can I? What do you think I am? The fence? Or the thief?

THE TRAVELLER. Who said anything about stealing? You're almost giving yourself away.

MARTIN KRUMM. Giving myself away? So you think I've got it? And do you know what it means to accuse an honest fellow of something like that? Eh?

THE TRAVELLER. Why do you have to shout like that? I haven't accused you of anything. You are your own accuser. Anyway, would I be so far wrong? Who was it that I caught a short time ago reaching for my watch?

MARTIN KRUMM. Oh, a man like you can't take a joke. Listen! [*Aside*] I hope he hasn't seen Lisette with it—she surely wouldn't be daft enough to show it around.

THE TRAVELLER. Oh, I can take a joke so well that I think you're joking with my snuff-box. But if you take a joke too far, it ends up turning serious. I'm sorry about your good name. Supposing

I were convinced that you meant no harm, other people might—

MARTIN KRUMM. Other people! Other people would have got fed up with this sort of reproach, long before now. But if you think I've got it, you can frisk me—go through my pockets—

THE TRAVELLER. That is not my job. Besides, one doesn't keep everything in one's pocket.

MARTIN KRUMM. All right! To show you I'm an honest fellow, I'll turn out my coat pockets for you. Just watch! [*Aside*] It can't fall out, unless the devil's in it.

THE TRAVELLER. Oh, don't give yourself any trouble!

MARTIN KRUMM. No, no, you'll see, you'll see. [*Turns out one of his pockets*] Any snuff-boxes there? Only breadcrumbs, that's all! [*Turns out the other pocket*] Nothing there, either! Oh yes—a bit of a calendar. I keep it because of the verses at the head of each month. They're a good laugh! But let's get a move on. Just watch: I'll turn out the third pocket. [*As he does so, two big beards fall out.*] Drat it! What have I dropped?

[*Tries to snatch them up, but the Traveller is quicker and seizes one*

THE TRAVELLER. What on earth is this?

MARTIN KRUMM [*aside*]. Damnation! I thought I'd got rid of that rubbish a while ago.

THE TRAVELLER. Why, it's a false beard. [*Tries it on*] Do I look like a Jew?

MARTIN KRUMM. Give it here! Give it here! Who knows what you might be thinking? I use it sometimes to give my little boy a bit of a fright. That's all it's for.

THE TRAVELLER. Be kind enough to let me keep it. I want to give someone a fright.

MARTIN KRUMM. Oh, don't play the fool with me. I must have it back.   [*Tries to grab it from him*

THE TRAVELLER. Go away, or else—

MARTIN KRUMM [*aside*]. Blast! I'm really in the soup now.—All right, all right! I see you've come here to do me down. But, damn my eyes, I'm an honest fellow! I'd like to know who can say anything bad about me. You mark my words! No matter what happens, I can swear that I didn't use the beard for anything wrong.   [*Exit*

Scene 17
THE TRAVELLER

THE TRAVELLER. That man arouses a suspicion in me which is much to his disadvantage. Might he not have been one of the masked robbers? But I'll be cautious in my conjectures.

Scene 18
THE BARON, THE TRAVELLER

THE TRAVELLER. Wouldn't you think that I'd been fighting with the Jewish highwaymen yesterday, and torn off one of their beards?   [*Shows him the false beard*

THE BARON. Whatever do you mean, sir? But why were you in such a hurry to leave me in the garden?

THE TRAVELLER. Forgive my impoliteness. I meant to return to you at once. I only went to look for my snuff-box, which I must have lost hereabouts.

THE BARON. I'm very sorry to hear it. To think of you suffering a loss in my house!

THE TRAVELLER. Not such a great loss—but look at this magnificent beard!

THE BARON. You've already shown it to me. Why?

THE TRAVELLER. I'll explain myself more clearly. I think—but no, I'll keep my conjectures to myself.

THE BARON. Your conjectures? Explain yourself!

THE TRAVELLER. No, I spoke too soon. I might be mistaken—

THE BARON. You're getting me worried.

THE TRAVELLER. What do you think of your steward?

THE BARON. No, no, don't change the subject. I implore you, by the kindness you showed me, tell me what you think, what you conjecture, what you might be mistaken about!

THE TRAVELLER. Answer my question first, and then I'll tell you.

THE BARON. What do I think of my steward? I think he's a very honest, upright man.

THE TRAVELLER. Forget that I was going to say anything.

THE BARON. A false beard—conjectures—the steward—how am I to connect these things? Doesn't it affect you when I implore you? You might be mistaken? Let's say you are mistaken; what kind of risk can you run with a friend?

THE TRAVELLER. You're pressing me too hard. So let me tell you that the steward dropped this beard by mistake; that he had another, which he hastily tucked away; that he talked like somebody who thinks he deserves his bad reputation; and that another time I caught him doing something that wasn't very scrupulous, or at least not very clever.

THE BARON. I feel as though my eyes were suddenly opened. I'm afraid you are not mistaken. And you had doubts about revealing such a thing to me? I'll go this very minute and do all I can to get at the truth. What if I had my murderer in my own house?

THE TRAVELLER. But don't be angry with me if, by good fortune, my conjectures should turn out to be wrong. You squeezed them out of me, otherwise I would certainly have kept them to myself.

THE BARON. Whether I find them right or wrong, I shall always be grateful to you.

Scene 19
THE TRAVELLER; *later* CHRISTOPH

THE TRAVELLER. I hope he doesn't deal with him too hastily! For however great the suspicion is, the man could still be innocent. I feel quite at a loss. Really, it is no small matter to make a master so suspicious of his subordinates. Even if he finds them innocent, he will never trust them again. When I think about it, there's no doubt, I should have kept silent. When they learn that I blamed him for my loss, won't they think that my suspicion was based on selfishness and revenge? I wouldn't mind being guilty of such things, if only I could prevent the investigation—

CHRISTOPH [*enters laughing*]. Ha, ha, ha! Do you know what you are, sir?

THE TRAVELLER. Do you know that you're a fool? What are you talking about?

CHRISTOPH. Very well! If you don't know, I'll tell you. You're a nobleman. You come from Holland, where you got into difficulties and fought a duel. You were lucky enough to stab a young puppy. The dead man's friends are having you pursued. You're on the run. And I have the honour of accompanying you on the run.

THE TRAVELLER. Are you dreaming, or raving?

CHRISTOPH. Neither one nor the other. For what I said was too intelligent for raving, and too fantastic for dreaming.

THE TRAVELLER. Who made you believe all this nonsense?

CHRISTOPH. I didn't say I believed it. But isn't it a wonderful invention? In the short time I had to think up lies, I couldn't have thought of anything better. It means you're safe from any further curiosity!

THE TRAVELLER. But what am I to make of all this?

CHRISTOPH. Just what you like; leave the rest to me. Listen, I'll tell you how it happened. They asked me about your name, your rank, your country, your plans; I didn't keep them waiting, I said all I knew; that is, I said I knew nothing. You can imagine that this information wasn't adequate, and they weren't satisfied with it. They pressed me harder; all for nothing! I kept my mouth shut, because I had nothing to keep it shut about. But finally I was offered a present, and that made me say more than I knew; that is, I told lies.

THE TRAVELLER. Scoundrel! I can see I'm in good hands with you.

CHRISTOPH. You aren't telling me that the lies I told happen to be the truth?

THE TRAVELLER. Impudent liar, you have put me in such confusion—

CHRISTOPH. You can get out of it by spreading the nice epithet you were pleased to give me just now.

THE TRAVELLER. But then, won't I be obliged to reveal who I really am?

CHRISTOPH. So much the better! That would give me a chance to learn who you are. But judge for yourself whether, with an easy conscience, I could have these lies on my conscience? [*He pulls out the snuff-box*] Look at this snuff-box! How could I have earned it more easily?

THE TRAVELLER. Show it to me! [*He takes it in his hand*] What do I see?

CHRISTOPH. Ha, ha, ha! I thought you'd be surprised. You'd tell a pack of lies yourself, wouldn't you, to earn such a snuff-box?

THE TRAVELLER. So it was you who stole it from me?

CHRISTOPH. What?

THE TRAVELLER. It's not your treachery that annoys me, so much as the premature suspicion that I have drawn upon an honest man. And you have the impertinence to try to tell me that it was a present, no matter how dishonestly you came by it? Get out, and never come near me again!

CHRISTOPH. Are you dreaming, or—I won't say the other thing, out of respect for you. Is it envy that puts such wild ideas into your head? You say this is your snuff-box? And I—saving your presence—stole it from you? If I did, I'd have to be an ass to boast of it to your face. Oh good, here comes Lisette! Here, come quick! Help me set my master to rights.

Scene 20
LISETTE, THE TRAVELLER, CHRISTOPH

LISETTE. Oh, sir, what a fuss you've stirred up among us! What has our steward done to you? You've made our master quite furious with him. They're talking about beards, snuff-boxes, robbery; the steward is crying and cursing, saying he's innocent and you weren't telling the truth. There's no appeasing our master, and now he's even sent for the mayor and the police, to have him put in chains. What does it all mean?

CHRISTOPH. Oh, that's nothing, just listen to what he means to do with me—

THE TRAVELLER. Yes, indeed, my dear Lisette, I was too hasty. The steward is innocent. It was only my godless servant who plunged me into these difficulties. It was he who stole the snuff-box that made me suspicious of the steward; and the false beard may have been part of a children's game, as he said. I'm off to give him satisfaction, I'll confess my error, I'll give him whatever he demands—

CHRISTOPH. No, no, stay where you are! You'd better give me satisfaction first. Hang it all, Lisette, open your mouth and say what really happened. I wish you and your snuff-box were on the gallows! Am I to let people call me a thief for your sake? Didn't you give it to me?

LISETTE. Yes indeed, and you can keep it, what's more.

THE TRAVELLER. So it's true? But the snuff-box is mine.

LISETTE. Yours? I didn't know that.

THE TRAVELLER. And so Lisette found it? and my carelessness is to blame for all this muddle? [*To Christoph*] I have said too much to you! Forgive me! I'm ashamed of being so hasty.

LISETTE [*aside*]. Well I never! I see what's up. He wasn't so hasty after all.

THE TRAVELLER. Come along, let us—

Scene 21
THE BARON, THE TRAVELLER, LISETTE, CHRISTOPH

THE BARON [*entering in a hurry*]. Quick, Lisette, give the gentleman back his snuff-box this instant! Everything is revealed; he's confessed everything. And you weren't ashamed to accept presents from a person like that? Well? Where's the snuff-box?

THE TRAVELLER. So it's true?

LISETTE. The gentleman has had it back for ages. I thought anyone who could give you service could give me presents. I knew him as little as you did.

CHRISTOPH. So my present has gone up in smoke? Easy come, easy go!

THE BARON. But, my dearest friend, how can I show my gratitude to you? This is the second time you have saved me from a great danger. I owe you my life. Without you, I would never have discovered the misfortune that was so close to me. The mayor, whom I thought the most honest man on my estates, was his godless accomplice. Just think, could I ever have suspected that? If you had left me today—

THE TRAVELLER. That's true—the help that I thought I gave you yesterday would have been very far from complete. I therefore consider myself extremely fortunate that Heaven has made me the instrument of this unexpected discovery; and I am as delighted now as earlier I trembled in fear of being wrong.

THE BARON. I admire your love of humanity as much as your noble-heartedness. Oh, if only what Lisette told me was true!

Scene 22
THE YOUNG LADY, *the foregoing characters*

LISETTE. Well, why shouldn't it be true?

THE BARON. Come, my daughter, come! Unite my request with yours: beseech my rescuer to accept your hand, and with your hand, my wealth. What more precious gift can my gratitude confer on him than you, whom I love as much as I do him? Don't be surprised at my making such a request. Your servant has revealed to us who you are. Grant me the inestimable pleasure of showing gratitude! My wealth matches my rank, and my rank matches yours. Here you are safe from your enemies, and are among friends who will worship you. But you look downcast? What am I to think?

THE YOUNG LADY. You aren't worried about me, are you? I assure you, I'll be only too happy to obey Papa.

THE TRAVELLER. Your noble-heartedness astonishes me. The magnitude of the reward you offer shows me how small a kindness I did you. But what am I to answer? My servant told you an untruth, and I—

THE BARON. Would to Heaven that you weren't even what he said you were! Would to Heaven your rank were lower than mine! My reward would thus become somewhat more precious, and you might be less reluctant to accede to my wish.

THE TRAVELLER [*aside*]. Why don't I reveal myself?—Sir, your nobility penetrates my entire soul. But ascribe it to fate, not to me, that your offer is in vain. I am—

THE BARON. Married already?

THE TRAVELLER. No—

THE BARON. What then?

THE TRAVELLER. I am a Jew.

THE BARON. A Jew? Cruel accident!

CHRISTOPH. A Jew?

LISETTE. A Jew?

THE YOUNG LADY. Why, what difference does that make?

LISETTE. Ssh, miss, ssh! I'll tell you later what difference it makes.

THE BARON. So there are cases where Heaven itself prevents us from showing gratitude?

THE TRAVELLER. The will suffices instead of the deed.

THE BARON. Then I'll at least do all that fate allows me to do. Take my entire wealth. I would rather be poor and grateful than rich and ungrateful.

THE TRAVELLER. This offer too is in vain, since the God of my fathers has given me more than I need. The only reward I ask is that in future you will judge my nation more mildly and less sweepingly. I did not conceal my identity from you because I was ashamed of my religion. No! But I saw that you liked me and disliked my nation. And the friendship of a human being, be he who he may, has always been priceless in my eyes.

THE BARON. I am ashamed of my behaviour.

CHRISTOPH. I was speechless with astonishment, but now I'm myself again. What? You're a Jew, and you had the face to employ an honest Christian in your service? *You* ought to have served *me*. That's what the Bible commands. By the Lord Harry! You've insulted all of Christendom in me. I wondered why my master wouldn't eat any pork while we were travelling, and got up to all manner of antics. You needn't think I'll accompany you any longer! I'll have the law on you, what's more.

THE TRAVELLER. I cannot expect you to think better than the rest of the Christian rabble. I shall not remind you of the misery from which I saved you in Hamburg. Nor shall I compel you to remain with me any longer. But since I am fairly pleased with your service, and besides I had unfounded suspicions of you earlier, you can keep as a reward the cause of those suspicions. [*Gives him the snuff-box*] You can have your wages too, and then go wherever you want!

CHRISTOPH. No, hang it all! There are some Jews who aren't Jews. You're a fine man. Done! I'll stay with you! A Christian would have kicked me in the teeth instead of giving me a snuff-box!

THE BARON. Everything I see in you delights me. Come, let's arrange for the guilty parties to be sent into safe custody. Oh, how admirable the Jews would be if they were all like you!

THE TRAVELLER. And how charming the Christians would be, if they all had your qualities!

[*Exeunt the Baron, the Young Lady, and the Traveller*

Last Scene
LISETTE, CHRISTOPH

LISETTE. So, my friend, you were lying to me earlier?

CHRISTOPH. Yes, and I had two reasons. First, I didn't know the truth; and second, a snuff-box that has to be returned doesn't deserve much in the way of truth.

LISETTE. And I daresay you're a Jew too, despite your disguise?

CHRISTOPH. A young lady shouldn't be so inquisitive. Come along!

[*He takes her arm, and exeunt*

MOSES MENDELSSOHN

Reply to Lavater

Moses Mendelssohn (1729–86) was the son of a Torah scribe in Dessau, a centre of the early Haskala (Jewish Enlightenment). Under the guidance of his scholarly teacher, David Fränkel, he studied not only the Talmud but also medieval Jewish philosophy, especially that of Maimonides. In 1743, when Fränkel moved to Berlin as chief rabbi, Mendelssohn followed him, and was allowed to continue his studies there at a time when the Jewish population of Berlin was officially restricted to 120 families (though 333 families were actually resident). There he met other Jews who were exploring secular knowledge; learnt standard German, besides French and Latin; studied Enlightenment thinkers, especially Leibniz, Locke, and Wolff; became friends with Lessing and the bookseller Friedrich Nicolai; moved freely in literary circles; and in 1755 published his first philosophical writings. His career, in which he became a successful manager of a silk-weaving factory, enabled him to marry in 1762 and support a large family, but was a burdensome distraction from his literary activities.

Mendelssohn's philosophical ability was first publicly acknowledged when, in 1763, he was awarded a prize by the Berlin Royal Academy for his essay about the kind of certainty possible for metaphysical truths, narrowly beating an entry by Kant. His Platonic dialogue *Phaedon* (1767), on the immortality of the soul, gained him a European reputation. Though scarcely found in biblical Judaism, the immortality of the soul was strongly upheld by Maimonides, and was part of the 'natural religion' professed by the Enlightenment. Mendelssohn not only satisfied a large public by defending it powerfully against the scepticism of materialists, but reconciled classical Jewish philosophy with Enlightenment deism. In 1771 the Berlin Royal Academy decided to propose to Frederick the Great that Mendelssohn should be elected a member; but the king did not approve the proposal. Mendelssohn also translated the Pentateuch into German, with a Hebrew commentary; he wanted to discourage German Jews from using Yiddish and to promote the use of Hebrew and German. He also tried to ameliorate the Jews' social position by persuading his friend, the Prussian civil servant Christian Wilhelm von Dohm, to write the treatise *On the Civil Improvement of the Jews* (1781). Mendelssohn's own last major work was *Jerusalem; or On Religious Power and Judaism* (1783), which described Judaism not as a religion, analogous to Christianity, with dogmas requiring faith, but as a revealed legislation requiring essentially the observance of strict morality and hence in no way contrary to the rationalism or the ethics of the European Enlightenment.

In 1769 Mendelssohn, now a well-known public figure, was challenged by the Swiss clergyman Johann Caspar Lavater (1741–1801) either to refute the proofs of Christianity supposedly advanced by Charles Bonnet (whose *Palingénésie philosophique* tries to resolve theological problems by a theory of reincarnation), or to accept Christianity. Mendelssohn, who shunned controversy, was embarrassed by this challenge. It put him in a false position where, by seeming publicly to oppose Christianity, he could bring official disfavour upon the Jews. His dignified and decisive reply to Lavater shows him reflecting on the relation between reason and toleration. While vulgar Enlighteners thought it the duty of reason to annihilate prejudice (irrational and merely traditional beliefs), Mendelssohn distinguishes between harmful prejudices and those which, though perhaps irrational, nevertheless provide the basis for moral living and cannot be extirpated without disorienting and demoralizing their adherents. Lavater, who had already made a blundering attempt to win the sceptical Protestant Goethe over to his own intense Christianity, found himself the object of general disapproval from Enlightened theologians, including Bonnet, and reluctantly withdrew from the fray.

———

Esteemed friend of humanity!

You have thought fit to dedicate to me your translation of M. Bonnet's *Study of the Evidence for Christianity*, and in your dedication, before the eyes of the public, to appeal to me in the most solemn manner: 'insofar as I find the *essential* arguments adduced in support of Christianity to be incorrect, to refute this book; but insofar as I find them correct, to do what prudence, veracity, and honesty bid me do—what Socrates would have done if he had read this book and found it irrefutable'; that is, to abandon the religion of my fathers and adopt the one defended by M. B. For certainly, even if my mind were base enough to make *prudence* a counterweight to veracity and honesty, I would in this case find all three on the same side of the balance.

I am entirely convinced that your actions proceed from pure motives, and *cannot* ascribe to you any but benevolent and humane intentions. I should be unworthy of the respect of any upright man if

I did not respond with a grateful heart to the friendly affection you display in your dedication. But I cannot deny that this step on your part has caused me great consternation. The last thing I expected from a Lavater was a *public* challenge.

As you will recall the confidential discussion which I had the pleasure of having with you and your worthy friends in my parlour, you cannot possibly have forgotten how often I tried to steer the conversation away from matters of religion to indifferent topics; how hard you and your friends had to press me before I ventured to express my sentiments on something so important to the heart. If I am not mistaken, assurances had previously been given that the words uttered on that occasion would *never* be used in public.— However, I would rather be wrong than blame you for breaking this promise.—But if I sought so anxiously to avoid making an explicit declaration in my parlour, among a small number of worthy men, of whose fair-mindedness I had reason to be assured, then it was easy to guess that a *public* declaration would be utterly repugnant to my character, and that I should feel *embarrassed* when the voice that *challenges* me to make one *cannot* be dismissed as contemptible. What then can have induced you, contrary to my wishes which were well known to you, to single me out from the crowd and lead me to the public lists which I so much wished never to enter?—And even if you ascribed my reserve to mere timidity or shyness, would not such a weakness deserve indulgence and charity from any benevolent heart?

However, my reluctance to enter into religious controversies has never consisted in fear or bashfulness. I may say that I did not begin to study my religion only yesterday. Very early in life I recognized it as a duty to examine my opinions and actions, and if, since my early youth, I have devoted my leisure hours to philosophy and humane learning, that was solely in order to prepare myself for such a necessary examination. I could have had no other motives. In the situation in which I found myself I could not expect learning to bring the slightest temporal advantage. I was well aware that I could not attain *worldly prosperity* by such means. And enjoyment?—O my esteemed friend of humanity! The position in society assigned to my co-religionists is so far removed from any *free* exercise of the intellect that one certainly does not increase one's happiness by learning the truth about the rights of mankind.—I will refrain from enlarging on this point. Anyone who knows our circumstances and has a human heart will feel more than I can say.

If, after all those years of research, my decision had not been in favour of *my own* religion, I must necessarily have made it known by a public act [i.e. baptism]. I do not see what could attach me to a religion that appears so strict and is so generally despised, if I were not convinced in my heart of its truth. Whatever the result of my inquiries might be, as soon as I did not consider the religion of my fathers to be true, I was obliged to abandon it. If I had been inwardly drawn to another, it would have been the most atrocious baseness to defy my inner conviction and *refuse* to confess the truth. And what could have misled me into such baseness? I have already admitted that in this case prudence, veracity, and honesty would all point in the same direction.

If I had cared nothing about either religion, and scorned or despised all revelation, then I should have known very well what prudence advises when conscience is silent. What could have prevented me?—Fear of my co-religionists?—Their worldly power is far too small to inspire me with fear.—Obstinacy? Indolence? Attachment to accustomed ideas?—Since I have devoted the greater part of my life to inquiry, people will give me credit for being intelligent enough not to sacrifice the fruits of my inquiries to such weaknesses.

You see, therefore, that if I had not believed sincerely in my own religion, the outcome of my inquiry must have shown itself in a public act. Since, however, it confirmed that of my fathers, I was able to proceed quietly on my way, without giving the world any account of my beliefs. I shall not deny that I have found in my religion human additions and abuses which, alas, too much obscure its glory. What friend of truth can boast of having found his religion free from all harmful human elaborations? All those of us who seek the truth recognize the corrupting breath of hypocrisy and superstition, and wish to remove it without detriment to the true and the good. But I am as firmly and unshakably convinced of the *essentials* of my religion as you or M. Bonnet or any of your associates can be of yours, and I hereby testify by the God of truth, your and my creator and preserver, that I shall adhere to my principles unless my entire soul shall change its nature. My remoteness from your religion, which I indicated to you and your friends, has not diminished in the

meantime, and my regard for the moral character of its Founder?—
You should not have ignored the qualification which I explicitly
added; for then I could now have repeated this concession. At some
point in one's life one must call a halt to certain inquiries in order to
get further. I may say that with respect to religion I reached this
point some years ago. I read, compared, reflected, and took my stand.

All the same, Judaism could have been demolished in every hand-
book of polemics, and been triumphantly demonstrated in every
scholastic exercise, without my ever entering into a dispute about it.
Every expert or amateur in rabbinic matters could have extracted
from dusty tomes that no sensible Jew now reads or even knows the
most absurd notion of Judaism for the benefit of himself and his
readers, without my raising the slightest objection. I should like to
refute the contemptuous opinion commonly held of a Jew through
virtue and not through polemical pamphlets. My religion, my philosophy, and my position in society give me every reason to avoid
religious controversies and to speak in my publications only of those
truths that must be equally important to all religions.

According to the principles of my religion, I *may not* try to convert
anyone who is not born under our law. This spirit of conversion,
whose origin some would like to blame on the Jewish religion, is
diametrically opposed to it.* All our rabbis are unanimous in teaching that the written and oral laws in which our revealed religion
consists are binding only on our nation. Moses brought *us* the law, it
is a legacy from the kindred of Jacob. All other nations of the earth,
we believe, have been instructed by God to keep the law of nature
and the religion of the patriarchs.* Those who conduct their lives in
accordance with the laws of this religion of nature and reason are
called *virtuous men of other nations*, and these are children of eternal
bliss.

Our rabbis are so far from any urge to make converts that even if
anyone voluntarily comes forward, they require us to dissuade him
by serious counter-arguments. We are to remind him that by this
step he would be unnecessarily submitting to a very wearisome burden; that in his present state he need only observe the Noahide laws
to attain eternal happiness, but by adopting the religion of the Israelites he would voluntarily be submitting to all the strict laws of this
faith, and would have either to keep them or await the punishment
which the legislator prescribed for their infringement. Finally we are

to give him a faithful account of the misery, the oppression, and the contempt in which the nation at present lives, in order to prevent him from taking a hasty step which he might subsequently regret.

The religion of my fathers, therefore, does not *wish* to be diffused. We are not to send missions to the East or West Indies or to Greenland to preach our religion to those distant peoples. Since the latter in particular, according to accounts of them, obey the law of nature better, alas, than we do, they are, by our doctrines, a blessed people. Anyone who is not born under our law may not live by our law. We alone consider ourselves bound to obey these laws, and that cannot offend any of our fellow men. Do our opinions seem incoherent? There is no need to dispute the matter. We act in accordance with our belief, and others are welcome to question the validity of laws which, by our own admission, do not apply to them. Whether it is proper, friendly, humane of them to cast such scorn on our laws and customs, may be left to their own consciences to decide. Since we do not seek to persuade others of our opinion, all dispute is futile.

If my contemporaries included a Confucius or a Solon,* I could, in accordance with the principles of my religion, love and admire the great man, without having the ridiculous idea of trying to *convert* a Confucius or a Solon. Convert him? To what? Since he does not belong to the *kindred of Jacob*, the laws of my religion are not binding on him, and we could readily agree on the teachings. Do I think that he could attain eternal happiness?—O! I hardly think that anyone who guides people to virtue in this life can be damned in the next, and I need not fear that any reverend College will arraign me for this opinion, as the Sorbonne did the honest Marmontel.*

I am fortunate enough to have as friends many excellent men who are not of my religion. We are sincerely attached to each other, although we guess and assume that in matters of religion our opinions vary widely. I enjoy the pleasure of their company, which I find improving and delightful. Never did my heart whisper to me: '*What a shame about their souls!*' Anyone who thinks that there is no salvation to be found outside his church must often find such sighs rising in his bosom.

It is, of course, the natural obligation of every mortal to diffuse knowledge and virtue among his fellow men, and to do his best to extirpate their prejudices and errors. One might think, in this regard, that it was the duty of every man publicly to oppose the religious opinions that he considers mistaken. But not all prejudices are equally harmful, and hence the prejudices we may think we perceive among our fellow men must not all be treated in the same way. Some are directly contrary to the happiness of the human race. Their influence on people's manners is obviously harmful, and not even an accidental benefit can be expected from them. These must be attacked outright by every friend of humanity. The best way to assail them is undoubtedly the direct one, and any delay resulting from circuitous methods is irresponsible. Of this kind are all people's errors and prejudices that disturb their own or their fellows' peace and contentment and kill every seed of the true and the good in man before it can germinate. On the one hand, fanaticism, misanthropy, and the spirit of persecution, and on the other, frivolity, luxury, and libertinism.

Sometimes, however, the opinions of my fellow men, which in my belief are errors, belong to the higher theoretical principles which are too remote from practical life to do any direct harm; but, precisely because of their generality, they form the basis on which the nation that upholds them has built its moral and social system, and thus happen to be of great importance to this part of the human race. To oppose such doctrines in public, because we consider them prejudices, is to dig up the ground to see whether it is solid and secure, without providing any other support for the building that stands on it. Anyone who cares more for the good of humanity than for his own fame will be slow to voice his opinion about such prejudices, and will take care not to attack them outright without extreme caution, for fear of overturning a moral principle that he finds dubious before his fellow men have *adopted the true principle* that he wishes to put in its place.

I can, therefore, perfectly well think that I perceive national prejudices and religious errors among my fellow citizens, and yet be *obliged* to remain silent, so long as these errors cause no *direct* damage to *natural* religion or *natural* law and are instead *accidentally* linked with the promotion of the good. Admittedly, the morality of our actions scarcely deserves this name when it is based on error, and the promotion of the good must always be effected much better and more securely by truth, *once it is acknowledged*, than by prejudice. But until it is acknowledged, until it becomes national, so as to affect the masses as powerfully as rooted prejudice, the latter must be held almost sacred by every friend of virtue.

Such restraint is all the more requisite when the nation that in our opinion upholds such errors has rendered itself estimable by virtue and wisdom, and includes a number of great men who deserve to be called benefactors of the human race. Such a noble part of humanity must be treated gently and with reverence, even when it falls into human error. Who is bold enough to ignore the merits of such a lofty nation and attack it where he thinks he perceives its weakness?

These are the motives which my religion and my philosophy supply for carefully avoiding religious disputes. If you consider also the social conditions in which I live among my fellow men, you will think me completely justified. I am a member of an oppressed people that must humbly rely for protection on the benevolence of the ruling nation, and does not always receive such protection, and never without certain restrictions. My co-religionists are happy to do without liberties that are accorded to every other human being; they are content to be tolerated and protected. If a nation accepts them under conditions that are tolerable, they must be grateful for a considerable benefit, since many states forbid them even to *reside*. Do not the laws of your home town forbid your circumcised friend even to visit you in Zurich? How grateful my co-religionists should then be to the ruling nation that includes them in its universal love of humanity and allows them to pray undisturbed to the Almighty in the manner of their fathers! In the state in which I live they enjoy the most respectable freedom in this regard; do you wonder that their members hesitate to oppose the religion of their rulers, that is, to attack their protectors on the side that for virtuous people must be the most sensitive one?

I decided always to act in accordance with these principles, and consequently to take the utmost care to avoid religious disputes, unless some extraordinary occasion should oblige me to alter my resolve. I have been bold enough silently to ignore private challenges from estimable men, and I felt that I could despise provocations from petty minds who thought that they could harass me in public because of my religion. But the solemn adjuration of a Lavater does compel me at least to present my views in public, so that nobody may mistake an unduly prolonged silence for *contempt* or *confession*.

I have read Bonnet's book, which you translated, with close

attention. Whether I was convinced is, after what I have just set out, no longer the issue. But I must admit that even as a defence of the Christian religion it did not seem to me to have the merit that you find in it. I know M. Bonnet from his other works as an excellent writer, but I have read many defences of the same religion, I will not say by Englishmen, but by our German compatriots, which struck me as much more thorough and philosophical than this of Bonnet's, which you recommend for the sake of my conversion. If I am not mistaken, most of this writer's philosophical hypotheses grew on German soil, and even the author of the *Essai de Psychologie*,* which M. Bonnet follows so faithfully, owes almost everything to German philosophers. Where philosophical principles are concerned, the German seldom needs to borrow from his neighbours.

The best-thought-out part of this work, in my judgement, is the general reflection with which M. Bonnet introduces it. For the way in which he applies and uses these reflections to defend his religion struck me as so improper, so arbitrary, that I scarcely recognized Bonnet. I am sorry that my judgement must diverge so much from yours. It seems to me that M. B.'s deep conviction and a praiseworthy zeal for his religion lent a weight to his arguments that another cannot find there. Most of his conclusions seem to follow so little from the premises that I would venture to adduce the same grounds in support of *any religion whatsoever*. The author himself should perhaps not be blamed for this. He can have been writing only for readers who share his conviction and read only to be *strengthened* in their belief. Once writer and reader are unanimous about the result, they can quickly agree on the reasons for it. But I may justly wonder at you, Sir, for thinking this book sufficient to persuade someone who, in accordance with his principles, must be committed to the opposite case. You cannot possibly have entered into the thoughts of such a person, who does not bring his conviction with him, but is supposed to derive it from this book. But if you did, and if you still think, as you give us to understand, that even a Socrates would have found M. Bonnet's arguments irrefutable; then one or other of us must be a curious example of the power that prejudices and education can exercise over those who sincerely seek the truth.

I have now set forth my reasons for so earnestly desiring never to dispute about religious matters; but I have also indicated that I certainly consider myself able to reply to the Bonnet book. If you press me, then I *must* set aside my misgivings and make up my mind to publish my thoughts about M. Bonnet's book and the case he defends in a set of *Counter-Reflections*. I hope, however, that you will release me from this unpleasant step, and will rather permit me to return to the peaceful situation which is natural to me. If you put yourself in my position, and consider the circumstances not from your viewpoint but from mine, you will concede the justice of my wishes. I should not like to be tempted to leave the limitations which I have deliberately imposed on myself.

I am, with the utmost regard,
Your sincere admirer,
Moses Mendelssohn.

Berlin, 12 December 1769.

SALOMON MAIMON

Recollections of Mendelssohn

Salomon Maimon (1754–1800), brought up near Nesvizh in what was then Poland, now Belarus, had a traditional education focused on Talmud study, in which he distinguished himself, and was married at 11, becoming a father at 14. He left his wife, worked as a private tutor, and eventually set off for Berlin in pursuit of the Enlightenment. On his way, at Königsberg, he met some Jewish medical students who were repelled by his strange appearance and his Yiddish, but were astonished when he picked up a copy of *Phaedon*, Mendelssohn's treatise on the immortality of the soul, read it aloud in German, and translated it on the spot into Hebrew. Refused entry to Berlin by the Jewish community, who rightly suspected him of being a freethinker, he begged his way through Poland and was eventually allowed by benefactors to return to Germany. This time he was taken up by Mendelssohn and enabled to study philosophy. After quarrels with his benefactors and further wanderings, he settled in Berlin and began to publish philosophical works, beginning in 1790 with a commentary on Kant's *Critique of Pure Reason*. He sent the manuscript to Kant, who said that 'a glance at its contents enabled me to appreciate its excellence at once and to recognize that none of my opponents have understood me and my essential meaning so well as Maimon'. This testimony founded Maimon's reputation and helped him to publish further philosophical works, including a Hebrew commentary on Maimonides's *Guide to the Perplexed*; it was in honour of Maimonides that he had changed his name from Shlomo ben Yehoshua to Salomon Maimon. Although in his later years he was supported by an aristocratic patron, Graf Kalckreuth, his hardships and dissipations had undermined his health and brought about his premature death.

Maimon's autobiography was first published in Berlin in two parts which appeared in 1792 and 1793, with an introduction by the educator and aesthetician Karl Philipp Moritz. Moritz's own lightly fictionalized autobiography, *Anton Reiser*, published between 1785 and 1790, clearly served as a model for Maimon's. Moritz was brought up in poverty as a member of a strict Pietist sect, obtained an education with great privations, and was eventually taken up by Goethe. Maimon tells us much about the improvidence of his grandfather, an innkeeper; about the misgovernment of Poland; about what he considers the superstitious tyranny exercised by the traditional Jewish authorities; and about his own serio-comic misadventures on the way to Berlin. His tribute to Mendelssohn is deeply serious. It provides both a sketch of Mendelssohn's character and an introduction to aspects of his philosophy. It is written, however, from a standpoint different to Mendelssohn's, for Maimon no longer considers himself part of the Jewish community and feels no obligation to observe its laws.

MENDELSSOHN

A chapter devoted to the memory of a worthy friend

Quis desiderio sit pudor aut modus tam cari capitis.*

The name Mendelssohn is so familiar to the world that I need not spend long describing the great intellectual and moral qualities of this famous man of our nation. Here I shall merely sketch those prominent features of his portrait that made the greatest impression on me. He was a good Talmudist and pupil of the famous Polish Rabbi Israel, who was denounced as a heretic by his nation, and who is known, after the title of a Talmudic work that he wrote, as *Netzach Israel* (the strength of Israel). Besides his great Talmudic ability and learning, this rabbi had considerable talent for the sciences, especially mathematics, of which, while still in Poland, he had acquired a thorough knowledge from the few Hebrew books about it, as can be seen from the work mentioned above. It contains solutions of many important mathematical problems which are needed either to explain obscure passages in the Talmud or to determine a law. Naturally our Rabbi Israel cared more about diffusing useful knowledge among his nation than about explaining or determining a law, using the latter merely as a vehicle. Thus, for example, he showed that it is not correct for Jews in our regions to face due east while praying; for since the Talmudic law requires one to face Jerusalem, people in our regions, which are north-west of Jerusalem, ought to face south-east. Hence he shows how in all regions this direction can be exactly determined by spherical trigonometry, and so forth. Both he and the famous Chief Rabbi Fränkel did much to help Mendelssohn develop his great abilities.

Mendelssohn possessed a thorough knowledge of mathematics; he valued mathematics, not only because of its demonstrable truth, but as the best exercise in rigorous thinking.

That he was a great philosopher is sufficiently well known. Although he was not an inventor of new systems, he had improved the old ones, especially the Wolff–Leibniz system,* and had success-fully applied them to many topics in philosophy.

It is hard to determine whether Mendelssohn possessed more ingenuity or profundity. He combined both these faculties in a very high degree. His exactness in definition and classification, his subtle distinctions, etc., are proofs of the former, and his profound philo-sophical treatises give proofs of the latter talent.

As regards his character, he was, as he himself confessed, natur-ally inclined towards passion, but had done much to control it through the prolonged exercise of Stoic virtue. Thus, one day young B., thinking Mendelssohn had done him an injustice, came to his house to reproach him, and made one impertinent remark after another. Mendelssohn stood leaning on a chair, looking steadily at him, and listened to all his impertinences with the utmost Stoic patience. When the young man's fury was exhausted, Mendelssohn went up to him and said: 'Be off! You see, you cannot attain your purpose; you cannot make me angry.' On such occasions, however, Mendelssohn could not conceal his sorrow at human weaknesses.

I myself was often too heated in my disputes with him and vio-lated the respect due to such a man, something I still regret.

Mendelssohn was a very good judge of character, which does not merely mean seizing a few unconnected character traits and repre-senting them theatrically, but rather discovering the essential fea-tures of a character from which all the rest can be explained and in some measure predicted. He could state exactly what springs and moral machinery governed a person, and thoroughly understood the mechanism of the soul. This left its mark not only on his social intercourse and dealings with other people, but also on his learned works.

Mendelssohn understood the useful and also agreeable art of entering into another's way of thinking. He knew how to supply the deficiencies and fill the gaps in someone else's ideas. He got on very well with Jews newly arrived from Poland, whose ideas are mostly confused and whose language is an unintelligible jargon. In conver-sation with them he adopted their words and expressions, he sought to adjust his way of thinking to theirs and thus to elevate theirs to his own.

He also understood the art of bringing out the best side of every person or incident. He often took pleasure in people whose company others shunned because of the irregularity in their use of their powers; and it was only entire stupidity and laziness that he detested. I once witnessed how he conversed for a considerable time with a man of the most irregular way of thinking and the most dissipated conduct. I lost all patience, and once he had gone, I asked Mendelssohn in amazement: 'How could you spend so much time with this man?' 'Why not?' he answered; 'we look attentively at a machine whose construction is unknown to us, and try to comprehend how it works; does not this man deserve just as much attention? Surely we should try to comprehend his strange utterances in the same way, since he must have springs and wheels, as much as any machine.'

When disputing with a rigid opponent, who adhered firmly to the system he had once adopted, Mendelssohn was himself rigid, and took advantage of the slightest fault in his opponent's manner of thinking. With a supple opponent, however, he was supple too, and he used commonly to end the dispute in the following words: 'We must attend to the matter, not to the words.'

He detested nothing so much as 'esprit de bagatelle'* and affectation, so that he could not conceal his dislike for them. When H——— once invited a group of people, among whom Mendelssohn was the leading figure, to his house and held forth the whole time about his hobby-horse, which was not of the best kind, he showed his dislike by denying this worthless creature any of his attention.

With Madame   , who affected an excess of sensibility and, as is the common practice, used to criticize herself in order to extort praise from others, he tried to bring her to her senses by forcefully pointing out to her how very mistaken this conduct was and how much she needed to reform.

He took little part in an inconsequential conversation, but followed his own thoughts and enjoyed other people's behaviour. However, if the conversation were coherent, he took part in it enthusiastically. He could also intervene skilfully so as to give the conversation a useful turn without interrupting it.

Mendelssohn's mind could never concern itself with trifles; he was kept in ceaseless activity by matters of the utmost importance—

the principles of morality, of natural theology, the immortality of the soul, and the like. In all these branches of inquiry that interest humanity, he achieved as much, in my opinion, as is possible within the philosophy of Wolff and Leibniz. In all these inquiries, the compass that he had constantly in view, and that guided his movement, was perfection.

The ideal of supreme perfection is his God, the ideal of supreme perfection is the basis of his morality. Sensuous perfection is the principle of his aesthetics.

As a faithful adherent of Maimonides,* before I became acquainted with the latest philosophy, I insisted on God's union of all positive qualities, which we can represent only within limits. I thus arrived at the following dilemma. Either God's qualities can be not only conceived by us but also apprehended, that is, represented as real concepts appropriate to an object; in which case He is not the most perfect being. Or else He is the most perfect being, in which case the concept of God can be conceived by us, but its reality can only be assumed theoretically.

Mendelssohn, on the other hand, insisted on the affirmation of all realities in God, which is possible in the philosophy of Wolff and Leibniz, because a concept, to be real, needs only to be conceivable (absence of contradiction).

My morality at that time was genuine Stoicism, the attainment of free will and the supremacy of reason over sensations and passions. The supreme purpose of man, sustaining his *differentia specifica*, was the apprehension of truth. All the other impulses that we share with the irrational animals were to be activated merely as means to this chief end. I did not distinguish the apprehension of the good from the apprehension of the true, since, following Maimonides, I considered only the apprehension of truth to be the supreme good worthy of man.

Mendelssohn, on the other hand, maintained that the concept of perfection which formed the basis of morality was far more extensive than the mere apprehension of truth. All natural impulses, abilities, and powers, being good in themselves and not merely means to something good, must be exercised as realities. Supreme perfection was the idea of the maximum or the greatest sum of these realities.

I considered the immortality of the soul, following Maimonides, as consisting in the union of the active intellect with the universal world spirit, according to the degree of the intellect's activity; so that only those people who sought to apprehend eternal truths, depending on the intensity of their search, could share in this immortality. On attaining this lofty immortality, therefore, the soul must lose its individuality. All my readers will readily take my word for it that Mendelssohn, in accordance with modern philosophy, thought differently on this point.

I can present his views about revealed or positive religion, not as a datum of which he informed me, but only insofar as I have been able to extract them from the remarks in his writings with the aid of my own reflection. For as I was then setting out as a freethinker, I declared all positive religion to be false in itself, and its usefulness, so far as I could discern any in Maimonides' writings, to be merely temporal; and, having no experience, I thought it would be easy to convince others, in spite of firmly rooted habits and age-old prejudices, and had no doubt that such a reformation would be extremely valuable. Mendelssohn, therefore, could not possibly discuss this subject with me, for he was bound to fear that (as others have done and still do) I would declare his counter-arguments to be mere sophistries and impute a hidden design to him. However, his remarks both in his preface to *Menasse Ben Israel** and in his *Jerusalem** make clear that, although he did not accept revealed doctrines as eternal truths, he did accept revealed laws of religion, and that he considered the laws of the Jewish religion, so far as circumstances allowed, to be the unalterable foundation of a theocratic constitution.

For my part, having reflected for myself upon the religion of my fathers, I entirely agree with Mendelssohn's reasoning on this subject. The basic laws of the Jewish religion are at the same time the principles on which its state is founded. They must therefore be obeyed by all who acknowledge themselves as citizens of this state and wish to enjoy the rights conditional on such obedience. Anyone, on the other hand, who separates himself from this state, wishing no longer to be considered a citizen of it and renouncing all the rights conferred by such citizenship (whether he is registered as a citizen of another state or betakes himself to solitude), is no longer obliged by his conscience to follow these laws. Mendelssohn does say, I grant, that a Jew who converts to the Christian religion cannot free himself from his religious laws, because Jesus of Nazareth himself commanded his followers to obey them. But what if a Jew no longer wishes to be a citizen of this theocratic state and adopts the religion of paganism or philosophy, which is none other than pure natural religion? What if, as a citizen merely of civil society, he accepts its laws and in turn demands his rights from it, without saying a word about his religion, since the civil state is rational enough not to require such a declaration (which is none of the state's business)? I do not think that in such a case Mendelssohn would still maintain that this Jew was obliged by his conscience to follow the laws of his ancestral religion, merely because they are the laws of his ancestral religion. Mendelssohn, who, so far as we know, lived in accordance with the laws of his religion, probably considered himself a citizen of the theocratic state of his fathers and was thus observing his duty; but anyone who leaves such a state is not neglecting his duty.

On the other hand, I declare that those Jews are acting wrongly who acknowledge the Jewish religion from grounds of family loyalty and self-interest and yet infringe its laws (when they do not think the laws in conflict with these motives). In the case of the Hamburg Jew who publicly infringed the religious laws and was therefore excommunicated by the Chief Rabbi of Hamburg, I therefore cannot understand how Mendelssohn can want to free him from excommunication, on the grounds that the church has no right to intervene in civil matters, and yet maintain the everlasting duration of the ecclesiastical Jewish state. What is a state without rights, and what, according to Mendelssohn, are the rights of this ecclesiastical state? 'How', says Mendelssohn in his preface to *Menasse Ben Israel*, 'can the state permit any of its useful and respected citizens to be made unhappy by the laws?' 'Not at all!' is my answer, 'that Hamburg Jew is not made unhappy by excommunication, he needed only to avoid saying or doing anything that incurred it, and he would have remained free from it; excommunication means only this: as long as you publicly oppose the laws of our community, you are excluded from it, and so you must calculate whether this public opposition or the other advantages offered by this community can most promote your happiness.' This cannot have escaped Mendelssohn, and I leave it to others to decide whether and how far one can be illogical for the good of humanity.

Mendelssohn also received a great deal of harm at the hands of otherwise estimable men from whom one would never have expected such behaviour.

Lavater's impertinence is well known, and has been condemned by all well-disposed and honest men.

The profound thinker Jacobi, being inclined towards Spinozism (which no one of independent mind can take amiss), tried to make Mendelssohn (and also his friend Lessing) out to be a Spinozist *malgré lui*,* and published an exchange of letters on this subject which was never intended to appear in print and be displayed to the public.* What was the point of this? If Spinozism is true, it is so, even without Mendelssohn's support. Eternal truths do not depend on a majority of votes; especially when the truth, in my opinion, is of such a kind as to be inexpressible.

Mendelssohn could not but be annoyed by such injustice. Indeed, a famous physician went so far as to maintain that it caused Mendelssohn's death, which, without being a physician, I can boldly deny. Mendelssohn behaved like a hero towards both Jacobi and Lavater. No, no! This hero died in Act Five.

After Mendelssohn's death, the ingenious Professor Jakob* in Halle published a book entitled *An Examination of Mendelssohn's 'Morning Hours'*, in which he shows that, according to the *Critique of Pure Reason*, all metaphysical assertions must be rejected as baseless. But why does this concern Mendelssohn more than any other metaphysician? All Mendelssohn did was to make the philosophy of Leibniz and Wolff more complete, apply it to many important subjects of human inquiry, and clothe it in a pleasing garb. It is just as though someone were to attack Maimonides, who wrote an excellent astronomical treatise setting out this science with the utmost precision according to Ptolemaic principles and applying it to the most important subjects, by writing a book entitled *An Examination of Maimonides' Hilchoth Kidosch Hachodesch* in order to refute him on Newtonian principles. But enough of this!

RAHEL LEVIN AND DAVID VEIT

Correspondence

Rahel Levin (1771–1833), known also as Rahel Varnhagen from her marriage to the diplomat Karl August Varnhagen von Ense in 1814, was the daughter of a wealthy Jewish financier. Her upbringing was sheltered but culturally limited. Early letters evoke a round of visits, dances, and trips to the theatre and concerts primarily as social events. Rahel satisfied her intellectual urges partly by private study. After her father's death in 1790 she opened a salon in the attic apartment of her mother's Berlin mansion, where aristocrats, academics, and cultivated women were drawn together by shared intellectual interests. It was the best-known of some ten Berlin salons, centring on Jewish hostesses, which flourished until the disruptions connected with the defeat and occupation of Prussia by Napoleon's troops in 1806.

During her lifetime Rahel published only anonymous fragments about Goethe and theatre reviews, but before her death she and Varnhagen prepared for publication a selection from her letters, which appeared in 1833 and, in a much expanded edition, in 1834. In the eighteenth century the personal letter was an important form of self-expression. No sharp distinction was yet made between fictional literature (poetry, drama, novels) and instrumental literature (letters, sermons, history), nor between public and private writing: not only letters but poems might circulate within a small group long before they were made available to a wider public; and it became increasingly common to publish letters, though usually after the deaths of the correspondents. Letter-writing also sustained, and was sustained by, the emotional cult of friendship. Rahel conducted long correspondences with her husband during his absence on diplomatic missions; with aristocratic male friends; with the emancipated Gentile Pauline Wiesel; and with Jewish friends like the novelist Rebecca Friedländer. In keeping with the convention exploited in epistolary novels by Richardson, Rousseau, and Goethe, her letters explore the working of her emotions rather than the external events which, in any case, were lacking from her over-protected life. She is often painfully frank about the sense of inferiority, resulting from many social slights, that she experienced as both a Jew and a woman. 'How horrible it is always to have to justify one's existence!' she writes to Friedländer in 1806. 'That's why it's so *repulsive* to be a Jewess!' And to the unconventional Pauline Wiesel in 1810: 'We've reached the same point by different routes. We are *alongside* human society.' Rahel's letters are remarkable for their raw emotion, the subtlety and intensity with which she reacts to her correspondents, and their often painful sincerity.

One of Rahel's early confidants was David Veit (1771–1814), who was studying medicine at Göttingen University. He was the nephew of Simon Veit, the Berlin banker who had married Moses Mendelssohn's daughter Dorothea. With his uncle he visited Weimar in 1793. The extracts given here from Rahel's letter of 1–2 April 1793 show her fascination with Goethe and other great figures of German classicism; her envy of Veit for being able to travel; her own frustration and sense of impotence; and her feeling that to be both Jewish and a woman is a great misfortune, though one which she tries not quite to accept.

Veit's letter quoted here reveals his own social uncertainty, his difficulty in modifying his natural liveliness to fit the decorum of Gentile Germans, his contempt for the trivial amusements of Gentiles, but also his ambivalence about the company of Jews. He keeps forgetting how little liberty of movement Rahel has, and must have caused her pain by his fantasy about how she should visit Goethe, who would become fond of her. He also reveals how much he relies on Rahel and admires her insight into character. Her kind advice in reply helps us to understand how throughout her life many young men, including Heine, who frequented her salon when studying in Berlin in the early 1820s, could confide in her. But she also responds to Veit's naivety with ironic, bitter, and opaque reflections on her desire for friendship, her reluctance to surrender herself, her self-destructive generosity, and, above all, her feeling that as a Jewish girl she cannot seem attractive. Since Veit, presumably meaning to compliment her wit, imagines her saying something ridiculous to Goethe, Rahel gives the barbed reply that for a Jewish girl to seek such an acquaintance is itself ridiculous.

Rahel's astonishing letter of 21–2 March 1795 conveys among other things her irritation with people like Veit who do not really understand her. In poor health, fretting even more than usual under the petty restrictions of Berlin, she talks of her identity as a Jewish woman as a curse imposed on her at her birth, analogous to a physical deformity, and one for which the world has no sympathy. In response to a letter in which Veit has compared her to Goethe's unconventional character Philine, Rahel defines the nature of her own unconventionality: she is perfectly well-behaved by her own standards, but she will never support any conventional party or faction; if she takes sides, it will be with the party of humanity, with the universalist ideals of the Enlightenment. She repeats three times the

Enlightenment's great key-word *Mensch* (human being, person, independent of nationality, class, or sex) and alludes also to Kant's newly published essay *Of Perpetual Peace* (1795).

The cult of Goethe, which Rahel was later influential in propagating, is already evident here. Veit regards him as a modern saint. Rahel constantly quotes him, especially the prison scene from his tragedy *Egmont*. 'The poet accompanied me unfailingly throughout my life, and what was split into unhappiness and happiness, and I could not hold together, he brought into a strong and healthy unity,' she wrote to Varnhagen von Ense in 1808. For Rahel, the self-divided Jewess, Goethe represented wholeness. Ironically, Goethe, a self-divided character, sought images of wholeness in sensitive and intelligent women ('beautiful souls'), like his fictional Iphigenie and the real Rahel, whom he described as a 'beautiful soul' for her combination of intellect and powerful emotion.

———

[In March 1793 David Veit visited Weimar, in the company of his uncle Simon Veit. He reported to Rahel in minute detail about his meeting with Goethe, describing Goethe's appearance, including the clothes which made him look like a civil servant, and mentioning his scandalous cohabitation with Christiane Vulpius. He also apologized in passing for his own lack of descriptive skill. Rahel replied:]

Berlin, 1 April 1793

I've just finished your letter. If only I could reply with something really enjoyable that would interest you as much! You wouldn't believe how grateful I am to you! All I can do is answer *straight away*; so that you see the entire impression your letter made; and that's what I'm doing while my sister-in-law is having her hair done; as soon as she's ready, it'll be my turn. We're going to Bouché's restaurant, they say the hyacinths are already flowering. Let me just tell you, I do know what you've done for me; first the *awful* looking at everything (but, believe me, you'll benefit from it as well) and describing it without any description. I know, believe me, I know what it's like on a journey, every minute is misplaced, everything's an effort, you could have made a wonderful use of the time, it's so difficult to describe details, however well one's observed them; in fact, that makes it all the harder. So you thought out the whole letter, wrote everything in it, for my sake, just to give me pleasure—no! satisfaction. I can't do more than that; I'll do the same for you. For some day

I must know something that you'd like to know, and *can* describe it *well*, and I will, I'll gladly give up the time for you. I believe *every word* you tell me.

Tuesday, 2 April

You always know so precisely what I'm thinking, and it's a pleasure to know that; if only there were people who told one that, then one might learn some sense. But now I'll say everything about your letter, you'll enjoy it. I'll begin with a dreadful piece of folly and show you how my mind works; I never thought Goethe went about in such antique clothes, like an inferior official (you see, I don't know any words); for someone who knows everything also knows this [i.e. how to dress], and why shouldn't he dress in a rather more domesticated fashion, especially as he lives at court and is in the most up-to-date society; it ought to come quite naturally, so I must suppose that he dresses differently on purpose, and I don't understand why. Of course things may be quite different, perhaps he dresses like that for comfort, perhaps he hasn't thought about such things for ages, perhaps he leaves such things to his servants; and then, he knows everything, and he may be like that. [. . .]

But how can you be so cruel as to tell me I must or should see that for myself; don't you know that I'm perishing, simply perishing, like something reaching its end? Can any decent person mistake Berlin's pavements for the world? Even this abominable windy climate (it's rained for the first time since the day before yesterday, and today the weather's fine), and can a female* help being a human being *too*? If my mother had been good-natured and tough enough, and if she'd had any foreboding of what I'd be like, she ought to have smothered me in the dust of this place as soon as I uttered my first cry. A *powerless* being that is supposed to sit at home like this *without it mattering*, and would have heaven and earth, mankind and animals against it if it wanted to go away (and it's got ideas like any other person), and has to stay nicely at home, and, if it makes perceptible *mouvements*, has to swallow all sorts of reproaches that are made with *raison*;* because it really isn't *raison* to shake oneself; for if the glasses, the spinning-wheels, the sewing fall down, everyone jumps on me. (Jettchen has just been here, she and Mrs Veit* are enchanted by you, *mais vraiment enchantées*; they enjoy the simplicity [of your letter] and the toil and attention you put into it, leaving no questions to be asked.) But for goodness' sake don't stop writing to me, especially about the beauty of the places you visit, and stay the same, if possible.

[. . .] I feel as if I were seeing it all for myself; I'll never quite grasp that I'm a *schlemiel** and a Jewess; since I haven't realized it after long years spent thinking about it, I'll never really know it. That's why 'the sound of the murderous axe is not gnawing at my *roots*',* that's why I'm still alive. I haven't told you all this, that's why I'm writing it to you, so as to give you pleasure. Dear Veit, do send me your address, I'd very much like to write to you myself, I can't stand adding enclosures to other people's letters. Even if our letters are broken open, nobody will understand them, and they won't interest a soul (once you've read them).

[Having transferred from the University of Göttingen to that of Jena, near Weimar, Veit wrote on 23 October 1794:]

[. . .] Your letter is a real companion; I had some hot chocolate made to go with it. (Write and tell me if that made you laugh; I'm laughing.)

I recently began a new exercise: I mean to acquire the habit of remaining completely silent; for the mixture of opinions with which I usually speak, the actual fun, makes people think very poorly of me; but that *won't do*. I take my meals in a professor's house (paying for them) in what is called very good company, and that's where I notice it. I'm truly embarrassed. I don't try to obtain an entrée to any house here, though I easily could; for I know in advance that I'll be bored. People often amuse themselves by—playing forfeits. Nevertheless, the town has fine qualities. I am the only Jew here. When there are no Jews, one has to relinquish many much more cultivated enjoyments; I'm very glad there are no *Jewish students* here.

In order to explain your *character* to the world, I shall have to publish a treatise, and if it's a success, I shall undoubtedly be made a Doctor of Philosophy...

I'm rereading your letter. Heavens, what truths you told me! How was it possible to know anyone so well! No, I can't make up my mind to be anything definite. You're right.—Dear Rahel, this evening I had a wonderful feeling. I thought that *you* are my friend and that *Goethe* believes I might come to something. At this moment, the only thing I'd beseech from Heaven is that the energy this feeling gives me should endure. I send you my best wishes. Get to know me intimately so that you can become more and more certain that I'm a high-minded person and your *true* and perhaps your *only friend*; but perhaps you're happier than I think. It is a great misfortune for you that Goethe does not know you. How he would like you! I don't suppose that's ever occurred to you? I'm suggesting it; for only yesterday I wrote to my sister: 'Anyone who does not know unhappiness has not learnt to grasp happiness and hold it fast.' If you ever come here, then call on him and venture to say something ridiculous; it's sure to be rewarded. A hundred years ago such people were painted with haloes round their heads; and isn't he a saint? Give my best wishes to Markus and his wife.* Adieu!

David Joseph Veit

[Rahel replied from Berlin on 31 October 1794:]

[. . .] I can't do anything with you, what should a thing like me do with *you*; still less can I take charge of you; but I'll tell you anything that occurs to me, and remind you of it whenever I can. So, first and foremost: don't think that you've changed, that you've made a choice, that you're now *something*; or rather, don't be in a hurry to be anything. You've gained enough by finding out about yourself; just turn over the soil in yourself, and let it become firm quite naturally and slowly. Through all kinds of foul weather, fair weather, whatever. The chocolate made me laugh myself into fits; it's funny from a thousand angles. Not speaking may be good; but one doesn't change; how often I've tried! Still, it does happen little by little. I positively *congratulate* you on the absence of Jewish students in Jena; by the way, I do enjoy what you say about that nation, and one has to get out. You mustn't *explain* my character; but you must say that I do good, and leave it to others to demonstrate my bad side, my dear Doctor of Philosophy... I don't know what you mean by saying 'perhaps you're happier than I think'; do you mean perhaps I've got a special friend? I don't need one. Somebody I could call by that name, and who treated me accordingly, would be delightful to *contemplate*! how beautiful! more than one should seek: good friends who are loyal to me are something I value more than anyone else: friends who can't leave me, because I support them, and they are attached to me in a nobler way. Anyway, I piece something together from this and that; and I regret all the beauty that one lacks when one thinks one has taste; but I'm not sure what I'm missing. Or perhaps even another person couldn't help me—I don't think I'd surrender myself to anyone as you surrender yourself to me, not if I could help it. And then my best side has a great defect: the great friend doesn't take, she only gives. An ugly spot, if it's true.—But it's amusing that I don't know Goethe; for he has known plenty of girls (I know that, I can see it from every one of his poems), and it would have been better if he had known me *instead*. The most amusing thing of all, though, is that I'm a girl, and in my situation, a Jewish girl. You're right; I could well make myself *ridiculous*, and you know I would hate that and would never get over it; but what would the *man* think, how would he regard me? I'd like to hear him talking to other people, but I can't manage that on my own. It's not only poor Klärchen who's unable to knock her head against damp walls and has the key to her door in her hand; she doesn't even wave the flag, and talks nonsense.*—You always sign with all three of your names, that's horrid.

Now I take my leave of you obediently, and take the liberty to call myself

Your friend.

[On 21–5 March 1795 Rahel writes a long, unhappy letter to Veit. Having told him that she is ill, described various plans for recuperating at country resorts, and expressed her longing to attend the great fair at Leipzig, she goes on:]

I hardly go out at all; because the air is never good enough for me, any social gathering that *I* can go to is *hateful*, the theatre is loathsome, and the concerts too. In society just listening is enough to make me ill with boredom and tiredness, it's the same in the theatre, also at concerts; at home I get a pain from reading, writing, or *whatever* I do, if my body has to be in the same position for even ten minutes. Air that's too dense, too thin, too hot, too cold, and every emotion, makes me sick, and so does every pain worthy of the name. I feel so fed up I could die, *vous sentez bien*—I'm forbidden to run away, how can anyone stand it! I couldn't be more irritable and oversensitive than I am. And yet! it must be impossible for me to have a fever, otherwise I would!—All this leads to exhaustion, which turns into pain, then I'm sick, then I'm exhausted, and it starts all over again. *I'm going to the country*. 'Closer to the earth, like the earth-born giant.'* Then there was so much I wanted to say in reply to your three letters, and that's laborious; but I didn't want to reply without an effort; for what are you to think unless you know these details; and giving them is a great effort for me, both thinking and writing. Now condemn me. Believe me—I'm not mad—there's *nothing wrong* with me in an ordinary way; the cause is always an immovable mountain, even if it can't be seen: *there's nothing wrong with me in an ordinary way*. I have such fantasies: as though, when I was driven into this world, a supernatural being had thrust these words with a dagger into my heart: 'Yes, have emotions, see the world as few see it, be great and noble, nor can I prevent you from constantly thinking, but *one* thing has been forgotten: be a Jewess!' And now my whole life is a process of bleeding to death; by keeping still, I can spin it out; every attempt to quench it is a new death; and immobility is possible only in death itself. These ravings are true, they can be translated. You may smile, or weep from compassion, I can trace every evil, every misfortune, every annoyance back to *that*; and I don't care if I look ridiculous in someone else's eyes. This opinion is my essence, and I must give you clear proof of it before I die. I can't deny myself the satisfaction. I'll reply to myself in your name, and let reason speak from your lips. 'Yes,' you'd say, 'you have suffered the greatest misfortune that could possibly strike you, you are a cripple: but listen, look, taste; if you keep looking at your legs, then it's you who are crippling yourself.' Yes, if I could live outside the world, without manners, without relationships, working hard in a village. Yes, the cripple would say, if I had no need to walk; but I don't need to live, and every step I want to take and can't reminds me not of the universal ills of humanity which I want to protest against, but rather I feel my own particular misfortune, doubly and tenfold, and the one keeps heightening the other. How ugly this makes me; after all, is the world wise? do people say: 'The poor fellow is a cripple, let's sympathize with him, oh what an effort every step must be for him, just look!' No; they ignore his steps, because it's not they who are taking them; they find them horrible because they see them, and they don't sympathize with him, because his struggles don't affect them, and it's their own struggles they find terrible. And the cripple, forced to walk—how can he not be unhappy? If I ever saw a lame comparison, it's this; it limps so badly that nobody could discern my own misfortune, if they didn't know it already.

[Three days later Rahel responds to some rather tactless remarks Veit has made about her. Both have been reading Goethe's novel *Wilhelm Meisters Lehrjahre* (*Wilhelm Meister's Apprenticeship*), which has just been published, and Veit has compared her to Philine, a female character, because of her unconventional behaviour and her difference from other women.]

You find Philine witty? I don't. She could be. I also notice the resemblance to myself. People write to me pointing it out from Strelitz, Vienna, and all over the place. A pity I'm neither so poor, nor very rich. That would be enough to make me prettier. I consider myself the best-behaved girl I know. Honestly! *encore un coup, mon cher ami,** I even think I've just unwittingly defined good behaviour; believe that, and one is well behaved. As for being different from other women, I could say a good deal about that. But it would be long, which is unpleasant. Just as one can't make oneself great, so one can't escape from one's sex; but Philines like to escape from anything entitled *esprit de faction et de corps,** party, guild, or whatever; but if party fights against party—and they *are* wretched—then they fight in its ranks, because it is better, more decent, and wiser, and the uniform of this nationality is the one we are born with, and they hate *all* standing armies without exception, and would like to see the advent of the perpetual peace, along with god-like reason, that lets person speak to person as a person. Read lots of wisdom into this, I mean it wisely...

THE BROTHERS GRIMM
The Jew in the Thorn-Bush

Jacob Grimm (1785–1863) and his brother Wilhelm (1786–1859) were philologists in the widest sense. They were dedicated to the study of the German past. Both originally studied law at Marburg University and were thus led to examine the institutions of medieval Germany which had been overlaid by the introduction of Roman law in the sixteenth century. The study of medieval institutions required the study of language and literature, not only as a practical necessity but because the Grimms, following Herder, believed that a single *Volksgeist* (spirit of the people) found expression in every form of culture. There was thus an organic connection between the study of medieval society, Jacob's research on the history of German grammar, the brothers' initiation of the historically based *German Dictionary* (equivalent to the *Oxford English Dictionary*, and completed only in 1960), Wilhelm's editions of German medieval literature, and their collection of German myths and folk-tales. After working for many years as librarians, both were appointed professors at the University of Göttingen in 1830. They were dismissed in 1837, along with five other academics, because their liberal principles forbade them to take a personal oath of loyalty to the King of Hanover which ran counter to the constitution.

The Grimms' *Tales* came partly from literary sources, partly from oral narrators, who tended to be not peasants but well educated women with a talent for storytelling and, in at least one case, some knowledge of Perrault's seventeenth-century French fairy-tales. However, the Grimms' absorption in Romanticism led them, in successive editions of their collection, to develop a simple, homely 'fairy-tale style' and a moral code in which modern critics have discerned the expression less of the *Volksgeist* than of the Grimms' own literary and social preferences. In 'The Jew in the Thorn-Bush' popular anti-Semitism intersects with Romantic nationalism. The popular imagination readily represented the Jewish trader as an untrustworthy alien (though relations with actual Jews in German small towns seem usually to have been harmonious), while the Grimms' commitment to eliciting and defining the German national spirit was compatible both with the liberal aspiration to a united Germany and with the construction of the non-German other.

Once there was a rich man, and he had a servant who served him diligently and honestly, was the first out of the bed every morning and the last in bed in the evening, and when there was an unpleasant job that nobody wanted to tackle, he was always the first to volunteer. And he never complained, but was content with everything and always cheerful. When the year was up, his master did not pay him, thinking: 'That's the smartest thing to do, I'll save something, and he won't go away, but will stay hard at work.' The servant said never a word, did his work the second year as he had done the first, and at the end of it, when once again he was not paid, he put up with it and stayed. When the third year was up, the master thought for a while and put his hand in his pocket, but fetched nothing out. Then at last the servant said: 'Master, I've served you honestly for three years, please give me what's rightly due to me: I'd like to go away and see more of the world.' Then the miser answered: 'Yes, my dear servant, you've served me without wearying, and you shall be liberally rewarded.' He put his hand in his pocket again and paid the servant three farthings, one after the other. 'There,' he said, 'you've a farthing for each year, that is a large and generous reward, such as few masters would have given you.' The good servant, who understood little about money, tucked his capital away and thought: 'Now your pockets are filled, why should you trouble yourself any longer with care or hard work?'

Off he went, up hill and down dale, singing and jumping for joy. Now it happened, as he came past a thicket, that a little man stepped forward and called to him: 'Where are you going, my cheerful friend? I see you have few cares.' 'Why should I be sad?' answered the servant, 'I've plenty of money, three years' wages are jingling in my pocket.' 'How much is your treasure?' asked the little man. 'How much? Three good farthings, if you count correctly.' 'Listen,' said the dwarf, 'I'm a poor, needy man, give me your three farthings: I can no longer work, but you are young and can easily earn your living.' And because the servant had a good heart and felt sorry for the little man, he handed him his three farthings and said: 'In God's name, I won't miss it.' Then the little man said: 'Because I see you have a good heart, I'll grant you three wishes, one for each farthing, and they will all come true.' 'Aha,' said the servant, 'you're someone who can do magic. Very well, if that's what must be, I wish first for a catapult that will hit whatever I aim at; second for a fiddle, and when

I play on it, everyone who hears the sound must dance; and third, if I ask for something, nobody can say no.' 'You shall have all that,' said the little man; he reached into the bushes, and just think, the catapult and the fiddle were lying ready, as if they had been ordered. He gave them to the servant and said: 'Whatever you ask for, nobody in the world will refuse you.'

'Heart, what more could you want?' said the servant to himself as he went cheerily on his way. Soon he met a Jew with a long beard like a goat's who was standing listening to the song of a bird perched high up on top of a tree. 'God's miracle!' he exclaimed. 'Such a small creature has a truly mighty voice! If only it were mine! If only someone could put salt on his tail!' 'If that's all you want,' said the servant, 'we'll soon have the bird down'; he aimed and hit the mark, and the bird fell down into the thorn-bushes. 'Go, you rogue,' he said to the Jew, 'and fetch out the bird.' 'My, my,' said the Jew, 'if the master sends the boy away, along comes a dog; I'll pick up the bird, because you hit it'; he lay down on the ground and began crawling into the bushes. When he was in among the thorns, the good servant felt mischievous, so he took his fiddle and started to play. At once the Jew started to lift his legs and caper about; and the more the servant played, the better went the dance. But the thorns tore his shabby coat, combed his goat's beard, and pricked him and nipped him all over his body. 'Oh my,' cried the Jew, 'that's enough fiddling! Stop fiddling, sir, I don't want to dance.' But the servant paid no attention, thinking: 'You've skinned people often enough, now the thorn-bush can do the same to you', and started fiddling again, so that the Jew had to jump higher and higher and the rags of his coat got caught on the thorns. 'Oy vey!' cried the Jew. 'I'll give you whatever you ask, sir, if only you'll stop fiddling, a whole bag full of gold.' 'If you're so free with your money,' said the servant, 'then I'll stop my music, but I'll say this much for you, your dancing is a sight for sore eyes'; and with that he took the bag and went on his way.

The Jew stood there looking after him and kept still until the servant was far away and quite out of sight, and then he shouted as hard as he could: 'You wretched musician, you tavern fiddler: wait till I catch you on your own! I'll chase you till you lose the soles of your shoes: you scoundrel, put a penny in your mouth, and then you'll be worth four farthings', and he went on cursing as hard as he could. And when he had got this off his chest and felt better, he ran to the judge in the town. 'Oy vey, your honour! Look how a godless person has robbed me and mauled me on the public highway: a stone on the ground would feel sorry for me. My clothes are in rags! My body is pricked and scratched! My scanty savings are taken along with my purse! All ducats, one more beautiful than the other: for God's sake, have the fellow thrown into prison.' Said the judge: 'Was it a soldier who gave you such a mauling with his sabre?' 'God forbid!' said the Jew. 'He didn't have a naked sword, but he had a catapult over his shoulder and a fiddle round his neck; the villain is easy to recognize.' The judge sent people to look for him, and they found the good servant, who had gone on his way very slowly, and they also found the bag of gold on him. When he was brought to trial, he said: 'I didn't touch the Jew and I didn't take his money, he offered it to me of his own accord, because he couldn't stand my music.' 'God forbid!' screamed the Jew. 'He tells as many lies as there are flies on the wall.' But the judge did not believe it either and said: 'That's a poor excuse, no Jew would do that', and sentenced the good servant to be hanged for committing a highway robbery. When he was being led away, however, the Jew screamed at him: 'You lazy-bones, you dog of a musician, now you're getting your well-earned wages.' The servant ascended the ladder with the hangman quite calmly, but on the last rung he turned round and said to the judge: 'Grant me one more request before I die.' 'Yes,' said the judge, 'provided you don't ask for your life.' 'Not my life,' answered the servant, 'but please let me play on my fiddle one last time.' The Jew started caterwauling: 'For God's sake, don't let him, don't let him.' But the judge said: 'Why shouldn't I grant him this brief pleasure? He can have it, and that's that.' Besides, he couldn't refuse because of the gift the servant had been given. But the Jew cried: 'Oy vey, oy vey! Tie me up, tie me firmly.' Then the good servant took his fiddle from round his neck, put it in position, and as soon as he made the first stroke with his bow, everyone started to shiver and shake, the judge, the clerk, and the usher, and the rope fell from the hand of the man who was tying up the Jew; at the second stroke they all raised their legs, and the hangman let go of the good servant and got ready to dance; at the third stroke everyone jumped up and started dancing, and the judge and the Jew led the dance and cut the best capers. Soon all the people who had come to the market-place out of curiosity joined in the dance, old people and young, fat people and thin ones together; even the dogs who had come running stood on their hind legs and hopped along. And the longer he played, the higher the dancers jumped, until they clutched each other and began to wail miserably. At last the judge cried, out of breath: 'I grant you your life, but just stop fiddling.' The good servant was won over, put away the fiddle, hung it round his neck, and climbed down the ladder. Then he went over to the Jew, who was lying on the ground gasping for breath, and said: 'You rogue, now confess where you got the money from, or I'll take my fiddle from round my neck and start playing again.' 'I stole it, I stole it,' he screamed, 'but you earned it honestly.' Then the judge had the Jew led to the gallows and hanged as a thief.

LUDWIG BÖRNE AND HEINRICH HEINE

On Shylock

Ludwig Börne (1786–1837) changed his name from Juda Löw Baruch when he converted in 1818. Born in the Frankfurt ghetto, he benefited from the extension of equal rights to Jews in Western Germany by the French occupying forces after the Battle of Jena in 1806, and was able to study public administration and work as a civil servant keeping police records; but in 1815, with the revocation of Napoleonic legislation, Börne lost his job and had to work as a freelance journalist. He founded and largely wrote a journal, *The Balance*, which ran from 1818 to 1821, when the authorities, tired of its frank expression of liberal opinions, closed it down. In establishing political journalism in Germany, Börne also politicized literary criticism, using his many theatre reviews as a pretext for discussing public issues, and divining the unacknowledged and often unwitting political significance of literary texts—an example later followed by Heine and Marx. Thus his antipathy to Weimar Classicism, whose ahistorical aesthetics he considered an expression of political reaction, led Börne to denounce Goethe and to interpret Schiller's Wilhelm Tell as the embodiment of bourgeois servility. In 1830, attracted by the July Revolution, he moved to Paris, where his major work of political and cultural commentary, the *Letters from Paris* (1831–4), was written. His relations with his fellow-exile Heine were tense: Heine thought Börne turned political commitment into narrow-minded zealotry, Börne thought Heine an irresponsible dilettante; after Börne's death Heine had the last word in *Ludwig Börne: A Memorial*, a sometimes scurrilous character-sketch which also defends Heine's own political stance.

Börne's essay on Shylock was written in 1828. Following a precedent established in the late eighteenth century in both Britain and Germany, it defends Shylock's character, making a subtle distinction between his hateful avarice and the humanity that is displayed, however perversely, in the desire for revenge, which Börne reads as a more than personal passion. He then takes Shylock to typify the power of finance capitalism, which by the nineteenth century exercises a malign power over the politics of the world. Similarly, commenting in the *Letters from Paris* on Rothschild's reception by the Pope, Börne ironically proposes that the European monarchs should be replaced by the Rothschild clan, thus acknowledging their real power and removing the danger of international conflict. In thus applying anti-Semitic stereotypes to the whole of modern society, Börne anticipates the argumentative strategy of Marx's essay *On the Jewish Question* (1844), where 'Jewish' commercialism is said so to pervade society that only Socialism, in emancipating us from commercialism, will emancipate the Jews from the Jewish spirit. Although Börne never denied his Jewish origins, he helped to found a radical critique of Judaism which can be seen as a version of assimilation.

Shylock the Jew in *The Merchant of Venice*

When the women came home after the end of the play, they recounted how the visiting actor who had played Shylock had had a curtain call, thanked the audience with the usual elegance, and said that fortunately such a monster as Shylock could never be found in real life. On hearing this, I was glad that a bad cough had prevented me from attending the performance. Still, perhaps the benevolent man had said this only because of his good nature. Many rich Jews live in this town, who are hated and mocked by their Christian fellow citizens. Since the visiting actor had satisfied the malice of the Christian inhabitants by choosing *The Merchant of Venice* for his benefit performance, he must have wanted to say something nice to the Jews who help to fill the theatre. But his extraordinary speech cannot have been meant seriously; for that would show that he did not understand the part in the least. Whether or not Jewish cannibals and vampires exist in nature is not the point; but it matters a great deal that people should not think the great poet wanted to earn money by showing us a little mirror of the Jews, in the manner of Hundt-Radowsky.* If heaven sends a prophet like Shakespeare to ignorant people like ourselves, that is not just so that he may teach us to read, but to convey a greater message. In any case, Shakespeare's mission does not consist in preaching and teaching. But if he ever did want to be a schoolmaster, then in *The Merchant of Venice* he certainly intended his lesson for the Christians rather than for the Jews.

Granting Shylock's Jewishness, this fine morality that despises all uncoined passions—nevertheless, despite himself, there is in him something great, something sublime, that may look down proudly on his own baseness. Shylock is a Jew who has risen on high, an avenging angel; his feelings have brought him to a height where he becomes able to do something that does not swell his money-bags, to do something for *everyone*. He wants to help his despised and downtrodden nation by taking revenge on their tormentors, the Christian people. In Shylock we detest the money-grubbing devil, we pity the tormented man, but we love and admire the avenger of inhuman persecution. Let no one think it a small matter to cut a pound of flesh from the breast of a good Christian man! It may be a small matter for an evil Christian, but not for a Jew. The Jew's mind may make him cruel, but never his heart: he has a soft heart, tender through much beating; he is compassionate; he cannot bear the sight of blood. Who can tell whether Shylock would have carried out his deed, or whether the knife he whetted so maliciously against his sole* would have dropped from his hand after the first drop of blood? Antonio could have afforded the risk. And how much Shylock sacrifices for the sake of his revenge! Three thousand, six thousand, nine thousand ducats! And the Jews' ducats are no ordinary ducats, but are worth much more than others; their love for them magnifies them in their eyes. And he risks not only this sum, he risks more, the interest on this sum; for the Jew values profit more than possession. Could Antonio not pay when his debt fell due? But Shylock places his trust in the gods of vengeance, in storms at sea and in the perilous winds of evil rumours, and they do not let him down. Nor should one be misled when Shylock says he hates Antonio because the latter is fool enough to lend money without interest, thus bringing down the rate of interest in Venice, and his trade will benefit by Antonio's elimination. No, that is not why Shylock hates Antonio. The Christian merchants in Venice, we may be sure, did not consist entirely of noble Antonios, and a single man, however rich, cannot diminish the value of money. Shylock is a Jew, he is ashamed in his own eyes to sacrifice hard cash for the sake of a humour, and therefore he tries to deceive himself. The Jew may give way to enthusiasm, for he knows he is sick. But in reality Shylock is not sick; in Antonio he is persecuting not his commercial but his religious antagonist, and deliriously giving up solid ducats for an airy humour.

The actor who assumes the part of Shylock will have his work cut out. The Jew's bloodthirsty hatred must terrify us, like all fanaticism, all madness; but it must not arouse loathing and disgust, like a physical illness. Shylock's accursed cupidity, and the paroxysms inflicted on his soul by thwarted selfishness, must offend our inmost selves, but we must not find it ridiculous—when the Devil appears in person, it is no laughing matter. But to show the god present in the devil, to advance through a sandy waste of sin to the tiny spring of love that trickles so far away in such concealment: that gives the actor plenty of work. For Shakespeare is not like ordinary people and ordinary poets who, indulging their hearts or their skill, behave like analytic chemists and reduce composite living things to dead elements by presenting *pure characters*, loving some and hating others, making some attractive and others repulsive—that is not Shakespeare's way. He does not take sides, he gives his assent only to morality, which never appears in life unsullied; instead, he lets his creatures dispute with one another and does not mingle in their quarrel. The poet has done his utmost to justify the Jew's hatred for Christians, and has exerted himself with equal labour to excuse the Christian's Jew-hatred. How could Shylock not hate Antonio, and hate him all the more, the better and nobler he is! Antonio is good, noble, benevolent, but not towards the Jew. He insults him in public and maltreats him wherever and whenever he meets him. Indeed, in the very moment when he needs his compliance and his money, he cannot bring himself to hide his hatred, his contempt, and the good and noble Antonio, who sacrifices everything for his friend Bassanio, is still not noble enough to say kind words to a Jew for his friend's sake. Then a Christian scamp runs off with Shylock's daughter; she robs and abandons her old father, and, resolving to become a Christian, she begins her conversion by despising her father because he is a Jew. That might well turn the blood of a dove into dragon's blood. The Christian hates the Jew, the Jew retaliates on the Christian, and Shylock, by doing so, avenges injured virtue in his own person. He gives money to avenge his nation and learns that gold does not rule the world, as the Jew believes, but that love is mightier than gold, even in the Jew.

Whenever I read Shakespeare I grieve that he does not live in our time, so that he could explain it to us. It is as though stories did not happen properly when there is no real master to tell them properly. A character or a situation that this great poet did not describe is like a book without a title, whose contents we must discover by reading it. Great ages often fail to find great historians, poets, or artists who could narrate, describe, or depict them in visual form. Grand stories are too proud, too restless, or too busy to sit quietly for their portrait to ordinary artists. These can only capture their features as they fly past, or must wait till the age is dead in order to take a cast from the corpse that is as lifeless as the original model. Before a painter like Shakespeare, however, the ages keep still, well knowing that nature owes its immortality only to art. How would Shakespeare have described *our* Shylocks, the great Shylocks with Christian decorations on their Jewish roquelaures!* How would he have drawn the Shylocks without roquelaures, who trade in paper, possess the flesh and blood of entire nations in notes, and instead of turning trash into paper, turn paper into trash! How devastatingly he would have painted the scoundrels for whom God is a Chancellor of the Exchequer, saying: 'Let there be...' and creating a world of paper; Adam, the Governor of the Bank; Paradise, the blessed state when state papers stand at par; the Fall, the first fall in the exchange rate; for whom the book of history is filled with share-certificates; for whom the Last Judgement marks the final settlement of accounts; for whom the god Mars, who sacrifices the calm of exchange rates for glory, honour, national happiness, faith, righteousness, and other vile things, is an accursed speculator who wants the markets to fall; Sultan Mahmud,* the protector of Christian papers, a great man, a mighty great man, a second Joshua; the *Austrian Observer*,* the sixth book of the Pentateuch! O, how Shakespeare, that great broker between nature and art, exchanging the former's cash for the latter's paper, would have disclosed the mysteries of Stock Exchange hearts! How he would have shown up our Stock Exchange dealers who call the Greeks* a 'nation of rogues'!—Do you hear Cato's* ashes laughing?—What did the Venetian Shylock do? Gave up three thousand good ducats for a wretched pound of Christian flesh; at least he paid dearly for his desire. But our Shylocks, of both the Old and the New Testaments, drown all Hellas, as though it were a blind kitten, for a few pence. Shylock of Venice was a lamb, a child, a worthy soul; and yet the actor in Frankfurt has just said that such a monster as Shylock does not exist in nature, and Shakespeare was a slanderer! O, my good actor! History lies in calling people Christians because their ancestors ate sausages; but Shakespeare does not lie.

[Heine's essay on Jessica comes from *Shakespeare's Girls and Women*, commissioned in 1838 by a French publisher who was issuing a volume of steel engravings illustrating female characters from Shakespeare's plays and wanted to bring out a German edition with a commentary by Heine. Having got carried away and written more than he had contracted for, Heine wrote only about the histories and tragedies, including *The Merchant of Venice* among the latter by interpreting Shylock as a tragic character. The essay follows the tactic, already used by Börne, of defending Shylock by contrast with his callous and frivolous antagonists. Heine shares Börne's association of the Jews with modern capitalism, though, perhaps more sensitive to its anti-Semitic implications, he ascribes it to a private letter which may be an invention or may be based on an actual letter from Rahel Varnhagen. Dialectically, however, Heine argues that the Jews have also overcome the national and nationalistic attachment to a place or a clan that was common to the ancient world and to modern Europe. If they typify the worrying mobility of modern finance, they may also embody the modern principle of cosmopolitanism which Heine hopes will supersede nationalism. He also argues, however, for a profound 'elective affinity' between the Germans and the Jews, based on their shared morality, a claim that was to be put forward most emphatically by the neo-Kantian philosopher Hermann Cohen during the First World War, and that may be found also in the Fitelberg episode of Thomas Mann's *Doctor Faustus*.]

Jessica (*The Merchant of Venice*)

When I saw this play performed in Drury Lane,* there was standing in the box behind me a pale and beautiful British woman who, at the end of Act Four, wept bitterly and cried out repeatedly: 'The poor man is wronged!' She had a face of the noblest Greek shape, and her eyes were large and dark. I have never been able to forget them, those large dark eyes that wept for Shylock!

When I recall those tears, however, I must count *The Merchant of Venice* among the tragedies, even though the play's framework is adorned by the most cheerful masks, satyr-faces, and amoretti, and the poet, too, really wanted to write a comedy. Shakespeare may have intended to delight the crowd by showing them a well-trained werewolf, a fabulous monster who in his thirst for blood loses his daughter and his ducats and is made a laughing-stock into the bargain. But the poet's genius, the world spirit that rules in him, is always higher than his individual will, and thus it came about that in Shylock, for all the broad grotesquerie, he pronounced the justification of an unfortunate sect that for obscure reasons has been burdened by providence with the hatred of the low and high rabble, and has not always returned love for hatred.

But what am I saying? Shakespeare's genius rises above the petty squabbles of two religious parties, and his drama really shows us neither Jews nor Christians, but oppressors and oppressed, and how the latter rejoice in mad agony when they manage to pay their arrogant tormentors back with interest for the injuries inflicted on them. There is not one trace of religious difference in this play, and Shakespeare shows us in Shylock only a man who is commanded by nature to hate his enemy, just as in Antonio and his friends he by no means presents the disciples of that divine doctrine that commands us to love our enemies. When Shylock speaks to the man who wants to borrow money from him in the following words:

> Signior Antonio, many a time and oft
> In the Rialto you have rated me
> About my moneys and my usances;
> Still have I borne it with a patient shrug,
> For suff'rance is the badge of all our tribe;
> You call me misbeliever, cut-throat, dog,
> And spit upon my Jewish gaberdine,
> And all for use of that which is mine own.
> Well then, it now appears you need my help;
> Go to, then; you come to me, and you say
> 'Shylock, we would have moneys.' You say so—
> You, that did void your rheum upon my beard
> And foot me as you spurn a stranger cur
> Over your threshold; moneys is your suit.
> What should I say to you? Should I not say
> 'Hath a dog money? Is it possible
> A cur can lend three thousand ducats?' Or
> Shall I bend low and, in a bondman's key,
> With bated breath and whisp'ring humbleness,
> Say this:
> 'Fair sir, you spat on me on Wednesday last,
> You spurned me such a day; another time
> You called me dog; and for these courtesies
> I'll lend you thus much moneys'?

To which Antonio replies:

> I am as like to call thee so again,
> To spit on thee again, to spurn thee too.

—Where has Christian love got to? Truly, Shakespeare would have composed a satire on Christianity if he had let it be represented by the people who are hostile to Shylock and yet are scarcely worthy to untie his shoelaces. The bankrupt Antonio is a feeble character without energy, lacking strength in his hatred and therefore also in his love, a dismal, worm-like heart, whose flesh is really fit for nothing better than 'to bait fish withal'. What is more, he does not return the three thousand ducats he borrowed to the cheated Jew. Nor does Bassanio give him back his money, and the latter is a real 'fortune-hunter', in the phrase of an English critic; he borrows money in order to dress up magnificently and capture a wealthy wife, a rich dowry; for, says he to his friend,

> 'Tis not unknown to you, Antonio,
> How much I have disabled mine estate
> By something showing a more swelling port
> Than my faint means would grant continuance;
> Nor do I now make moan to be abridged
> From such a noble rate; but my chief care
> Is to come fairly off from the great debts
> Wherein my time, something too prodigal,
> Hath left me gag'd.

And as for Lorenzo, he is an accomplice in an infamous burglary, and the Prussian law-code would sentence him to fifteen years of penal servitude with hard labour, as well as having him branded and put in the pillory; although he is very responsive not only to stolen ducats and jewels but also to the beauties of nature, moonlit landscapes, and music. As for the other noble Venetians who appear as Antonio's companions, they likewise seem not averse to money, and when their poor friend falls into misfortune they have nothing for him but words, coined air. On this point our good Pietist Franz Horn* makes the following feeble but correct observation:

Here it is proper to raise the question how it was possible for Antonio's misfortune to be so severe. All Venice knew and esteemed him; his good friends were well aware of the terrible bond, and that the Jew would not relent on a single point of it. Yet they allow one day to go by after another until the three months, and therewith all hope of rescue, are at an end. These good friends, whom the royal merchant seems to have in great hordes, would have found it quite easy to raise the sum of three thousand ducats to save a human life, especially such a life as this; but such actions are always a little inconvenient, and so his dear friends, being merely self-styled friends, or, if you prefer, half-hearted or three-quarters-hearted friends, do nothing whatsoever. They are heartily sorry for the excellent merchant who laid on such beautiful parties for them, they denounce Shylock with all the severity of which their hearts and tongues are capable—another proceeding that incurs no danger—and then they evidently consider that they have done everything friendship requires. However much we are to hate Shylock, we could not blame even him for despising these people a little, as he no doubt does. Indeed, he seems finally to confuse Gratiano, whose absence gives him an excuse, with the others and to lump them all together, when he condemns their earlier inactivity and their present loquacity with the cutting answer:

> Till thou canst rail the seal from off my bond,
> Thou but offend'st thy lungs to speak so loud;
> Repair thy wit, good youth, or it will fall
> To cureless ruin. I stand here for law.

Or should Launcelot Gobbo perhaps be taken as the representative of Christianity? Strangely enough, Shakespeare nowhere expresses himself on this topic so clearly as in a conversation between this rogue and his mistress. To Jessica's remark, 'I shall be sav'd by my husband; he hath made me a Christian,' Launcelot Gobbo replies:

Truly, the more to blame he; we were Christians enow before, e'en as many as could well live one by another. This making of Christians will raise the price of hogs; if we grow all to be pork-eaters, we shall not shortly have a rasher on the coals for money.

Truly, with the exception of Portia, Shylock is the person in the whole play who deserves most respect. He loves money, he does not hide his love for it, he shouts it aloud in the public market-place... But there is something he values above money, and that is the satisfaction for his offended heart, the just retaliation for unspeakable degradations; and although he is offered the borrowed sum ten times over, he refuses it, and he does not regret the three thousand, the ten times three thousand ducats, if he can buy with them a pound of flesh from his enemy's heart. 'What's his flesh good for?' asks Salerio. And he replies:

To bait fish withal. If it will feed nothing else, it will feed my revenge. He hath disgrac'd me and hind'red me half a million; laugh'd at my losses, mock'd at my gains, scorned my nation, thwarted my bargains, cooled my friends, heated mine enemies. And what's the reason? I am a Jew. Hath not a Jew eyes? Hath not a Jew hands, organs, dimensions, senses, affections, passions, fed with the same food, hurt with the same weapons, subject to the same diseases, healed with the same means, warmed and cooled by the same winter and summer, as a Christian is? If you prick us, do we not bleed? If you tickle us, do we not laugh? If you poison us, do we not die? And if you wrong us, shall we not revenge? If we are like you in the rest, we will resemble you in that. If a Jew wrong a Christian, what is his humility? Revenge. If a Christian wrong a Jew, what should his sufferance be by Christian example? Why, revenge. The villainy you teach me I will execute; and it shall go hard but I will better the instruction.

No, Shylock does love money, but there are things he loves much more, including his daughter, 'Jessica, my child'. Although in the extreme passion of anger he curses her and would like to see her lying dead at his feet, with the jewels in her ears and the ducats in her coffin, he still loves her more than all the ducats and jewels. Forced out of public life, from Christian society, into the narrow confines of domestic happiness, the poor Jew has nothing but family affection, and that is manifested in a touchingly heartfelt manner. He would not have given the turquoise, the ring that was a present from his wife Leah, for 'a wilderness of monkeys'. When Bassanio, in the court scene, speaks the following words:

> Antonio, I am married to a wife
> Which is as dear to me as life itself;
> But life itself, my wife, and all the world,
> Are not with me esteem'd above thy life;
> I would lose all, ay, sacrifice them all
> Here to this devil, to deliver you

—when Gratiano likewise adds:

> I have a wife whom I protest I love;
> I would she were in heaven, so she could

Entreat some power to change this currish Jew

—then Shylock begins to feel anxious about the fate of his daughter, married to one of these people who are ready to sacrifice their wives for their friend, and he says to himself, not out loud but 'aside':

These be the Christian husbands! I have a daughter—
Would any of the stock of Barrabas
Had been her husband, rather than a Christian!

This passage, these soft-spoken words, justify the condemnation which we must pronounce on fair Jessica. It was not an unloving father whom she left, whom she robbed, whom she betrayed... Shameful betrayal! She even made common cause with Shylock's enemies, and at Belmont, when they say all manner of bad things about him, Jessica does not cast down her eyes, Jessica's lips do not blench; no, it is Jessica who says the worst things about her father... Appalling crime! She has no heart, only a taste for excitement. She was so bored in the locked, 'sober' house of the bitter-hearted Jew that in the end she thought it a hell. Her wanton heart was too strongly attracted by the merry sounds of the drum and the wry-necked fife. Was Shakespeare here trying to depict a Jewess? No indeed; he is depicting only a daughter of Eve, one of those pretty birds that, as soon as they are fledged, flutter from the paternal nest to find their beloved male. Thus Desdemona followed the Moor, thus Imogen followed Posthumus. That is how women behave. In Jessica's case we particularly note a certain hesitant shame that she cannot overcome when she has to put on a boy's clothes. In this characteristic one might wish to recognize the strange modesty that is peculiar to her tribe and lends its daughters such wonderful charm. The Jews' modesty perhaps results from their immemorial opposition to those Oriental rites of the senses and sensuality that once flourished so exuberantly among their neighbours, the Egyptians, Phoenicians, Assyrians, and Babylonians, and has persisted to the present day amid perpetual transformations. The Jews are a modest, self-denying, I might almost say an abstract people, and in the purity of their manners they are closest to the Germanic tribes. The chastity of Jewish and Germanic women may have no absolute value, but as it manifests itself, it makes the most charming, delightful, and moving impression. For example, it moves one to tears when, after the defeat of the Cimbri and Teutons, their women beseech Marius not to hand them over to the soldiers but to give them to the priestesses of Vesta as their slaves.*

There is indeed a strikingly close elective affinity prevailing between the two moral peoples, the Jews and the Germans. This elective affinity did not arise historically, because the Jews' great family chronicle, the Bible, served the entire Germanic world as a textbook; nor is it because Jews and Germans were from early times the most implacable enemies of the Romans, and hence natural allies: it has such deep foundations, and both peoples are originally so similar, that one might regard ancient Palestine as an Oriental Germany, just as one might regard present-day Germany as the home of the holy Word, the motherland of prophecy, the citadel of pure spirituality.

But it is not only Germany that bears the physiognomy of Palestine: the rest of Europe, too, is rising to the Jews' level. I say 'rising', for the Jews have always borne within them the modern principle which is only now unfolding visibly among the European nations.

The Greeks and Romans were intensely attached to the soil, to the fatherland. The subsequent Nordic invaders of the Greek and Roman world were attached to the person of their chieftains, and classical patriotism was replaced in the Middle Ages by feudal loyalty, by attachment to the prince. The Jews, however, were attached from time immemorial only to the law, to the abstract idea, like our modern cosmopolitan republicans, who respect neither the land of their birth nor the person of their prince, but regard the laws as supreme. Indeed, cosmopolitanism really sprang from the soil of Judaea, and Christ, who, despite the ill-humour of the Hamburg spice-dealer* mentioned earlier, was a true Jew, really founded a system of propaganda to make people citizens of the world. As for the Jews' republicanism, I recall reading in Josephus* that there were republicans at Jerusalem who were opposed to the royalist Herodians, fought most bravely, called nobody 'master', and hated Roman absolutism most fiercely; their religion was freedom and equality. What a delusion!

But what is the ultimate basis of the hatred that we observe in Europe, even today, between the adherents of the Mosaic laws and those of Christ's teaching—the hatred of which the poet, conveying the general through the particular, has provided a hideous image in

The Merchant of Venice? Is it the original fraternal hatred that we see flaring up between Cain and Abel, just after the creation of the world, on account of their different ways of serving God? Or is religion nothing but a pretext, so that people hate each other for the sake of hating, as they love for the sake of loving? Which side is to blame for this enmity? To answer this question, I cannot forbear communicating a passage from a private letter* which also justifies Shylock's antagonists:

I do not condemn the hatred with which the common people persecute the Jews; I condemn only the unhappy errors that gave rise to this hatred. The people [*Das Volk*] is always right about the fundamental issue; its hatred, like its love, is always based on a sound instinct, but it cannot formulate its feelings properly, and instead of the issue, its enmity is aimed at the person, the innocent scapegoat of temporal and local ills. The people suffers want, lacks the means to enjoy life, and although the priests of the state religion maintain 'that we are placed on earth in order to suffer, and to obey the authorities despite hunger and thirst,' the people secretly longs for the means of enjoyment, and hates those who keep them stored in chests and cupboards; it hates the rich and is glad when religion allows it to vent this hatred from the bottom of its heart. In the Jews the common people have always hated only the possessors of money; it was always their piles of metal that drew the lightning of popular rage down upon the Jews. The spirit of the age, whatever it might be, always supplied a slogan for such hatred. In the Middle Ages the slogan bore the gloomy colour of the Catholic Church, and the Jews were killed and their houses plundered 'because they crucified Christ'—with the very same logic that allowed some black Christians, during the massacre on San Domingo,* to run about carrying an image of the crucified Saviour and shouting fanatically: 'les blancs l'ont tué, tuons tous les blancs.'*

My friend, you laugh at the poor negroes; I assure you, the West Indian planters found it no laughing matter, and they were slaughtered to atone for Christ, as the European Jews had been a few centuries earlier. But the black Christians on San Domingo were equally right about the fundamental issue! The whites were living in idleness surrounded by pleasures, while the negro had to work for them in the sweat of his black brow, receiving only a little rice and many whiplashes as his reward; the blacks were the common people.

We are no longer living in the Middle Ages, and the common people, too, are more enlightened, no longer kill the Jews, and no longer mask their hatred with religion; our age is no longer so naively warm in its faith, traditional enmity is clad in modern clichés, and the rabble, both in beer-halls and parliaments, declaims against the Jews with mercantile, industrial, scholarly, or even philosophical arguments. It is only double-dyed hypocrites who nowadays still give their hatred a religious tinge and persecute the Jews for Christ's sake; the masses frankly admit that their enmity is based on material interests, and they seek to prevent the Jews by every possible means from exercising their industrial abilities. Here in Frankfurt, for example, only twenty-four adherents of the Mosaic faith are permitted to marry annually, so that their population will not increase and provide excessive competition for the Christian shopkeepers. Here the real basis of Jew-hatred appears with its real face, and its face is not the gloomy mien of a fanatical monk, but the easy, enlightened features of a grocer, who is afraid that his business will be outdone by the commercial talents of the Israelites.

But is it the fault of the Jews that their commercial talents have developed so alarmingly? The fault lies with the madness of the Middle Ages in ignoring the importance of industry, regarding trade as something ignoble and moneylending as something disgraceful, and therefore placing the most profitable of these branches of industry, that is, moneylending, in the hands of the Jews; so that, being barred from all other employment, they could not help becoming the most crafty merchants and bankers. They were forced to grow rich and then hated for their wealth; and although nowadays Christendom has discarded its prejudices against industry, and the Christians have become as great knaves as the Jews in trade and finance, and as rich as the Jews: nevertheless, the latter are still the objects of traditional popular hatred, the people still see in them the representatives of money and hate them. In the history of the world, you see, everybody is right—both the hammer and the anvil.

HEINRICH HEINE

Jehuda ben Halevy
(translated by Hal Draper)

Heinrich Heine (1797–1856) belongs, with Börne and Marx, to the first generation of assimilated Jews whose link with Jewish tradition was loose and who, unable to find a secure place in German society, were attracted by journalism and radical politics which led them into exile. Born in Düsseldorf, and sent to university at Bonn, Göttingen, and Berlin after displaying a complete lack of business talent, Heine was attracted both to the German historical and legendary past that had been reanimated by Romantic scholars, including the Grimms, and by the exploration of the Jewish past ('Wissenschaft des Judentums') being undertaken by friends in Berlin. There he met leading intellectuals in the salons of Rahel Varnhagen and other hostesses. Of his own writings, his poems, collected in the *Book of Songs* (1827), are increasingly subtle, often ironic refinements of Romantic motifs, which have since been made internationally famous by composers; while the witty, dense, associative prose of his *Travel Pictures* (4 volumes, 1826–31) includes brilliant if barbed social comedy focusing on over- and under-assimilated Jews. The difficulty of earning a living in Germany, the dangers his political radicalism might incur, and the attraction of the 1830 July Revolution, made Heine move in 1831 to Paris, where he lived for the rest of his life. He remained largely aloof from the German radical exiles led by Börne, mixed easily in French cultural life, and informed the French about the political implications of German Romanticism and idealist philosophy in long essays which appeared both in French and German. Reportage on French events, short Sternean novels, diverse essays, and many amatory and satirical poems, notably the narrative satires *Atta Troll: A Midsummer Night's Dream* (1843, revised 1847) and *Germany: A Winter's Tale* (1844), form the bulk of his work in the 1830s and 1840s. As he became dissatisfied with the unequal democracy of the July Monarchy, his political opinions moved from utopian socialism to an ambivalent attachment to the hard revolutionary communism represented by Marx, whom he got to know in 1843. The year of revolutions, 1848, coincided, however, with Heine's collapse from spinal tuberculosis. Bed-ridden for the last eight years of his life, and harassed by money worries and family feuds, he experienced a return to a non-denominational religious faith, and produced a large body of dazzling satirical poetry which ranges throughout history to ask ultimate questions about the meaning and purpose of life. Still Germany's wittiest writer, he has been particularly popular in the English-speaking world, where George Eliot and Matthew Arnold were among his early admirers. In Germany his reputation has been inconstant, attacked on one hand by conservatives and nationalists, on the other by fastidious critics unduly influenced by Karl Kraus's polemic *Heine and the Consequences* (1910), which lambastes Heine for blurring artistic boundaries by introducing the 'French disease' of journalism into Germany.

'Jehuda ben Halevy' is the central poem of the three 'Hebrew Melodies' which in turn form the third and last section of *Romanzero*, the first book of poetry composed by the bed-ridden Heine. It appeared in 1851. The poems owe their overall title, but little else, to the *Hebrew Melodies* by Byron, whom Heine admired and felt akin to. The first, 'Princess Sabbath', draws an affectionately humorous, occasionally bitter contrast between the hardship of the Jew's working week and the Sabbath evening when he can be fully human. The third, 'Disputation', describes one of the public disputations arranged in medieval Spain between priests and rabbis. 'Jehuda ben Halevy', the longest, is in the artful, seemingly rambling style that the late Heine cultivated in his long poems from *Atta Troll* onwards, and keeps intercutting between the present and various layers of the past: Heine plays his poetic identity off against that of the great medieval poet properly called Judah Halevi, and compares his sickness to the sufferings of Job. By its apparent meanderings, the poem achieves immense historical depth. In particular, two epochs of Jewish history are made to reflect each other. One is medieval Spain, where Jews often enjoyed good relations with their Christian neighbours and also had ready access to the Arab world, participating fully in its intellectual culture. The other is early nineteenth-century Berlin, where as a student Heine had enjoyed the company both of Rahel Varnhagen and of Hegel, and where we are shown the convert Hitzig mingling not only with Heine but with Adalbert von Chamisso, who, as a German writer of French descent, also testifies to the virtues of cultural hybridity.

These poems were written when Heine, crippled by a painful illness, had found his way back to a strange, ambivalent, personal relationship with God and attained an attitude of detachment, sometimes humorous and sometimes cynical, from the world and its strivings. The life of Jehuda ben Halevy and his yearning for Zion are ironically placed within a cosmos that is apparently meaningless and allows such random disasters as the casual murder of Jehuda by a passing Arab. The futility of history, a theme of many poems in *Romanzero*, is figured by the string of pearls which the conqueror Alexander gathered up with the rest of his booty and which found their way via the follies of Thais and Cleopatra to Europe, where the Arabs were eventually driven out by the Christian kings and these in turn succumbed to the financial power of Jewry, illustrated by the financier Mendizábal and by the Jewish baroness (supplanting the traditional European aristocracy) who wears the pearls at a court function in Paris. History can be interpreted as a tale of greed and folly, as a narrative of decline, or, ironically, as a story in which Alexander's military conquests are eventually counterbalanced by the financial victories of the Rothschilds. In this world the poet is helpless, fated to be an unlucky *schlemiel*.

Jehuda ben Halevy

'Dry with thirst, oh let my tongue cleave
To my palate—let my right hand
Wither off, if I forget thee
Ever, O Jerusalem—'*

Words and melody keep buzzing
In my head today, unceasing,
And I seem to make out voices
Singing psalms, I hear men's voices——

Sometimes, too, I catch a glimpse of
Shadowy long beards in darkness—
Phantom figures, which of you
Is Jehuda ben Halevy?*

But they scurry by me quickly—
Ghosts will shun with fear the clumsy
Consolations of the living—
Yet I recognized him there—

I could recognize his pallid
Forehead, proudly worn with thinking,
And his eyes, so gentle-stubborn—
Pained, inquiring eyes that pierce me—

But I recognized him mostly
By his enigmatic way of
Smiling with those rhyming lips,
Which are found in poets only.

Years come round and years go fleeting.
Since Jehuda ben Halevy
Saw the light, the world has counted
Seven hundred years and fifty;

It was in Castile's Toledo
That he came into the world,
And the golden Tagus crooned him
Lullabies beside the cradle.

His strict father early nurtured
His development and thinking,
And his education started
With the book of God, the Torah.*

And the youngster read this volume
In the ancient text, whose lovely
Picturesquely hieroglyphic
Old Chaldean squared-off letters

Are derived out of the childhood
Of the world, and for this reason
Show familiar, smiling features
To all childlike minds and spirits.

This authentic ancient text
Was recited by the youngster
In the old, original singsong
Known as *Tropp** down through the ages—

And with loving care he gurgled
Those fat gutturals right gladly,
And the quaver, the Shalsheleth,*
He trilled like a feathered warbler.

As for Onkelos's Targum,*
Which is written in that special
Low-Judaic idiom
That we call the Aramaic

And which bears the same relation
To the language of the prophets
That the Swabian has to German—
In this garlic-sausage Hebrew

Was the boy instructed likewise,
And this knowledge soon provided
Solid service to his efforts
In the study of the Talmud.

Yes, his father early led him
To the pages of the Talmud,
And thereby he laid before him
The Halacha,* that prodigious

School of fencing, where the greatest
Of the dialectic athletes
In the Babylonian contests
Used to carry on their war games.

Here the boy could master every
Art and science of polemic;
And his mastery was later
Witnessed by his book *Kuzari.**

But the heavens shed upon us
Two quite different kinds of lustre:
There's the sun's harsh-glaring daylight
And the milder moonlight—likewise,

Likewise, shining in the Talmud
Is a double light, divided
In Halacha and Haggada.*
Fencing school I called the former,

But the latter, the Haggada,
I would rather call a garden,
A phantasmagoric garden
That is very like another

That once bloomed and sprouted also
From the soil of Babylonia—*
Queen Semiramis' great garden,*
That eighth wonder of the world.

Queen Semiramis was brought up
As a child by birds, and always
Later on retained a number
Of their birdlike traits and temper,

And so she refused to walk on
Lowly ground like common mammals
And insisted on the planting
Of a garden in the air:—

Rising high on giant pillars
Cypresses and palm trees flourished,
Orange trees and beds of flowers,
Marble statues, even fountains,

All secured with cunning braces
Formed by countless hanging bridges,
Made to look like vines and creepers,
On which birds would swing and teeter—

Big and bright-hued birds, deep thinkers
Much too solemn-faced to warble,
While around them fluttered bands of
Little finches, gaily trilling.

All of them were blithely breathing
Air distilled of balsam fragrance,
Unpolluted by the reek of
Earth's miasma and malodours.

The Haggada is a garden
Of such childlike airy fancy.
And the young Talmudic scholar—
When his heart felt dry and dusty,

Musty from the noisy squabbling
Over the Halacha, over
Quarrels on the plaguy egg
That a hen laid on a feast day,

Or about some other question
Equally profound—the youngster
Fled for solace of the spirit
To the blossom-filled Haggada,

With its lovely olden fables,
Tales of angels, myths and legends,
Tranquil stories of the martyrs,
Festive songs and wise old sayings,

Droll exaggerations also,
Yet it all had faith's old power,
Faith's old fire—Oh, how it sparkled,
Bubbling with exuberance—

And the youngster's noble spirit
Was enraptured by the sweetness,
Wild and wonderful adventure,
And the strangely aching gladness,

And the fabled thrills and shivers
Of that blissful secret world,
Of that mighty revelation
Which we title poesy

And the art of poesy—
Gaia scienza,* gracious talent
That we call the poet's art—
Also worked upon his spirit.

Thus Jehuda ben Halevy
Grew to be not just a scholar
But a master of poetics
And a great and mighty poet.

Yes, he was a mighty poet,
Star and beacon for his age,
Light and lamp among his people,
And a wonderful and mighty

Pillar of poetic fire
In the vanguard of all Israel's
Caravan of woe and sorrow
In the desert waste of exile.

Pure and truthful, without blemish,
Was his song—his soul was also.
On the day his Maker fashioned
This great soul, He paused contented,

Kissed the soul whose beauty sparkled;
And those kisses still go thrilling
Through the poet's every measure
Hallowed by this grace and bounty.

Both in poetry and life,
It's the gift of grace that governs—
He who has this highest good can
Never sin in prose or verse.

Any poet who possesses
This, God's grace, we call a genius:
Monarch in the realm of thought, he
Is responsible to no man.

He accounts to God, God only,
Not the people; both in art
And in life, the people can
Kill us but can never judge us.

ii

'By the Babylonian waters
There we sat and wept—our harps were
Hung upon the weeping willow...'*
That old song—do you still know it?

That old tune—do you still know it?—
How it starts with elegiac
Whining, humming like a kettle
That is seething on the hearth?

Long has it been seething in me—
For a thousand years. Black sorrow!
And my wounds are licked by time
Just as Job's dog licked his boils.*

Dog, I thank you for your spittle,
But its coolness merely soothes me—
Only death can really heal me,
But, alas, I am immortal!

Years come round and years pass onward—
In the loom the spool is whirring,
Busy flying hither-thither—
What it weaves no weaver knows.

Years come round and years pass onward,
And men's teardrops trickle slowly
Into earth, and earth absorbs them
In a dark and greedy silence—

Seething mad! The lid blows off—
Hail to him, the man 'that taketh
All thy little ones and dasheth
This young brood against the stones.'*

God be thanked! the steam is cooling
In the kettle, which now slowly
Quiets down. My spleen subsides,
That black Western–Eastern* spleen—

And my wingèd horse is neighing,
Glad once more, and seems to shake off
Baleful nightmares from his spirit,
And his knowing eyes are asking:

'Shouldn't we go back to Spain now,
To the young Talmudic scholar
Who became a mighty poet—
To Jehuda ben Halevy?'

Yes, he did become a great one,
Sovereign ruler of the dream world,
Monarch of the mind and spirit,
Poet by God's grace and bounty,

Who, in God-imbued *sirventes*,
Madrigals and sweet terzinas,
Canzonets and sultry ghazels',*
Poured out incandescent ardours

From his God-kissed soul and spirit!
Yes indeed, this troubadour
Was the equal of the greatest
Lutenists in old Provence,

In Poitou, or in Guienne,
Roussillon,* or all the other
Lovely lands of orange blossoms
Of our gallant Christendom.

Ah, our gallant Christendom's
Lovely lands of orange blossoms!
Ah, how fragrant, shining, plangent
In the twilight of remembrance!

Lovely world of nightingales!
Where men worshipped not the true God
But the false god Love, him only,
And bowed down before the Muses.

Clerics, with their wreaths of roses
On bald pates, sang psalms and hymnals
In the blithe tongue of Provence;
And the noble knights, the laymen,

Trotted proud on lofty chargers,
Mulling over rhymes and verses
Made in honour of the ladies
Whom they served with jocund hearts.

There's no love without a lady,
And a lady was essential
To a troubadour, like butter
To a piece of bread and butter.

So too he, the hero sung here,
So Jehuda ben Halevy
Had a ladylove he honoured—
But she was a special case.

She was not another Laura,*
Whose sweet eyes—those mortal starlets—
On Good Friday in the duomo
Lit a blaze now celebrated;

She was no chatelaine, presiding
In the flower of youth and beauty
Over tournaments and jousting,
Handing out the knightly laurels;

Nor a casuist who lectured
On the legal code of kissing
Or some other law or dogma
In a learned Court of Love.

She, the rabbi's love, was just a
Sad and wretched little darling,
Woeful image of destruction—
She was named Jerusalem.

Even in his early childhood
She had all his love already,
And his heart already quivered
At the word Jerusalem.

Then the boy would stand and listen,
Scarlet flames on cheeks, when pilgrims
Journeyed through Toledo coming
From a far-off Eastern country,

And told people how defiled and
Devastated were the places
Where the soil still glowed with radiance
From the footsteps of the prophets,

Where the air was still imbued with
The eternal breath of God—
'What a lamentable sight!' once
Cried a pilgrim, whose long beard

Flowed down silver-white, though strangely
At its tip the hair was growing
Black again, and almost seemed to
Undergo rejuvenation*—

Yes, a curious-looking pilgrim*
Must this man have been, whose eyes
Held a thousand years of sorrow;
And he sighed, 'Jerusalem!

'She, the crowded holy city,
Has become a desolation
Where wood demons, werewolves, jackals
Carry on their vile existence—

'Snakes and birds of night are nesting
In its mouldering walls and ramparts;
From the windows' airy arches
Foxes gaze in carefree comfort.

'Here and there one sometimes glimpses
Ragged peons of the desert
Letting their old humpbacked camels
Pasture on tall-growing grasses.

'On the noble heights of Zion
Where the golden stronghold towered
Whose majestic splendour witnessed
To the great king's pomp and glory—

'There the weeds grow rank and only
Grey old ruins still are standing,
Looking so forlorn and woeful
One might fancy they were weeping.

'And it's said they really do weep
One day every year, upon the
Ninth day of the month of Ab—.*
I myself, with hot eyes streaming,

'Saw the heavy teardrops seeping
Slowly from the mighty stone blocks,
And I heard the lamentations
Of the broken temple pillars.'—

Stories from such pious pilgrims
Wakened in the youthful bosom
Of Jehuda ben Halevy
Yearnings for Jerusalem.

Poets' yearnings! dreamy bodings,
Ominous as was the longing
That once at his Chateau Blaye
Filled the noble-souled Vidame,

Noble troubadour Rudel,*
When—to knights who had returned from
Eastern lands, midst clinking goblets—
He presented this assertion:

'Paragon of grace and breeding,
Pearl and flower of all women
Is the lovely Melisande,
Tripoli's enchanting countess.'

Everyone knows that this lady
Was the troubadour's belovèd,
That he sang her praise, and felt that
Chateau Blaye was cramped and straitened.

Longing drove him forth. At Cette
He took ship, but on the water
He fell sick, and, close to dying,
Made his way to Tripoli.

Here he saw his Melisande;
Finally his eyes beheld her
But that selfsame hour the shadow
Of grim death closed them forever.

Thus he sang his final love-song,
And he died there at the feet of
Melisande, his longed-for lady,
Tripoli's enchanting countess.

Wonderful is the resemblance
In the fate of these two poets!
Save that one was in his old age
When he launched his pilgrimage.

And Jehuda ben Halevy
Also died at his love's feet,
And his dying head lay resting
On Jerusalem's fair knees.

iii

When the battle of Arbela*
Ended, Alexander took the
Lands and peoples of Darius,
Court and harem, horses, women,

Elephants and jingling darics,
Crown and sceptre—golden rubbish—
And he stuck it all into his
Baggy Macedonian breeches.

In the tent of great Darius,
Who had fled lest he himself be
Stuck away with other booty,
Our young hero found a casket.

This small golden chest was graced with
Miniatures and filigree work
And was splendidly adorned with
Cameos and crusted jewels.

Now, this chest, itself a treasure
Of inestimable value,
Served to hold the monarch's treasures,
All his precious body jewels.

Alexander gave these jewels
To brave soldiers in his army,
Smiling at the thought that men get
Childlike joy from coloured pebbles.

One rich jewel of the fairest
He sent to his cherished mother;
Once the signet ring of Cyrus,*
It was now set in a brooch.

And he sent to Aristotle,
Teacher and the world's rump-thumper,
A big onyx for his noted
Natural history collection.

Also in the chest were pearls,
Strung into a wondrous necklace,
Which were once to Queen Atossa*
Given by the bogus Smerdis;

But the pearls themselves were real—
And the gleeful victor gave them
To a beauty of a dancer,
Come from Corinth, name of Thaïs.*

Thaïs wore them in her tresses,
Which streamed loose like a bacchante,
On the night of fire when, dancing
At Persepolis, she boldly

Flung her torch at the king's castle,
So that flames shot up and crackled
In a noisy conflagration
Like the fireworks on a feast-day.

On the death of lovely Thaïs—
Which took place in Babylon
Of a Babylonian ailment—
The pearl necklace was disposed of

At a local public auction.
There a priest from Memphis* bought them,
Took them on to Egypt, where they
Turned up somewhat later, on

Cleopatra's dressing table;
She then crushed the finest pearl and
Mixed it into wine and drank it,
Just to chaff Mark Antony.*

With the last of the Omayyads*
Came this string of pearls to Spain,
And they coiled it round the turban
Of the Caliph in Cordova.*

Abderam the Third then wore it
As his favor at the tourney
Where he pierced the thirty golden
Circlets and Zuleima's heart.

With the Moorish empire's downfall
The pearl necklace also passed on
To the Christians, and it wound up
In the crown jewels of Castile.

Their most Catholic Majesties, the
Queens of Spain, adorned their persons
With the pearls on court occasions,
Plays and bullfights and processions,

And at auto-da-fés* also,
Where on balconies in comfort
They regaled themselves with fragrant
Whiffs of old Jews slowly roasting.

Later on, the son of Satan,
Mendizábal,* put these pearls
Out to pawn, to cover certain
Deficits in state finances.

At the Tuileries the necklace
Showed up for its last appearance,
Shimmering on the neck of Madame
Solomon, the baroness.*

So it went with these fine pearls.
Less adventurous was the story
Of the casket: Alexander
Kept it for his very own.

In it he enclosed the poems
That ambrosial Homer chanted,
Favourites of his; at night-time
At the head of his hard pallet

Stood the chest; while he lay sleeping
Radiant forms of heroes rose up
From the casket and they drifted
Into Alexander's dreams.

Other times, and other birds—
I too once loved just as keenly
All those songs about the deeds of
Great Achilles and Odysseus.

In those days my heart was sunny
And the world shot through with crimson,
And my brow was wreathed in vine leaves,
And the air was filled with fanfares—

Hush, enough!—all smashed to pieces
Is my proud triumphal chariot,
And the panthers that once drew it
Are all dead—likewise the women

Who, with drums and cymbals clashing,
Danced about me; I myself
Writhe here on the ground in torment,
Cripple's torment—hush, enough!—

Hush, enough!—our story's subject
Is the casket of Darius.
In my own mind I was thinking:
If I ever owned that casket

And were not compelled to sell it
Right away for ready money,
I would keep enclosed within it
All the poems of our rabbi—

All Jehuda ben Halevy's
Festal songs and lamentations,
Madrigals and travel pictures
Of his pilgrimage—I'd have it

All engrossed on purest parchment
By the greatest scribe that's living,
And I'd place this manuscript in
That same golden little casket.

I would put it on a table
At the head of my hard pallet,
And when friends came round and marvelled
At the little box's splendours,

At the bas-relief's rare beauty,
So minute and yet so perfect
Both at once, and at the size of
The encrusted precious jewels—

Smiling then I'd tell them: This is
Nothing but the roughhewn shell that
Holds the greater treasure in it—
Here within this chest are lying

Diamonds whose radiant lustre
Is the mirror of the heavens,
Rubies burning red as heart's blood,
Turquoises of flawless beauty,

Emeralds of glowing promise—
Yes, and pearls of purer water
Than were once to Queen Atossa
Given by the bogus Smerdis,

Or than those that later shimmered
On a host of noted figures
Of this moon-encircled planet—
Thaïs, say, or Cleopatra,

Priests of Isis, Moorish princes,
Queens of Spain and other monarchs,
And at last the worthy Madame
Solomon, the baroness—

These world-famous pearls are merely
Whitish slime secretions from a
Hapless oyster lying sea-deep
Suffering from some stupid ailment;

But the pearls within this casket
Are the lovely product of a
Beauty-mantled human soul that's
Deeper than the ocean chasms;

For they are the teardrop pearls that
Once Jehuda ben Halevy
Let fall over the destruction
Of his love, Jerusalem—

Pearly teardrops, strung together
By a golden thread of verses,
Made into a song by labours
In the poet's golden forge.

This, his song of pearly teardrops,
Is the famous lamentation
Sung in all the tents of Jacob,
Scattered far through all the world,

On the ninth day of the month that's
Known as Ab, the year's remembrance
Of Jerusalem's destruction
By Vespasian's scion Titus.

Yes, it is the song of Zion,
Which Jehuda ben Halevy
Sang amid the holy ruins
Of Jerusalem, and died.

Clad in penitential raiment
He sat barefoot on the fragment
Of a crumbling fallen column;
Flowing down upon his bosom

Like a grey wildwood his tresses
Cast fantastic shadows over
His pale face where anguish peered out
Like a ghost from haunted eyes.

Thus he sat and sang; he seemed like
Some old prophet of past ages,
Just as if old Jeremiah
Had arisen from the graveyard.

Even birds around the ruins,
Hearing his wild song of anguish,
Were made tame—the vultures listened
And approached, as in compassion——

But a Saracen came riding
Brazen-souled along the roadway;
Rocking back high on his charger,
Down he swung a shining lance

Into the poor singer's bosom,
And the deadly shaft was fatal;
Then he rode off at a gallop
Like a shape of wingèd shadow.

Tranquil flowed the rabbi's lifeblood,
Tranquilly he sang his song out
To the end, and his last dying
Sigh breathed out: Jerusalem!—

There's an ancient legend stating
That the Saracen was really
Not an evil human being
But an angel in disguise,

Sent from Heaven to deliver
God's own favourite from this world,
And to expedite his painless
Passage to the Blessèd Kingdom.

Up above, it states, a special
Flattering reception waited
To accord the poet honour—
What a heavenly surprise!

Festively a choir of angels
Came to greet him playing music,
And the hymn he heard in welcome
Was a poem of his own—

His own Sabbath hymeneal,
Synagogal nuptial song,
With the well-known merry-lilting
Melodies—what strains of gladness!

Little angels blew on oboes,
Little angels played the fiddle,
Others strummed upon violas,
Beat the drum or clashed the cymbals.

And it all went ringing, singing,
Sweetly echoing through the distant
Spaces of the realm of Heaven:
'L'khah dodi likras kallah.' *

iv

My good wife's dissatisfaction
With the chapter just concluded
Bears especially upon the
Precious casket of Darius.

Almost bitterly she comments
That a husband who was truly
So religious would have cashed in
That old casket on the instant,

And would certainly have purchased
For his lawful wedded wife
That fine cashmere shawl she needed
With such monumental urgence.

And Jehuda ben Halevy,
In her view, would have been honoured
Quite enough by being kept in
Any pretty box of cardboard

With some very swanky Chinese
Arabesques to decorate it,
Like a bonbon box from Marquis*
In the Passage Panorama.

'Strange!' she adds in further comment,
'That I never heard the name of
This great poet that you speak of,
This Jehuda ben Halevy.'

And I answered her as follows:—
Dearest child, your lack of knowledge
Is quite sweet, but shows the defects
Of the French-type education

That the boarding schools of Paris
Give to girls, those future mothers
Of a freedom-loving people,
Who are thoroughly instructed

On old mummies, or the pharaohs
Who were stuffed in ancient Egypt,
Merovingian shadow-monarchs,*
Or unpowdered wigs on ladies,

Or the pigtailed lords of China,
Porcelain-pagoda princes—
All of this is crammed into them,
Clever girls! but, oh ye heavens—

If you ask them for great figures
In the golden age of glory
Of the Arabic-Hispanic
Jewish school of poetry—

If you ask about the trio
Of Jehuda ben Halevy
And of Solomon Gabirol*
And of Moses Ibn Ezra—*

If you ask about such figures,
Then the children stare back at you
With their goggling eyes wide open—
Like the cows along a hillside.

I'd advise you, my belovèd,
To make up what you've neglected,
And to learn the Hebrew language;
Drop the theatre and concerts,

Go devote some years of study
To this subject—you'll be able
To read all of them in Hebrew,
Ibn Ezra and Gabirol

And of course Halevy also—
The triumvirate of song, who
Once evoked the sweetest music
From the harp that David cherished.

Alcharisi*—who no doubt you
Also do not know although he
Was a Gallic wag who out-wagged
The *Makamat* of Hariri

And in this department shone as
A Voltairean six hundred
Years before Voltaire was fathered—
This same Alcharisi stated:

'It's through thought Gabirol sparkles
And it's thinkers that he pleases,
Whereas Ibn Ezra sparkles
In his art, and suits the artist—

'But Jehuda ben Halevy
Has both qualities together,
And he is a mighty poet
And a favourite of all.'

Ibn Ezra was a friend
And I think also a cousin
Of Jehuda ben Halevy;
In his travel book he sadly

Heaps laments that in Granada
He once vainly tried to search out
His good poet-friend, but only
Found his brother, the physician,

Rabbi Meyer, poet also
And the father of a beauty
Who enkindled Ibn Ezra's
Heart with flames of hopeless passion.

To forget his little cousin,
He took pilgrim's staff and wandered
Like so many of his colleagues,
Living vagrantly and homeless.

Faring toward Jerusalem,
He was set upon by Tartars,
And they bound him on a horse and
Bore him to their native steppes.

There he had to render service
Hardly worthy of a rabbi
And still less so of a poet—
Namely, he was milking cows.

Once, as he was stiffly squatting
Underneath a cow's big belly,
Busy fingering the udder
To spray milk into the bucket—

An undignified position
For a rabbi or a poet—
Melancholy overwhelmed him
And he sadly started singing,

And he sang so well and sweetly
That the Khan, the tribal chieftain,
Passing by, was moved to pity,
And he gave the slave his freedom.

And he also gave him presents:
A long Saracen mandolin,
One fox pelt, and travel money
To insure his safe return.

What a fate's reserved for poets!
Star of evil, deadly gadfly
Of Apollo's sons, and one that
Did not even spare their father

On that day when, chasing Daphne,
He reached out for her white body
And instead embraced a laurel—
What a big divine Schlemihl!*

Yes, the highborn Delphic god is
A Schlemihl; indeed, the laurel
That enwreathes his brow so proudly
Is a sign of this Schlemihldom.

What the word Schlemihl denotes is
Known to us. Long since, Chamisso*
Saw to it that it got German
Civic rights—I mean the *word* did.

But its origin is still as
Far from known as are the sources
Of the holy Nile; I've pondered
Many a night upon this subject.

Many years ago I travelled
To Berlin to see Chamisso,
Our good friend, for information
From the dean of the Schlemihls.

But he could not satisfy me
And referred me on to Hitzig,*
Who had been the first to tell him
What this Peter-without-shadow

Had for surname. So I straightway
Took a droshky and rushed to the
Court Investigator Hitzig,
Who was formerly called Itzig.

Back when he'd been still an Itzig,
He had dreamed a dream in which he
Saw his name inscribed on heaven
With the letter H in front.

What did this H mean? he wondered—
Did it mean perhaps *Herr* Itzig,
Holy Itzig (for Saint Itzig)?
Holy's a fine title—but not

Suited for Berlin. Brain-weary,
Finally he made it Hitzig;
It was only faithful friends who
Knew a saint hid in the *Hitzig*.

'Holy Hitzig!' said I, therefore,
When I saw him, 'Kindly tell me
What the etymology of
This odd word Schlemihl may be.'

Long the saint talked round the question—
Couldn't quite remember—piled up
One excuse upon the other,
Always Christianlike—until I

Finally burst all the buttons
On the breeches of my patience,
And I started roundly swearing
With such blasphemies and curses

That the godly Pietist,
Pale as death and knees atrembling,
Promptly granted what I wanted,
And this tale is what he told me:

'In the Bible it is written*
That, while wandering in the desert,
Often Israel made merry
With the daughters born of Canaan;

'So it came to pass that one day
Phinehas saw noble Zimri
Fornicating with a woman
Of the Canaanitish stock,

'And he straightway boiled with anger,
Seized his spear, and thrust it into
Zimri, killing him instanter—
So it tells us in the Bible.

'But the people have a different
Oral version of this story,
Namely, that it was not Zimri
Who was slain by Phinehas,

'But that he, made blind by fury,
Unawares struck not the sinner
But an innocent bystander,
One Schlemihl ben Zuri-shaddai.'—

Well now, this Schlemihl the First is
Forebear of the race and lineage
Of Schlemihls. We are descended
From Schlemihl ben Zuri-shaddai.

To be sure, we have no mention
Of heroic deeds by this one;
We know only what his name was,
And that he was a Schlemihl.

Still, one's family tree is valued
Not for the good fruit it turns out
But for age—how far it goes back—
Ours can boast three thousand years!

Years come round and years pass onward—
Full three thousand years have fleeted
Since the death of our forebear,
Herr Schlemihl ben Zuri-shaddai.

Phinehas is long dead also—
But his spear is ever with us,
And we constantly can hear it
Swishing round above our heads.

And the hearts it smites are noblest—
Like Jehuda ben Halevy's;
It smote Moses Ibn Ezra
And it smote Gabirol also—

Yes, Gabirol, that truehearted
God-enraptured minnesinger,
Pious nightingale who warbled
To the God who was his rose—

That sweet nightingale, who carolled
Tenderly his lilting love songs
In the rayless darkness of the
Gothic medieval night!

Unaffrighted and untroubled
By the goblin shapes and phantoms,
By the maze of death and madness
Haunting us through that long night—

That sweet nightingale thought only
Of his heavenly belovèd
Unto whom he sobbed his passion
Whom his songs of praise exalted!—

Here on earth, Gabirol lived through
Thirty Springs, but Fama's trumpet
Blazoned forth his name and glory
To the people of all nations.

In Cordova, where he dwelt, he
Had a Moor as nearest neighbour
Who wrote verses too, and so felt
Envy of the poet's fame.

When the poet sang, the Moor was
Filled with rancour on the instant,
For the sweetness of the songs was
Bitter to this jealous grudger.

So he lured the hated poet
To his house by night, and killed him,
And then buried his poor body
In the garden to the rear.

But behold, from out the ground where
He'd consigned the corpse to darkness,
There precisely grew a fig tree
Of the most supernal beauty.

All its fruits were strangely long and
Of a strangely spicy sweetness;
All who tasted them were spellbound
In a dreamy haze of rapture.

Whispered talk and muttered rumours
Made the rounds among the people,
Till at last the tittle-tattle
Reached the Caliph's noble ears.

He made use of his own tongue to
Test this fig phenomenon,
And in consequence appointed
A commission of inquiry.

They went straight to work. The owner
Of the tree got sixty lashes
With a cane upon his foot soles,
And confessed the dreadful crime.

Thereupon they tore the fig tree,
Roots and all, up from the soil,
And Gabirol's murdered body
Was discovered to the light.

With all pomp they reinterred him,
And his brethren stood in mourning;
On that selfsame day the Moor was
Hanged upon Cordova's gallows.

[*End of fragment*]

KARL EMIL FRANZOS

Schiller in Barnow

Karl Emil Franzos (1848–1904) gained international fame for his fictional and journalistic accounts of traditional Jewish life in Eastern Europe. His father, a doctor, was posted first to Czortkow (now Chortkov) in what was then the eastern extremity of Galicia, where Franzos was born, and then in 1859 transferred to Czernowitz (the capital of the Bukovina; now Chernovtsy). The Franzos family were assimilated: they observed none of the ritual laws and never attended synagogue, though they ensured that Franzos learnt Hebrew. His knowledge of traditional Jewish culture was that of an ethnographically informed outsider. His family's assimilationist ideals were directed towards Germany; Franzos learnt to consider the Austro-Hungarian Empire a backward, corrupt, and redundant state, and Galicia its most benighted province. After his father's death Franzos studied law in order to support his close relatives, but as he could not practise law without converting, he turned to journalism and acquired fame by describing the Eastern Jewish world of which he so disapproved. His most successful collection of stories, *The Jews of Barnow* (1877), was translated into twelve languages. Among his many novels, the outstanding achievements are *Judith Trachtenberg* (1891), the tragic story of a mixed marriage, and *Der Pojaz* (*The Clown*, 1905), completed in 1893 but published only posthumously, which tells how a gifted boy from a Hasidic community surreptitiously learns German, reads the German classics, and tries to become an actor, only to be frustrated by his failing health (he dies of tuberculosis) and by the loyalty that forbids him to leave his mother.

Franzos coined the name 'Half-Asia' for the vast area of Eastern Europe stretching from Poland across Galicia and the Ukraine to the Black Sea. In his fiction, essays, and travel sketches he campaigned for its inhabitants, especially the Jews, to be freed from religious obscurantism and corrupt bureaucracy. He particularly condemned the Polish aristocracy, who ruled over the Ukrainian-speaking 'Ruthenian' farming population of Galicia, for their extravagance and immorality. He saw the solution in the spread of German culture in the emancipatory spirit of Lessing and Schiller. Many autobiographies confirm that the humane ideals and the enthusiastic, occasionally bombastic verse of Schiller's plays and philosophical poems were intensely popular among Eastern European Jews seeking a foothold in Western (which meant primarily German) culture. Franzos goes further by showing how, in the spirit of Enlightenment universalism, a love of Schiller brings together members of three oppressed groups: the Jew Israel Meisels, the unhappy monk Franciscus (a victim of clerical tyranny), and the Ruthenian schoolmaster Basil Woyczuk. Their favourite Schiller text, appropriately, is the 'Ode to Joy' (familiar from Beethoven's Ninth Symphony), with its appeal to all humanity to join in an embrace.

————

Altogether, counting both German and Polish texts, there are five copies in the town. The single library, that of the Dominicans, does not contain any. But there are good reasons for that. First of all, Schiller was not a Catholic. Secondly, everyone knows that *The Robbers** is a very immoral play. Thirdly, there is no good Polish translation. And fourthly, most of the monks cannot read. But other people own these works: the local Count, Herr Alexander Rodzicki; Herr Dr Artur Tulpenblüh, the town physician; Madame Kasimira von Lozinska, wife of the district magistrate; and Schlome Barrascher. The latter cannot be called 'Herr', because only the nobility and the officers call him that, and only when they want to borrow money from him. Usually they call him 'Jew', because he wears a kaftan and does not permit himself any luxuries: he does not even call himself 'Salomo'... So that makes four. As for the fifth copy, a single slim volume containing the poems, it is one of the most curious books to be found anywhere, not just in Barnow near Tarnopol in Austrian Podolia. It is badly printed and badly bound, with many ink-stains, and many hot, heavy tears, hastily wiped away, have made the bad print even more smudgy. If a second-hand bookseller gave you a penny for it, he wouldn't know his business; and yet there are three people for whom this little book is their most precious treasure. They own it jointly, and each of them might part with his heart's blood sooner than with his share in this little book. How could it be otherwise! The three were in darkness and yearned for light, they were in the wilderness and thirsted for a spring. They yearned and thirsted, words cannot say how sorely, how desperately! And such light and refreshment as shines and flows into their poor, sombre lives, comes from these pages resembling blotting-paper. Alas, you educated people in the great cities, what do you know of the value that a volume of Schiller's poems can sometimes acquire in a wretched, remote corner of the globe?

I am going to tell you about this pitiful little book, mentioning the other four copies in passing. And I shall tell you about it today, for the anniversary of Schiller's birth* has come round again. It is only this day that we celebrate, and rightly so, for what do we care about Schiller's death? As far as we are concerned, he was only born, he has not died and never will die, until yearning and thirst are extinct among humankind. Perhaps there will come an age of satiety, of horrible satiety, when Schiller is dead; some signs speak for it, some against; at any rate, that age is still a long way off. Today he is still alive for millions and is born anew every year in thousands upon thousands of hearts and lifts up these hearts and is their true saviour and redeemer, raising them from the depths of prejudice and dull hardship to the heights of free humanity. The story of how this happened to those three people in Barnow may fill a modest page on the day that commemorates his genius.

But first, something about those four copies.

To deal with Count Alexander Rodzicki first of all, he owns the handsome twelve-volume edition published by Cotta. He did not acquire it from any interest in literature, although he himself is one of the most energetic writers in Galicia; he writes a great deal for the Jews, trifles whose value consists only in his signature; no, the reason why he ordered the books from Tarnopol ten years ago was that Countess Wanda wanted to be loved by him just as Schiller loved Laura.* Just like that, without a jot of difference. Now he cared a great deal about this lady; he would often say: 'Either she marries me, or I'll shoot myself!'—and he said this not only to others, but also to the only person he never lied to, himself; for he was so completely ruined that the very buttons on his shirt were no longer his. Admittedly, Wanda was of mature years, but 'trente ou quarante'*—the Count knew these figures from Homburg* and Monte Carlo. So Alexander wanted to, and the enthusiastic Wanda wanted to, but first she wanted samples of this literary passion. The Count was quite at a loss, for he knew only that Schiller was 'some German poet or other', but how this poet had loved his Laura he had no idea. Well, that is why, with a heavy heart, he bought the complete works. What he found there, and what use he made of it, is his secret. Suffice it to say that Wanda gave him her hand and her dowry; he passed on the latter and kept the former. That is the strange tale of how the works of the noblest poet came into the possession of the most unsavoury of people. Now the handsomely bound volumes stand in a corner of the dreary empty room known as 'the library' in the decaying mansion of Barnow, slowly rotting alongside Casanova, whom the Count no longer likes reading either. Nowadays he finds these memoirs much too honest and tedious. But the day is fast approaching when the whole 'library' will be resurrected under the auctioneer's hammer. For the Count is a most industrious writer, and his works are reissued whenever his debts fall due.

The same edition has had a different fate in the possession of the town physician, Dr Artur Tulpenblüh. There is not a speck of dust on the neat books; they are only seldom read, but when they are, their effect on a heart that is not easily touched is one that would surely have pleased their great, kindly creator. He is a strange person, this town physician, and yet at bottom a typical figure. The son of a poor tailor in Brody, he fought his way out of grinding poverty, and for fourteen years he had a sorrowful companion; on the arduous road from 'mensa, mensae' to his doctoral diploma she never left him for a day, whatever pains he took. This companion was poverty. And poverty makes people hard. Aaron Tulpenblüh was a poor boy without a crust of bread. And therefore he never knew the light-heartedness of youth, nor its enthusiasm; he never read a poet, except in German lessons at grammar school; the intoxication of the first bottle was as unknown to him as the intoxication of first love; Aaron Tulpenblüh was a dreadfully poor boy. Now, at the age of thirty, the doctor at last returned home. His first thought was to seek a job; he found one in Barnow. His second was to choose a wife; he did not need to look, the marriage-brokers made sure of that. Ten thousand, twenty thousand, fifty thousand pounds; can you blame this man for choosing the richest girl? He was concerned only that she was honest; her external appearance did not worry him. Nor did he ask what she was feeling as she stood beside him under the wedding canopy. And what was she feeling? Well, Melanie Feigelstock was a real, true, educated Jewish girl from the East, and so she was very sentimental. She had read and dreamed a great deal; perhaps she might once have sent an extravagant letter to a poet who had particularly moved her, and kept his laconic, polite reply close to her heart for years. But these girls are not only very sentimental, but also very honest, and their good sense may be concealed, but it is not lacking. Dr Tulpenblüh did not match her ideal; but she resolved to be an honest wife to him, and she faithfully kept her promise. There were only two requests she made to her fiancé that were a touch romantic. She wanted him to call himself Artur instead of Aaron. He consented with a smile. Then she wanted his permission to buy a small library and take it with her, especially Schiller, Börne, Heine. He encouraged this plan; perhaps he thought: 'The books may offer her what I can't offer her.' But once they were married things took a different turn, a very strange turn. Melanie first read her favourites only rarely, then not at all; the household took up too much of her time, along with the children and coffee with the neighbours. But her husband, in one of his few moments of leisure, went to the bookcase and took out a volume of Schiller and began reading. When others did this kind of thing, he had always condemned it as a waste of time, and now he read for two hours and put down the book only because he had to. Not that the first impression was so magical; in truth, the poor man, who had never been young, only had a sense of astonishment. He had peeped into a world whose existence he had never suspected, a world entirely foreign to him. The next time he had leisure, he took up the same book, then a second and a third. His wife was beside herself with wonder at her husband's suddenly being such a keen reader, and teased him about it. But he only shook his head, smiling quietly, perhaps at himself. For gradually a great change was taking place in him: he was learning to comprehend the world that at first had so surprised him; he realized that in truth it was the very world he knew, but seen with such different eyes! When he read Schiller, he felt like a short-sighted man who, by putting on a pair of spectacles, can find beauty and life in the very things that seemed dead and hideous to the naked eye. And truly, what splendid things he perceived; he saw the stream of enthusiasm flowing, the roses of love flowering, and the shady bower of a proud and noble philosophy arching overhead. And if at first he had only wondered in astonishment: 'Did this man walk on clouds? Did he never feel life's harshness?', he gradually comprehended why Schiller remained so unspeakably good and eternally young, although there was so much conflict, suffering, and hardship in his life. There is no saying what the doctor of Barnow learnt from his Schiller, whom he began to read only at the age of 40. It did not make him into a man of feeling, nor into an idealist, but he did become a better and happier person. He did indeed at times feel a kind of gentle sorrow for his youth, in which he had been so dreadfully old; but then his heart softened again, and he felt as though the verses of his favourite poet were flowering into September roses, since the roses of May had been denied him...

It is unlikely that Madame Kasimira von Lozinska noticed the scent of roses when she read 'Sziler' in her bad Warsaw translation. Nor did she need to, for she was herself a rose—a canker rose. Long ago, when she left the convent to be married to Herr Hippolyt von Lozinski, she may not yet have been corrupt, she may even have had a heart. But the district magistrate had none, nor any ear for the voice of another's heart. And so their marriage gradually became a truly pitiful one. Herr Hippolyt's soft felt hat was crowned by a mighty pair of horns, but he wore them like a decoration. It was a good thing for the lovely Kasimira that her husband was so pitiful; that made people speak much more mildly about her, as did, perhaps, their fear of her poisonous tongue. But in truth, it may not have been only a base impulse that drove this woman, with her voluptuous, supple, serpentine body and her dully glowing eyes, into a different man's arms almost every year; perhaps she was really longing for a heart. For she was a Pole, and among this nation the women seem to have all the emotional life, leaving the men empty-handed. This may be confirmed by her strange way of reading Schiller. Sometimes, shedding tears, she would read some heart-rending poem such as 'Resignation', declaiming in feeling tones that her life's May, too, had faded. But straight afterwards she would leaf through *The Robbers* till she found the story of the assault on the convent, and would enjoy it with a knowing smile. Then she would think about the person who had given her the book, a fair-haired young adjutant of German stock, who soon afterwards died of consumption; and she would weep. She wept bitterly, and reached for Paul de Kock,* and laughed once more. For this book had been given her by a tanned hussar, and he was still alive and in the pink of health.

Schlome Barrascher treated his Schiller very differently, almost as the King of Thule treated his goblet.* 'He prized it above all things', and his eyes were often moist as he read these books. A strange person, so kindly, so confused, so unhappy! He was an enthusiast, and the spring that kept him moving was very thin and elastic, too thin; when fate slammed down its clumsy fist, the spring broke. He is

very rich and never complains, and yet his destiny may evoke profound compassion. His father was a *rendar*, an innkeeper dealing in
brandy, and had acquired a substantial fortune. And because the old
man could hardly read his prayer-book, the young man must become
a light in Israel. So Schlome became a Talmudist, although he
showed many other talents, especially for an art that the Jews normally ignore, that of drawing. It was driven out of him; but there was
something else that neither his father's blows nor the treatises of the
Talmud could drive out of him: his great heart, and in his heart a
great thirst. At 18 he was married, at 19 he was the father of a little
boy, at 20 he ran away from Barnow and became a pupil of the lowest
Latin form in Czernowitz. He stayed there two years, but he never
entered the third form: during the holidays his mother and his dear
little boy died, the spring was broken... A 22-year-old pupil in the
second form of the grammar school who cannot enter the third form
because his son has died—heavens! what tragicomic figures appear
in the struggle that has begun in the East, the struggle between
nationally minded Jewry and culture!... Schlome was defeated. He
lived like other people, he even lent money at interest, except that he
also enjoyed reading Schiller, very much, more even than the town
physician. For Schlome was the other way round: he was familiar
with the poet's world; but he peered into reality with the shy gaze of
the enthusiast. And his eyes are not getting any sharper, even when
he puts on his big horn-rimmed spectacles. For he always has these
spectacles on his nose when a bill of exchange is signed in his presence, and yet Count Rodzicki and Lieutenant Domossy have cheated
him shamelessly. But Barrascher has plenty of money left; he can
read his Schiller without worrying. And how he reads him! No
words can say what this poet is for this man. No spring confers its
fragrance, no love can stir his heart, his bosom is neither refreshed
nor renewed with the courage for life and strife—poor man! But
when he reads these books, his eye gleams, he raises his head. And
his face is flushed when he softly reads aloud the apostrophe to the
blessed ones:

> Just as in seven gentle rays
> The light is beauteously refracted,
> As seven rays of rainbow hue
> Are in white radiance compacted,

> So let a thousand vistas clear
> Enchant the viewer's dazzled sight,
> So let a single bond of truth
> Compose a single stream of light!*

At such times he is no longer a tired, lonely failure; these inspiring words seem to have been written for him, and he is a link in the chain of those good and noble people. Happy man!

... To come at last to the little book, one thing must be repeated: no bookseller would give you a penny for it, if he knew his business. A bad Viennese reprint from the Greiner* printing-works, and so dog-eared and stained! What's more, the book contains pencil markings, and on the back of the title-page there are four inscriptions. First, in a girl's dainty, curly handwriting: 'To her dear cousin Franz, from Josephine.' Beneath that a cross is painted, with the words 'Sustine et abstine'* in thick letters, and the signature 'Franciscus'. Then a rough drawing of an axe, and beneath it the signature 'Basil Woyczuk'. Finally, there is something resembling a lighted torch, drawn in ink, and beneath it, in clumsy handwriting: 'Thies bouk belongs allso to Israel Meisels, bicos his good frends have let him.' And that is at the same time the story of the little book; it only needs to be explained.

Josephine was a very beautiful girl. She had big blue eyes and brown curly hair, and when she laughed, in her deep, splendid voice, it sounded so heart-warming that nobody could resist and everyone had to laugh with her. Her cousin Franz Lipecki joined in the laughter, though that was by no means in his nature; he was a quiet, shy boy. But as he grew older and reached the sixth form in the grammar school, he no longer laughed. His cousin kept growing prettier, and he kept growing uglier. Then Josephine too forgot how to laugh; her father, who was Imperial and Royal Deputy Assistant Director of Charities in Lemberg,* died, and she and her mother were reduced to dire poverty. Franz had a compassionate heart and helped the two helpless women, so far as a poor law student could, and far beyond his powers, but a strange happiness came over him; you might almost have thought he was glad that his cousin was so poor. It was at that time that she gave him the wretched little book, which had been found among her father's belongings, as a present for his twenty-second birthday, but she accompanied it with such affectionate words and glances that it was the most beautiful present with which any person can gratify another. And three months later she became engaged to a rich landlord. Franz congratulated her heartily, but in writing, and then face to face, though he looked rather green about the gills and hence much uglier even than usual. The happy bride did not notice, but her mother asked him with concern whether he was ill. Just a little, he replied, but he was about to take some medicine which he was sure would have excellent results. And two weeks later he entered the Dominican monastery at Lemberg.

But that was bad medicine. His poor, battered heart hurt him just as much in his monastic cell as it used to in his student's garret. He had indeed inscribed the cross, along with Augustine's admonition, not only in his beloved's book, but also deep in his heart. But it is not so easy to practise renunciation at the age of 22; the poor young heart goes on lamenting and accusing. And he had another sorrow. As long as he had studied Justinian's Institutions* he had kept his faith, on the side, because he did not think about it much. But now that this faith was the only rock in which he put his trust, everything else having broken and collapsed, he felt, felt with horror, that this rock, too, was trembling... Seldom has anyone been overwhelmed by greater sorrow than poor Franciscus. He lay there in his cell, wrestling with his fate; he had sought balsam for his wounds, and found poison. He did not leave the monastery, but only because he thought: 'It isn't worth the trouble, it won't last much longer; whether I go or stay makes no difference, except to the kind of funeral I get.' He kept growing paler and weaker, and coughed a great deal. His superiors noticed this and resolved to send him to the monastery at Barnow, either because the air there was better or because a death causes such inconvenience.

So the monk Franciscus had come to Barnow in order to die there. But perhaps the air really was healthful, or the passing of time alleviated the pain of his soul; anyway, he recovered. And not only his body. He could not regain his faith, but he rescued his God and revered Him in the prescribed forms and ceremonies. He must have found the right God, because his heart grew softer, not happy but peaceful. And now he understood that saying of Augustine for the first time; perhaps he drew a deeper meaning from it than the man who uttered it. He realized how much misery there is on earth, and that there is only *one* light that can illuminate all the darkness, the light in one's own good, compassionate heart. And in this mood he found the courage to face the past and once again to seek out that little book and to read it.

The impression he received was prodigious. The gospel of pure enthusiasm, the gospel of love for humanity, which had fought its stammering way from his poor struggling heart, now rang out to meet him. Schiller is indeed a poet for the poor and heavy-laden. From that moment on, the young monk Franciscus was no longer lonely, as he had hitherto been all his life. He now had a friend who spoke to him. And in what voices!

But this friend was to bring him two others, real heartfelt friends, who till now, like him, had been groping in the darkness and thirsting in the wilderness. One September day the monk had gone out on to the heath. Alone and aimless, he was marching along, with no sound near him but the whistling of the wind. Summer was dying on the heath, but it was an easy death. The grass was slowly fading, the leaves were quietly dropping from the bushes, and far, far away the farewell song of migrant birds was dying away in the air... The pale young monk felt very quiet. He sat down among the heather and closed his eyes. He felt as though he could look into his own heart and see the last trace of bitterness softly and gently dissolving.

Then suddenly he heard voices. It must be two people crossing the heath and talking in monotones to themselves, first one and then the other, then both together. The sounds were unfamiliar. And as they approached, Franciscus could understand these people, for both the wanderers were conjugating Latin verbs.

He opened his eyes in astonishment: they were very strange students. A square-built, defiant lad in peasant costume, and a young Jew in a tattered kaftan. He stood up; the two caught sight of him and stayed where they were, rigid with terror at being overheard. But the young monk went kindly up to them and asked what their names were and what books they were using.

The Jew looked at him shyly and remained silent, but the young man in peasant costume replied defiantly: 'That's none of your business.' 'Why not?' 'Because you're a Pole, a Catholic monk.' 'But a human being as well,' said Franciscus. 'And is the world so full of sympathy that you can afford to reject any?' There must have been something in his voice that supported the gentleness of these words. 'Why shouldn't we tell you?' began the Jew. 'This man is called Basil

Woyczuk. He's the Ruthenian schoolmaster of Koczince. But I, by your leave, am a Jew from Barnow, and my name is Israel Meisels. We got together because we both want to learn something. But we have no teacher, and no book but this one here.' He showed him an elementary Latin grammar. 'And what makes you want to learn?' asked the monk. 'We just thought,' came the answer, 'why shouldn't we learn? We'd like to learn a lot—everything! Besides, Basil wants to enter Parliament as a leader against the Poles. But I'd like to study medicine.'

From that moment on the two pupils had a teacher. And a friend as well. He instructed them not merely in Latin, but in many other things that are not to be found in any book, but only in the depths of a noble heart. At first he gave them lessons on the heath, but in winter in Basil's parlour in Koczince. It was a long way, but the Jew and the monk were happy to undertake it.

When they had truly become his friends, he shared with them his greatest treasure, the poems of Friedrich Schiller, and words can hardly say how much the poet came to mean to these poor people. Since he was a shared spiritual possession, they wanted some external sign of this. Basil was allowed to write his name in the little book alongside the axe, the symbol of the free Ruthenian. And then Israel wrote his piece, humbly and gratefully.

This happened about a year after their first meeting, on the evening of the tenth of November, in Basil's parlour. Then they read the 'Ode to Joy' with tears in their eyes. That was the only Schiller celebration ever held in Barnow. Does anyone know a finer?

FERDINAND VON SAAR

Seligmann Hirsch

Ferdinand von Saar (1833–1906) came from an Austrian family which had served the Habsburgs as bureaucrats, and at first he continued their tradition by serving in the army. After the war of 1859 in which Austria lost its northern Italian territories Saar left the army and took up a literary career. Although he wrote historical tragedies and a varied body of poetry, much of it in classical metres, his main achievement is his large body of Novellen, many collected as *Novellen from Austria* (1877; the enlarged edition of 1897 included 'Seligmann Hirsch'). Despite the gradual recognition accorded to his fiction by discerning readers, Saar was disappointed by his failure as a dramatist and subject to depression, accentuated by prolonged early poverty, by the suicide of his wife in 1884, by his reading of Schopenhauer and other pessimistic philosophers, and by a chronic illness from which he escaped by suicide.

In contrast to the many Novellen of his better-known North German contemporary Theodor Storm, where the narrator is often a small-town recluse and the atmosphere lyrical and melancholy, Saar, as befits his background, writes with attractive worldly sophistication and invokes a wider range of human experience. His narrators, as in 'Seligmann Hirsch', are usually experienced observers who can skilfully guide the reader's understanding of the strange characters or emotional entanglements that they describe.

To help us appreciate his main character, Saar alludes to several models. One is literary: Hirsch's relations with his children resemble those of King Lear, and the comparison, like the Shakespearean references in other nineteenth-century Novellen (Turgenev's *A Lear of the Steppes*, Leskov's *Lady Macbeth of Mtsensk*, Keller's *A Village Romeo and Juliet*), lends tragic dignity to the pain of obscure people. Another is scientific: Saar followed with interest the development of Darwinian theories, and the vagaries of evolution are illustrated by the Hirsch family, where old Hirsch's appearance is reproduced in his grandson while his granddaughter is a striking beauty. Hirsch himself, by implication, corresponds to the species that lose the struggle for survival and become extinct. Hence the frequent animal imagery: Hirsch in Venice is 'like a rhinoceros in an aquarium'; earlier he is as bored as a 'pug-dog', and snores 'like a bear'.

These frames add significance to the rise of the Hirsch family. Old Hirsch, unlike his pious Hasidic wife, breaks away from his traditional background, though being 'a man of the Enlightenment' evidently means for him only escaping from religious restrictions, adopting Western manners, and eating pork. To the narrator he is still an uncouth and exotic figure, resembling at first sight an Armenian or Bulgarian. His children are thoroughly assimilated, one to Magyar culture (like many Hungarian Jews), the other to Viennese high society, with ennoblement and a change of name to Baron Hirtburg. To them the old man is now an embarrassment. Saar hints at a tragic dynamic in the very process of Jewish emancipation: having discarded his traditional background, Hirsch finds with dismay that his children have taken the next step and discarded all but the hypocritical semblance of familial loyalty.

I

In the small spa where, on my doctor's advice, I had been taking the 'cold-water cure', the season was nearing its end. One by one, all the defective human specimens drawn here by an excess of hope and confidence had departed. Persons of high rank with ineradicable ailments, young men about town whose vital fluids were disordered, anaemic ladies with nervous complaints, and finally some who had come to the delightful valley simply to enjoy a summer holiday with all its social amusements—all were gone. Only a few visitors were staying as long as I, a late arrival: a surly Financial Councillor, tormented by congestions, who always went about hatless and at certain times barefoot as well; a rather dubious lady from Vienna who was using a highly conspicuous toilette to display the remains of her erstwhile beauty; an elderly fop and habitué of spas who was paying court to her; and, last but not least, a witty, semi-paralysed *bel esprit* whose wheelchair made him the object of general feminine sympathy, but who had driven me to distraction with his incessant literary conversation: even these four stalwarts unanimously fled before the sudden onset of inclement autumn weather, reinforced by a heavy snowfall—and I was left alone. The door of the pump room was practically slammed in my face, for the chief medical officer had long since completed his preparations for resuming his winter practice in the provincial capital. But that gave me small concern. I had enjoyed plenty of massages and compresses, in consequence of which, to tell the truth, I felt extremely well, and since I liked the area, I resolved to stay a while longer—a resolution that met with hearty approval from the proprietor of the Three Monarchs Hotel, where I was lodging; for at least he retained *one* guest whose bill matched the scale of charges usual in the spa.

In addition, as I had foreseen, the premature herald of winter had been followed by magnificent weather, a veritable Indian summer. The sky was cloudless and blue, the mountain peaks shimmered in gentle sunlight, and a mild warmth overspread the fields and forests, while the latter, with their colourful adornments, recalled the words of the poet:

> The breezes stroke the wood with gentle hands,
> Coaxing him to discard his faded fronds.*

What a pleasure it now was to rove in secure solitude amid the lofty beeches and spruces! How rewarding to climb a hill and look down at the picturesquely situated village or gaze at the distant mountain ranges without being disturbed by outbursts of clichéd enthusiasm! How agreeable to breakfast on the hotel patio and, instead of the clattering of my neighbours' cups and spoons along with the obligatory gossip, to hear the plashing of the silvery river below, as it wound its way amid green meadows! It was as though the entire landscape were only now presenting itself in its full, undisturbed beauty. Even my room, which had previously resembled a compartment in a dove-cote, felt quite snug and homely now that the hotel was empty. In order to increase my comfort, I rented another, smaller one next door, and thus I at last found myself restored to the congenial state of active solitude which I have throughout my life considered the most desirable.

Late one afternoon—I was in the habit of eating about that time—I was sitting over my coffee and cigar in the hotel dining-room, immersed in the newspapers which the postman had just brought. The hanging lamp over the billiard table in the middle of the room had already been lit, and the cosy silence was disturbed only now and again by the sounds of a glass being demanded and filled in the bar, where some harmless local worthies were sitting in largely silent sociability. Suddenly the steps of someone entering the bar could be heard—and thereupon a very loud, grating voice.

'Ha! ha! Still the same old company together! The carpenter and the tanner! Good afternoon to you both! And to you, Herr Gamil-schegg!' This was the local grocer. 'Glad to see you all again!'

The speaker did not seem put out by the very restrained response to his greeting, and continued:

'And pretty Cilli's still here!' This was for the benefit of the bar-maid, who also performed the services of a waitress. 'Not married yet, hey? And you won't have many admirers now the patients have left, so you'd better be patient!' He accompanied his own joke with loud, self-satisfied laughter. 'You might even have to fall back on an old chap like myself! Or maybe your wife has reason to be jealous, Herr Matzenoer?' This was addressed to the proprietor, whose name was Matzenauer; but the newcomer seemed sometimes to pronounce the diphthong *au* as if it were *o*.* 'Let's hope not! And how are things inside? All present and correct, as usual?'

Heavy, shuffling steps approached the open door leading to the dining-room, and the sturdy, broad-shouldered shape of a man became visible, standing on the threshold and spitting far into the room.

He might have been about sixty. His red, fleshy face, with its bushy eyebrows, prominent cheekbones and large, ill-shapen nose, was framed in a greying beard known as a *collier grec*.* On his head he had an extraordinary travelling cap, askew and crushed; he wore a long, unbuttoned overcoat with a fur collar, which revealed well-worn, none-too-clean trousers, as well as a large, bejewelled brooch and a massive golden watch-chain. In his hand, whose short fingers were overloaded with rings, he held an enormous amber cigar-holder, which he sucked on with a loud intake of breath. His feet were encased in wide boots with felt lining. There was something grotesque and also foreign about his whole appearance: the man looked like an Armenian or Bulgarian.

He cleared his throat and spat again, then he entered the room. On catching sight of me—I was sitting at one side—he started, but did not offer a greeting, although as he walked slowly round the billiard-table he kept his glance turned suspiciously sideways on me. He then sat down on a chair some distance away and stared at me. I did not like his inspection and turned aside.

Now he got up once more, took down an illustrated magazine that was hanging in a frame on the wall, turned his back on the billiard table, put on a pair of pince-nez, and began looking at the pictures.

Little by little the text also absorbed his attention. While reading, he moved his lips, as many old people do, as though silently repeating every word. Gradually he also began emitting a noise. First it was a dull muttering, then he could be heard spelling out the words, and finally, getting into the swing as it were, he began reading aloud. Only now did I recognize him, by his curiously sing-song and long-drawn-out pronunciation, as a Jew. This was not apparent from the way he talked to others, which was that of someone used to moving in the world; but now that he was left to himself, the specific features were apparent. Although his voice did not lack a certain sonority, it was so disagreeably loud and penetrating that it set my teeth on edge and brought all my nerves into agitation. Unable to control myself any longer, I cried: 'Sir, let me point out that you are not alone!'

He gave a start and gazed at me open-mouthed. Then he raised his cap humbly and stammered: 'Pardon me.' Immediately after-wards, however, he assumed a dignified posture and said patroniz-ingly: 'Would you care for the paper?'

'I've already seen it, thanks.' With these words I turned my back on him.

I could hear him putting the magazine aside, walking up and down, as though irresolute, beside the billiard table—and then heav-ing a sigh and stealing out of the room so quietly that I already regretted speaking to him as I had done.

Outside in the bar, however, he promptly assumed his noisiest, most jovial manner. 'Well, Herr Matzenoer, what's for dinner? Any trout?'

'I'm afraid not, Herr von Hirsch. At this time of year—'

'I'm with you! I'm with you! No demand just now! No guests? But your lady wife will be able to catch a chicken for me, hey?'

'Of course, Herr von Hirsch.'

'Chicken, then! With salad! I expect it'll take a while, so I'll go upstairs in the meantime. Cheers, gentlemen! Au revoir!'

These last words were directed at the assembled company, who, however, remained completely silent.

Once he had gone I knocked on a glass, whereupon Herr Matzenauer appeared. As a genuine country hotelier, he served his guests in person as far as possible.

'Do tell me, who on earth was that?' I exclaimed.

'A Herr Hirsch from Vienna,' he replied with his usual frank smile tinged with slyness. 'Don't you know him?'

'Good grief, how can anyone know all the Hirsches! But what on earth is he doing here?'

'He is expecting his son, who is at present in Italy with his family. They are planning to meet here and then travel back to Vienna together.'

'And when will that be?'

'I couldn't say. Perhaps in a week.'

'Where have you put him?'

'Room 5.'

'What? So close to mine?'

'I was going to put him in room 12; but he insisted on having the room he had before.'

'The room he had before?'

'He's an old acquaintance. He took the waters here two months ago; he left just as you arrived. I don't know where he's been in the meantime. Probably in Graz.* At least, that's where he's just come from. But excuse me, I must see to the kitchen.'

With these words Herr Matzenauer went away smiling, leaving me in a very bad humour. For this unexpected guest would in any case have required me to behave sociably and thus forfeit my happy, peaceful mood, but, worse still, the new arrival was not a particularly agreeable man. Finally I got up and went to my room. There I lit the lamp and picked up a book. But I could not read; my thoughts kept straying back to this Herr Hirsch, whom I could hear quite distinctly moving about in his room; probably he was unpacking his suitcase. And this reminded me how thin the walls were and how much I had previously suffered from the noises that had assailed me from all sides. In mild desperation I went to the window and looked out, in order to see whether at least an evening stroll was possible. The area was buried in pathless darkness; so I was a prisoner. Then I recalled that I had some necessary letters to write, a task that I had already been putting off for an unconscionable time. One can make oneself do such things—and I made myself. As I sat down at the desk, my neighbour left his room and stumped downstairs. Now I could breathe—and soon I was so immersed in my subject that some two hours later, when Herr Hirsch returned, guided by the landlord, it took me a moment to remember the circumstances.

'Good night, then, Herr Matzenoer!' he shouted. 'Cilli's the one who ought to have lighted my way upstairs—but you're a cautious chap!' These words were accompanied by a thunderous laugh.

Herr Matzenauer took his leave. Herr Hirsch, however, walked up and down in his room, noisily moving some objects. He then started whistling an aria from *Norma** and singing it in different keys. At last there was quiet, and I guessed that he was starting to take his clothes off; sure enough, presently his heavy boots crashed to the ground. There soon followed a loud, long-drawn-out 'Aah!' of comfort, a sign that he had stretched out in bed. I promptly prepared for rest, slipped under the covers, and blew out the light. I was already half asleep when I was suddenly startled into wakefulness by a dreadful croaking sound, as though someone next door were being throttled. Had something happened to the old man? I was about to leap out of bed. But my fears were baseless. For I soon realized that this croaking was only the prelude to the most powerful snoring I have ever heard in my life. It resounded in every modulation: sometimes like the regular, jerky sound of a saw-mill, sometimes in deep, tremulous gurglings and snortings, and sometimes in such frightful, prolonged rattling, as almost to shake the foundations of the quiet, restful house.

II

In the morning I had made up my mind: I could not stay under the same roof as this man. The only question was what to do. But hadn't I made up my mind long before to visit Graz? After all, I had to supply myself with many necessities, particularly with certain books that I hoped to find in that town. It also occurred to me that I had a relative living there whom I was really duty-bound to visit, now that I was so close. I could stay away for several days, for a week—and by that time Herr Hirsch would doubtless have left or at least not be here for much longer. Off to Graz, then! I hastened to put this saving thought into practice by taking the next train, dressed quickly while my neighbour was still emitting audible sounds of slumber, and went down to breakfast, where I told Herr Matzenauer of my decision.

'What?' he cried in alarm. 'You're leaving? But surely not because of Herr Hirsch?'

'Yes indeed.'

'You mustn't. Wait till you know him better. He has his little ways, but he's a very good-humoured old man.'

'He snores like a bear.'

'You'd soon get used to that. Besides, you could move to another room.'

'That's too much trouble,' I said dismissively.

'Well, it was just an idea. You can understand how sorry I am to lose you; I was hoping you would stay over New Year. But if you really mean to come back—'

'Of course I'll come back. I'll leave my things and take only what I really need. I was going to pay a short visit to Graz in any case, because I've things to do there. So don't say anything to Herr Hirsch; I shouldn't like to hurt anyone's feelings.'

Half an hour later I left with my plaid and valise.

On my return, my first question was: 'Has he gone?'

'Not yet,' replied Herr Matzenauer, embarrassed and visibly annoyed. 'He had a letter from his son, who was planning to stay in Venice for a few days longer.'

'I might have known!' I cried in vexation. 'But what's the matter with you? You look quite cross.'

Herr Matzenauer scratched his head.

'I must admit,' he said, 'that I've had about enough, too.'

'How's that?'

'Well, look: I keep a hotel, so I have to think about making money. So I was very pleased when a new guest turned up. Herr Hirsch is a rich man—or rather his son is—and the old man lives pretty well. But you wouldn't believe how much he demands in return. He wants all the furniture in his room you could possibly imagine; no chair is soft enough for him, no bed is long or wide enough, something has to be changed almost every day. And he constantly wants delicacies to eat. But they're hard to get hold of in the country, especially for just one person; first and foremost, they cost money. And since Herr Hirsch minds his pennies, even though he likes a good life, he always thinks he's being overcharged. My wife is threatening not to cook for him any more because the food is hardly ever to his liking; I have to go down on my knees to her.'

'Hm—'

'He wasn't nearly so difficult in the summer. Of course, he had to follow a certain diet, and he had to restrain himself when the other guests were there, because the pump room was still fresh in his mind.'

'The pump room?'

Herr Matzenauer blushed.

'I kept it from you earlier—but now you had better know. None of the visitors to the spa could endure him. Everyone avoided him, especially the ladies—and finally they couldn't stand him even at dinner in the pump room. He resorted to me in order to get something to eat.'

'There you are! But what's the use?' I continued, feeling resigned. 'We must be patient. After all, he won't stay here for ever.'

'I hope not. So long as he doesn't drive my few regulars away from the bar. In winter they're worth twice as much to me. They're quiet, serious people, and now that the evenings are drawing in, they enjoy a game of tarock.* But since Herr Hirsch is bored to death and is also as mad on card games as the Devil himself, he always wants to take part. The others won't let him, though; here in the country there's still a certain antipathy to the—you know what I mean. And anyway, they don't want to play with someone they don't know. Still, they can't prevent him from sitting beside them and watching the game. And it might be all right if only he would keep quiet. But he won't stop making observations and objections, so that people get confused and annoyed. Only the day before yesterday, the carpenter said to me—and he's pretty plain spoken: "Herr Matzenauer, if you don't keep that old Jew away from our table, we'll move to the Sun." Just think, that wretched ale-house at the far end of the square! After that I told Hirsch pretty clearly what the matter was—but the next day he was back. We'll have a scandal before it's all over!'

With this exclamation Herr Matzenauer brought his explanation to a close and hurried away, as he was wanted outside.

However, I remained seated with the glass of beer that I had had brought into the dining-room on my arrival. Evening was approaching. The last rays of the November sun fell obliquely through the glass panes on to the floor of the room; a small fire, suitable for the season, was flickering in the stove; from the bar the ticking of the Black Forest clock could be heard, along with the occasional word or exclamation showing, along with the soft rustling of cards, that the winter regulars had already begun their meditative game of tarock.

All this felt quite snug and homely, and only the awareness that Herr Hirsch was still in the hotel prevented me from feeling completely comfortable.

Then I heard him entering the bar.

'Aha! The card-sharps are already at it! Good luck, Herr Gamil-schegg! You had rotten luck yesterday. But then your playing was terrible. Just wait, I'll sit beside you. You'll get on much better!'

The leading shopkeeper of the village muttered something I did not catch. Herr Hirsch, however, moved his chair very audibly as the game proceeded. And it was not long before he started criticizing.

'But why a colour, Herr Gamilschegg? You should have played a tarot. Now make it tarot! But not so low—higher! higher!'

'You're getting me all muddled, Herr von Hirsch—'

'Never mind! Just go on like that—stay with tarot!'

'It's easy for you to give advice, Herr Hirsch,' interjected a gruff voice which obviously belonged to the carpenter. 'You can see every-one's cards!'

'See?' cried Hirsch, accentuating specific sounds as he grew excited. 'I can't see a thing! Nothing at all! Right, Herr Gamil-schegg! And now the trump! You've won! What did I tell you?'

The cards were shuffled and dealt again. But Herr Gamilschegg still did not seem to play to his mentor's satisfaction, for the latter abounded in rebukes and advice. This went on for a while, but finally the rest seemed to have had enough. Cards were thrown on to the table, and immediately the same voice growled: 'Either you shut your trap, or we stop playing!'

For a moment there was silence. No doubt Herr Hirsch was unprepared for words like these. Finally he stammered: 'Don't be so rude, carpenter.'

'Rude or not, we don't need anyone to tell us what to do!'

'Tell you what to do? I'm not telling you what to do!'

'I'm afraid you are disturbing the game, Herr von Hirsch,' inter-jected the grocer politely, as though by way of apology.

'I didn't mean any harm! I was trying to help—'

'We don't need your help!' thundered the carpenter. 'Herr Gamil-schegg knows himself how to play. The long and the short of it is: get lost, or we'll show you where the door is.'

Having been reprimanded so brutally, Herr Hirsch did not wait to see this threat made good, for he promptly appeared in the dining-room, pale and weak at the knees. He staggered laboriously to a chair near the window, sank down upon it, and covered his face with his ring-laden hands.

'God of justice! Nobody can stand me—everyone chases me away—whatever am I to do, a poor, beaten man!'

This semi-audible outburst of deep, despairing agony was very moving. To be quite honest, I had been following the dramatic scene next door with a touch of malicious enjoyment, but now my feelings changed into compassion. I made a movement.

He now noticed me for the first time and gazed at me for a while with increasing attentiveness, obviously searching his memory, but without success. Finally he stood up, came closer to me, and said without the least sign of shame or embarrassment, in a reproachful and accusing tone: 'Did you hear how they treated me out there?'

'I'm afraid I couldn't help hearing it. But don't take it to heart. You shouldn't have got involved with those people.'

'You're quite right! They're common as dirt. But you see, I have no prejudices and don't care about differences of rank—though I have every reason to do so. For I've spent my life in the most dis-tinguished company. Only recently I was present at a game of whist in which a general and two Court Councillors took part.'

'All the more reason for being careful.'

'Right! Quite right! I should have been careful! But that's what I've never been! But with whom do I have the honour of speaking?' he went on, suddenly assuming a proud posture.

I mentioned my name.

He stared pensively into space and then shook his head, in order to indicate that he had never heard this name.

'And are you from here?'

'No.'

'From where, if I may ask?'

'From Vienna.'

'From Vienna!' he exclaimed, spreading out his arms as though to fold me in an embrace. 'From Vienna! Then you must know my son!'

'I haven't the pleasure.'

'What? You don't know Hirsch? Ritter von Hirsch? Wholesaler and director of the —— Bank? But perhaps you don't belong to the business world?'

'No, I do not belong to the business world.'

'And what do you do, if I may ask?'

'I have a private income.'

I had already given this answer to quite other people than Herr Hirsch.

'Oh, I see! And what are you doing here?'

'Staying in the country—'

'Staying in the country? Now? At the beginning of winter? Strange taste! If I hadn't arranged to meet my son here—he's in Venice just now—I wouldn't have set foot in a hole like this.' Then, suddenly: 'Do you play cards?'

'Never.'

'What? A Viennese, and you don't play cards? Shame on you! What about billiards, then, hey?'

'Well, now and again—when the occasion arises—'

'Fine! Then we can amuse ourselves right away!' And he rushed over to the billiard table.

I was about to demur.

'No, no! You mustn't refuse! You've *got* to play with me!'

And since I still appeared reluctant, he continued in an imploring tone: 'Please play with me!'

'Very well! Five games.'

'Bravo! Five games! But we need some light—it's getting quite dark. Herr Matzenoer! Herr Matzenoer!'

And when the latter appeared, anxious to be of service: 'Light the lamp! I'm going to play billiards with this gentleman!'

Herr Matzenauer looked at me in astonishment, lit the lamp, and returned to the bar, which the guests seemed by now to have left.

'Right, now we can start,' cried Herr Hirsch, pulling a billiard cue out of the drawer. 'Choose a good cue—that's the main thing. I'll lead off. And now show what you can do.'

'Don't expect too much. I'm very out of practice.'

'Modesty! Pure modesty! I'm quite sure you're an excellent player. But you'll meet your match in me.'

'I don't doubt it,' I replied, making the first stroke.

'First-rate! Just see how you hit it! But look out, it's my turn now!'

With these words, Herr Hirsch leant all his weight on the billiard-table and took aim very slowly. But as he aimed too low and struck much too hard, the ball bounced up and jumped over the edge.

'Oho! It isn't greased! Nothing like elbow-grease!'

He laughed at this stale pun.

The game proceeded. Herr Hirsch praised his own playing extravagantly, but always tried to outdo me with 'dodges' which he announced boastfully. However, since they almost all misfired, it happened that I was the victor. I was about to put down the cue, but my opponent would not let me. He said that he could not admit defeat, and we would have to play another five games. I gave way gracefully, but as I was dreadfully bored and therefore played inattentively, it was Herr Hirsch who won this time.

'And now the tie-breaker!' he cried.

'What?'

'Of course! We're neck and neck; we need another game to decide.'

I did not care, so, in order to bring things to an end, I let him win.

'You see,' he cried, radiant with triumph, 'what did I tell you! But now let's have dinner! You must be ready to eat, and I'm sure you'll let me join you.'

I could make no objection, and allowed him to summon the landlord.

'Herr Matzenoer, I'm going to dine with this gentleman! You know what to serve me. And a small bottle of Bordeaux!'

As I had had a very early lunch in Graz, I ordered something as well.

Once we were seated at the newly laid table, Herr Hirsch filled his glass and raised it to drink my health.

'To our acquaintance!' he said with emphasis. Suddenly, however, he paused and stared at me. 'Strange! I must have seen you somewhere before.'

'Of course,' I replied with a smile. 'A week ago in this very room.'

Herr Hirsch's expression underwent an indescribable alteration, like a kind of collapse.

'That was *you*?' he stammered. Then he fell silent, and his lower lip hung down. All of a sudden, however, he burst out laughing, placed his hands on his hips, and exclaimed: 'Whatever did you think of me?'

I shrugged my shoulders evasively.

'No, no! Spit it out! You thought I had no manners.'

'Well—since you put it like that—'

'I was right, hey? Oh, I know, I know! That's what everyone thinks of me. But I tell you, I *have* got manners—I *must* have manners, for in Vienna I move in the most select circles. In the country, mind you, where I don't know anyone, I let myself go.'

As though to confirm this statement, he shoved his knife into a small mountain of caviar which had been served on a little dish, and put the blade in his mouth.

'First-rate! Genuine Astrakhan!* You must taste it! I ordered it specially for myself. But do try it!'

Not wanting to hurt him, I took a little of the large-grained roe, which was indeed excellent.

'You are a gourmet,' I said.

'Yes, that's my weakness—my only weakness. If you live as long as I have, you'll come to realize too that a tasty morsel is the most solid pleasure. And I can take it. There's nothing wrong with my digestion. How old do you think I am?'

'Sixty, perhaps—'

'Wrong! Wrong by a mile! Seventy, I tell you, seventy! Seventy-two! Yes, you wouldn't think it to look at me. Apart from a bit of arthritis in my legs, I'm perfectly healthy, and more than a match for many a young man. But now what do you think I've ordered to follow the caviar?'

'Well, what?'

'Wild boar! Some delicious wild boar, which a gamekeeper near here has delivered to the kitchen. It's just the season for it. You're looking at me? You're laughing? You're surprised that I eat such things as a Jew.'

'That never entered my head.'

'Oh yes it did! But you aren't looking at an Orthodox Jew, although I grew up among them in Galicia. I've always been a free-thinker, a man of the Enlightenment, and there was a time when I raised a lot of hackles on that account—of course, things are different now. Especially my wife! She—may God give her rest—she was so strict about such things—a real Hasid!* If you ate anything that offended the ritual laws, she thought that was the greatest crime you could commit. Seligmann, she'd often say, when I'd committed such a sin, Seligmann—that's my name, by the way—you're an apostate! To say nothing of the Sabbath! That was when she gave me a real hard time. I couldn't light a pipe—people still smoked pipes in those days—couldn't write a letter, not even read one! Mind you, she was a splendid woman. They don't make 'em like that any more. And beautiful with it! I cried, I cried like a child, when they cut off her jet-black hair* on our wedding day. What nonsense! But in those days there were no two ways about it. Yes, what a woman my Gittel was!' He ruminated, and his eyes grew moist.

Now the roast boar appeared. Herr Hirsch looked up. 'Well? Doesn't it look appetizing? Take a bit for yourself!' And despite my remonstrances he put a slice on my plate and continued, while heartily enjoying his dinner: 'It's funny how things sometimes work out. My wife was a Jewess through and through, though, as I said, I was never a particularly good Jew myself. My son is a much better Jew than I am—and just fancy, he's got a wife who's ashamed of being Jewish. She comes from a very posh, very grand family—and educated, you wouldn't believe! Speaks every language—and reads books neither you nor I have ever heard of. But she's vain as well, very vain. Everyone who is anyone in Vienna gets invited to her house: statesmen, scholars, artists and writers. And most of them come—though people are still very prejudiced against us—and the ones who try to hide it, they're the worst. All these people turn up in her salon all right, and they don't mind sitting at her table—but the moment they're outside again, they start laying into the Jews as they go down the steps. I know they do. And my daughter-in-law knows it too, though she won't admit it. That's why she secretly feels annoyed and humiliated. And my son loves her. It's like a fairytale the way he loves her. Ten years they've been married, and he's still as passionate, still worships her, like he did on the first day. And she's not beautiful in the least. She's got brains, mind you –brains and energy. She'll end up making my son get baptized—or at least their children, so that they don't run about in the world as Hebrews.'

'And would you object to that very much?'

'Object? Me? Good Lord, you know I'm not a fanatic, and years ago I horrified the community by saying publicly that in the end none of us would have any choice. And even if I didn't like it, what could I do to stop it? You've got to let your children have their way.' He sighed and pushed his plate aside reflectively.

'Have you several children?' I asked after a pause.

'I used to! I used to! Four in all, but two of them died very young. I've only got this son left—and a daughter.' He was silent for a while, then asked suddenly: 'Do you know Shakespeare's King Lear?' (He pronounced them 'Lee-ar' and 'Sheekyspir'.)

'Yes, I know the play.'

'Well then, I'm another King Lee-ar! But no,' he continued, hastily qualifying his words, 'you mustn't think my daughter is a Recha or Gonovril*—but she's no Ophelia, either. I'll tell you all about it.' He leant back and continued after a pause: 'As you see me before you, I'm a poor man. At least, it depends—I've got what I need. But I was once a rich, a very rich man. Twice, in fact. The first time was in Poland. I had contacts with the whole nobility, and they asked for my help when they got into difficulties. And I was too good-natured; I couldn't say no—and so I lost almost my whole fortune. With what was left—my wife was dead by this time—my children and I went to Vienna. You can't begin to imagine how hard it was for people like us to find a foothold there in those days. But I managed it. Little by little I developed business contacts, till I was wealthy Hirsch again. By this time my Sarah—that's my daughter—was ready for a husband. A beauty, I tell you! Quite different from her mother, mind you—but a beauty. Painters nowadays, who only paint women with red hair, would have fought over her. You see plenty of dyed hair these days; but hers was red gold by nature, and when it was loose, it fell to the ground like a bridal train. Well, I had a business acquaintance called Mandel—worth a pretty penny, a lot more than I was. He had a son, and of course this son promptly fell in love with Sarah. One day old Mandel comes to me and says: "Look'ee here, Hirsch, you give your daughter to my son. Me, I'll buy him an estate in Hungary"—this was after 1848*—"and your Sarah, she can be the lady of the manor." I didn't say yes and I didn't say no. It was a good match, a very good one—but I didn't care for young Mandel. He was too unattractive, too ugly for my taste—a real scarecrow, saving your presence. So I called Sarah and said: "Sarah," I says, "young Mandel's asking for your hand in marriage. It's up to you as far as I'm concerned. If you want him, take him; if you don't, don't." Now I thought she'd throw up her hands and run out of the room. But not a bit of it! She answered quite coolly: "Why shouldn't I take young Mandel, father? I'll take him." Soon afterwards they had their wedding, a brilliant wedding. But I spent the time skulking in a side-room, because I was ashamed of my daughter for taking such an *untam** for her husband, and everyone else thought I'd gone aside to shed quiet tears of happiness because of the wealthy match. So people have never understood me—never!' As he said these words, he pulled a cigar-case from his breast-pocket with a violent gesture, and prepared to have a smoke.

After blowing some immense clouds of smoke, he continued: 'That wedding was the beginning of my next misfortune. For soon afterwards I suffered losses—enormous losses. The Stock Exchange! What was I to do! I was a beggar, but I was ashamed to go on the streets. My son had to look after himself, and though he had just graduated in law, he went into the textile trade—and as for *me*—well, I went to Hungary to stay with my daughter. They gave me a very decent reception—very decent, I'll give them that. But it wasn't long before things went awry. I've always been an active kind of man, and I could never just be an onlooker. So I wanted to give my son-in-law a hand in managing the estate; for in Poland I'd learnt quite a lot about farming. But my daughter put her oar in straight away. "Please don't tell Aladar"—my children still said "please" to me at that time—"please don't tell Aladar"—his real name's Aaron—"what to do, dear father; you're a *schlemiel*."* That hurt, coming from my own flesh and blood. But she was right enough! I *was* a *schlemiel*. So I kept my mouth shut and didn't bother about anything else. But what was I supposed to do the whole day long in that dreary castle on the Hungarian *puszta*?* I sometimes visited a small town in the neighbourhood where the local country gentry used to meet in a café. There was plenty of gambling there, especially on market-days. I wasn't penniless, for my son was already earning, and now and again he sent me whatever he could spare—so I took part. But misfortune was after me, and that was that. I lost, until I had a gambling debt to pay. Not a very big one, but I couldn't pay it, and, like it or not, in this fix I had to turn to Sarah. Now she'd had a substantial dowry from me; but I knew she'd always been mean, very mean. "Why do you need to gamble, father? I'll give you the money this time, but you mustn't gamble any more; you're a poor man now." That was the second blow. But she was right enough: I *was* a poor man. Never touched the cards again. But that wasn't the end of it. It turned out that I was too choosy about my food and drink, and one day, when I happened to cough a bit, they said: "You smoke too much, father. Why do you smoke so much? It will do you harm." I could take a hint—and that was the last straw. Take my cigar away, and you take my life. I answered never a word, though my heart was like to burst; but the next day I was off, leaving Sarah alone with her Aladar. For they haven't any children.'

While telling this story he had got excited, and on falling silent he breathed heavily. His beloved cigar had gone out, but he made no attempt to light it again, and stared straight ahead. 'You might almost say,' he continued presently in a toneless voice, 'that that's God's way of punishing her. For my daughter is a real Jewess: she can't bear being infertile.'

Trying to cheer him up, I said: 'Still, you seem to have all the more happiness from your son.'

He looked up, startled. 'From my son? Oh yes, of course! My son is a noble person—*he* will give me anything I want. But'—he struck a pose—'he has a lot to thank me for. I never skimped on his education; I even kept a private tutor for him. As I said, he's a lawyer, and he could have gone into the civil service, like lots of others, and had a good career. Last year people were desperate to elect him to parliament. But he preferred to remain a merchant and nothing else. And there's no one to match him. His schemes, his enterprises, they're magnificent. He's already a millionaire.'

'Congratulations. And do you live with him in Vienna?'

'Naturally! Naturally! That's to say, I used to. But once again, my daughter-in-law was the stumbling-block. You can understand it: the double jealousy of a wife and a mother. That woman knows how highly my son thinks of me—and then, the grandchildren! Oh, if you knew my grandchildren!' he continued with shining eyes. 'A boy and a girl. Real angels! Especially the little one, Jenny—she's seven. Charming, I tell you, charming! And they idolize their old grand-father! So there was always envy and strife in the house, and finally I decided I'd rather live on my own. But close by, close by; any moment I can—' Suddenly he broke off, as though he were out of breath, and fidgeted uneasily on his chair, immersed in his thoughts.

I made no reply, and so a long silence ensued. He seemed to have entirely lost his communicative mood and scarcely paid me any attention. His eyes had a glazed, lifeless look, his cheeks were sunken, his features loose—suddenly he really looked very old.

Then, without warning, he stood up and said: 'I'm going to bed. Are you staying here too?' and without waiting for my answer or saying goodnight, he was gone.

I stayed in my chair, pondering. I had undoubtedly touched the old man on a very sore point, and after some reflection I had no difficulty in working out how matters stood. Despite his foibles and uncouth ways, he inspired me with sympathy; for I felt that he was an unhappy man. When Herr Matzenauer came to clear the table and asked me with some irony how I had got on with Herr Hirsch, I did not answer. Soon afterwards, having reached my room, I heard my neighbour already snoring. But not so dreadfully as last time. Or was that just my impression?

III

The next day, when I returned from my usual morning stroll, Herr Hirsch was standing at the front gate. He again looked fresh and cheerful, and had a brand-new top hat perched rakishly over his right ear; in his hand he was holding a small valise. He scarcely seemed to recognize me, and returned my greeting almost as though I were a stranger.

'Well, how did you sleep?' I asked, taken aback.

'Exceedingly well!' he rejoined patronizingly. 'And now I'm going to M———. It's a little frosty today, but that doesn't matter. Do you know the town?'

I replied in the negative.

'A handsome market-town, where officials from the surrounding estates meet every day. They've set up a kind of casino, and it's very jolly. I was there quite a lot this summer, and I don't understand why I didn't seek out these people long before now, instead of getting bored here like a pug-dog. Would you like to come too? There's a convenient train service; we'll be back by ten this evening.'

I thanked him, but refused.

'Well then, adieu!' He put a finger to the brim of his hat and set off for the station, which lay outside the town and was to be reached by a short walk.

Last night this man had poured out his heart to me, and this was how he behaved today! However, his decision to go to M——— could only be agreeable for me. For despite the sympathy I had begun to feel for him, I had been anticipating a renewed invitation to play billiards, and similar convivial demands, with a certain nervousness.

When he returned in the evening, I was sitting in my room reading.

'I've had a wonderful time—wonderful!' he cried, addressing someone in the hall, probably Herr Matzenauer, so loudly that I could hear it upstairs. 'Quite different people from this lot. I'm going back tomorrow!'

Indeed, there was no sign of Herr Hirsch the following day, nor on the day after that—and on the third day he even stayed away overnight.

'Herr Hirsch has deserted you,' I said to our landlord at breakfast.

'God forbid!' he rejoined in irritation. He seemed not to like the wealthy guest taking his money elsewhere. 'But do you know what he does in M——? He gambles, and for pretty high stakes. There's a regular gang there. The steward and the head forester, as he calls himself, from a baronial estate, both as deep in debt as the owner himself, and a pettifogging lawyer who's gone to the dogs but who used to be a local magistrate—these three are fleecing the old fellow for all he's worth. Yesterday he already had to borrow a hundred gulden* from me, and he must have got so carried away that he missed his train. I hope he's back by lunchtime. There's a telegram for him—probably from his son.'

Herr Hirsch did indeed turn up at midday. 'A telegram? A telegram?' he yelled, clattering up the stairs to his room. 'Where's the telegram?' Then after a pause: 'My son's coming! My son! Now look sharp, Herr Matzenoer! Do your hotel some credit! You did warm the other room in the last few days, as I ordered? And then a carriage! A carriage at six o'clock! I'm afraid my son's coming by himself—not with his family, as he hoped—but you can't expect him to walk. No, he won't walk! And tell your wife to make a bit of an effort. The food must be exquisite. A dinner! A proper dinner! My son will have an appetite; for I know he never eats anything while travelling.'

Left on his own, he rushed to and fro, sometimes in his own room, sometimes in the room intended for his son. I thought that, in his state of excitement, he might come over to me in order to inform me of the great event. But that did not happen; it was obvious that he had already forgotten me.

Still, I was somewhat curious about Herr Hirsch junior, and as my dinner-time coincided with the arrival of the train, I could be sure that I would see him in the dining-room.

I had just finished my meal when the carriage arrived, and

immediately afterwards the father and the son entered; the latter cut a distinguished but rather modest figure. Smaller and much more slightly built than his father, he bore not the faintest resemblance to the latter. Seen in profile, his features looked sharp and decidedly Jewish; his lofty, broad forehead was made even more expressive and imposing by his prematurely receding hairline; his somewhat tired eyes were assisted by fine steel spectacles. He took his seat noiselessly at the table which Herr Matzenauer had laid with great care, and on which four candles were burning in a silver-plated candelabrum.

'This is the dining-room, you see!' cried Herr Hirsch senior in oratorical tones. 'Not elegant, I admit, but comfortable. Have a glass of beer; I know you like it. It's excellent, too—the only good thing to be had here, if truth be told. But you should have brought Richard with you!'

'I've already told you, dear father,' replied the other in a low voice, 'that both the children have very bad colds, and so we must do our utmost to get them home as soon as possible.'

'All right, all right—but I could surely have seen them at the station.'

'That would have meant taking the slow mail train, which is most unpleasant for women and children. The express train stops here only during the bathing season.'

'True enough, true enough—anyway, I'll be able to give the little darlings a big hug tomorrow in Vienna!'

The son made no reply. He seemed pensive, and sipped inattentively at the beer that had been brought for him. However, I no longer wished to be a witness of this familial conversation, which the old man, in his usual unrestrained manner, conducted at the top of his voice, so I rose and went away.

Outside the moon was shining. I walked up and down for a while, finishing my cigar, on the deserted village square; then I retired to my room.

After an hour had elapsed, the other two came upstairs and went straight into the room that had been prepared for the newcomer. There a discussion began which grew more and more heated, so that the sound of the voices reached me ever more clearly. Suddenly I heard the old man exclaim:

'To Venice? What am I to do in Venice?' As he spoke, he entered his own room and marched heavily up and down in it.

His son, obviously not suspecting that anyone besides them was staying on this floor, had followed him, and now said soothingly: 'But, dear father, you've often expressed the desire to see Venice.'

'Yes, with you! I'd like to see it with you—I wanted to travel with you. But on my own? What's an old man like me to do in Venice all on his own? I can't speak a word of Italian.'

'That isn't necessary. You'll feel quite at home with this family. They will take care of you in every way—and so you'll gradually become pleasantly familiar with the city's distinctive life.'

'But I don't want to! What's life in Venice to me? My own is quite enough. And I don't want to stay with these scroungers!'

'They are not scroungers. The husband has a very reputable position in one of the local banking houses.'

'But who got him his position? You did! You did! I see it all. I'm to be kept in custody. They'll watch every step I take!'

'You're just imagining that.'

'I'm not imagining anything! You're plotting behind my back! You're sending me into exile! Oh, I know, I know! You wouldn't let me spend this summer with you in Hietzing,* though the villa was big enough, and that's how the doctor came to prescribe the cold-water cure and a long stay in the mountains. There's nothing wrong with me! I'm perfectly healthy!'

'God be thanked that you are, dear father. You will enjoy yourself all the more in Venice.'

'But I don't want to! And even if I wanted to, how could I—so far from you! Bernhard!' he continued in imploring tones, 'dear Bernhard, don't send me away! I know the suggestion doesn't come from your heart, it's your wife who wants to be rid of me!'

'You are mistaken. The position I am currently striving for, and the contacts which I am therefore obliged to maintain—in a word, circumstances make it imperative for you to spend this winter away from Vienna.'

'I won't be there—nobody will know I'm there! I'll rent a room somewhere in the suburbs, and no one will set eyes on me! Just let me visit you for a quarter of an hour once a week, so that I can see you—and embrace my little grandchildren!'

'How often you've said that already! Such undignified and unnatural arrangements would not be necessary if you would only be reasonable. But there we have it. If you cannot be in the house the whole day, if you are not invited to every dinner and every party, you feel deeply injured, you cover us with reproaches and make the most unedifying scenes. And then—I am very sorry to have to say this to you again—'

He stopped; for I had cleared my throat extremely loudly. I was already finding my involuntary role of eavesdropper highly embarrassing. They immediately withdrew into the adjoining room and closed the connecting door.

Now all was quiet. But not for long. The scene continued at three rooms' remove from me. Admittedly, I could no longer follow what was being said; but the old man's voice reached my ears now and again, lamenting, threatening, or beseeching. Finally there was a muffled shout—then complete calm ensued.

Soon afterwards Herr Hirsch crept into his room and went to bed. But his usual snoring did not follow. I heard him sighing, giving a low groan, and, as I thought, weeping softly, until I fell asleep.

Next morning the new arrival had already left. His father had accompanied him to the station and was now returning in the carriage. He entered the dining-room, where I had just been breakfasting; he looked very pale and worn-out. On catching sight of me he made an effort to cheer up, and placed his hat above his right ear with pretended merriment. 'Aha! You're here, are you? Good morning! Good morning! Did you see my son? He's already left—he's got to be in Vienna tonight. And where do you think *I'm* off to for a change? To Venice! What about that? To Venice! I've always wanted to go there, and now my son has enabled me to spend the winter there. I'm going to live with a very posh family and not miss anything the wonderful city has to offer. I'm already looking forward to floating in a gondola. Pity I'm not younger—they say there's nothing to beat a Venetian woman!' He tried to utter a light-hearted laugh, but suddenly fell silent; one could see that he was close to tears.

I wished him a good journey and left him alone.

That same day Herr Hirsch departed without further leave-taking. I, however, as winter descended in all its rigour, remained in the Three Monarchs Hotel.

IV

A great ball was being held in the rooms of the Vienna Musical Society. It was one of those brilliant charity events that are now being put on more and more often because of spreading poverty—no doubt also because of increasing vanity. For a good many years I had ceased to take part in such festivities, mainly because I was often absent from Vienna for long periods. Today, however, I had turned up in order to enjoy the 'great world' again and to observe its younger and youngest denizens. The latter were in the overwhelming majority, and hence I soon felt out of place and lonely amid the colourful bustle that was surging through the radiant halls. Even older acquaintances had some difficulty in calling me to mind, and then they merely gave me their hand in passing with a casual 'So you're back!'

I was greeted at more length, albeit in similar words, by a distinguished-looking gentleman who came up to me as I was about to withdraw into a corner.

This man was a well-known personality throughout the city, with a peculiar position in society. The scion of a respected Jewish family, he had been endowed by his fathers with wealth, but not with the gift of increasing or even keeping it. He had set out early on travels, lived for a while in Paris, and then returned to Vienna, where he happily exhausted his fortune on all manner of noble passions. However, as he was related or otherwise connected to virtually the entire financial aristocracy, the latter, unable to drop him, provided the poor fellow with all manner of commercial sinecures which imposed on him only the duty of collecting his appointed dividends at appointed times. Consequently he was able to retain his previous habits, though on a more modest footing, and was very popular about town among both gentlemen and ladies, and also in artistic circles, on account of his lively mind and witty repartee; otherwise he was held in small regard. Since he felt this more and more deeply, as he grew older he became hungry for revenge, which he took by pouring the acid of his mockery on all and sundry, not least upon his fellow-Jews. A thorough-going anti-Semite could not have attacked the Jewish character more savagely than Herr X did on every occasion and with the most perfect enjoyment.

'Where have you been hiding all this time?' he asked. 'In the country? You'll turn into a rustic if you're not careful. But what do you think of the cream of present-day society? Our modern great men? Our modern beauties? Rubbish! *Pofel!** Brilliant *pofel!* That's all! And don't you think the *national element'* (he meant the Jewish element) 'has become very conspicuous? I wouldn't mind betting that two-thirds of the assembled company belong to the Mosaic confession, to borrow the euphemism that was current in my young days. And the patronesses of the ball are half of them Jewesses.' He pointed to a group of ladies who were standing and chatting not far from us. 'Do me the favour of looking at these noses! These round shoulders! The good Baroness Hirtburg is of the party. For ten years it was her dearest wish to figure as patroness alongside Princess M—— —and now she's made it. She's made up in jewellery for what she lacks in deportment. There—I mean the stout person talking to the Princess. Doesn't she look as though she were set in jewels?'

I glanced at the lady he was referring to; she had indeed mounted a positively fabulous display of clothes and diamonds.

'Her husband is close by, as usual,' continued X with a side-glance. 'A most remarkable man. They say he's worth twenty million. And he may make even more, if our friends the anarchists don't intervene. For he's an exceptionally smart fellow—a kind of financial genius. But every lotus has its stem. That's to say, everybody has his own particular stupidity. So does he. He loves his wife to excess. Just look at him standing there and revelling in the sight of her. You'd think he was in ecstasies!'

I had turned in the direction he indicated and looked hard at the gentleman. The longer I gazed at him, the more familiar he seemed. 'What did you say the lady's name was? Baroness Hirtburg? Isn't that gentleman called Hirsch?'

My cicerone burst out laughing. 'I can see you live in the back of beyond! His name was Hirsch—it's now Hirtburg. He acquired the name along with the Baroness—or bought it, rather. He was on the point of getting baptized, too. But that would have ruined his credit; for these days Israel takes more pride than ever in staying away from water.'

'And do you know what happened to his father? Is he still alive?'

'Old Seligmann? Did you know him?'

'Very superficially. I met him somewhere years ago.'

'Be thankful you didn't get to know him better. A quite impossible individual. Do you really not know how he ended up?'

'No.'

'Then I'll tell you. Even if you only saw him *once*, you'll understand that one can't have a father like *that* in one's house. It could all have been sorted out. But the old stock-jobber, who once had quite a tidy fortune, couldn't stop playing the markets. I've no idea how often his son paid for his losses, but finally he'd had enough. Then, in order to satisfy his passion, Papa resorted to all kinds of strange resources—finally he even fell back on the seamy moneylending with which he had started his career, and he was in danger of getting into conflict with the courts. How compromising for the future baronial household! So they had to get him out of Vienna at any price. First they sent him to small bathing resorts—then they interned him in Venice! Now just imagine old Hirsch in Venice! A rhinoceros in an aquarium! But joking apart, the weak-minded old chap, who, like all Jews, clung to his family as the white of egg does to the yolk, went mad, though the people who were supposed to be keeping an eye on him didn't notice it at first. One fine morning, when he was shaving his beard with his own hands, as he usually did, he put the knife an inch too low down and gave himself a tiny little cut on the throat. And that cut, you see, is the sore point for the house of Hirtburg. Sore point? It's a bottomless abyss, and the Baron would happily pour two millions into it if he could, for—and this is incomprehensible, too!—he loved his father very much indeed. But lo and behold: the youngest Hirtburg!' He glanced across at a young man who was approaching the Baron. 'What do you think of that specimen? Isn't he his grandfather *in nuce*?* It's all explained in Darwin. Who'd want a son like that? But that makes the daughter all the more charming. She's positively enchanting. I've no idea where she gets it from. One of the few Jewish beauties I can admire. Come on, I'll show her to you,' he added, standing on tiptoe. 'If I'm not mistaken, she's dancing with yet another young diplomat, a marquis of the *république française*. He seems to have his eye on her golden hand.'

He took me by the arm, and we forced our way through the circle of onlookers that had formed around the dancers.

'Do you see the tall, slender girl with tea-roses on her dress? Well, what do you say? What a figure! What movements! Grace itself. And that profile! Those eyes—that hair—'

'A wonderful creature, indeed!'

'*Voilà*: the granddaughter of the late lamented Seligmann Hirsch.'

THEODOR HERZL

An Autobiography

Theodor Herzl (1860–1904) was born in Budapest, where his parents were unusual among Hungarian Jews in resisting Magyarization and remaining loyal to the German-language culture of the Austrian Empire. In 1878 they moved to Vienna, where Herzl, as a law student, was an enthusiastic German nationalist with an admiration for Prussia, Bismarck, and Wagner. He belonged to a student duelling society, 'Albia', but left it in 1883 after a commemoration of Wagner was accompanied by a public affirmation of anti-Semitism. While he was forging his career as journalist and dramatist, his notebooks and letters show a continuing preoccupation with the 'Jewish question', which was heightened by his experience as Paris correspondent of the leading Viennese liberal newspaper the *Neue Freie Presse (New Free Press)*. Anti-Semitism in France was outspoken, and seemed justified by Jewish involvement in financial scams like the Panama scandal. Although Herzl witnessed the degradation of Captain Dreyfus for alleged treason, his conviction that anti-Semitism was ineradicable in Europe was formed well before the Dreyfus affair. In 1895, in feverish excitement, he drafted a visionary plan for a Jewish state, initially imagining it as located in Argentina, where unsuccessful Jewish agricultural colonies had recently been formed. He published *The Jewish State* in 1896, and a year later, in August 1897, held the First Zionist Congress in Basle. Thereafter he combined his journalistic career with negotiations with Jewish notables and European potentates (to whom his association with a major European paper gave him ready access), seeking support for a Jewish state which, he increasingly felt, had to be situated in Palestine, then a distant province of the Ottoman Empire. His conviction that Jewish life in the Diaspora was untenable found expression in his play *The New Ghetto*, written in 1894, while his utopian novel *Altneuland (Old-New Land*, 1902), set twenty years in the future, describes in great detail the workings of a liberal democratic Jewish state which by then dominates the Middle East and includes a contented Arab population. In many ways, though, Herzl's most remarkable literary work is his Zionist Diary, which records not only his negotiations but his dreams and fantasies. These show him to be a political visionary in the mould of Cecil Rhodes, to whom he drafted a letter saying: 'You, Mr Rhodes, are either a politician full of fantasy or a political fantasist,' a judgement that applies also to Herzl.

This short autobiography was first published in English in the London *Jewish Chronicle* on 14 January 1898; the translation has been revised.

———

I was born in 1860 in Budapest, in a house next to the synagogue, where recently the Rabbi denounced me from the pulpit in very strong terms, because, believe it or not, I am trying to obtain for the Jews more honour and greater freedom than they enjoy at present. On the front door of the house in the Tabakgasse where I first saw the light of the world, twenty years hence a notice will be posted up with the words: 'This house to let.'

I cannot deny that I went to school. First of all I was sent to a Jewish preparatory school, where I enjoyed a certain authority because my father was a wealthy merchant. My earliest recollection of that school consists of a caning which I received from the master, because I did not know the details of the exodus of the Jews from Egypt. At the present time a great many schoolmasters want to give me a caning, because I recollect too much of that exodus from Egypt.

At the age of ten I went to the Realschule (a grammar school where the modern side is more looked after than classics, in contradistinction to the Gymnasium, a grammar school where the study of Latin and Greek is more cultivated than Euclid and natural science). De Lesseps* was then the hero of the hour, and I had conceived the idea of piercing the other isthmus, that of Panama. But I soon lost all my former love for logarithms and trigonometry, because at that time a very pronounced anti-Jewish tendency prevailed at the Realschule. One of our masters explained to our class the meaning of the word 'heathen' by saying: 'To that class belong the idolaters, Mohammedans and Jews.' After this peculiar definition, I had quite enough of the Realschule, and wanted to become a classical scholar. My good father never constrained me into a narrow groove for my studies, and I became a pupil of the Gymnasium. But for all that I had not yet quite done with Panama. Many years later, as the Paris correspondent of the *Neue Freie Presse*, it became my duty to write about the notorious incidents of that scandalous episode* in the history of France. At the Gymnasium, which was called the Evangelisches Gymnasium, the Jewish boys formed the majority, and therefore we had not to complain of any Jew-baiting. In the upper seventh I wrote my first newspaper article—anonymously, of course, otherwise I would have been 'kept in' by the headmaster. While I was in the highest class in the Gymnasium, my only sister died, a girl of eighteen; my good mother became so melancholy with grief that we moved to Vienna in 1878.

During the Shivah* week Rabbi Kohn called on us and asked me about my plans for the future. I told him that I intended to become an author, whereupon the Rabbi shook his head, just as dissatisfied as he was when disapproving of Zionism only the other day. A literary career, concluded the discontented Rabbi, is not a proper profession.

In Vienna I studied law and took part in all the student follies, including wearing the coloured cap of a *Verbindung*,* until the association one day passed a resolution that no Jews should henceforth be admitted as members. Those who were members already they kindly permitted to remain in the *Verbindung*. I said goodbye to these noble youths and began devoting myself seriously to work. In 1884 I took my degree as Dr Juris and took up an unsalaried appointment at the lawcourts as a judicial clerk.

I held this appointment in the law-courts of Vienna as well as in Salzburg. In Salzburg the work seemed to be much more attractive, the scenery in and around the town being most beautiful. My office was in an old castellated tower just under the belfry, the chimes sounded sweetly pretty to me three times every day.

Of course I wrote much more for the theatre than for the lawcourts. In Salzburg I spent some of the happiest hours of my life; I would have liked to stay in the beautiful town but, as a Jew, I could never have advanced to the position of a judge. I therefore bade farewell to Salzburg and to the legal profession at the same time. Again I caused a great deal of worry to the Rabbi in Budapest; for instead of going in for a real profession or for art, I began travelling and writing for newspapers and for the theatre. Many of my plays were performed at different theatres; some met with great applause, others fell flat. Even now I cannot understand why some of my plays met with success while others were hissed off the stage. However, this varying reception of my plays taught me to disregard altogether whether the public applauded or hissed my work. One's own conscience must be satisfied with one's work; all the rest is immaterial. I disown at present all my plays, even those which are still applauded at the Burgtheater*; I no longer care about any of them.

In 1889 I married. I have three children, a boy and two girls. In my opinion my children are neither ugly nor stupid. But of course I may be mistaken.

While I was travelling in Spain in 1891, the *Neue Freie Presse* invited me to become its correspondent in Paris. I accepted the position, though until then I had detested and despised politics. In Paris I had occasion to learn what the word politics means, and I expressed my views in a little book, *The Palais Bourbon*. By 1895 I had had quite enough of Paris and returned to Vienna.

During the last two months of my residence in Paris I wrote the book *The Jewish State*, to which I owe the honour of your request for some biographical data. I do not recollect ever having written anything in such an elevated frame of mind as that book. Heine says that he heard the wings of an eagle beating over his head while writing certain verses. I do believe that something also beat its wings above my head while I was writing that book. I worked at it every day until I was completely exhausted; my only relaxation in the evening consisted in listening to Wagner's music, especially to *Tannhäuser*,* an opera which I went to every time it was performed. Only on the evenings when there was no performance at the Opera did I feel doubts about the correctness of my ideas.

At first I had conceived the idea of writing my pamphlet concerning the solution of the Jewish question only for private circulation among my friends. The publication of these views did not enter into my plans until later; I had not intended to begin a public agitation for the Jewish cause. Most people will be surprised at present to learn that this was my original intention. I considered the whole matter as only fit to be acted upon, not to be talked about. Public agitation should only be my last resort if my private advice was not heeded or obeyed.

When I had finished my book I asked one of my oldest and best friends to read the manuscript. While reading it he suddenly began to cry. I found this emotion quite natural, as he was a Jew, and I had also cried several times while writing the book. But to my dismay I found that he gave quite a different reason for his tears. He thought that I had gone mad, and, being my friend, was deeply saddened by my misfortune. He ran away without saying another word. After a sleepless night he came back to me the next morning and besought me to 'leave the matter alone,' as everybody would consider me crazy. He was excited to such a degree that I promised him anything to calm his feelings. He then advised me to ask Nordau* whether my plan was the conception of a responsible person. 'I shall ask nobody,' was my reply; 'if my ideas have that effect upon a cultivated and devoted friend of mine, I shall abandon my plan.'

I then passed through a very serious crisis; I can only compare it to the throwing of a red-hot body into cold water. Of course, if that body happens to be iron, the process makes it into steel.

My friend of whom I spoke above had to make up my accounts for the cost of telegrams. When he gave me the account, consisting of an immense array of figures, I saw at a glance that he had added up the sums incorrectly. I pointed this out to him, and he started to do the sums all over again. Only after a third or fourth attempt did his sums agree with mine. This fact restored my self-confidence. If I was able to do sums more correctly than he, my reason could not have deserted me entirely.

On that day my troubles with *The Jewish State* began. During the two years and more since then I experienced many, many sad days, and I am afraid there are many more sad days to come.

In 1895 I began keeping a diary; four stout volumes have already been filled. Should I ever publish them, the world will be surprised to learn what I had to put up with; who were the enemies of my plan; and who, on the other hand, stood by me.

But one thing I consider certain beyond a doubt: the movement will last. I do not know when I shall die, but Zionism will never die. Since the days at Basle the Jewish people again has a popular representation; consequently, the Jewish state will arise in its own country.

THOMAS MANN

The Blood of the Volsungs

Thomas Mann (1875–1955), son of a prosperous patrician of Lübeck and his more artistic South American wife, chose a literary rather than a professional career and soon made a name for himself as the author of the subtle and ironic short stories collected as *Little Herr Friedemann* (1898), and of the family chronicle *Buddenbrooks* (1901), which has sold more copies than any other twentieth-century German novel. His later master-pieces, including *Death in Venice* (1912), *The Magic Mountain* (1924), the tetralogy *Joseph and his Brothers* (1933–42), and *Doctor Faustus* (1947), accompanied a career as an increasingly public figure. In 1914 Mann enthusiastically affirmed Germany's part in the First World War and rejected 'Western' liberalism. After the war, recognizing the reality of defeat and the threat of anarchic violence, he transferred his support, despite misgivings, to the precarious Weimar Republic. Forced into exile, first in Switzerland and later in the United States, by the Nazi seizure of power, he became an internationally famous spokesman against the Hitler regime and in favour of the humane values of German culture.

Mann's public utterances were also consistently philo-Semitic. In 1907, in a forum on the Jewish question, Mann declared himself 'a convinced and unequivocal philo-Semite', while in 1936 he said that he numbered Jews among his closest friends and his worst enemies; by the latter he meant the critics Alfred Kerr and Theodor Lessing, who attacked his work maliciously. Throughout the Nazi period Mann condemned the mal-treatment of Jews. In 1943 he asserted that no cultivated German could be an anti-Semite, for the Jews, along with the Catholic Church, represented an international element in a nation disposed towards isolation and intro-spection. He urged the United States to change its immigration laws to save Jews from Europe. And at the end of the War, besides expressing horror and contrition at the opening of the death camps, he denounced the signs that anti-Semitism was persisting.

The scandalous story 'The Blood of the Volsungs', written in 1905, depicts a highly cultivated and wealthy Berlin Jewish family with a dis-turbing resemblance to the Pringsheims of Munich, whose daughter Katia married Thomas Mann in 1905. Mann's father-in-law, an academic, was an authority on Wagner; the Pringsheims too had a room hung with

Gobelin tapestries; Katia even had a twin brother, and held hands with him at meals. Mann's letters to his brother Heinrich show how impressed he was by the family's sophistication: he sums them up as 'Tiergarten with genuine culture', referring to the exclusive Berlin district where his story is set; and he may occasionally have felt as much out of his depth as Beckerath. However, Mann seems to have been remarkably insouciant about possible resemblances; he had long been in the habit of using his family and acquaintances freely as materials for fiction. The story was due to appear in the *Neue Rundschau* (*New Review*), Germany's most prominent literary periodical, but its contents became known prematurely because some faulty proofs were used as packing-paper and sent to a Munich bookshop, where they were discovered and pieced together by an employee. Rumours circulated that Mann had taken revenge for humiliations supposedly endured in the household of his wealthy Jewish in-laws. Under pressure from the latter, Mann withdrew the story from publication. It appeared in a limited edition in 1921, and was not made available to the general public until after Mann's death.

The story illustrates how Jewish stereotypes were so ingrained in realist fiction as to blind Mann to its possible reception. Herr Aarenhold comes from a remote Eastern locality, and has made a fortune by dubious business deals and by his indomitable determination; Frau Aarenhold embarrasses everyone by her foreign appearance, elaborate hairdo, ostentatious jewellery, and Jewish syntax and vocabulary. The children, who despise their parents and their own Jewish blood, have ultra-Germanic names—Kunz, Märit, Siegmund, and Sieglinde (or Sieglind; both forms are used interchangeably)—and 'Jewish' physiques: protruding lips, hooked or flat noses, and dark hair and eyes. Their conversation is relentlessly intellectual and sophisticated, displaying a command of logic and an unrestrained capacity for aggression—the result, the narrator suggests, of an innate defensiveness—together with a contempt for the mass of humanity. Towards the end of the story Mann becomes increasingly explicit about the Jewish appearance of the twins, and his original ending (the version translated here) shows Siegmund's features, syntax, and vocabulary becoming caricaturally 'Jewish' at a deciding moment. This ending alarmed Oscar Bie, the editor of the *Neue Rundschau*, who asked Mann to change it. Mann reluctantly substituted: 'he should be grateful to us. He will lead a less trivial existence from now on.'

Surprise at the original ending should not prevent attentive readers from perceiving that Siegmund's aggressiveness is the obverse of a deep loneliness and insecurity. Outwardly assimilated, he has no friends; he and Sieglinde are sheltered from an outside world that he regards as threatening. He feels secure only with his sister. Their incest is an act of revenge on the Gentile world, a search for a real experience that has hitherto been absent from Siegmund's empty existence, and an attempt to realize their companionship to the full before it is destroyed by her marriage. The comparison of their appearance to that of Egyptian statues recalls the sibling incest practised in late Egyptian royal dynasties and invokes the conception of the Jew as Oriental. But their identification with the incestuous siblings Siegmund and Sieglinde in Wagner's *The Valkyrie* discloses the richest new seam of meaning. The twins are not, as one might suppose, symbolically identifying themselves with triumphant and heroic Germanic figures. For Wagner's Siegmund is a hunted and desperate man, his Sieglinde is unhappily married to the brutal Hunding, and the siblings belong to the Volsung family, the chosen race of the god Wotan, who is nevertheless compelled by destiny to harass and persecute them. Mann thus hints at a strange analogy between Wagner's characters and another chosen people whose god allows them to suffer incessant persecution.

As it was seven minutes to twelve, Wendelin entered the anteroom on the first floor and sounded the gong. Legs wide apart, in violet knee-breeches, he stood on a prayer-mat faded with age and belaboured the metal with the drum-stick. The brazen din, wild, barbaric, and too loud for its purpose, penetrated everywhere: into the drawing-rooms to right and left, the billiard room, the library, the conservatory, up and down all over the house, whose uniformly temperate atmosphere was thoroughly impregnated with a sweet and exotic perfume. At last it fell silent, and Wendelin went about other tasks for seven minutes longer, while Florian in the dining-room put the finishing touches to the breakfast table. But on the stroke of twelve the warlike summons rang out for the second time. And thereupon the family appeared.

Herr Aarenhold came with short steps from the library, where he had been busy with his old printed books. He was constantly acquiring literary antiquities, first editions in every language, precious and musty tomes. Gently rubbing his hands, he asked in his subdued and somewhat pained manner: 'Is Beckerath not here yet?'

'He's coming all right. Why wouldn't he come? It saves him breakfast in the restaurant,' replied Frau Aarenhold, ascending the stairs noiselessly on the thick carpet and passing the ancient miniature church organ on the landing.

Herr Aarenhold blinked. His wife was impossible. She was small, ugly, prematurely aged, and seemed to have been shrivelled under a foreign, hotter sun. A diamond necklace lay on her sunken bosom. She wore her grey hair, with many twists and cornices, arranged in a laborious and towering coiffure, in which, somewhere on the side, was fastened a large, colourfully sparkling diamond clasp, itself adorned with a white plume. Herr Aarenhold and the children had more than once condemned this hairdo in well-chosen words. But Frau Aarenhold adhered obstinately to her taste.

The children came: Kunz and Märit, Siegmund and Sieglind. Kunz was in a braided uniform, a handsome, tanned man with curling lips and a menacing duelling-scar. He was spending six weeks exercising with his regiment of hussars. Märit appeared in an uncorseted gown. She was a severe, ash-blonde girl of twenty-eight, with a hooked nose, the grey eyes of a bird of prey, and a bitter mouth. She was studying law, and insisted on going her own way, with a contemptuous expression.

Siegmund and Sieglind came last, hand in hand, from the second floor. They were twins, and the youngest: slender as wands and childlike of build despite their nineteen years. She was wearing a claret-coloured velvet dress, too heavy for her figure, and close in cut to the fashion of Cinquecento Florence. He wore a grey jacket suit with a raspberry-coloured raw silk tie, patent-leather shoes on his narrow feet, and cuff-links studded with small diamonds. His thick, dark facial hair was shaved, so that his thin, pale face with its dark, frowning eyebrows shared the ephebic character of his body. His head was covered with dense, dark curls, forcibly parted at one side, and growing far down over his temples. In her dark-brown hair, combed down over her ears in a deep, smooth fringe, lay a golden circlet, from which a large pearl hung down over her forehead—a present from him. Round one of his boyish wrists was a heavy golden chain—a present from her. They were very like each other. They had the same slightly flattened nose, the same full lips resting softly one upon the other, prominent cheekbones, dark and gleaming eyes. Most similar of all were their long, slender hands—so much so that his displayed no more masculine form, only a redder tinge than hers. And they constantly held each other's hands, undisturbed by the fact that the palms of both tended to perspire...

The family stood for a while on the carpets in the hall, scarcely speaking. At last von Beckerath, Sieglind's fiancé, came. Wendelin opened the vestibule door for him, and he came in wearing his black frock-coat and apologized in every direction for his late arrival. He was a civil servant and from a good family—small, canary-yellow, with a pointed beard and zealous good manners. Before beginning a sentence, he would suck in air through his open mouth while pressing his chin on to his chest.

He kissed Sieglind's hand and said:

'You too, Sieglinde, please forgive me! It's such a long way from the Ministry to the Tiergarten...' He was not yet allowed to be informal with her; she did not care for that. She replied without hesitation:

'Very long. And in view of its length, might you consider leaving your Ministry a little earlier?'

Kunz added, and his dark eyes became flashing slits:

'That would have a distinctly enlivening effect on the pace of our domestic life.'

'Oh, good Lord... so much to do...', said von Beckerath wearily. He was thirty-five.

The siblings had spoken promptly and sharply, with a seeming aggressiveness that was perhaps only an innate habit of defence, wounding, but probably only enjoying the precise use of words, so that it would have been pedantic to bear them a grudge. They accepted his wretched answer as though it were adequate for him, as though his sort did not need wit as self-defence. They made for the table, led by Herr Aarenhold, who wanted to show Herr von Beckerath that he was hungry.

They took their seats, they unfolded their stiff napkins. In the enormous, carpeted dining-room, surrounded by eighteenth-century *boiserie*,* with three electric chandeliers hanging from the ceiling, the family dinner-table with its seven places was dwarfed. It had been moved beside the big French window, beneath which, behind a narrow railing, skipped the dainty silver jet of a fountain, and which offered an extensive view over the still-wintry garden. The upper part of the walls was covered by Gobelin tapestries showing pastoral idylls, which, like the panelling, had in days of yore adorned a French chateau. The chairs round the table were low; their broad, yielding cushions were covered with Gobelins. Beside each set of cutlery on the strong, gleaming white, impeccably ironed damask cloth stood a tapering glass vase with two orchids. With his lean and careful hand Herr Aarenhold fastened his pince-nez half-way down his nose and read the menu, of which three copies lay on the table, with a mistrustful expression. He suffered from an infirmity of the solar plexus, that nerve-centre located below the stomach which can be the source of grave discomfort. He was thus obliged to scrutinize closely what he consumed.

There was beef-marrow bouillon, sole au vin blanc, pheasant, and pineapple. Nothing more. It was a family breakfast. But Herr Aarenhold was content: they were good, wholesome things. The soup came. A dumb-waiter attached to the sideboard bore it noiselessly down from the kitchen, and the servants, stooping and with expressions of concentration, handed it round the table, in a kind of ecstasy of service. It was in tiny cups made of the most delicate, translucent porcelain. The whitish lumps of marrow floated in the hot, golden-yellow liquid.

Herr Aarenhold felt stimulated by the warmth to release a little air. With cautious fingers he put the napkin to his mouth and cast about for words to express what was on his mind.

'Take another cup, Beckerath', he said. 'It's nourishing. Anyone who works has the right to look after himself, and enjoy it... Do you like eating? Does it give you pleasure? If not, it's your loss. For me every meal is a little feast. Someone said life is beautiful because it's so arranged that you can have four meals a day. A man after my own heart. But to appreciate this arrangement takes a certain youthfulness and gratitude that not everyone knows how to preserve... We get old; all right, there's nothing to be done about that. But what matters is that things should still feel new, and that you shouldn't take anything for granted... Now,' he continued, placing a little beef-marrow on a crumb from his roll and sprinkling salt on it, 'your circumstances are about to change; the level of your existence is due to rise not inconsiderably.' (Von Beckerath smiled.) 'If you want to enjoy your life, really enjoy it, consciously, artistically, then do your best never to get used to your new circumstances. Getting used to things is death. It means tedium. Don't get accustomed to things, don't let them become a matter of course, retain a childlike taste for the sweetness of prosperity. You see... For many years now I've been able to allow myself a few of life's comforts' (von Beckerath smiled), 'and yet I assure you that even now, every morning that God brings, when I wake up I feel my heart skipping because my blanket is of silk. That's youthfulness... I know how I got where I am; and yet I can gaze round like an enchanted prince...'

All the children exchanged glances, so openly that Herr Aarenhold could not help noticing and became visibly embarrassed. He knew that they were united against him and that they despised him: for his origins, for the blood that flowed in him and that they had received from him, for the way he had acquired his wealth, for his hobbies, which they considered unsuitable for him, for his self-indulgence, to which they likewise thought him not entitled, for his loose and poetic loquacity which lacked the restraint of good taste... He knew this, and in a way he agreed with them; he felt some measure of guilt towards them. But in the last resort he had to assert his own personality, had to lead his own life and be free to talk about it, especially the last. He had been a worm, a louse, he had indeed; but the very ability to feel this so fervently and with such self-contempt had been the cause of that tough, never-satisfied perseverance which had made him great... Herr Aarenhold had been born in a remote Eastern locality, had wed the daughter of a well-endowed businessman, and by dint of bold and prudent enterprise, of grandiose machinations, centring on a mine, on the exploitation of a coal deposit, he had guided a mighty and inexhaustible torrent of gold into his treasury...

The fish course descended. The servants hastened with it from the sideboard through the expanse of the room. They handed round the creamy sauce that accompanied it and poured out hock that tingled gently on the tongue. The conversation turned to Sieglind's and Beckerath's wedding.

It was imminent: it was to take place in a week. The trousseau was mentioned, a route was mapped out for the honeymoon in Spain. In fact it was Herr Aarenhold alone who discussed these subjects, supported by well-mannered docility on von Beckerath's part. Frau Aarenhold ate voraciously and, as was her wont, answered questions only with counter-questions that were less than helpful. Her speech was laced with strange, guttural words, expressions from the dialect of her childhood. Märit was full of silent antipathy towards the church ceremony which was being planned and which offended her entirely enlightened beliefs. Herr Aarenhold, too, regarded this ceremony with some reserve, since von Beckerath was a Protestant. A Protestant ceremony, in his view, had no aesthetic value. It would have been a different matter if von Beckerath had professed the Catholic faith.—Kunz remained mute, because his mother embarrassed him in von Beckerath's presence. And neither Siegmund nor Sieglind displayed any interest. They held each other's slender, moist hands between their chairs. Now and again their glances met, fused, struck an accord which excluded all outsiders. Von Beckerath was sitting on Sieglind's other side.

'Fifty hours,' said Herr Aarenhold, 'and you can be in Madrid, if you want. Progress never stops, it took me sixty by the shortest route... I assume you prefer the overland route to the sea journey from Rotterdam?'

Von Beckerath hastened to prefer the overland route.

'But you can hardly bypass Paris. You could travel direct via Lyons... Sieglinde knows Paris. But you should not let slip the opportunity... I leave it up to you whether you want to make an overnight stay before that. The choice of the place where you begin your honeymoon may fittingly be referred to you... '

Sieglinde turned her head, turned towards her fiancé for the first time: openly and frankly, quite unconcerned about whether anyone was watching her. She looked into the polite face beside her with big dark eyes, scrutinizing, expectant, inquiring, with a grave, luminous glance that for those three seconds spoke without thought, like that of an animal. But between their chairs she was holding the slender hand of her twin brother, whose linked eyebrows formed two black creases at the base of his nose...

The conversation slid away, skirmished fitfully to and fro for a while, touched on a consignment of fresh cigars which, packed in zinc, had arrived from Havana expressly for Herr Aarenhold, and then circled round a point, a purely logical question which Kunz had raised casually: whether, if a was the necessary and sufficient condition for b, b must also be the necessary and sufficient condition for a. They disputed this, analysed it keenly, cited examples, treated the matter from every possible angle, attacked each other with a steely and abstract dialectic, and became exceedingly heated. Märit introduced a philosophical distinction between the real and the causal ground into the debate. Kunz, raising his head and talking down at her, dismissed the 'causal ground' as a pleonasm. Märit insisted irritably on the value of her own terminology. Herr Aarenhold sat upright, lifted a scrap of bread between thumb and forefinger, and undertook to explain the whole matter. He suffered a complete fiasco. The children laughed at him. Even Frau Aarenhold rebuffed him. 'What are you talking for?' said she. 'Did you learn that? You never learnt nothing!' And when von Beckerath pressed his chin on to his chest and sucked in air through his mouth in order to deliver his opinion, the conversation had already moved on.

Siegmund was speaking. He was talking in a tone of ironic tenderness about the winning simplicity and naturalness of an acquaintance who had remained ignorant of which article of clothing was termed a sports jacket and which a dinner jacket. This Parsifal* talked about a checked dinner jacket... Kunz knew a yet more touching case of unspoiled innocence, involving someone who had turned up for afternoon tea in a dinner suit.

'A dinner suit in the afternoon?' said Sieglinde, curling her lip... 'That's on the animal level.'

Von Beckerath laughed zealously, especially since his conscience reminded him that he himself had been to tea in a dinner suit... Thus, over the game course, the conversation moved from general cultural questions to art: to the visual arts, of which von Beckerath was a connoisseur and amateur, to literature and the theatre, which enjoyed the highest esteem in the Aarenhold household, although Siegmund went in for painting.

The discussion became lively and general, the children took a decisive part in it, they spoke well, their gestures were energetic and imperious. They marched in the vanguard of taste and demanded the utmost. Mere intentions, feelings, dreams and determined struggle were mercilessly dismissed; they were ruthless in requiring ability, achievement, success in the savage contest of talents, and they hailed the victorious work of art without admiration, but with appreciation. Herr Aarenhold himself said to Beckerath:

'You're very good-natured, my dear fellow. You stand up for good intentions. *Results*, my friend! You say: "What he does may not be first-rate, but he was only a peasant before he took up art, so even this is astonishing." Not a bit of it. Achievement is absolute. There are no mitigating circumstances. Let him either do something first-rate, or shovel shit. How far would I have got with your kindly outlook? I could have said to myself: "You were penniless when you started; if you work your way up to manage your own office, that's impressive." Well, I wouldn't be sitting here now. I had to force the world to take note of me; very well, I expect people to force me to take note of them. Here's Rhodes; be good enough to dance!'*

The children laughed. For a moment they did not despise him. They sat in deep, soft chairs round the dining-room table, in indolent attitudes, with spoiled, capricious expressions, they sat in secure luxury, but they talked as sharply as in places where it matters, where clarity, toughness, self-defence, and watchful wit are necessary for survival. Their praise was qualified agreement; their criticism, agile, alert, and irreverent, disarmed their opponents in a flash, checked enthusiasm, left it speechless and silly. A work whose unrelenting intellectuality seemed to forestall any objection was deemed 'very good', and ineptitude resulting from passion was mocked. Von Beckerath, who tended to show defenceless enthusiasm, had a hard time, especially since he was older. He kept shrinking on his chair, pressed his chin on to his chest and breathed through his open mouth, distressed and oppressed by their cheerful superiority. They never failed to contradict, as though they thought it impossible, pitiable, shameful, not to contradict; they were adept at contradicting, and their eyes became flashing slits as they did so. They would pounce on a word, a single one, that he had used, tear it to shreds, throw it away, and produce another, deadly in its aptness, that whirred, hit the bull's-eye, and stuck there quivering... By the time breakfast was over, von Beckerath's eyes were red and he looked bemused.

Suddenly—they were sprinkling sugar on the pineapple slices—Siegmund said, screwing up his face, as he was wont to do while speaking, like someone dazzled by the sun:

'Oh, listen, Beckerath, before we forget, one thing... Sieglind and I crave a boon from you... It's *The Valkyrie* tonight at the opera... Sieglind and I would like to hear it together once more... may we? Of course it depends on your grace and favour... '

'How thoughtful!' said Herr Aarenhold.

Kunz drummed the rhythm of the Hunding motif on the tablecloth.

Von Beckerath, dismayed at having his permission asked for anything, replied zealously:

'But of course, Siegmund... and you, Sieglind... I think that's a very good idea... you absolutely must go... I shouldn't mind joining you... It's an excellent cast tonight.'

The Aarenholds bent over the plates, smiling. Von Beckerath, left out, blinking, and struggling to see the joke, tried as best he could to share their mirth.

Siegmund said quickly:

'Actually, I think the cast is bad. For the rest, be fully assured of our gratitude; but you've misunderstood. Sieglinde and I are asking to be allowed to listen to *The Valkyrie* one last time *alone* together before the wedding. I don't know if you... '

'But of course... I quite understand. That's charming. You absolutely must go... '

'Thank you. We're most grateful.—So I'll order Percy and Leiermann to be harnessed.'

'Permit me to remark,' said Herr Aarenhold, 'that your mother and I are going out to dinner at the Erlangers', and using Percy and Leiermann. You will deign to make do with Baal and Zampa and to use the brown coupé.'

'And seats?' asked Kunz.

'I booked them ages ago', said Siegmund, tossing back his head.

They laughed, looking the bridegroom full in the face.

Herr Aarenhold unwrapped a belladonna powder* with his pointed fingers and shook it cautiously into his mouth. Thereupon he lit a fat cigarette, which at once diffused a delicious fragrance. The servants leapt up to draw back the chairs behind him and Frau Aarenhold. Orders were issued to serve coffee in the conservatory. Kunz, in a sharp voice, demanded his dog-cart so that he could go to the barracks.

Siegmund was dressing for the opera. It had already taken him an hour. He possessed an extraordinary and continual urge to cleanse himself, so much so that he spent a considerable part of each day at the wash-basin. He was now standing in front of his large Empire mirror with its white frame, dipping his powder-puff into its embossed box and powdering his chin and his cheeks, which were freshly shaved; for his facial hair grew so fast that when he was going out in the evening he was obliged to rid himself of it a second time.

He was a colourful sight standing there: in pink silk underpants and socks, red morocco slippers, and a padded smoking-jacket with a dark pattern and light grey-fur lapels. And around him was his large bedroom, furnished with elegant and practical white-painted objects, and behind its windows lay the bare and misty massed tree-tops of the Tiergarten.

As darkness was falling fast, he switched on the lamps, which, arranged in a large circle on the white ceiling, filled the room with milky radiance, and drew the velvet curtains in front of the twilit window-panes. The light was reflected in the highly polished watery depths of the cupboard, the washstand, the dressing-table; it flashed in the facets of the cut-glass bottles on the tiled shelves. And Siegmund continued working on himself. Now and again, when a thought struck him, the linked eyebrows at the base of his nose would form two black creases.

His day had passed as his days usually passed: emptily and swiftly. As the opera began at half-past six and he had begun changing at half-past four, he had scarcely had an afternoon. After resting from two to three on his chaise-longue, he had taken tea and then used the extra hour, reclining in a deep leather armchair in the study he shared with his brother Kunz, to read a couple of pages in each of several newly published novels. Although he had judged one and all to be lamentably feeble performances, he had sent a couple to the book-binder to have them artistically bound for his library.

Besides, he had worked in the morning. He had spent the hour from ten to eleven in his professor's studio. This professor, an artist of European reputation, was developing Siegmund's talent for drawing and painting and received two thousand marks a month from Herr Aarenhold. Nonetheless, what Siegmund painted was laughable. He knew that himself and was far from attaching any ardent expectations to his artistry. He was too acute not to realize that his mode of life was hardly the most conducive to the development of a creative gift.

The furnishings of his life were so rich, so manifold, so overladen, that hardly any room was left for living. Each item of furnishing was so precious and beautiful that its pretensions surpassed the purpose it served, caused bewilderment, consumed attention. Siegmund had been born to superfluity, he was undoubtedly used to it. Yet it remained the case that this superfluity never ceased to preoccupy and excite him, to stimulate him with constant pleasure. He was in the same situation, whether he liked it or not, as Herr Aarenhold, who practised the art of never getting used to anything...

He liked reading, coveted the word and the spirit like weapons to which he was directed by a deep-seated compulsion. But he had never surrendered to a book and lost himself in it, as happens when this one book seems to you the single most important thing, a little world that you cannot see beyond and in which you become absorbed and immersed, in order to draw sustenance even from the last syllable. Books and periodicals came to him in floods, he could buy them all, they rose in heaps around him, and when he wanted to read, he was disturbed by the quantity that still had to be read. But the books were bound. In embossed leather, adorned with Siegmund Aarenhold's handsome *ex libris*, they stood in self-sufficient splendour, weighing down his life like a possession he could not master.

The day was his, was free, was given to him with all its hours from sunrise to sundown; and yet within himself Siegmund found no time to desire anything, let alone to accomplish anything. He was no hero, he did not command a giant's strength. The preambles, the luxurious preparations for whatever might be real and serious, consumed what energies he had available. How much care and cogitation were expended on a perfect and painstaking toilette, how much attention went on monitoring his wardrobe, his supplies of cigarettes, soap, perfume, how much decisiveness was used in the moments, recurring twice or thrice a day, when what counted was choosing a tie! And it did count. It mattered. Let the country's blond citizens go about heedlessly in elastic-sided boots and soft collars. He of all people, he must be unassailable and without reproach in his outward appearance from top to toe...

In the end, no one expected any more from him than that. Now and again, when unease about what might be 'real' stirred faintly in him, he felt it being deadened and dissolved by this lack of others' expectations... In their house time was so organized as to make the day elapse quickly and forestall a feeling of emptiness. The next mealtime was always approaching. Dinner was before seven; the evening, when one could idle with a good conscience, was long. The days slipped away, and the seasons came and went just as rapidly. Two of the summer months were spent in their little castle on the lake, the broad and magnificent garden with the tennis-courts, the cool paths in the park, and the bronze statues on the close-cropped lawns; and the third by the sea, in the mountains, in hotels that sought to surpass the extravagance of home... Recently, on a few winter days, he had had himself driven to the university to hear a conveniently timed lecture on art history; he no longer went, for his olfactory nerves deemed that the other gentlemen took far too few baths...

Instead he went for walks with Sieglinde. She had been at his side since the dawn of memory, she had been close to him since the two had lisped their first words, taken their first toddling steps, and he had no friend, had never had one, save her who had been born with him, his richly bejewelled, dark and adorable likeness, whose moist and slender hand he held while the sumptuous days slipped past them with sightless eyes. They took fresh flowers on their walks, a bunch of violets or lilies of the valley, at which they sniffed alternately or sometimes both together. As they walked, they breathed in the sweet scent with voluptuous and careless self-abandonment, coddling themselves with it like egoistic invalids, seeking intoxication as people do who have lost all hope, dismissing the malodorous world with an inner gesture and loving each other for the sake of their exquisite futility. But what they said was sharp and sparkling; its targets were the people they met, the things they had seen, heard, read, the things done by others who existed merely to expose their works to words, definitions, witty contradictions...

Then von Beckerath had come, employed in the Ministry and from a good family. He had sought Sieglind's hand, supported by Herr Aarenhold's benevolent neutrality, Frau Aarenhold's advocacy, and the eager assistance of Kunz the hussar. He had been patient, assiduous, and infinitely well-mannered. And at last, after telling him many times that she did not love him, Sieglind had started looking at him with mute, expectant scrutiny, with a gleaming dark glance that spoke without thought, like that of an animal—and had said Yes. And Siegmund himself, her lord and master, had encouraged this outcome; he despised himself, but he was not opposed, because von Beckerath was employed in the Ministry and from a good family... Now and again, while he worked on his toilette, his linked eyebrows formed two black creases at the base of his nose...

He stood on the polar-bear skin that stretched out its paws beside his bed, his feet disappearing into its fur, and took the folded dress-shirt after washing himself all over with toilet-water. His yellowish torso, over which the starched and shimmering linen slid, was as thin as a boy's and shaggy with black hair. He then clad himself in black silk underpants, socks of black silk and black garters with silver buckles, put on the ironed trousers whose black fabric gave off a silky shimmer, fastened white silk braces over his narrow shoulders and began, his foot placed on a stool, to do up the buttons of his patent-leather boots.—There was a knock.

'Can I come in, Gigi?' asked Sieglinde outside...

'Yes, come', he answered.

She entered, her toilette already complete. She was wearing a dress of shining sea-green silk with a wide border of ecru embroidery round its angular neckline. Above her belt two embroidered peacocks, facing each other, held a garland in their bills. Sieglinde's deep dark hair was now without ornament, but a large egg-shaped jewel on a thin pearl chain lay on her bare throat, whose skin was the colour of smoked meerschaum. Over her arm hung a heavy shawl interlaced with silver.

'I shall not conceal from you', she said, 'that the carriage is waiting.'

'I should not scruple to maintain that it can exercise a few more minutes' patience,' came his repartee. It was soon ten minutes. She sat on the white velvet chaise-longue and watched him working more zealously.

From a colourful jumble of ties he chose a white piqué band and began knotting it in front of the mirror.

'Beckerath', she said, 'still wears his coloured ties knotted cross-wise, as the fashion was last year.'

'Beckerath', he said, 'is the most trivial existence into which I have ever cast a glance.' Then he added, turning round to her and screwing up his face like someone dazzled by the sun:

'By the way, I should like to ask you to make no further mention of that Germanic type in the course of the evening.'

She gave a short laugh and replied:

'You may rest assured that I shall have no difficulty in complying.'

He put on his piqué waistcoat with its deep neck-line and pulled on the dress coat which had been tried on five times and whose soft silken lining caressed his hands as they slipped through the sleeves.

'Let me see which set of buttons you've chosen', said Sieglind, going over to him. They were the amethyst buttons. The buttons of his shirt-front, his cuffs, and his white waistcoat matched them.

She contemplated him with admiration, with pride, with devotion—a deep, dark tenderness in her shining eyes. As her lips were resting so softly one upon the other, he kissed them. They sat down on the chaise-longue to fondle each other for a moment, as they loved to do.

'You're quite, quite soft again', she said, stroking his shaven cheeks.

'Your little arms feel like satin', he said, running his hand over her delicate forearm while breathing in the violet scent of her hair.

She kissed him on his closed eyes; he kissed her on the throat, next to the jewel. They kissed each other's hands. Each loved the other with sweet sensuality for their pampered and precious elegance and their good fragrance. Finally they played like puppies, biting each other with their lips. Then he stood up.

'Don't let's arrive too late this evening', he said. He squeezed the mouth of the perfume bottle on to his handkerchief, rubbed a drop between his slender red hands, took his gloves, and declared himself ready.

He put out the light and they went: along the pink-lit corridor, where old, dark paintings hung, past the organ, and down the stairs. Wendelin, gigantic in his long yellow greatcoat, was standing in the ground-floor vestibule, waiting with their coats. They let him help them into them. Sieglinde's dark little head half disappeared in the silver-fox collar of hers. They went, followed by the servant, through the stone-paved hallway and stepped outside.

It was mild, with a little snow, in the whitish light, falling in large, ragged flakes. The coupé was halted close to the house. The coach-man, his hand on his cockaded hat, bent down slightly from the box while Wendelin ensured that the siblings climbed in safely. Then the door closed, Wendelin swung himself up beside the coachman, and the carriage, promptly attaining a rapid pace, crunched over the gravel of the front garden, glided through the high and wide-open lattice door, turned to the right-about in a supple curve, and rolled away...

The small, soft space they were sitting in was gently heated.

'Shall I close the curtain?' asked Siegmund... And when she agreed, he drew the brown silk curtains across the polished panes.

They were in the heart of the city. Lights flew past behind the drapes. All round the regular, rapid hoof-beats of their horses, the silent speed of their carriage bearing them springily over the uneven ground, the great mechanism of life roared, shrieked, and thundered.

And sequestered from it, softly sheltered from it, they sat motionless in the padded brown silk cushions—hand in hand.

The carriage drew up and halted. Wendelin was at the door to assist them in descending. In the brightness of the arc-lamps, grey, shivering people watched their arrival. They passed between their inquisitive, hostile glances, followed by the servant, through the vestibule. It was already late and quiet. They climbed the staircase, threw their outer garments over Wendelin's arm, lingered for a second side by side in front of a tall mirror, and stepped through the little box door into the row of seats. The clattering of the chairs, the last upsurge of conversation before silence, received them. At the moment when the usher pushed the velvet armchairs under them, the auditorium was swathed in darkness, and down below, with a wild accent, the overture began.

Storm, storm... Having been wafted there in an easy, privileged manner, not distracted or worn out by hindrances, by small irritating mishaps, Siegmund and Sieglinde found their bearings immediately. Storm and raging thunder, wild weather in the woods. The god's harsh command rang out, was repeated, distorted with anger, and the thunder crashed obediently. The curtain flew up as though blown open by the gale. There was the heathen hall, with the hearth glowing in the darkness, the outline of the ash-tree's trunk towering in the centre. Siegmund, a rubicund man with a bread-coloured beard, appeared in the wooden doorway and leaned, exhausted from pursuit, against the doorpost. Then his strong legs, wrapped in pelts and thongs, bore him forward with tragic, trailing steps. His blue eyes under his blond brows, the blond forelock of his wig, were directed at the conductor with a glazed look as though issuing an appeal; and at last the music fell back, fell silent, to let his voice be heard, sounding clear and brazen, although he lowered it panting. He sang briefly that he must rest, no matter whose the hearth; and with the last word he dropped heavily on to the bearskin and lay there, his head resting on his fleshy arm. His chest heaved as he slept.

A minute passed, filled by the singing, speaking, telling surge of music, rolling its flood at the feet of the events... Then Sieglinde entered from the left. She had an alabaster bosom that rose and fell wonderfully in the neckline of her fur-draped muslin dress. She caught sight of the strange man with astonishment; and she pressed her chin on to her breast so that it formed creases, placed her lips in position, and gave voice to her astonishment in notes that rose from her larynx, soft and warm, to be shaped by her tongue, her mobile mouth...

She tended him. Bending down to him, so that her breast blossomed towards him from her rough pelt, she gave him the horn with both hands. He drank. The music spoke movingly of refreshment and cooling kindness. Then they contemplated each other with an early rapture, an early, dim recognition, silently absorbed in the moment, which resounded down below as a deep, drifting song...

She brought him mead, touched the horn first with her lips, and then watched him taking a long draught. And once more their glances met and melted, once more the deep melody down below drifted and yearned... Then he took his leave, gloomy, painfully repulsing her, went to the door with his bare arms hanging down, to take his sorrow, his solitude, his persecuted, pariah existence away from her, back into the wilderness. She called to him, and when he did not hear, she recklessly revealed, with upraised hands, the confession of her own misfortune. He stood. She lowered her eyes. At their feet a dark tale was told of sorrow uniting them both. He stayed. His arms crossed, he stood before the hearth, awaiting his fate.

Hunding came, paunchy and knock-kneed like a cow. His beard was black with brown tufts. His iron-clad motif announced his coming, and there he stood, sombre and clumsy, leaning on his spear, and gazed with a buffalo's eyes at the guest whose presence he then welcomed from a kind of primitive civility. His bass was rusty and colossal.

Sieglinde prepared the dinner; and while she worked, Hunding's slow and suspicious gaze went back and forth between her and the stranger. This booby could see clearly that they resembled each other, were of one and the same kind, that footloose, unruly, and extraordinary kind that he hated and felt unequal to...

Then they sat down, and Hunding introduced himself, explaining in a few simple words his simple, orderly, universally respected existence. But he thus compelled Siegmund to present himself likewise, which was incomparably more difficult. Yet Siegmund sang—sang clearly and enchantingly about his life and sorrow and how he had been born as two, a twin sister and himself... assumed a false name, in the manner of people who have to be a little careful, and gave an excellent account of the hatred, the malice, with which his foreign father and he had been persecuted, of the burning of their hall, the disappearance of his sister, the outlawed, harried, maligned existence of the old and the young man in the forest and how in the end he had mysteriously lost his father as well... And then Siegmund sang the most painful part: his desire for people, his yearning and his infinite loneliness. For men and women, he sang, for friendship and love, he had appealed and yet always been rebuffed. A curse had lain on him, the stigma of his strange descent had always marked him out. His language was not that of others and theirs was not his. What he found good, annoyed the great mass, what they held in high honour, roused him to rancour. Fighting and fury had been his portion, always and everywhere, contempt and hatred and scorn were hard on his heels, because he was of a strange kind, hopelessly different from the others...

Hunding's attitude to all this was entirely characteristic of him. No sympathy and no understanding emerged from his answer: only resentment and sombre suspicion of Siegmund's dubious, eccentric, and irregular mode of existence. And when he realized that he had in his own house the outlaw whom he had been summoned and sent to pursue, he behaved just as his four-square pedantry would lead one to expect. With the civility that suited him so badly, he again declared that his house was holy and would shelter the fugitive tonight, but that tomorrow he would have the honour of slaying Siegmund in combat. Thereupon he harshly ordered Sieglinde to spice his night-draught and wait for him in bed, barked out two or three further threats, and then departed, taking all his weapons with him and leaving Siegmund alone in the most desperate situation.

Siegmund, leaning forward in his armchair and bending over the velvet-covered balustrade, cupped his dark boyish head in his red and slender hand. His eyebrows formed two black creases, and one of his feet, poised on the heel of his patent-leather boot, was in continual nervous motion, restlessly turning and vibrating. He checked it on hearing a whisper next to him: 'Gigi... '

And as he turned his head, there was an impudent twist to his mouth.

Sieglind was offering him a mother-of-pearl box of brandy cherries.

'The maraschino beans are underneath', she whispered. But he took only a cherry, and as he undid the silk-paper wrapping, she bent down to his ear once more and said:

'She comes back to him immediately.'

'I was not entirely unaware of that,' he said, so loudly that several heads turned angrily towards them... Below them, the great Siegmund was singing alone in the dark. From the depths of his chest he called for the sword, the shining weapon which he could swing if the feelings locked in his angry heart should one day break into open revolt: his hatred and his yearning... He saw the sword's hilt gleaming in the tree, saw its glitter go out with the fire on the hearth, sank down into desperate sleep—and propped himself on his hands in delicious alarm when Sieglind crept over to him in the dark.

Hunding was sleeping like a stone, drunk and drugged. They rejoiced together at outwitting the clumsy blockhead—and their eyes had the same way of contracting in a smile... But then Sieglind glanced covertly at the conductor and received her cue, placed her lips in position, and sang in great detail of how things were—sang heart-rendingly of how the solitary girl who had grown up strange and wild had been given to the coarse and gloomy man and still been told to think herself lucky at making such a respectable marriage that might make people forget her obscure origins... sang in deep, comforting tones of the old man in the hat and how he had thrust the sword into the ash-tree's trunk—for the one who alone was destined to free it from its confinement; if only he could be the one, she sang, beside herself, he whom she thought of and knew and longed for in grief, the friend who was more than her friend, her comforter in distress, the avenger of her disgrace, he whom once she had lost and for whom she had wept in shame, her brother in sorrow, her rescuer, her deliverer...

Then Siegmund enfolded her in his two fleshy, rubicund arms, pressed her cheek to the pelt on his chest and sang over her head, in a voice unleashed and ringing like silver, proclaiming his jubilation to the skies. His chest was heavy with the oath that bound him to her, his sweet companion. All the yearning of his much-maligned life was satisfied in her, and all that had been insultingly denied him when he forced himself on men and women, when he begged for friendship and love with an impudence springing from shyness and the consciousness of his stigma—he had found it all in her. Her disgrace matched his sorrow, she was dishonoured as he was outlawed, and revenge—their sibling love should now be their revenge!

A gust of wind snarled, the great wooden door flew open, a flood of white electric light poured into the hall, and suddenly, stripped of darkness, they were standing there and singing the song of spring and its sister, love.

They crouched on the bearskin, they looked at each other in the light and sang sweet endearments. Their bare arms touched, they held each other by the temples, gazed into each other's eyes, and their mouths were close together as they sang. Their eyes and their temples, their brows and their voices, they compared them and found them alike. Urgent, increasing recognition wrested from him his father's name, she called him by his: Siegmund! Siegmund! He swung the liberated sword above his head, she blissfully sang to him who she was: his twin sister Sieglinde... he stretched out his arms in ecstasy to her, his bride, she sank on his heart, the curtains came swishing together, the music swirled in a raging, roaring, foaming frenzy of furious passion, swirled and, with a mighty crash, was still!

Hearty applause. The lights came on. A thousand people rose, covertly stretched, and applauded, their bodies already making for the exit, only their heads still turned to the stage and the singers, who appeared side by side in front of the curtain, like masks outside a fairground stall. Hunding emerged too and smiled politely, despite all that had been happening...

Siegmund pushed back his chair and stood up. He felt hot; a red glow was smouldering on his cheekbones, under his pale, thin, and close-shaven cheeks.

'As far as I am concerned,' he said, 'I shall now seek more salubrious air. Incidentally, the Siegmund was almost feeble.'

'And the orchestra', said Sieglinde, 'felt impelled to drag out the spring song insufferably.'

'Sentimental,' said Siegmund, shrugging his narrow shoulders under his dinner jacket. 'Are you coming?'

She hesitated for a minute, sitting propped on her elbows and gazing over at the stage. He looked at her as she rose and picked up the silver shawl in order to go with him. Her full lips, resting softly one upon the other, were twitching...

They went into the foyer, moved amid the sluggish crowd, greeted acquaintances, promenaded down the stairs, sometimes hand in hand.

'I should like an ice,' she said, 'if it were not exceedingly likely to be mediocre.'

'Impossible!' he said. And so they ate some of the sweets from their box, brandy cherries and bean-shaped chocolates filled with maraschino.

When the bell rang, they looked askance with a kind of contempt at the crowd as it was seized by haste and blocked the doorways; they waited till the corridors were quiet and entered their box at the last minute, as the light faded and darkness settled, silencing and quelling the confused animation of the auditorium... The bell rang softly, the conductor stretched out his arms, and the sublime sounds at his command once more filled the ears that had now had a little respite.

Siegmund looked at the orchestra. The sunken space was lighted by contrast with the listening auditorium and filled with work, with hands fingering, arms fiddling, cheeks puffing and blowing, with simple, zealous people humbly accomplishing the work of a great, sorrowful creative force—the work that was manifest up above in childlike lofty visions... A work! How was a work created? There was pain in Siegmund's breast, a burning or gnawing pain, a kind of sweet anguish—for what? It was so obscure, so disgracefully unclear. He felt two words: creativity... passion. And as the heat throbbed in his temples, he sensed a yearning insight that creativity stemmed from passion and again took the form of passion. He saw the pale, exhausted woman on the lap of the fugitive man to whom she had yielded herself, saw her love and distress and felt that life had to be like that in order to be creative. He looked at his own life, that life composed of softness and wit, indulgence and negation, luxury and contradiction, material opulence and mental clarity, wealthy security and playful hatred, that life with no experiences, only logical games, no feelings, only deadly definitions—and a burning or gnawing pain was in his breast, a kind of sweet anguish—for what? For the work? Experience? Passion?

Swishing curtains, grand finale! Light, applause, a rush for the exits. Siegmund and Sieglind spent this interval like the last. They said hardly anything, walked slowly along the corridors and up and down the stairs, sometimes hand in hand. She offered him brandy cherries, but he would not take any more. She looked at him, and as he fixed his gaze on her she withdrew hers, walking silently and in a somewhat tense posture at his side and letting him contemplate her. Her childlike shoulders, under the silver lacing, were a little too high and vertical, like those of Egyptian statues. On her cheekbones lay the same heat that he could feel on his own.

They again waited until the crowd had dispersed and occupied their armchairs at the last moment. Gale, racing clouds, grotesque heathen hallooing. On the rocky stage eight ladies, somewhat subaltern in appearance, represented virginal and laughing savagery. Brünnhilde's terror turned their merriment into fearfulness. Wotan's rage, approaching in dread, swept the sisters away, descended on Brünnhilde alone, almost annihilating her, spent its fury and was slowly, slowly soothed into mild melancholy. The end was close. A great vista, a sublime intention was revealed. All was epic and religious consecration. Brünnhilde slept; the god descended the crags. Burly flames, darting up and dispersing, blazed all round the boards. In sparks and red smoke, with the fire's soporific jingle and lullaby dancing and flickering magically around her, the Valkyrie, covered by mail-coat and shield, lay outstretched on her mossy bed. But in the womb of the woman whom she had found time to rescue it was stubbornly germinating, the hated, irreverent, and divinely chosen race, from which the twins had sprung to unite their distress and sorrow to form such free rapture...

As Siegmund and Sieglinde left their box, Wendelin was standing outside, gigantic in his yellow greatcoat, holding their outer garments in readiness. He descended the stairs, a towering slave, behind the two dainty, warmly wrapped, dark, curious creatures.

The carriage was standing ready. The two horses, tall, elegant, and exactly similar, were waiting on their slender legs, quietly gleaming in the misty winter night, only occasionally tossing their heads proudly. The small, heated, silk-cushioned space enfolded the twins. The door closed behind them. For a moment, barely a second, the coupé stood quivering from the gymnastic feat with which the practised Wendelin swung himself up beside the coachman. Then it glided softly and swiftly forwards, and the portals of the theatre were left behind.

And again that noiseless, rolling speed accompanied by the regular, rapid hoof-beats of the horses, carrying them gently and springily over the uneven ground, tenderly sheltering them from the shrill life all around. They were silent, sequestered from daily life, as though still on their velvet chairs opposite the stage, and still breathing the same atmosphere. Nothing at hand could estrange them from the world of raw and exuberant passion that had cast its spell on them and drawn them into it... At first they did not realize why the carriage had come to a halt; they thought there was some obstacle in the way. But they had already stopped outside their parents' house, and Wendelin appeared at the door.

The porter had emerged from his lodge to open the gate for them. 'Are Herr and Frau Aarenhold back yet?' asked Siegmund, looking over the porter's head and screwing up his face like someone dazzled by the sun...

They were not yet back from dinner at the Erlangers'. Kunz was not at home either. As for Märit, she was likewise absent, no one knew where, since she insisted on going her own way.

After being helped out of their coats in the ground-floor vestibule, they went up the stairs, through the first-floor ante-room, and into the dining-room. Its enormous splendour was veiled in semi-darkness. Only one chandelier was lit, above the table, already laid, at the further end, and Florian was waiting there. They strode quickly and noiselessly over the carpeted expanse. Florian pushed the chairs under them as they sat down. Then a sign from Siegmund conveyed that he was no longer needed.

On the table were a plate of sandwiches, a bowl of fruit, a carafe of red wine. The electrically heated kettle, surrounded by accessories, was purring on an immense silver tea-tray.

Siegmund ate a caviar sandwich and drank a hasty draught of the wine that was glowing darkly in his delicate glass. Then he complained, in an irritated voice, that the combination of caviar and red wine was uncivilized. With curt movements he took a cigarette from his silver case and began to smoke, leaning back with his hands in his pockets and screwing up his face as he slid the cigarette from one side of his mouth to the other. His cheeks, under their prominent bones, were already beginning to assume a darker hue from the growth of his beard. His eyebrows formed two black creases at the base of his nose.

Sieglinde had made tea for herself and added a drop of Burgundy. Her full, soft lips enveloped the thin edge of the cup, and as she drank, her large, moist, dark eyes gazed across at Siegmund.

She put down the cup and cupped her dark, sweet, exotic head on her slender, pinkish hand. Her eyes remained fixed on him, so expressively, with such flowing and persuasive eloquence, that what she actually said seemed less than nothing in comparison.

'Won't you have anything more to eat, Gigi?'

'Since I am smoking,' he replied, 'it is implausible to assume that I intend to eat anything more.'

'But you've taken nothing since teatime, except sweets. At least a peach...'

He shrugged his shoulders and rolled them to and fro in his dinner jacket like a stubborn child.

'This is boring. I'm going upstairs. Goodnight.'

He drank the rest of his red wine, threw the napkin away, stood up, and disappeared, ambling peevishly through the twilit room with his cigarette in his mouth and his hands in his pockets.

He went into his bedroom and put on the light—not much, he switched on only two or three of the lamps which formed a large circle on the ceiling, and then stood still, wondering what to do next. His parting from Sieglind had not been final. This was not how they were accustomed to say goodnight to each other. She would come back, that was certain. He threw off his dinner jacket, put on his fur-trimmed smoking jacket, and took a new cigarette. Then he stretched out on the chaise-longue, sat upright, tried lying sidelong with his cheek on the silk cushions, threw himself on his back once more, and lay in this position for a while with his hands under his head.

The subtle and acrid fragrance of tobacco mingled with that of the cosmetics, the soap, the toilet water. Siegmund breathed in these scents floating in the tepid air of the room; he was aware of them and found them sweeter than usual. Closing his eyes, he surrendered to them like someone painfully enjoying a touch of bliss and delicate happiness amid his harsh and unusual fate...

Suddenly he rose, threw away his cigarette, and stepped in front of the white wardrobe, which had immense mirrors let into its three parts. He stood in front of the middle one, very close, eyeball to eyeball with himself, and contemplated his face. He scrutinized every feature carefully and curiously, opened both wings of the wardrobe and, standing among three mirrors, saw himself in profile as well. He stood there for a long time, scrutinizing the distinguishing marks of his blood, the slightly flattened nose, the full lips resting softly one upon the other, the prominent cheekbones, his dense, dark hair, forcibly parted at one side, and growing far down over his temples, and his eyes themselves under the strong linked eyebrows—those large, dark, moist, shining eyes, into which he put an expression of plaintiveness and weary sorrow.

Behind him he caught sight in the mirror of the polar-bear skin that stretched out its paws beside his bed. He turned, went over with tragic, languid steps, and after a moment's hesitation he sank down at full length on the bearskin, his head resting on his arm.

For a while he lay quite still; then he propped himself on one elbow, cupped his cheek on his slender, pinkish hand, and remained thus, absorbed in the sight of his mirror-image on the cupboard. There was a knock. Startled, he blushed and was on the point of rising. But then he sank back, let his head fall again on to his outstretched arm, and was silent.

Sieglind entered. Her eyes sought him in the room without finding him straight away. Finally she caught sight of him on the bearskin and was alarmed.

'Gigi... what are you doing?... Are you ill?' She ran to him, bent over him, and, stroking his forehead and hair with her hand, she repeated: 'You're not ill, are you?'

He shook his head and looked at her from below, lying on his arm, stroked by her.

She had come in slippers, half ready for night, from her bedroom, which was across the corridor from his. Her unbound hair fell down over her open, white dressing-jacket. Under her lace chemise Siegmund saw her small breasts, their skin the colour of smoked meerschaum.

'You were so horrid,' she said; 'you went away so crossly. I wasn't going to come to see you. But then I did come, because that wasn't a proper goodnight just now...'

'I was waiting for you,' he said.

Still standing bent double, she grimaced with pain, which made the physiognomic peculiarities of her kind extraordinarily conspicuous.

'Despite which,' she said in the accustomed tone, 'my present posture is causing me a not inconsiderable pain in the back.'

He tossed himself to and fro in protest.

'Don't, don't... Not like that, not like that... It shouldn't be like that, Sieglind, don't you see... ' His voice was strange, he could hear that himself. His head was hot and dry, his limbs moist and cold. She was now kneeling beside him on the bearskin, her hand in his hair. Sitting half upright, he had one arm round her neck and was looking at her, contemplating her as he had just contemplated himself, her eyes and temples, forehead and cheeks...

'You're just like me,' he said with paralysed lips, swallowing because his throat had dried up... 'Everything is... like it is for me... and what... experiences are for me... Beckerath is for you... things are even... Sieglind... and finally it's... the same thing, especially as regards... revenge, Sieglind... '

He strove to clothe what he was saying in the garb of logic, and yet it was queer and venturesome like a wild dream.

To her it did not sound unfamiliar nor strange. She was not ashamed to hear him say such unpolished, such murky and muddled things. His words gathered round her mind like a mist, drawing her down to the place they came from, to a deep realm she had never yet reached, but to whose frontiers, since her engagement, expectant dreams had occasionally borne her.

She kissed him on his closed eyes; he kissed her on her throat under the lace of her bodice. They kissed each other's hands. Each loved the other with sweet sensuality for their pampered and precious elegance and their good fragrance. They breathed in the sweet scent with voluptuous and careless self-abandonment, coddling themselves with it like egoistic invalids, seeking intoxication as people do who have lost all hope, lost in caresses that exceeded their bounds and turned into a hurried turmoil and finally no more than a sobbing—

She was still sitting on the bearskin, her lips apart, propped on one hand, and brushing her hair out of her eyes. He was leaning on the white chest of drawers with his hands behind his back, swaying with his hips and gazing into the air.

'But Beckerath... ' she said, trying to arrange her thoughts. 'Beckerath, Gigi... what about him?'

'Well,' he said, and for a moment the distinguishing marks of his race stood out on his face very sharply, 'what about him? We've jewed him—the goy!'

ELSE LASKER-SCHÜLER

From *Hebrew Ballads*

(translated by Robert Newton)

Else Lasker-Schüler (1869–1945), the greatest woman poet of twentieth-century Germany, was brought up in an assimilated Jewish family in Elberfeld (now part of Wuppertal in the Ruhr). Her life was overshadowed by the premature deaths of her dearly loved mother and her gifted son; both her marriages—first to a Berlin doctor, then to the literary editor 'Herwarth Walden' (Georg Levin)—were unhappy. Her oriental costumes and impulsive behaviour made her a conspicuous and, for some, embarrassing figure in Bohemian circles in Berlin. Having suffered physical ill-treatment by the Nazis, she moved first to Switzerland and then, in 1939, to Palestine. Much of Lasker-Schüler's life and writing expresses the desire to regain a lost paradise which she identified with her early childhood and sought to recreate in her love poetry. Throughout her life she remained childlike in her love of play and disguises, her frankness, and her emotional vulnerability. She devised an exotic fantasy world in which she assumed the androgynous identities of Tino of Baghdad and later Yussuf, Prince of Thebes. Her poetry attempts to construct a private domain of feeling with rich and colourful imagery which has often been called 'Oriental', but in fact derives from German Romanticism and the *fin de siècle*. Yet this poetic home is threatened by loneliness and fear that make her long for 'God's blue spaces'; these feelings find perhaps their most poignant expression in her last collection, *My Blue Piano* (1943).

Lasker-Schüler's writings show her developing awareness of her dual, German–Jewish identity. Her most 'German' work is *The River Wupper* (1909), a basically Naturalist drama of class conflict, written partly in the dialect of her native Rhineland and steeped in a lyrical atmosphere. Encouraged by Martin Buber's vitalist conception of Judaism, she distanced herself from assimilationism and celebrated the 'wild Jews' of the Bible in *Hebrew Ballads* (1913). On her first visit to Palestine in 1934 she found the reality disappointingly different from her fantasies, and compensated with the charming, fanciful travel-book *The Hebrews' Land* (1937), which represents modern immigrants to Palestine as renewing the identity of the ancient Hebrews.

The first poem in the *Hebrew Ballads*, 'My People', helps the reader to bridge the gulf from the degenerate present to the world of the Old

Testament. The remaining poems are parts of a mythic narrative involving separation from God and the attempt to re-create the lost unity through the experience of love. The fall into separation from God is prefigured in Adam's uneasy dreams, whose groans disturb Eve as she bends over him, and its consequences are seen in 'Abel', where 'the city ditches pass through the body of Cain': Cain, having killed the pastoralist Abel, prefigures a modern, urban civilization built on violence. Abraham is still close to God and nature, building a city from such innocuous materials as 'earth and leaf', and entertaining angels (Genesis 18); but the child Isaac, torturing animals under the pretence of playing at sacrifices, represents the antithesis of Abraham's piety—the *yetser ha-ra* or 'evil impulse' which, it seems, is present in the supposed innocence of childhood and even underlies the invention of some religious ceremonies.

Other poems use natural imagery, especially that of plants, to celebrate the peaceful union of lovers. Thus David and his 'playmate' Jonathan are 'like the buds on the love-psalms'. The most passionate, complex, and inventive of these poems is 'Pharaoh and Joseph'. Spoken by Joseph (the figure with whom Lasker-Schüler identified), it describes Pharaoh's head giving off a scent of corn as it rests on Joseph's shoulder 'in the wheat of our morn', and combines the images of blood and water as does 'My People': Pharaoh's eyes are like waves of the Nile, his heart 'lies in my blood' and 'roars on my riverbed'. Violence is suggested by Pharaoh's anger against Joseph's brothers, the 'ten wolves' who threw him into the pit. The lovers' union has quietened but not removed Pharaoh's own potential for violence. Elsewhere Lasker-Schüler seeks ways of making violence acceptable. The animal energies of the 'buffalo' Jacob are humanized when he learns to smile. Moses dies 'when his tired lion's soul cried out to God', having first appointed the 'wild Jew Joshua' as his successor. Violence constantly threatens to disrupt Lasker-Schüler's myth, and she seeks ways of accommodating it in a primitive, full-blooded conception of Jewish existence.

―――――

My People

The rock begins to crack
From which I spring
And my divine songs sing...
Steep from the path I plunge
And trickle, all in me,
Far off, alone over grieving stone,
Toward the sea.

So much I've streamed away
Of my blood's
Early fermentation.
And always and again the echoing
In me,
When shuddering towards the East
The crumbling skeleton of stone,
My people
Cries to God.

Abel

Cain's eyes are not well pleasing unto God;
But a golden garden is Abel's countenance;
Abel's eyes are nightingales.

So brightly does Abel always sing
To the strings of his soul
But the city ditches pass through the body of Cain.

And he'll slay his brother—
Abel, Abel, your blood will deeply dye the sky.

Where is Cain, for I would storm him:
Did you slay the sweet-bird
In the face of your brother?!!

Abraham and Isaac

Abraham built himself on Eden's sod
A city raised of earth and leaf
And practiced converse with his God.

The angels pleased to rest before his holy home
And Abraham knew every one;
Their wingèd steps left symbols in the loam.

Until they then once heard in fearful dreams
The bleating of tormented rams
Where Isaac was playing sacrifice behind the licorice trees.

And God admonished: Abraham!
From the ridge of the sea he broke off sponge and clam
To trim the altar towering up in stone.

And bound on his back he bore his only son
Since that his Lord's command did him compel—
The Lord, however, loved his servant well.

Hagar and Ishmael

The little sons of Abraham took shells
And floated boats made out of mother-pearl;
Then Isaac leaned in fear on Ishmael.

And mournfully sang the two black swans
Quite gloomy notes around their brilliant world,
And the banished Hagar quickly stole her son.

Poured into his small tear her larger one,
And their hearts murmured like a sacred well
And could the swiftest ostriches outrun.

But the sun on the desert dazzled like a brand,
And into its yellow fur the boy and Hagar fell
And their white negroes' teeth bit burning sand.

Jacob and Esau

Rebecca's maiden is a heavenly stranger.
A garment of rose petals garbs the angel
And in her face a star.

And she looks upward at the light afar,
And her soft hands and gentle
Are shelling a pottage of golden lentil.

Jacob and Esau blossom from her being,
Nor seek those sweetnesses with quarrelsome zeal,
That in her lap she breaks to make the meal.

One brother sells the younger undismayed,
His hunt and heritage to serve the maid;
Bursts shouldering through the thicket and away.

Jacob

Jacob was the buffalo of his herd.
When he thundered with his hooves
Earth beneath him rocked and stirred.

Bellowed, left his many-coloured brothers,
Ran through jungle to the cool lagoons,
Staunched the blood there of his ape-bite wounds.

Fever forced him to sink down a while
Under heaven, to rest his painful bones;
And his ox-face bore the world's first smile.

Pharaoh and Joseph

Pharaoh dismisses his blossoming wives;
They are fragrant as Amon's gardens.

His royal head rests upon my shoulder,
Which sends forth the scent of grain.

Pharaoh is golden.
His eyes come and go
Like shimmering waves of the Nile.

His heart, though, lies in my blood;
Ten wolves went to my watering place.

Pharaoh thinks always
Upon my brothers
Who cast me into the pit.

In sleep his arms become pillars
And threaten!

But his dreamer's heart
Roars on my riverbed.

Wherefore my lips are thick with words
Of very sweetness
In the wheat of our morn.

Moses and Joshua

When Moses was as old as God
He took the wild Jew Joshua
And anointed him king of his multitudes.

Then a soft longing went through Israel,
For Joshua's heart refreshed them like a well.
His altar was the body of the Bible's Jews.

With maidens the brother king was popular—
Like holy thornbush did his hair burn sweet;
His smile did greet the homeland's beckoning star,

Which Moses' dying eye still lived to see
When his tired lion's soul cried out to God.

David and Jonathan

In the Bible we are written
In bright embrace.

But our boyish games
Survive in the star.

I am David.
You my playmate.

Oh, we dyed
Our white ram-hearts red!

Like the buds on the love-psalms
Beneath holiday skies.

But your leave-taking eyes—
You always depart with a wordless kiss.

And what should your heart do
Without mine too—

Your sweet night
Without my song.

David and Jonathan

O Jonathan, I pale in your embrace;
My heart is draped in dark and solemn folds.
In the temple of my brow—care for the moon!
And from the stars receive their gold!
You are my heaven, mine, you mate of grace.

I've only viewed the cool world in the streams,
Indolent, as if from far above...
But since in my eye it now no longer gleams,
Being thawed out by your love...
O Jonathan, you, take the royal tear!
It shines rich as a bride, soft as a dove.

O Jonathan, you blood of the sweet fig,
You aromatic pendant on my twig,
You ring, through my lip interwove.

Esther

Esther is slender as a palm.
The blades of wheat take from her lips their balm,
And the feast days that in Judah fall.

At night her heart reposes on a psalm;
The idols hearken in the hall.

The king looks, smiling, when she comes—
For everywhere God watches Esther.

The young Jews compose love songs to their sister,
Which they incise in the pillars before her room.

GERSHOM SCHOLEM

From His Diaries

Gershom Scholem (1897–1982), the historian of Jewish mysticism, was originally Gerhard Scholem, born into an assimilated Berlin family; his father was a printer, and one of his brothers, Werner, became a Communist and perished in a Nazi concentration camp. Scholem's rebellion took a different form. Even before the First World War he was drawn to Zionism, being active in a Zionist youth movement called Young Judaea; but he disliked the emotional, aestheticizing Zionism of Martin Buber, thinking it insufficiently founded on the study of Jewish tradition. To remedy this deficiency, Scholem turned his attention from 1915 onwards to the Kabbalah, the tradition of Jewish mysticism. Nobody in Germany could guide his studies; although he qualified in Semitic studies at Munich University, which had a large collection of Kabbalistic manuscripts, he wrote his thesis on the twelfth-century *Book of Bahir* largely unaided, and based his subsequent researches on his own collection of Kabbalah texts, of which he issued an important bibliography. In 1923 he emigrated to Palestine and worked first as librarian at the new library of the Hebrew University, then, when the University was officially opened in 1925, as lecturer, later professor, in Jewish mysticism. His virtually single-handed construction of his academic field is not only a towering scholarly achievement but a devastating rejoinder to the emancipatory tendency, established by Mendelssohn, to identify Judaism with ethical and rationalistic deism in order to prove the Jews' fitness for assimilation.

Besides his great works *Major Trends in Jewish Mysticism* (1941) and *Sabbatai Sevi, the Mystical Messiah* (1973), the latter a study of the seventeenth-century impostor who set all the Jews of Europe in an apocalyptic frenzy, Scholem wrote many important and controversial essays on aspects of Jewish history and religion; special mention should be made here of his pungent polemic 'Against the Myth of the German–Jewish Dialogue'. In the 1920s he belonged to the small group of intellectuals, Brit Shalom, which sought a bi-national Arab–Jewish state, and in his later years he denounced the messianism of the Gush Emunim, the religious nationalist movement in Israel. As a controversialist Scholem took no hostages, and his forthright and embattled personality is vividly present in his letters, his autobiography *From Berlin to Jerusalem*, and his remarkable memoir of his friendship with Walter Benjamin.

Now that Scholem's early diaries have been published, we can see another facet of his character. The young Scholem appears as a tormented God-seeker, a reader of Rilke, Tolstoy, Nietzsche, Kierkegaard, even St Francis, in some ways a typical member of the Expressionist generation. The extract translated here records the commitment to Zionism formed during a walking tour in the Alps in August 1914. There are many literary echoes. Scholem's scorn for tourists clutching their Baedekers recalls the fun poked at tourists by Heine in *The Harz Journey* (1826), which includes a description of the sunrise seen from the summit of the Brocken. The mountain landscape and the high-flown rhetoric are reminiscent of Nietzsche's Zarathustra and of the biblical psalms and prophecies that provided Nietzsche's linguistic inspiration. Scholem betrays also the influence of Gerhart Hauptmann's novel *The Fool in Christ Emanuel Quint* (1910), about a Christian visionary who comes to believe that he is himself Christ, inspired especially by sunrise in the mountains, and who dies alone in a blizzard on the St Gotthard Pass. Like the reference to the false Messiah Sabbatai Zvi (Sevi), the subject of Scholem's later study, and the closing celebration of Herzl, this allusion shows the young Scholem's concern with the moral ambiguity of assuming a calling: how does one know that one's vocation may not be false? Any doubts, however, are soon submerged in the ardent rhetoric with which Scholem takes up his mission on behalf of the Jewish people.

17.8.1914

The thoughts written down here were not thought out at my desk. I have not arranged them in order and placed them in an intelligible sequence; I have not related them to the co-ordinates of Whence and Whither, nor squeezed them into the thumbscrews of an argument, that is, an inadequate causal connection. All our experience can be fitted into a pattern retrospectively—it has been said that every revolution looks like evolution to later generations*—but these lines are intended to retain thoughts as they sometimes burst upon us, uninvited and unstoppable, and place their yoke on our necks. They come from high in the mountains, from pure pleasure, and sink into the crevasse at your feet. But their essential feature for you is not that they come and go, come from the eternal ocean of unknown necessity and go into the abyss of oblivion: their essential feature is only the short span in between, an eternal moment of blissful experience.

Here is the necessary minimum. I have spent four weeks in a high

Alpine valley of the St Gotthard massif, remote from the great stream of tourists that pours through Switzerland every year. Its magnificence, which gives it—forgive my bitterness!—a star in Baedeker, means that climbers lingering here in their thirst for beauty are sometimes granted the company of civilized people—still civilized at a height of 2,000 metres! Four weeks: isn't that an eternity for a young man who has fled from city and school, from utilitarian machinery and artificial harmony into the magnificent wildness of the high mountains, and whose only marching orders, uttered in doctors' surgeries in Berlin, are: solitude. On my solitary wanderings through the stony and snowy wastes of the Windgälle and the Düssistock I had sufficient leisure to pursue my own thoughts, which some call childlike and others eccentric, until the rumour of war aroused a hideous echo even in the Maderaner Valley, and the Brisenstock sent down continual avalanches as a clear sign of its anger at the disunity of the world. And the Brisenstock is a man to be taken seriously.

Since I regarded my journey not as a holiday but as a voyage of discovery like that of Prometheus, who is said to have fetched down fire from heaven for mankind, you will understand why I have included thoughts here that would not be expected of a traveller. You will understand that amid this solitude I have pondered the same things that I always carry in my mind. I have sought up here for the God who, in David Strauss's words, has been made homeless down below,* and you will understand my thoughts.

The path that leads far up into the Maderaner Valley ends in a magnificent setting, on a rocky outcrop. Right before the walker's face there extends a glacier, a mighty sea of ice pitted by crevasses. The huge mountains tower into the sky like petrified giants. The icefields are covered by dazzling fresh snow. Nothing lives in these mountains but chamois and marmots, and it takes an experienced eye to detect them. People? They stay far away from the clefts and cliffs; nature breathes its everlasting breath. God's nature. Everything is quiet; only on this path through the valley is there any coming and going. Cultivated people, culture: that is not, as you might suppose, a goddess who imposes sacred silence on all who visit this place, preserving its purity from profane eyes. O no, fool, how could you believe that! Culture is a book with a red cover. 'What sort of book is that?' you say in astonishment, opening it at the title-page.

Did you think that the book they carry with them at every step was the Bible? No, my friend, culture is Baedeker.

They stand there and gaze. Yes, they gaze. Perhaps at the mountains, seeking for the God who dwells there, perhaps at the glacier, hoping that from its depths may come answers to the questions that mankind has pondered since time immemorial? Or are they gazing into a realm without space, overwhelmed by the magnificent spectacle and turning away from it as the climber does from the gleaming of snow in sunlight? Behold, they are opening their mouths, and their lips are filled with words. Surely they will stammer sacred truth in awestruck words, and the ineffable will cast its radiance on what they say. They will praise Him who dwells above the mountains and displays His magnificence in the glow of dayspring. Their stammering will be of God's freedom and God's nature, and they will be thankful for being found worthy to behold the holy. Measuring their smallness by the greatness of the setting, they will grow, and recognizing it, they will fall silent!—You who are strong in unreason, ascend a high mountain; you who prophesied falsehoods by the measure of your folly, cast yourself over dreadful cliffs into the abyss. You do not know the world that here opens its mouth and serves the Lord God after its fashion. These people are not gazing at nature and its beauty; they are looking at the red book, which will proclaim the thoughts that civilized man should have in this place. At the end of the valley: rocky outcrop, fine view. With a star. That's that. They are not gazing at the glacier and its blue crevasses, they are not thinking that tomorrow one crack will have closed and another will yawn elsewhere, and that their life's path resembles the glacier; they are thinking. 'Splendid view of the Hüfi Glacier (seven or eight hours' walk in length) which has recently retreated considerably and joins the Clariden Icefield at the top.' Yes, they are thinking that and reading it aloud. And no angel descends from the mountains with a flaming sword to drive them away, out of the paradise they have profaned, the mountains do not fall on the blasphemers—for have they not blasphemed against God by failing to speak of Him at the place of His throne!—and the earth does not open to swallow them up!*

When Sabbatai Zvi wanted to prove to himself and others that he was the Messiah, he went to the market-place at Smyrna and uttered the name of God with his head uncovered. For the people believed that none, unless he were the Redeemer himself, could pronounce the Tetragrammaton* without being struck by the lightning of heavenly wrath. But when nothing of the sort occurred, he believed in himself and they in him.—These people are the same; they carry their delusions ever further. They speak of the mountains, but not of their sublimity nor their beauty, they are satisfied to know their names! They utter one name after another, and are thankful for knowing so many names. And once they have thus completed their programme, as they are wont to say, they generously add: 'Really quite beautiful', or some other such ejaculatory prayer. At home, however, they will speak in lofty tones of what they have seen, and if anyone conceals his experience within his bosom, they will say scornfully: 'He has no feeling for beauty—what's more, they say he goes on holiday without Baedeker!'

... The mountains are still shrouded in cloud and mist, with the occasional ridge appearing drowsily through the white blanket. Only half an hour ago the sea of stars were still guarding their prince, but now the clouds in the east are assuming a reddish hue. On some high meadows the four-footed beasts are stirring and staring at passers-by with eyes whose language has been unknown since the days of King Solomon.

Far in the east the sun has appeared: I cannot see it, I can only guess at it, for its rays, piercing the mist, clearly announce its presence. Here and there on the Wetterwand a stream becomes visible, and golden masses of light burst forth and cast their reflections on the snow. It is not one of the 'great' sunrises of the mountains; certainly not. But is not the modest beauty, revealed daily in the east, more essential than the short-lived beauty of an exceptional day?

At various places in *Emanuel Quint* Hauptmann tells how God's holy fool prostrates himself before the rising sun, overwhelmed by ecstasy. Truly, this Quint served his God better than those who built special houses and locked Him in there, because they were unable to find Him in nature... Why do they build churches and chapels in the high mountains? Is not every mountain a church and every hill a chapel? Did not God call to them: 'The heaven is my throne, and the earth is my footstool: what manner of house will ye build unto me? and what place shall be my rest?'*

But you have travelled far to the mountains to seek beauty; you have set forth, and yet you sleep at sunrise? When is the world beautiful, if not when it appears in youthful radiance? When are you young, if not early in the morning, and when is your world young, if not at sunrise? Your cows and oxen, which you say lack reason, they are awake, but you, to whom reason is given, are asleep. How are you to find beauty if you do not look for it!

A storm in the high mountains! A black wall of cloud rises menacingly above the glacier up there. Scraps of cloud fly and are broken on the precipices. The snow on the icefields gleams in strange darkness, as a sea sucks up the last rays of sun before the hurricane. The wind is whistling down in the valley and round the mountains up here. People hide from the storm as Adam did from the voice of God.* Water streams from the heavens as in the days of the Flood. Lightning flashes from many places at once, and the thunder's echo rolls awesomely in the lonely corries. The Wild Hunt is rushing above my head, the God of the mountains is approaching in the storm. You solitary child of man, why are you standing here, did not the thunder call to you: 'Turn back'? Will not the spirits and the elements be enraged against you for disturbing them and eavesdropping on their combat? No, I shall not yield! For the storm is why I came. Now you are chaos, but the eternal will shall bring forth renewal from you. Only amid danger is God to be found. I stand here waiting for Him, so that He may carry me through the heavens like Enoch,* who the ancients say was all eyes and wings.

Who can find himself without descending into the abyss and seeking himself amid danger? Who will find chaos, save in the raging of the mountains? Far from me be the security of those who keep themselves intact! Continually reborn, mantled in unity, I rise again from the combat into the life of the secure. From you, you mountains, I can learn. The Wild Hunt is already vanishing again from the firmament, a new radiance has broken from the sluice-gates of the heavens to welcome their mighty warriors. Nature breathes again, like God, who they say created the world in six days so that He might rest on the seventh. Renewed by God's demonic spirit, the mountains rise from combat and resume their former places, the rushing of the Stäuber Falls can again be heard from the ravine behind me. The secure ones emerge from the ark and look pityingly at the fools: 'Fancy being out in this weather.' Oh, you clever ones...

Renewal! An old word that resounds from old books. Is not the sun its symbol, creating the world and its creatures anew every time?

There is an old saying in our hands, as old as the first word, and it says: 'The Lord God does not do the same thing twice.' New things rise from the turmoil of events: the material is old, but the sign is always new. But this is renewal: *that which is* is single and unique. It emerges new and unbeen, the flood of gestations is its maternal womb, to which it returns, unrepeatable. Everything reappears, but everything is transformed. But its transformation is this: You stamp the mark of eternity indelibly on its brow, not as a thing to the things of earth, but as a star to the stars in heaven...

Solitude! I should like to chant a song of songs in its praise, standing among the mountains, if only I could. Not praising the solitude of man alone with his self, in which all measures are lost, but that of man surrounded by nature, the quiet solitude of holy ecstasy. Anyone who has walked through the high mountains, in pathless and trackless places, over scree-slopes and snowfields, with the mountains for brethren and the heavens for his father, climbing through the mist to reach the light, cut off from the branching tree of community, knows the thoughts that arise then. He understands why Moses had to bring the teaching down from the wilderness of the mountains and why he stayed up there for forty days and forty nights; he understands why men of spiritual greatness sought solitude, though spiritually they were already alone.

God dwells in the mountains. Not the God they invoke down there, in stuffy houses, without the magic of the right direction, not the God whom they forced to bear the world on His shoulders because they found it too heavy, but the God of experience, the God of myth, that God with Whom one must wrestle in order to receive His blessing, and Whom one redeems by living Him.

Ecstasy dwells in the mountains, and that is union with this God. As you stride along, mighty shudders permeate your soul, the scraps of cloud rushing by turn into demons, fighting overhead for your soul with the God of the mountains. You free your God from the demons' embrace, and they disappear. And He kisses you, as He kissed Moses* in death. You are one with Him, an everlasting moment, and you discover yourself in His embrace. And you rise and cry out your inmost self. But the cry breaks impotently on the iron mountains of necessity, and does not return to you. With a gleam in your eye and death in your heart, you turn your steps to the community, unable to interpret the mystery of grace...

In God's free, solitary nature, there you stand, you happy man, now staying in the Swiss mountains for the fifth time, but down in the city which is your home there are millions waiting for redemption. Were you not struck by their misery when you saw them, with sunken cheeks and hungry bellies, glazed eyes and dead thoughts, vegetating in poverty-stricken Berlin! How could you journey with a contented heart, forgetting misery, misfortune, and your own people, as it reels towards its downfall in the back alleys of Europe and America! Never do so. Who can find oblivion who has once walked along the Grenadierstrasse* with a bleeding heart and looked into the eyes, the four-thousand-year-old eyes of his brethren. Such a one should be struck out of the book of redemption! But no one has ever walked along that street and forgotten it. No, I shall never forget my people, subjugated and bleeding to death. How could I! That same sun whose rays produce wondrous symphonies of colour on the eternal snow above my head, doesn't it try its best—alas, seldom successfully—to penetrate Whitechapel's narrow alleys, where my people curses the earth on its deathbed? No, I shall not forget you. Did I not come here for your sake, to draw strength, strength from the mountains, so that I might accomplish the work of redemption down below? I shall fetch fire from the mountains, the fire of myth, that of humanity's soul. It is close to extinction among you, and then you would have to die. I am not making this journey for myself alone, I am making it for ten million others.

We who want to set our people free, all those of us who are young and have sacrificed our youth to it, we must go to the mountains and seek God. We must seek Him and find Him. For He must descend with us from His place and lead us. Some from Berlin and others from Vienna, those of Kishinev* and those of Cracow. He must go ahead of us once more as a cloud by day and a pillar of fire by night. We are going.

When Moses was roaming about in solitary mountain deserts to seek God, he heard a voice saying: 'Put off thy shoes from off thy feet, for the place whereon thou standest is holy ground.'* And Moses went and brought God back to his people. You who seek God on your lonely paths, hear this saying. In the stony deserts where you roam, on the rocky slopes and snowfields, remember that God can meet you wherever you seek Him. And therefore take off your shoes from your feet, strip off whatever oppresses you, all half-measures and all compromises, be undivided on your paths, and renew yourselves from the spirit of unremitting severity, that God may again be to you what He was to Moses: a devouring fire!

Yes, he will be a mighty poet, star and beacon for his age, light and lamp to all his people, and a wonderful and mighty pillar of poetic fire, going on before Israel's caravan of woe and sorrow in the desert waste of exile (Heine).*

Ten years ago, at this time in summer, Theodor Herzl* was buried in the Jewish cemetery at Döbling. They took him to his last resting-place, but the journey from Vienna out to Döbling, on which the best members of his people accompanied him, along with thousands of his brethren, was not his last journey. He will make another great journey: when his people will return to the land of their fathers, to their own earth and their own ways, they will take on their journey a coffin from the Jewish cemetery at Döbling. That is what he asked of us, and we swore at his grave to do so. When God once more sends His angel ahead of us, we shall accompany him on his last journey, as our fathers took their ancestor Joseph with them when they left Mizraim,* the house of bondage, for the Promised Land. . . When will the journey be? 'Soon and in our days,' as our pious men say in their prayers? We do not know, but we shall prepare the way for the angel who is coming, so that another Herzl may arise for us, the later-born, one who is whole to guide his hesitant brethren.

He provided youth with a hope, old age with a dream, mankind with something beautiful... We raised no monument to him, we have never erected monuments, not to Moses son of Amram nor to the man from Nazareth, nor to Moses da Leon* or Israel ben Eliezer,* and we shall raise no monument to him either. For we have no need to know who he was, whence he came and whither he went. What shall live in us without form or shape is a monument of everlasting substance: that we know the rhythm of his life that cried renewal; that we bear the myth of Theodor Herzl within ourselves like a sacred fire. It is not *what* he wanted, but *that* he wanted, that concerns us... In the afterword to *Old–New Land*￼* are the words: 'If you want it, it is not a fairy-tale.' You who have the will and the direction, did he not intend these words for you? Do you want always to let the fire die down to the embers? He left you the flag, and is not the flag an order to begin the march? 'Yes, he left us the flag, but for ten years we have been looking for God to carry it.'

FRANZ KAFKA

Jackals and Arabs

(translated by Malcolm Pasley)

Franz Kafka (1883–1924) was born into a Jewish family that was largely assimilated to the dwindling German-speaking minority in Prague, then the capital of Bohemia, the most industrialized province of the Austrian Empire. His knowledge of Czech enabled Kafka to continue in his career as a civil servant, responsible for the insurance of industrial workers against accidents, after his native country become the First Czechoslovak Republic, though the tuberculosis that eventually killed him was diagnosed in 1917 and his later life included long stays in sanatoria. The circumstances of his life are transformed in his writings, which consist of extensive diaries and notebooks, many short stories and sketches, and three novels which remained incomplete and which, because of his perfectionism, he did not wish to be published; thanks to the disobedience of his devoted friend and supporter Max Brod, they did appear after his death. The first, known in English as *America*, subjects the reports of travellers (including some enterprising relatives who had emigrated there) to humorous exaggeration, depicting an ultra-modern, mercilessly competitive society which is also the setting for a narrative about innocence and injustice. *The Trial*, written mainly in 1914, draws on Kafka's legal training and bureaucratic experience to evoke a mysterious agency which intervenes in the life of Josef K. and finally condemns him by an authority incomprehensible to his morally limited awareness; while *The Castle*, whose rural setting recalls that of the Slovakian sanatorium where Kafka wrote it in 1922, takes the administrative staff of a castle seemingly deserted by its owner to represent, humorously and sceptically, the strange behaviour of supernatural powers. Kafka's literary breakthrough came in September 1912 with the compact short story 'The Judgement', where a familiar conflict between son and father acquires cryptic and metaphysical overtones; it was followed three months later by the tragicomic 'Metamorphosis', where the son of an ordinary household is transformed into an unspecified insect.

Animals serve many purposes in Kafka's fiction: they may embody the more primitive, non-rational side of humanity that is in danger of suppression in an increasingly rationalized, bureaucratic world; menacing but thrilling energies, like the carnivorous horses in 'An Old Manuscript' and the panther in 'A Hunger Artist'; the irruption of the supernatural, like the unearthly horses in 'A Country Doctor'; or, as in the traditional beast-fable, they may serve to ironize the vanity of human endeavour, as in 'Investigations of a Dog' and 'Josefine the Singer or the Mouse Folk'. In the latter story the mice also illustrate the sympathy with small nations which Kafka gained from his experience of Central European nationalism, and particularly from his acquaintance with Yiddish culture, first through a troupe of itinerant actors and later through meeting refugees who had fled from Galicia to Prague during the First World War.

'Jackals and Arabs' was first published, along with 'A Report to an Academy', under the heading 'Two Animal Stories', in the October and November 1917 issues of the Zionist monthly *The Jew*. Its editor was Martin Buber, whom Kafka had already met and liked. His decision to publish there confirms that by 1917 he had been persuaded by Brod to assume a sympathetic attitude to Zionism. Later Kafka took lessons in modern Hebrew and talked of emigrating to Palestine. Both stories are indirect and humorous treatment of themes that concerned Zionists. In 'A Report', the ape who has, or claims he has, become a human being, satirizes the assimilation to European society which Zionists thought doomed to failure. 'Jackals and Arabs' satirizes half-hearted conceptions of Jewish identity. In their loyalty to their old 'teaching', their insistence on letting animals die naturally, and their repeated calls for purity, the jackals resemble Orthodox Jews who follow the prescriptions for ritual purity laid down in the Torah. As parasitic animals who rely on others to provide their food, they typify the lack of self-reliance ascribed by Zionists to Western Jews. Their absurd messianic expectations, shown when they beseech the traveller to cut the Arabs' throats and thus end an ancient dispute, serve to criticize the Orthodox for awaiting the coming of the Messiah instead of improving their condition for themselves. Such beings are bound always to lead a timid, marginal existence in their host society. By satirizing its opposite, the story supports the Zionist programme of active self-improvement through developing one's Jewish consciousness and helping in the colonization of Palestine which was favoured by readers of *The Jew*.

––––––

We were encamped in the oasis. My companions were asleep. An Arab, a tall figure in white, strode past; he had been seeing to the camels and was going to his sleeping place.

I flung myself on my back in the grass; I wanted to sleep; I could not; the wailing howl of a jackal in the distance; I sat up again. And what had been so far off was suddenly close at hand. A seething mass of jackals around me; dull golden eyes gleaming out and fading away; lean bodies in orderly and nimble motion, as if controlled by a whip.

One came up from behind me, pushed through under my arm, pressing against me as if he needed my warmth; then he stepped almost eye to eye in front of me and spoke:

'I am the oldest jackal, far and wide. I am glad I'm still able to welcome you here. I'd almost given up hope, for we've been awaiting you for countless ages; my mother waited and her mother and every mother as far back as the first mother of all the jackals. Believe me!'

'I am surprised,' I said, forgetting to light the pile of firewood lying ready to keep the jackals off with its smoke, 'I'm very much surprised to hear it. I've only come down from the far north by chance, and I'm making a short journey. What is it you want then, jackals?'

And as if these words, perhaps all too friendly, had given them courage, they drew their circle closer round me; they were all breathing fast with a snarl in their throats.

'We are aware,' began the eldest, 'that you come from the north; that is just what we build our hopes on. People up there understand things that aren't understood by the Arabs down here. From their cold arrogance, I can tell you, no spark of understanding can be struck. They kill animals in order to eat them, and carrion flesh they despise.'

'Don't talk so loud,' said I, 'there are Arabs sleeping near.'

'You really must be a stranger here,' said the jackal, 'or you'd know that never in all history has a jackal been afraid of an Arab. Why, do you think we should be afraid of them? Is it not misfortune enough to be banished among such creatures?'

'Perhaps, perhaps,' said I, 'I don't presume to judge things so remote from my concerns; it seems to be a most ancient feud, so it probably runs in the blood; so maybe blood will be needed to end it.'

'You are very wise,' said the old jackal; and they all breathed even faster; their lungs straining, although they were standing still; a sour smell came from their gaping mouths which at times I had to grit my teeth to bear, 'you are very wise; what you say accords with our ancient teachings. So what we shall do is take their blood, and the feud is ended.'

'Oh!' I exclaimed, more vehemently than I meant to, 'they'll defend themselves; they'll shoot you down in packs with their muskets.'

'You misunderstand us,' said he, 'after human fashion, which seems to persist in the far north as well. Killing them is not at all what we have in mind. All the waters of the Nile would never suffice to wash us clean. The mere sight of their living flesh is enough to send us running off, out into a purer air, out into the desert which is therefore our home.'

And all the jackals standing round me, their number now increased by many others come up from afar, lowered their heads between their forelegs and polished them with their paws; it was as if they were trying to conceal their revulsion, a revulsion so terrible it made me want to leap clean out of their circle.

'What do you propose to do, then?' I asked, trying to get to my feet; but I was unable to do so; two young beasts behind me had fastened their teeth in my coat and my shirt; I had to remain seated. 'They are carrying your train,' explained the old jackal gravely, 'it's a token of respect.' 'They must let me go!' I cried, turning now to the old jackal, now to the youngsters. 'Of course they will,' said the old one, 'if you so wish. But it will take a little time, because as custom requires they have bitten in deep and first they must gradually loosen their jaws. Meanwhile, pray hear what we ask.' 'Your behaviour hasn't put me in a very receptive frame of mind,' I said. 'Don't hold our clumsiness against us,' said he, and now he began to make use of his natural wailing tone, 'we are only poor creatures, we have nothing but our teeth; we depend for all that we want to do, the good and the bad, on our teeth alone.' 'What is it that you want, then?' I said, only slightly appeased.

'Master,' he cried, and every jackal set up a howl; the howling from the furthest distance seemed to reach my ears like a melody. 'Master, you are to end the strife that is dividing the world. You are exactly the man our ancients described as the one to accomplish it. We must be granted peace from the Arabs; air that we can breathe; the whole round of the horizon purified of their presence; never again the piteous cry of a sheep slaughtered with an Arab knife; every manner of beast must die in peace; we must be left undisturbed to drink them empty and cleanse them to the bone. Purity, purity is our sole desire'—and now all of them were crying and sobbing— 'how can you endure it in this world, you noble heart and sweet entrails? Filth is their white; filth is their black; a thing of loathing is their beard; the corner of their eye is enough to make you spit; and when they lift an arm, all hell gapes in their armpit. Therefore, O master, therefore, beloved master, with the help of your all-powerful hands, with the help of your all-powerful hands, take up these scissors and cut their throats!' And in obedience to a jerk of his head a jackal came trotting up, from one of whose corner-teeth there dangled a small pair of sewing scissors, covered in ancient rust.

'Right, so we've come to the scissors at last, and that's enough of it!' cried the Arab leader of our caravan, who had been creeping up to us against the wind and now cracked his gigantic whip.

All the jackals ran off in haste, but some distance off they stopped, cowering close together; the many beasts so stiff and tight-packed that it looked like a narrow hurdle, wreathed in flickering will-o'-the-wisps.

'And so, master, now you too have seen and heard this spectacle,' said the Arab, laughing as heartily as the reserve of his race allowed. 'So you know what the creatures are after?' I asked. 'Of course, master,' said he, 'that's common knowledge; for so long as there have been Arabs these scissors have wandered the desert, and they will go on wandering with us until the end of time. Every European is offered the scissors to perform the great work; they imagine that every European is the very one called to perform it. They have an insane hope, these animals; they are fools, veritable fools. And we love them for it; they are our dogs; more beautiful ones than yours are. Now look, a camel has died in the night, I have had it brought along.'

Four bearers arrived and threw the heavy carcass down in front of us. Hardly had it touched the ground when the jackals raised their voices. As if they were drawn, each one, on a cord, irresistibly, they came hesitatingly forward, their bellies to the ground. They had forgotten the Arabs, forgotten their hatred; all else was obliterated by the presence of the reeking carcass that held them in its spell. One jackal was already hanging at the camel's throat and his first bite found the artery. Each muscle of his body twitched and jerked in its place, like a frenzied little pump that is utterly and hopelessly committed to the quenching of a raging fire. And by now they all lay piled up high on the carcass, each one labouring away.

Then out lashed the leader with his biting whip, fiercely to and fro across their backs. They raised their heads; still half numb in their ecstasy and stupor; saw the Arabs standing before them; now they were made to feel the whip on their muzzles; they sprang back and retreated a little. But already the blood of the camel was lying in pools, steaming high; in many places its body was torn wide open. They could not resist; back they came once more; once more the leader raised his whip; I caught hold of his arm.

'You are right, master,' he said, 'we will leave them to their task; besides, it's time to break camp. Now you have seen them. Wonderful creatures, aren't they? And how they do hate us!'

RICHARD BEER-HOFMANN

From *Jacob's Dream*

Richard Beer-Hofmann (1866–1945), one of the most accomplished writers of the Viennese *fin de siècle*, was the son of a lawyer. Since Richard's mother died at his birth, he was brought up and later adopted by her sister Berta and her husband Alois Hofmann, whence the double name. None of his family were observant Jews except his paternal grandmother, whom he describes reading a prayer-book by candlelight on Friday evenings. Beer-Hofmann, however, retained and developed his Judaism. His Gentile wife converted to Judaism in order to marry him. Disappointing his father's hopes that he would also become a lawyer, Beer-Hofmann explored Judaism through his literary works. His novel *George's Death* (1900) shows the protagonist, an assimilated Jew, regaining contact with a primordial, passionate Jewishness surviving in his unconscious racial memory. His play *The Count of Charolais* (1904), adapted from a seventeenth-century English drama by Massinger, *The Fatal Dowry*, rather incongruously includes a Jewish creditor who delivers a Shylock-like tirade recalling how *his* father was burnt by the Inquisition. From 1898 on, Beer-Hofmann contemplated a pentalogy of biblical dramas with the title *History of King David*. The only parts completed are the disappointingly diffuse *The Young David* (1933) and the prelude, *Jacob's Dream*, written between 1909 and 1915 and premiered in the Vienna Burgtheater in 1919.

The play focuses on Jacob, grandson of Abraham and father of the founders of Israel's twelve tribes, in order to inquire into the election of the Jewish people, into the Jews' relations with other peoples, and into the justification for Jacob's obtaining the birthright due to Esau (here called Edom, indicating that he also stands for the Gentiles). It falls into two parts. In the first and shorter, Jacob has already received his father's blessing and set out for Haran; the slaves discuss the incident before the return of Edom, who remonstrates with Rebekah and resolves to pursue Jacob with hounds that are to tear him to pieces. The play links the transference of the blessing to Jacob with his moral superiority. Edom is a brutal, violent, sensual man, who invokes pagan goddesses as he sets out to hunt down his brother; Jacob is described, by his and Edom's mother, as a man of active piety and universal compassion:

He does not banish God to distant heavens,
But wrestles with Him daily, heart to heart!
You merely hunt, make sacrifices, *murder*!
He blenches at the suffering of all beings,
He speaks to all, and all things speak to him...
Hence *he* bears both the blessing and its burden!

The meaning of 'its burden' is explained in the second part, set on the night when Jacob, on his way to Haran, sleeps on the hill later called Beth-El. Edom arrives and repeatedly challenges Jacob to fight, but Jacob, by standing unmoved and unafraid, eventually obliges Edom to kneel before him and plead for reconciliation. Jacob offers him the ceremony of blood-brotherhood, but refuses to expiate his deceit by being sacrificed: 'The Lord won't *take* me as an offering!' In rejecting sacrifice, Jacob is affirming complete non-violence. His election separates him from the cycle of violence and sacrifice in which Edom—and, by extension, the Gentile world—is caught. It also accompanies his acute awareness of the suffering that pervades the world.

Am I elected so that every being
That suffers may send me its supplication?
Even the dying gaze of helpless beasts
Silently asks me '*Why?!*'

Accordingly, the dream that forms the core of the play, based on Jacob's dream of angels ascending and descending the heavenly ladder in Genesis 28: 12, centres on the question of God's responsibility for suffering, not only human pain but also that of animals and even inanimate beings like the stream and the stone that address Jacob. It offers a strange and bold theodicy, with echoes from the Book of Job, via the drama enacted by the archangels who announce Jacob's election, the fallen angel Samael who condemns the world God has made, Jacob's disconcerting reluctance to accept his election, and the final, paradoxical intervention of the voice of God.

The section here translated begins with Jacob composing himself for sleep at Beth-El, and continues to the end of the play. In the original, Beer-Hofmann set out to make his characters more unfamiliar by Hebraizing their names, so that Jacob is 'Jaákob', a trisyllable; but rather than call him 'Ya'akob', with the resulting difficulties for pronunciation and scansion, I have given the names in the forms customary in English (except that, again because of scansion, I have kept 'Uru-Shalim' for Jerusalem); they are in any case less familiar to most readers now than in Beer-Hofmann's time. Dramatically, the play owes much to German and Austrian models. It recalls the 'Prologue in Heaven' of Goethe's *Faust* and Faust's confrontation with successive spirits in the 'Night' scene, while the arrival of the archangels recalls the supernatural machinery of Austrian Counter-Reformation drama, confirming Beer-Hofmann's own remark: 'In substance I am very much a Jew, and functionally very much an Austrian.'

———

JACOB [*steps forward and bends over the steep slope that he has ascended*].

How thickly the white mists are rolling in!
Nothing to see. Road, hillside, bushes, brook,
Are all enveloped in the milky flood
That fills the vale on every side. This hilltop
Is like a lonely island! [*More softly*] All alone!

> *He walks towards his sleeping-place.*

Nothing but mist and rock, and clouds and stars!

> *He loosens his belt and slips down onto his sleeping-place.*

Stone, you are hard—the earth is wet with dew!
A chilly welcome's all that either gives!

> *He stretches out, then looks up at the sky.*

I never saw a night of such deep blue!
How thick you crowd, the stars above my head...
With so much light, I cannot go to sleep,
And yet I'm tired! And first I have to pray,
My mother says that prayer helps you rest!

> *He draws a deep breath.*

Then let me pray!

He pauses; then the words slip from his mouth, with little emotion, more and more quietly.

> O you Unknown—Unseen—

God of my fathers—do You hear me too?
And do You know me? When I quake with dread,
Am I but grass that quivers in the breeze?
The murmurings of the streamlet in the valley—
Are my words any more to You than these?
Who knows! The tree may think its leaves address You
When they are moved by Your tempestuous air;

So—in me—You may speak—unto Yourself—
Your self-communing, Lord, shall be my prayer!

*He falls asleep. The mists have risen, and white swathes are hanging in
the treetops that project from below. The deep blue of the starry sky is
visible between thick clouds edged with light. The moon is hidden behind
the clouds, and as they float slowly past it in irregular forms, it casts an
irregular, shifting light on the rocky hilltop. Only a faint light falls on the
place where Jacob is sleeping. The stream, whose gurgling becomes audible
in the silence, shimmers brightly amid the dark moss.*

JACOB [*starting up in his sleep, softly*]. What calls me in the dark?
    What speaks?
  Am I not on my own?

*From the plashing of the stream there emerges a clear voice full of
emotion.*

THE STREAM. Because your name is Jacob, friend,
  You cannot be alone!
JACOB. Who's speaking?
THE STREAM.   You can understand
  The words that I can say
  Because your name is Jacob, friend!
  I wander on my way,
  Sprung from the hidden heart of earth
  And flowing over stone,
  But since you understand my words,
  I need not be alone!
  Plants hear me not, nor beasts nor rocks,
  The Lord is far, unseeing;
  But Jacob, listening, frees me from
  My solitary being!
JACOB. Are you so mournful?
THE STREAM.   What I am,
  My friend, I do not know,
  But you are Jacob, and you care
  For all things, high and low—
  And if you have not time for me
  In busy daytime's light,
  Then let my murmuring follow you
  Through Jacob's dreams at night...

*A deep gruff voice comes in a low growl from the stone on which Jacob's
head is resting, and interrupts with passionate anger.*

THE STONE. Don't heed the stream, though his whispering soft
    May stir you with longing and dread!
JACOB. Who's muttering there?
THE STONE.   It is I, the stone
    Where a blessed one lays his head!
    Don't call me hard—don't call me cold—
    I used to be heat and flame!
THE SURROUNDING ROCKS [*in a low, defiant mutter*]. We were aglow
    with heat once too!
THE STONE. Silence! We aren't the same!
    Spewed aloft by volcanic fires,
    You are rocks of lowly birth,
    But I was a star—and, Jacob, *why*,
    Why did I fall to earth?
JACOB. Leave me alone...
THE STONE [*restraining its sobs*]. That you know of my pain,
    That is all I can ask.
JACOB. Don't choose *me*!
THE STONE.   Yes, Jacob, I do;
    What else is your holy task?
    Do you heed only the murmuring stream,
    Blandishing, soft and low?
    I was sibling to stars and suns,
    Resonant, proud, aglow—
    Did I *have* to fall?
JACOB [*groaning*]. Leave me, you stone!
    Who gave you power to torment me thus? [*Tossing and turning on
        his bed*]
    I want to sleep and not to dream!
TWO WHITE-WINGED ANGELS *are kneeling to Jacob's right and left.*
THE FIRST ANGEL [*in a clear voice*]. Dream on,
    Jacob, dream on—
THE SECOND ANGEL [*joining in, in a deeper voice*].
                    —but for this night alone!
A faint, low groaning is heard far away, fading in the depths of the earth.
THE STONE. I was a star...

THE ROCKS. We burned now bright, now dim...

JACOB [*fearfully*]. You white-winged, swaying figures—can you be...

THE SECOND ANGEL. We are—

THE FIRST ANGEL.   You know it: messengers—

A THIRD ANGEL *bends over the stone on which Jacob's head is resting. He spreads out his wings so that they overshadow Jacob's head.*

THE THIRD ANGEL.   —from *Him*!

THE FIRST ANGEL. Your head is resting on a stone; sit up...

THE SECOND ANGEL. And lay your head against our downy wings!

JACOB *raises his head a little; the two kneeling angels slip their arms under his head so that their wings meet and support Jacob in a half-sitting position.*

JACOB [*shuddering*]. I must be waking—I can feel you!

THIRD ANGEL.   *He*

Awoke you, Jacob—He, to dream such things!

A distant rushing sound approaches; brief gusts of wind drive dark and lighted clouds across the sky, tearing some apart and blowing others together. During the words that follow, the wind, fed by other winds that hasten to its aid, swells into a gale.

THE FIRST ANGEL. Hearken!

JACOB [*fearfully*].   I hear the clash of silver shields
That strike together in a desperate fight!
I hear the rushing wings of migrant birds
Far overhead...

THE SECOND ANGEL. And do you see the light?

THE FIRST ANGEL. A glittering stream amid the clouds...

JACOB [*in terror*].   The stars—
They're fading—going out!

THE SECOND ANGEL.   No! They're still there!
Their light is only dimmed by that new radiance
That bursts from clouds to form a mighty stair!

THE FIRST ANGEL. Look there!

JACOB [*turning away*].   I'm dazzled!

THE THIRD ANGEL [*reprovingly*].   Others may be blind,
Your mission, Jacob, is to see! Look there!

JACOB. I'm trembling, shivering in the icy wind,
That roars as when a thunderstorm is nearing! [*Shaken*]
Is that Thy gale, O God?

THE THIRD ANGEL [*in a powerful voice*]. Behold the answer!
THE FIRST ANGEL. The lightning flashes...
JACOB.   What a storm I'm hearing—
It's swooping down—at last it touches ground!

> *He utters a cry and hides his face in his hands.*

Too near—too near!

> *He rises from his bed, reeling, as though about to flee.*

THE SECOND ANGEL [*hastily*]. Speak to it!
THE THIRD ANGEL [*in a powerful voice*]. Kneel and bow!
THE FIRST ANGEL [*urgently*]. Speak to it!
JACOB [*kneeling, with bowed head*]. I'm afraid!
THE THIRD ANGEL [*wrathfully*].   Speak to it!
JACOB [*stammering, struggling for breath, then with profound emotion*].
    Thou—
Before me, girt with gold and robed in white,
With eyes and brow beneath a helmet's shade—
Kindly or menacing? I cannot tell!
A fire envelops you, yet does not burn...
I shudder, yet I'm drawn to you—pure light—
Tell me your name! [*Humbly, beseechingly, in a lower voice*]
                Or how should I salute you?

> *On radiant steps, whose rays penetrate the drifting clouds, stands*
> GABRIEL *with outspread wings, bent slightly forward, as when he*
> *touched the ground. From under his golden helmet there emerge auburn*
> *curls which shade his eyes and brow. He has golden sandals on his feet,*
> *and golden greaves on his arms and thighs. His armour is almost con-*
> *cealed beneath a long sleeveless garment of white linen with slits at the*
> *side and a loose belt. From his belt hangs a golden vessel resembling a*
> *quiver. He is unarmed.*

GABRIEL. I am Gabriel—the strength of God!
His sword, His hammer—arrow, bow, and spear!
His outstretched arm and His creating rod—
He speaks through me the words for man to hear!
> *He folds his wings together and stands upright.*
JACOB [*tremulously*]. Then is He near at hand?
GABRIEL [*almost reprovingly*]. He is not near—He is not far!
Neither the past nor present holds Him!

You, we, the stars, the worlds, have bounds,
But neither space nor time enfolds Him!

To GABRIEL*'s left, but standing on a higher stair,* RAPHAEL *becomes visible. A radiant helmet hides his brow and eyes.*

RAPHAEL [*joining in, in a gentler voice*]. And yet He reads your heart and knows your feelings
As though He were yourself, and you—His child!

JACOB. O mild and gentle one, your words are healing...
Who are you?

RAPHAEL. What He made me, soft and mild!
Young Jacob, you are still a budding shoot,
But you must grow and ripen—you must flower!
I, Raphael, then may stand beside your bed,
Healing and soothing with my peaceful power!

The clouds to GABRIEL*'s right are parted by mighty wings.* URIEL *becomes visible on a level with* RAPHAEL. *His eyes and brow are overshadowed by his radiant helmet. His dark hair is blowing in the wind. His voice is clear and joyful.*

URIEL [*turning to* RAPHAEL]. He is beginning—do not speak of ending!
Our joyful tidings shall to him be given!
Jacob, look up—around you are extending
The sheltering wings of all the hosts of heaven!
I, Uriel, send my tempests down to wreak
Destruction on the dwellers in the vale,
But you must struggle upwards to the peak
Above the pain and torment of the gale!

Far overhead the clouds are torn asunder. MICHAEL *becomes visible. He is in full armour. His bright mail, composed of scales like an animal's shell, shimmers with silver, mother-of-pearl, and opal. His weapons are a buckler and a bare, flaming sword. His brow and eyes are hidden by his helmet.*

MICHAEL. Restrain your revelry, you winds—be calm! [*Looking upwards*]
Hurt not his eyes, you glowing light—be dim!

GABRIEL [*bending down to Jacob, in a low voice*]. The words of your protector—

THE THIRD ANGEL [*softly*]. Radiant
  In arms!
THE FIRST ANGEL [*in a whisper*]. Michael has spoken!
THE SECOND ANGEL [*blissfully*].   List to him!

The torrents of light that have been plunging from above now surround
the angels' forms more mildly; the deep midnight blue of the starry
heavens can again be made out. On RAPHAEL's *left, overtopping him*
slightly, SAMAEL *becomes visible. The outlines of his figure, not con-*
cealed by a robe, are lost in the darkness; a pallid light lies only on his
pale, calm, youthful face. His wide eyes gaze over his surroundings into
the obscure distance.

JACOB [*hesitantly*]. I waited long for such a visitation,
  And now it's come, I tremble none the less!
  Did you descend from heaven just for me?
GABRIEL. For your sake—all of us!
ALL THE ANGELS [*joining in loudly*]. All of us!
MICHAEL.   Yes!
JACOB [*catching sight of* SAMAEL]. And you as well, whose gaze no
    helmet hides?—
  You will not speak to me? [*Turning to the angels*] You shining
    ones —
  Your splendid glory stands on stairs of light—
  But that pale being, beside you, in the dark,
  Where rests his foot?
SAMAEL [*His voice carries through space, clear and calm*]. I stand on
    ancient night!
JACOB. I know you not, yet when I see your eyes,
  Some ancient memory lingers in my brain—
SAMAEL [*unmoved*]. You know me not, you never saw me, and
  That which you recognize in me—is pain!
JACOB. You are not one of these! Your face is fair,
  But grief, not jubilation, is your token!
  I do not see your wings!
SAMAEL [*impassively*]. I cannot fly;
  I too had wings like these—but they were broken!
URIEL [*in sudden anger*]. What, do you raise your head again? Be
    silent!
GABRIEL. You vile corruptor!

SAMAEL [*bitterly*]. Why this timid tone?
For are you not the mighty hosts of heaven?
And I— [*overcome by pride and defiance*] I say it gladly—am alone!

MICHAEL [*in a powerful voice*]. Are you still proud? I once could
    have destroyed you,
But spared you from the death-blow I had planned!

SAMAEL [*with gloomy scorn*]. What, you? It was not I who bade you
    spare me!
Another—One who needs me—stayed your hand!

MICHAEL. Don't listen to him, Jacob!

GABRIEL.   From his mouth
Come blasphemy, rebellion—

URIEL.   Abhorred!

RAPHAEL. Why do you come between us and the boy?

SAMAEL [*drawing himself up; in a powerful voice*]. Why did you come
    between me and the Lord?

*He forces himself to be calm, filled by a pain that is stronger than his
scorn.*

I speak no blasphemy! I *cannot* praise!
You sun yourselves in His eternal reign,
And yet your trumpetings and shouts of joy
Are drowned by the atrocious howls of pain [*Almost groaning*]
Rising perpetually from the world
That He created! Wonderful indeed!
I do not envy Him the bloodstained mess
Composed of lust and hatred, fear and greed! [*With increasing
    passion*]
Is pain a punishment? What law was broken
By beasts that die in silent agony?
You happy beings! Tell me, for what crime
Are infants born with sores and venomed wounds?
Sing praises to His kindness, love and power—
This riddle leaves me horrified! Could He
Not make things different? Did He will them thus?
Does He not shudder at his dreadful works?
Did He create this globe for pleasure? Now,
Slipped from His hands, it rolls through space and time,
But to what end? Complaisant lackeys, how,

How can you praise this plaything that He made—
And botched it—for He lacked the strength for better!
MICHAEL [*holding up his gleaming sword menacingly; in a firm voice*].
      Mock not the world's creator and begetter!
He has not finished—He is still creating!

The voices of invisible angelic hosts from far and near echo the words:
    He is still creating!
MICHAEL. And he has called on us...
URIEL.   Rejoice!
MICHAEL.   To help,
To help him shape—
URIEL [*jubilantly*].   The universal frame!

The angels' voices succeed one another in ever-growing blissful confidence.

GABRIEL. His messengers, the lights that wing their way
    Through empyrean heights to praise His name!
URIEL [*more forcefully*]. And fire that flashes from the sombre clouds,
    The raging floods, the peaceful murmuring rill,
    The gale, the gentle breezes—one and all
    He summoned, His instructions to fulfil!
RAPHAEL [*more gently*]. And metal flowering in the earth's recesses,
    And all that seeds and sprouts and seeks the sun,
    And what you feel, your laughter and your tears,
    All serve His plan, unknowing, every one!
GABRIEL [*in a powerful voice*]. The silent will that animates the
    beasts,
    Our songs of praise—the envious looks you send,
    Did you but know, you gloomy being, help
    Create his world, with Him...
MICHAEL.   ... World without end!
URIEL [*forcefully*]. Look at us, Jacob! Turn your face away
    From him who was condemned...
SAMAEL [*with deeply injured pride*]. Not so, I say!
    Cast out, but not condemned! And still at one
    With Him, your Master—not the servile choirs
    Who sing His praise with tedious jubilation!
    God cast me out because He needs a shadow
    To loom across the brightness of creation! [*Appealing anxiously,
    almost tenderly*]

Boy! Do not sell yourself to strength and light
And splendour...

RAPHAEL [*imploringly*]. Jacob, hark to us—to *us*!
For only once...

URIEL [*in warning tones*]. Just once!

RAPHAEL.   ... comes such a night!

GABRIEL [*solemnly*]. A wide domain was promised to your fathers,
 And now to you is made the self-same pledge:
 From northern wastes where snow eternal gathers,
 Extending to the southern desert's edge!
 A land whose meadows suck the dew of heaven,
 And hundredfold reward the tiller's toil—

URIEL [*almost shouting for joy*]. A land that flows with waters,
 springs, and wells,
 With milk and honey, corn and vines and oil!
      JACOB *gets to his feet.*
You hear?

JACOB [*in a low voice*]. I hear!

URIEL.   No answer?

JACOB [*softly, then more loudly*].   Who am I,
 That I should dare to answer such as you?
 It is a father's blessing: corn and cider,
 The fatness of the earth, the heaven's dew. [*Stirred by profound
  emotion*]
 Yet since the heavens' canopy has parted
 To send you shining ones to speak to me,
 I crave a different blessing at your hands,
 Another gift—whatever it may be!
 [*Bitterly*]. My youth was spent in restless pride and sorrow,
 Awaiting Him—awaiting you, and now?—
 I must have sought too high a grace. Dismiss me!
 To silent torpor I myself resign!
 Call Edom hither, and bestow on Edom
 The happiness that should be his, not mine!

URIEL [*angrily*]. Boy, wait till we have done, before you speak!

GABRIEL [*in a powerful voice*]. From your loins there shall spring a
 tribe, a nation;
 The sea will part that they may cross dry-shod!
 And when they travel through the pathless waste,

Their guide shall be the fire and smoke of God,
Until they gain the land, the towns and castles
Where now the Jebusite makes his abode;
On Uru-Shalim's rock a royal throne
Shall seat the kings who come from Jacob's blood!

SAMAEL [*quietly*]. Power must end, and nations disappear...

JACOB [*dismissively*]. That does not matter...

GABRIEL [*to* SAMAEL]. Quiet! [*To* JACOB, *kindly*].

                                             What do *you* say?

JACOB [*with gloomy reserve*]. He chooses, He decides; was I
    consulted?
What can I say to envoys now they're here?

URIEL [*in fury*]. Dare you defy the Lord, whose wondrous power
Places a radiant crown upon your head
And casts a royal mantle round your shoulders?
Humility should be your word instead!

JACOB [*in pain, throwing back his head*]. How can the chosen one of
    God be *humble*? [*In an agony of vexation*]
O angels, send me back to sleep, I pray!
That is the only service I request!
But if you can, then show my soul the way
To Hebron, where its dear departed rest!

> RAPHAEL´s *shape has separated itself from the clouds and is now
> standing behind Jacob.*

RAPHAEL [*softly, with his hand on* JACOB's *head*]. You're still a child,
    my dear, and that is why
You'd throw your life away—because you're young!

> *He bends over* JACOB, *takes him by the shoulders, and pulls him
> upright.*

Come, take a deep, calm breath, and do not cry,
And if you're feeling hurt, tell us what's wrong!

JACOB [*closing his eyes, softly*]. I seem to know your voice. When I
    was small,
My mother spoke to me such gentle things...

> *He rests his head on* RAPHAEL's *shoulder.*

RAPHAEL [*walking slowly backwards with him*]. Lean on me—so—
    and let me guide you—there—

And sit down in the shadow of our wings!

He is standing at the same spot as before. He lets JACOB *slide slowly to
the ground.* JACOB's *head rests against* RAPHAEL's *knees.*

RAPHAEL [*looking up at* MICHAEL]. Speak, Michael! You are by the
  Lord appointed
As his protector for all time to come—
Ask him yourself...

JACOB [*shuddering*]. But do you need to ask me?
Surely you know me—surely God must know me?
As I grew up, did I not always turn
To Him, as flowers turn towards the sun?
Have not three generations felt His presence?
Does He not know my blood? Does He insist
On my confessing, stammering and shameless,
What He already knows? [*In injured pride*]
                        Are we the mere
Recipients of glory? Is my blood
Good for no more than to engender kings?
I do not wish to be a ruler here!
Babel, Mizraim,* and the royal coast—
Does He suppose I envy that domain?
I do not envy your angelic bliss... [*In agony*]
Could I be happy in a world of pain?
Awake or dreaming, I am hard beset:
Men, animals, and plants, all things that live,
The very stones cry out, demanding answers
From me—the answers only He can give!

        He looks up to the angels as though imploring help.

And that, I think, is why all suffering things
Are sent to me, a boy, untried and tender:
For He is far away in heaven's height,
Pavilioned in glory, throned in splendour...
From my blood there shall spring a noble shoot,
That through all time shall grow and flourish still,
And never fade— [*With growing assurance*] my lips shall evermore
Proclaim the word of His eternal will!
And that is why He broke my carefree youth,
That I, with human steps, should here below

Retrace the distant path that God must go,
And be the voice of His eternal truth...

URIEL [*bursting into rage*]. You say 'eternal' when you soon must
    rot?

GABRIEL [*in a powerful voice*]. Eternal is the Lord, and you are dust!

URIEL. We shall not bear such words before His throne!

JACOB [*bitterly, breathing fast*]. I know, I know—your hand is
    close—I must

Go to the land from which there's no return—
You breathe on me—and I approach the dead!
I'm but a worm! And yet, from him to me,
From me to him—your mission I recall:
You are not lords, but messengers instead!

URIEL. He's raving!

JACOB.   You may bar my way to God,

But not for long—and He will hear my plea!

URIEL. Impertinence—you slave!

JACOB.   No slave am I;

God chose me, for He wants me to be free!

URIEL. What blasphemy! Fall down upon your face,

Your brow and hair in earthly dust to hide!
Repent, recant, and beg forgiveness!

JACOB [*jubilantly*].   Never!

God chose me, for He wants my honest pride! [*Resolute and
    submissive*]

God, here I stand, and if I've sinned, condemn me!
The vow You made my forebears—take it back!
I set You free, God, from the oath You swore!
God, throned amid the thunder, let Your fire
Blast me and slay me! And my soul shall die:
Too wild, too wild was my imploring cry!

*Amid low thunder, black clouds descend, shot through with flashes of
lightning, and cover everything with roaring darkness. Then silence. The
air clears. The* ANGELS *become visible; their heads are bowed. Only*
JACOB *is standing upright as before. His hands are resting on his breast,
he is breathing quietly and deeply. He is surrounded by light. The*
ANGELS *stand upright, first* MICHAEL *with a jerk, then the others
more slowly.*

RAPHAEL [*softly*]. No lightning struck him, Uriel!

GABRIEL.   There's light
Upon his brow!

RAPHAEL.   And flowing all around him!

MICHAEL. The radiance of the Lord is on his head!

SAMAEL [*in a low voice; grave, without hatred*]. *Your* light is dimmed
by *his* exceeding brightness!

GABRIEL [*in a low voice, to himself*]. You'd lure him, tempter, with
your flattering tongue?

MICHAEL [*calling loudly*]. O Jacob, hearken!

THE ANGELS' VOICES *succeed one another, each clearer and more jubilant than the last.*

RAPHAEL. Hearken!

GABRIEL.   Hearken!

URIEL.   Hearken!

MICHAEL. Upon my lips the Lord has set these words:
Your choice is one the Lord will not refuse!
The coastal kings shall perish, Mizraim
And Babel's towers shall be to ruin hurled!
But you alone, the Lord's eternal nation,
Shall roam for ever His eternal world!

SAMAEL [*urgently*]. Do *not* accept it, Jacob! Don't accept!

MICHAEL. The mighty nations of today shall crumble
To dust, and be forgotten and forlorn!
None may endure save you! You shall be slain
A thousand times, and every time reborn!

SAMAEL [*with a bitter laugh*]. You may endure! You *may*! Thanks to
His kindness
Your soul desires the fate He'll make you suffer!
You think you're choosing freely in your blindness! [*Imploringly*]
Do not accept it! Other nations too
Endure, although their names may change: like rivers
Enriched by tributaries, ancient blood
Can mingle with the life that youth delivers!
And they are able to forget their fates—
While you alone remember and regret...
They *may* remember ancestors; you *must*,
For you're the nation that cannot forget!
Dragged at God's heels through every age and time—

He looks upwards and nods, with satisfaction in his voice.

Yet why fear solitude? Why feel alone?
Do not accept it! Though it sounds like bliss,
It's hell!

JACOB.   I take this fate to be my own!

URIEL [*bursting out in rapture*]. Hail to you, Jacob!

MICHAEL [*with a kind of jubilation repeatedly breaking through the
     steely gravity of his voice*].

                                    By the Lord appointed
As witness to his wonders—you'll proclaim them
To mainland, islands, every land and clime,
Till every knee shall bow before the Lord
And every tongue attest His holy word!
Thanks to the cry that sprang from your despair,
Dumb suffering at last can find a voice;
Your word shall sanctify a royal crown,
And help the grateful nations to rejoice! [*More rapidly and
     eloquently*]
Your word shall punish, comfort, and reward,
Shall bless the cradle, consecrate the dead—
You shall become an everlasting torch
Flaming above the paths all nations tread!
The Lord will make you stubborn and stiff-necked;
Your burdens will be great—your strength no less!
You'll light the nations, help the blind to see,
Set prisoners free from darkness and duress...
He'll heat and hammer you for His good pleasure,
A steadfast rock Time's waves shall beat in vain;
You shall become a monument and measure
For faith, for hope, for suffering and pain!
You shall...

SAMAEL [*interrupting with vehement scorn and anger*]. 'You shall'! *I'll*
     tell you what will happen!
All that is true! Yes, men will hear your words,
But smash the mouth that uttered them to pulp!
Yes, you shall roam! But will you ever rest?
'Home' is an empty word that cannot help!
You shall become the nation all exploit,
All men will wound you, none will hear your cry;

Your soles will tread an earth as hard as iron,
Above your heads shall stretch a brazen sky...
Too stubborn to betray your single God,
You shall be driven out and made the mock
Of mangy beggars who are glad to boast
That they are not from *your* ignoble stock! [*Carried away with
   hatred and bitterness*]
You chosen race, you blessing to the nations,
You'll suffer every misery and distress;
All men shall hate and loathe your minds and bodies,
Spit in your very face...

JACOB [*rising in revolt*]. No! No!
SAMAEL [*as though stabbing with a knife*]. Yes! Yes!
   They will! And every nation where you lodge
   Shall burn you like an ulcerated sore...

His words fall like whiplashes on JACOB'*s bowed head, which shudders
                         under them.*

Though men hate poison, plague, and rabid beasts,
God's favourite, they'll hate you even more!
They'll burn your parents till they're charred to ash,
Your mutilated wife will die in shame,
Your unborn child shall be ripped forth and smashed,
Men will exterminate your race and name! [*With a jubilant cry*]
Such are His blessings!

JACOB [*with a shriek of despair*]. Messengers of God,
   Have you no answer?
SAMAEL.   Dare to say I'm wrong!
JACOB. Don't leave me with this monster, all alone!
SAMAEL. You're God's elected whipping-boy, you fool!
   The blows He heaps upon your patient body
   Make other nations quail before His throne! [*With terrible gravity*]
   Appalled by what He has Himself created,
   He needs you faithful servants to proclaim
   To all the nations that the pain they suffer
   Is punishment, and He is not to blame!
   You are His victim! Only good for this:
   When He has left you bleeding in the dust,
   You serve Him as a witness who is still

Prepared to praise your God for being—*just*!
You keep on hoping: only one more trial,
Then God will cease to scarify your nation...
Abandon Him! No judge records your woes
To pay you back with equal compensation! [*With a loud cry*]
Abandon Him!

JACOB [*standing erect*]. Abandon Him? I can't!

[*With a blissful smile*]. You thing of pain, have *you* abandoned
   Him?
Your hatred brings you closer to His throne
Than all the rapture of His cherubim!
You're warning me, but my ancestral blood
Speaks in me, and I love Him—as He is! [*Fervently*]
A God at once compassionate and cruel—
Radiant light—a deep and dark abyss!
I won't abandon Him! I'm His for ever!
Fear can't repel me, favours can't allure:
For deep within me, past the reach of words,
There sleeps what you have lost: a faith that's sure! [*In absolute
   self-surrender*]
Hear me, my God! Your messengers are silent—
Then *I'll* speak! I won't leave You on Your own!
A dim reflection of Your distant fate—
That is my destiny, and mine alone!
Hear me, my God! Your messengers are silent— [*Bursting into
   jubilation*]
You chose me, I chose you—You, the Most High—
Tell them that in our anger, doubts, and quarrels,
We two are joined for ever—You and I! [*In a more subdued tone*]
God, You are full of grace, and want to share it:
Let Your three currents flow into my blood,
Strength, pride, and patience, in a sacred flood;
And, if You're bowed by guilt, I'll help to bear it: [*Spreading out
   his arms*]
Upon my shoulders place Your guilty load! [*Bowing his head upon
   his chest*]

SAMAEL [*with a sneer*]. You think He's proud? Mind—He'll accept
   your offer!
He'll pile on burdens till your shoulders crack!

You'll rise again from scourging—He'll look on!
You'll drag yourself in agony—He'll let you,
Nor give your parching tongue a single drop!
He won't have any mercy on you!

MICHAEL [*bursting out*].

Liar!

GABRIEL, URIEL, RAPHAEL [*and the other three* ANGELS *in a united shout of fury*]. You lie!

Hastening to their support from the air, near and far, high and deep voices join in a wild crescendo.

THE ANGELS' VOICES. You lie!

A ray of light that darkens everything else pierces the clouds, descends steeply, and focuses on Jacob. At the same time, A GENTLE VOICE, *clear and calm, breaks through the tumult, which falls silent in its presence.*

THE VOICE.   Samael's words are *true*!

The angels are swathed in cloud, only JACOB *is visible. His hands are resting on his chest, his head is bowed.*

When others kneel to me and beg for grace,
I spare them, as a lord his slave; but *you*
Shall stand before your Father face to face
And get no mercy! Ask me for your *due*!
In my name you shall suffer woes beyond all count,
But, even in torment, you shall know that you're my own!

The VOICE *becomes deeper, with infinite love emerging from its resonance.*

My debt of guilt to you, my son, must always mount,
Till high above all others I raise you—to atone!

URIEL. Your morning gales, O Lord, will soon be blowing!

Clear high ANGELIC VOICES *all round.*

THE ANGELIC VOICES. Lord! Lord! Your starry light is fading fast!

URIEL. Must the gales pause, O Lord?

THE ANGELIC VOICES.   ... The stars keep glowing?

THE VOICE. Let stars and winds perform their wonted task!
All things join hands to dance a sacred round
Pursuing courses I myself decreed—
Let my sun's rays across the heavens resound—

Distant thunder

This night's appointed work is now complete!

*The ray vanishes. The morning wind blows white clouds round the hilltop.
The light grows.* THREE ANGELS, *previously stationed around
Jacob's sleeping-place, are now surrounding him.* GABRIEL *emerges from
the clouds.*

GABRIEL. Sink down once more, my Jacob, on your stone,
    A brief repose is all you can afford!

JACOB, *his eyes closed, sinks back into the arms of the angels, who let
    him slide onto his sleeping-place.* GABRIEL *bends over him.*

Remember, when you fight yourself or others:
This very night you strove with God the Lord!
The memory of this night, thus He commands,
Will shake the seed that in your loins shall dwell!

He looks up.

His dawn is breaking. Time your eyes should open!
Now, walk, behold, and hearken, Israel!

*Gathering clouds conceal the hilltop. The rustling of great wings fades
away in the distance. The clouds dissolve into swathes of mist and sink
slowly into the valley. The grey light of early morning surrounds the
hilltop.* JACOB *is alone and asleep. He breathes heavily and with
difficulty. Against the roar of the morning gale the faint sound of distant
cow-bells can occasionally be heard.*

JACOB *rises unsteadily from his sleeping-place, his eyes still closed; he is
struggling for breath, his words come uncertainly and hesitantly from his
lips.*

JACOB I'm walking—hold me, do not shake, my knees!

Opens his eyes wide

And I behold—the cloud and mist; I hear
The wind of morning— [*Touching the stone on which he rested*]
    Did they not arise,
A gallery of heavenly hosts, just here? [*In a lower voice*]
Are you still muttering, stone of my repose?
You were a star—do you lament your fall?
You think the Lord rejected you? He chose
This very stone, most dignified of all,

To be His heaven's threshold here below! [*With a sigh*]
It's past. The gate is shut!

He turns to the East.

His mighty day
Unfolds, as though the world were new created!
His gale rejoices! His great light approaches
And opens petals still in slumber curled. . . [*Breathing deeply, with his head thrown back and his eyes closed*]
Bright morning, you have never heard of grief—
I breathe you in, you new created world! [*Looking upwards; in a lower voice*]
Was I too bold in what I said last night?
Was I too proud in thus addressing You?
Behold, Creator, every dawn You send
Makes me fall down and worship You anew!

The wind carries the ringing of many cow-bells, louder than before, up from the valley. Amid their sound can be heard the song played by the shepherd SHUA *on his flute.*

I lie here, Lord! I, Jacob, whom You summoned!
Your choice, and yet a child of earth as well!
Does my way now lead downward to the dale?
And am I summoned by my cattle's bell?
My shepherd down there, is your song intended
To wake me? Shepherd, I'm awake all right!
I'm coming! I must bid farewell to ground
That was made holy—in a holy night!

IDNIBAAL'S VOICE [*from the valley*]
Where are you, master?

JACOB [*who has got to his feet*]. Idnibaal, I'm coming!
Just wait for me a moment—more is waiting
Upon the road that starts for me down there! [*Beginning in a lower voice*]
Lord! Whatsoever Your command imposes
Shall never bow my back, but crown my head!
My blood may serve You as a fiery torch
Flaming above the paths all nations tread...
Lord, do not let my blood's remote descendants
Forget the choice that You Yourself have made!

But if they should forget, if by the wayside
They fall, then spare them from a coward's death! [*In a powerful
    voice*]
Call to them, Lord, O call, and from my blood
A leader or a preacher shall come forth
To fan the embers, kindled by Your breath,
The sacred, hidden glow that smoulders still,
And tell them— [*Frowning in an imperious and threatening manner*]
            tell them why they have been chosen
For evermore to do Your holy will. [*Imploringly*]
O Lord, lend force to what his lips can say!
From Your divine magnificence and bliss
Cast on his words, O Lord, a single ray, [*In pride and humility*]
And do it, Lord, for Your sake—not for his!

*He turns round swiftly and steps behind the stone. He picks up one after
the other the silver cup filled with wine, the skinful of milk, the ram's
horn containing oil, and lets some drops of each trickle onto the stone. His
                    voice is clear and proud.*

With this land's fruit and blessing I anoint you,
O stone— [*Recollecting joyfully*] With *my* land's wine... and milk...
    and oil!
IDNIBAAL'S VOICE [*from the valley*]. Where are you, Jacob?
JACOB, *still bending over the stone, suddenly springs to his feet. With
rapid steps he approaches the brow of the hill. He reaches for his long
shepherd's crook which is lying on the ground. Turning to the East,
standing erect, he calls down to the valley in a jubilant voice:*
                            I'm no longer Jacob!
For he who strove with God—is Israel!
                It is broad daylight.

ELSE LASKER-SCHÜLER

The Wonder-Working Rabbi of Barcelona

'The Wonder-Working Rabbi of Barcelona', written in 1921, is an elliptical and often obscure tale which draws on many aspects of Else Lasker-Schüler's rich imaginative life. Like many European Jews, including Heine and Herzl, she liked to think that her ancestors were not Ashkenazic Jews from Germany or Poland but dignified and learned Sephardic Jews from Spain. Her imaginary Spain is entirely unhistorical. Similarly, although her father was a private banker, she liked to imagine him as a builder or architect, the profession assigned here to Arion Elevantos. The builder's daughter, Amram, has affinities with Lasker-Schüler herself. Bearing a man's name (that of Moses' father, Exodus 6: 20), she joins the male figures such as Tino of Baghdad and Yussuf Prince of Thebes whom Lasker-Schüler invented to signify an androgynous self-conception. Her love for Pablo is close in spirit to Lasker-Schüler's many love poems, like 'Pharaoh and Joseph' and 'David and Jonathan', which evoke an intense feeling of being in love rather than exploring a concrete relationship; and the ship that appears in the market-place to carry Amram and Pablo away represents Lasker-Schüler's recurrent fantasy about love as a rescue from the pain and deprivation of actual experience.

Although love unites two representatives of the Christian and Jewish communities, it has no effect on anyone else. The pogrom still breaks out, recalling the massacre evoked by Heine in his unfinished historical novel *The Rabbi of Bacherach*, and the Jews are slaughtered. Their devout leader Eleazar does not protect them; indeed, it is when he is absorbed in devout contemplation that the Jews are sure to be persecuted. The advice he offers is religious. Instead of leading them to the Holy Land, he tells them they need to have the Holy Land in their hearts; this may be seen as Lasker-Schüler's answer to Zionism, anticipating her disappointment on visiting Palestine in 1934 and finding the settlers very different from the 'Hebrews' and 'wild Jews' of her imagination. At the end, however, Eleazar does avenge his people. After fervent prayer, he and his house fall on the city and crush its inhabitants as Samson did the Philistines. The end of the story thus contrasts this heaven-sent miracle with the prosaic 'enlightenment' professed by the Christians of Barcelona. As a whole, the story, with its lyrical and often enigmatic style, is an attempt to revive a religious, legendary understanding of the Jewish people and Jewish history, and thus to overcome the rationalism which the German Jews themselves adopted as part of the Enlightenment which had originally admitted them to Western society.

The poem 'Pablo', which forms part of the story, is given here in the translation by Robert Newton.

———

During the weeks that Eleazar spent in pious contemplation in old Asia, the people of Barcelona took pains to persecute the Jews. It was they, once again, who made it hard for Spanish merchants to charge excessive prices, but, at the same time, spread their redemptive ambitions among the poor of the city. Apostolic figures among them preached equality and fraternity, and they broke their hearts in their bosoms and gave them to the poor, as Jesus of Nazareth shared the bread of his blue heart with them. But no matter how the Jews behaved, they aroused resentment, which in truth originated with a single disappointed Spaniard who had once clashed with a Hebrew, and was transferred to the people. This year, as before, Eleazar, the wonder-working rabbi, returned to Barcelona at the stated time. His dignified head, mysteriously enlarged and made more real as though seen through a magnifying-glass, and framed by the arched window of the palace, nodded kindly to everyone who passed, whether Jew or Christian. Rumours about Eleazar were whispered throughout the Spanish town. He was said to be Gabriel, the great archangel, who never died; the unmelting snow of his beard enveloped the Ark of the Covenant. The Jews, however, were more familiar with Gabriel; they often saw the wonder-working rabbi smiling; once he jubilantly clapped his slender, delicate hands, even in prayer before the altar, for he had seen Jehovah... and he became a child The old Jews, heirs of their fathers, had inscribed on the calendar of the hearts the day on which their supreme rabbi had been born to them. On the seventh of the month of Gam* children and grandchildren made a pilgrimage up the hill to the Jews' palace, to bring their wonder-working priest branches from the woods, hung with sweet and bitter berries, for Eleazar loved the wild corals and liked to inhale their scent, whereupon he would satiate his hunger and refresh himself with the pure flesh of the humblest fruit, and have all the other foodstuffs distributed to the needy of Barcelona. This year, however, the Jews intended no longer to conceal from their sacred jewel the sufferings that awaited them annually in his absence. On that same wet and misty evening, the hard-pressed Jewish nobility, assembled in a cellar, resolved to leave this world. Scattered everywhere, planted, a flavouring to the dough, tired of sweetening it for the sake of a slight, bitter aftertaste, a whole people, tired of being humiliated for millennia. Thus the tormented Jews were dimly conscious of their destiny. The yearning for their lost country, which they had possessed only on sufferance, rose higher in them all, and each of them solemnly watered the bed of his recollection; even their wonder-working rabbi could not tell them where they would land; for some young Jews had taken roots in the soil of Spain, in the enchanting perfume of roses, and their sisters with Jerusalem eyes had given Christians a painful awakening. But Eleazar replied to the worried community: 'Anyone who does not bear the promised land in his heart will never get there.' And this God, he said, revealed Himself to all men as their noblest and most ancient quality. And when asked how this could be, since most creatures were so godless, the highest priest said with heartfelt sorrow that only a few were able to be gardeners for their God, to honour and tend their most precious seeds. And there was no greater impoverishment on earth than to allow the heavenly blossom of the heart to wither.

Whenever Eleazar, the wonder-working rabbi, called out the awe-inspiring name of Jehovah, the Jews heard it devoutly, down to the grain of their pulses, and all their good deeds awoke and they repented of their bad actions. The Spaniards, however, shut their ears to the redeeming sound, which scratched the temples of the Jews to let them drink divine lymph, and exacted a drop of blood as payment from many a one whom the sound shook to the core.— Among the Jewish people of Barcelona there lived a poetess, the daughter of a distinguished man who had the task of building the watchtowers of Spain's great cities. Wishing for an heir to his building skills, Arion Elevantos brought up Amram, his daughter, like a son. Early each morning Amram and her father ascended the incomplete buildings, the highest skeletons of the town, so that she often thought she had been paying a visit to God. And her eyes had gazed up into the domes of wood from Lebanon and pure gold which Arion extended over the roof of the splendid house, a present from the wealthy Jews, to shield their wonder-working rabbi from

mischance. Descending the ladder that led from the still unattached
crest, little Amram in her haste fell from the sacred building on to a
sandy hillock where Pablo, the little son of the mayor, was playing.
And the boy thought pale Amram was an angel that had tumbled out
of a cloud in the kingdom of heaven, and looked at her in astonishment. After that Amram smiled in her dreams whenever Pablo
thought about her.

Pablo, at night I hear the palm leaves
Rustle beneath your feet.

Sometimes I have to cry a lot
From happiness about you.

Then a smile grows
On your hooded eyelids.

Or a rare joy opens for you:
Your heart's black aster.

Whenever past the gardens
You see the end of your pathway, Pablo,

—It's my eternal thought of love
Desiring to join you.

And often a glow will fall from heaven,
For in the evening my golden sigh goes searching for you.

Soon the languishing month arrives
Over your dear city;

Under the garden tree there hang
Flocks of birds like gaily coloured grapes.

And I too wait enchanted
Hung about by dream.

You proud native, Pablo,
I breathe from your countenance strange sounds of love;

But on your brow I want to plant my fortunate star,
Rob myself of my luminous blossom.

As the Señor grew up, signs appeared to him unexpectedly in ancient
harp-writing. The officials, his father's subordinates, interpreted

them scornfully as the writing of dogged, obdurate Jews who pestered his father, the supreme councillor, with rebellious writings. The mayor's son would have liked to knock at the palace of the wonder-working rabbi, to assure him of the unshakeable respect he felt for his people, but he feared the gossip of the townsfolk and, above all, his father's anger. Once, however, he disguised himself to follow a Jewish caravan that was making its way up the hill into the Jew's palace, and he felt in his heart the benefit of the blessing. The Spaniards only reluctantly allowed the synagogue among the houses of their city and felt it to be an alien member, this timid building on their roads. The Jews' mysterious prayer-house lay concealed behind an inn where Spanish students danced and shouted in the upper rooms or practised fencing within the walls. Sometimes the riotous crew, inflamed by hot wine, would kick the door of the synagogue on Friday evening. The women behind the railings quaked gently, and Amram felt a foreign continent growing between her and Señor Pablo, the mayor's son. The commandments in the Jews' prayer-books were read from the outside to the inside, and so, ever since their birth, their Jewish eyes had to be pointed in a different direction from those of all other nations. Eyes that dared not remain fixed on their object, eyes that hid in the book's stitching, always fled back to the column. 'Eyes that steal'—declared the mayor firmly to his blenching son. For the latter was recalling the secrecy of the time when they were still children and Amram his 'bride', when this she-angel of the heavenly hosts had girded herself, with light in her eye, and told him that she had murdered the tailor with her little dagger and buried him in the sand, as the prophet did the Egyptian who maltreated the Jews under his yoke of slavery. 'Tailor' was the children's name for the bony, skinny-legged sweet-seller, who kept his little shop behind the school and was notorious for often having attacked Jewish children. He accused the innocent creatures of theft, after he had magically put sweets in their pockets like a wizard. Threatening to tell their parents about his crimes, the young, wailing victims, whom he dragged into a dark subterranean hole in his house, let him satisfy his filthy lust on them.

One day a big ship was standing in the market-place. Human effort, horses, and ox-power could not remove the mysterious vessel from the city, though it damaged trade and the market. But the excited

Spaniards advised their mayor to consult old Gabriel, the wise magician, and they pointed out the Jews' glittering house, with pure sunshine bleeding from its windows. And the Spanish patricians, the citizens and workers, along with many Jews, and Pablo's worthy father, the mayor of Barcelona, at their head, stood outside the gate of the golden palace; they were so busy that they had overcome their inexplicable shyness. Since the previous evening, however, the small, decent company of the Jewish elders had been with Eleazar, for they had resolved to tell their wonder-working rabbi gently about their fears, and to ask him not to leave the town this year. From the blessed hilltop Barcelona could be seen, empty and starved, lying in its valley. Only the mayor's big, long-haired dog, Abraham, was hurrying through the town, through the streets of Barcelona, constantly sniffing at the ship that had given ear to two people's yearning overnight. At the helm, Señor Pablo and Amram, the Jewish poetess, were playing unconcernedly in the sun, just as after the little accident on the sacred hill outside Eleazar's palace they had so often delighted in their notions when they were children. Transfigured by immense love, they remained invisible behind the wing of the sail. And only the dog witnessed how the seas' enormous messenger, moved by love, passed lightly across the market-place, through the streets of the town that stretched out devout arms, then vanished through the gate as carefully as a solemn bridal carriage. Eleazar refused to receive the mayor with his mass following, for what was the use of talking to sleepers! And the small number of Jews who did not behave in a restrained and timid way, as is proper for heirs of an ancient people, cared for him, strengthened by the stories of the Jewish elders who had surreptitiously left the garden door of the supreme palace. During the night, spurred on by the wonder-working rabbi's refusal, the Christians now felt justified, the pogrom began. Raising their fists to form a hill, the Spaniards cried that Gabriel, the false archangel, the wicked magician, had drawn the great ship from the sea and in this trickery he had had the assistance of none other than Arion Elevantos, who, having built the Jews' palace, knew all its archways, secrets, and passageways, and the evil powers of its denizen, which could petrify the breath of the people of Barcelona. Even in the Bible the devil hid behind the score of his sins, and kill him, 'Kill him, the old procurer'!!! The bewildered Christians superstitiously confined themselves to breaking the windows of their good, cheerful master builder; forgot that he gave shelter in his buildings to many thousands of the poor of Barcelona, taking nothing in return. They gagged him; but he laughed in his dismay, as he used to rejoice in his boyhood, when a playmate grabbed him in a game of cops and robbers; till the mayor's wife approached and stirred up the people, alarmed though they were, to kill the father of the Jewish girl who had abducted her son. She herself tore the heart from the innocent victim's bosom to be a red foundation stone where masterless dogs should do their business. And the Jews, who had kept waking anew on hearing the name of Jehovah, all lay mutilated, savaged, their faces separated from their bodies, children's hands and tiny feet, tender human foliage, here and there in the alleys, into which these poor souls had been driven like cattle. But the evening breezes, the sweet liars who sang outside the palace of the great wonder-working rabbi, told tales that were dreamlike and false. 'Your sons are sitting by the hedges, Eleazar, suspecting nothing, counting the days and the hours that separate them from Palestine, and the delicate daughters of David are embroidering cushions with silk and pearls for the blessings of your hands. The feast of Passover is approaching, and the bakers are baking pious unleavened bread for your table, great wonder-working rabbi.' He leafed through the atlas of creation and read how at the beginning of things the Father made the world of earth and water and squeezed it into a ball, his 'wedding manna-cake', with all the golden ingredients of His heavenly blood, and how He took man from the great shape of the world and from him in turn He power-fully drew the nations and the nations' nations and the nations' nations' nations and invited them all to eat together. By His heart, however, He placed the Jews, for though they were few, of all the nations it was they who had turned out most in accordance with His orders and hence they were more obedient to him and more tender. 'And the all-loving Father', praised Eleazar singing, 'plucked a star from His robe, and lifted up the child among the nations and placed the light on his brown forehead. With this little light on the divine body of the world's guardian, the Lord made the enlightened Jews into the people of the prophets, to serve Him in every land, in every nation, on every road. Amen. For the great sibling nations, however, instead of the glorious ray, He made a home for them amid the green foliage of the august earth, in the rocking, refreshing rest of the water and beneath the pure winter snow of the breezes, to maintain a loving order, and every man, amid the men of all nations, should point to men above the nations.' The great hermit closed the faded book, whose commandments had fallen asleep in the hearts of most creatures, even in the blood of Judah. He loved his people and he constantly evaded their questions about home. Forced to leave the cities where they had been primordially destined to sow God, the Jewish thoughts that were still awake took refuge in the lap of the High Priest. But that Palestine was only the observatory to watch the stars of their home, that was something of which the wonder-working rabbi dared not remind the weary chosen people.

Now Eleazar's eyes, fixed on Barcelona—in the lightning of terror—split... wept. 'Lord, in truth, the boat on the waves of the sea awakened the awe of Your name.'

In immense yearning for the third time in his life the prophet cried out the awe-inspiring name of his Lord. And at the redeeming sound of Jehovah's name the dead of the dead awoke. They were the Christians and through them all the Christian nations of Christendom. Yet he mistrusted the penitent brother nations and their reawakening! The omnipotence of his great Lord made him angry.

* אין תקר לדרכי אדני

Unfathomable are the ways of the Eternal... 'You let your dearly beloved son be slaughtered ever and again and again, that the trumpet of Your holy name may awaken the nations of the Christians, and You reward their atrocities with enlightenment.' And Eleazar waited in the forecourt of his palace for God, the yearned-for guest. At last the Invisible One offered the impatient one His fatherly hand. But in the midst of the interior of the solemn chamber the priest's trembling, kneeling servant saw his great and holy maestro reaching out to the air's cool semblance, seizing it as the brave torero seizes the bull's horn in the arena—and then—on the stone arabesques lay the wonder-working rabbi bleeding. All night he went out wrestling in riddles with God; darkened and broke away from Him. The priest shook the pillars of his house till they broke like arms. The roof rolled down in heavy blocks and shattered the houses in the street. An enormous quarry, He, the great wonder-working rabbi, a nation plunged from the sacred hill, which was transfigured by the golden fragments of the dome's mosaic, upon the Christians of Barcelona, who were penitently laying the last tortured Jew to rest, and extinguished their enlightenment, crushed their bodies.

The angels spread a cloud-white tablecloth for the heavenly meal,
God took the heart of the high homecomer from its dish
To test the stubborn consecrated ore,
O Eleazar's heart was rubbed on heart,
Setting his stone ablaze!
Into his jug, Jerusalem, pour your wine
And let it ferment, stored up in the vale.

STEFAN ZWEIG

Book-Mendel

Stefan Zweig (1881–1942) was brought up in a highly assimilated home, the son of a successful textile manufacturer who had moved to Vienna from the Bohemian provinces, and received no religious training. He said in a 1931 interview: 'My mother and father were Jewish only through accident of birth.' He was not attracted to Herzl's Jewish nationalism, and regarded many expressions of Jewish pride as mere disguised insecurity, yet he felt at ease as a Jew and equated conversion with disloyalty. Foreseeing Hitler's annexation of Austria, Zweig emigrated in 1933, first to London, then to New York, and finally to Petropolis in Brazil, but the fall of Singapore in 1942 made him fear that no part of the world was safe from Nazism, and he and his wife committed suicide. Although Zweig did not directly address the 'Jewish question', his major works on Jewish themes, the biblical drama *Jeremias* and the Novelle 'Book-Mendel', reveal much about his assimilation.

Although Zweig's autobiography, *The World of Yesterday*, gives an extremely selective account of his life, with no reference, for example, to his marriage, it memorably evokes the 'golden age of security' before the First World War, when Zweig began developing his international humanism. His values have been summed up by David Turner: 'first, an emphasis on personal freedom together with a condemnation of those forces which restrict or destroy it; second, a high regard for intensity of experience and passionate commitment as opposed to emotional indifference; third, an ideal of the rounded personality, of wide human and cultural interests, in contradistinction to narrow-mindedness of any kind; fourth, an affirmation of human brotherhood across all man-made barriers of race, creed or class.' To this Turner adds compassion for individuals, a virtue evident in the story of Mendel the book-dealer. One must add Zweig's commitment to a European ideal of culture, evident in his many studies of artistic and historical figures from Erasmus and Montaigne to Tolstoy and Freud.

In his day Zweig was a popular and successful writer, especially with his historical biographies, and he has gained a reputation for facility which is seriously unjust to his best Novellen. 'Book-Mendel' belongs in a Viennese tradition of Novelle-writing, founded by Franz Grillparzer with

'The Poor Minstrel' (1848) and continued by Ferdinand von Saar in stories like 'Seligmann Hirsch'. A worldly narrator, with the experience of humankind only available in city life, gradually explores the character and life-story of an apparent eccentric, and sometimes has the limitations of his own worldliness exposed by the eccentric's hidden depths.

'Book-Mendel' is a meditation on memory. Hence the long preamble in which the narrator, finding himself in once-familiar surroundings, describes the unpredictable but powerful workings of his memory. His procedure of casting hooks into the depths of memory and eventually fishing up his prey closely recalls the study by John Livingston Lowes, *The Road to Xanadu* (1927), of the mysterious workings of Coleridge's 'tenacious and systematizing memory' which produced 'Kubla Khan'. Thus the narrator establishes in advance a contrast between his own mind and the perfectly functioning, machine-like memory possessed by Mendel. With his devotion to books, Mendel does typify the life of the spirit, in an extreme and specialized form. But though the narrator admires Mendel, Mendel also makes him uneasy. His encyclopaedic knowledge of books that is confined to their titles offers a parallel to Zweig's vast collection of manuscripts by writers whose creative powers he knew were superior to his own. Zweig projects into Mendel the fear of the assimilated Jew that his assimilation may be only external, that he may be unable to absorb and reproduce the essence of his adopted culture.

At the same time, 'Book-Mendel' is a fine document of Zweig's humanism. It reminds us to appreciate the gifts and the humanity of humble people whom we might be inclined to overlook: not only Mendel but also Frau Sporschil, the old toilet attendant whose warm heart puts the narrator to shame. The story also attacks the unimaginative inhumanity shown by the Habsburg bureaucracy in mistaking the innocent Mendel for a Russian spy. In his indifference to national divisions, Mendel half-humorously anticipates the international humanism which is Zweig's ideal, and he falls victim to narrow-minded soldiers who—as in subsequent wars—are prompt to thrust inoffensive foreigners into internment camps, or, as Zweig here baldly terms them, concentration camps.

Back in Vienna and returning home from a visit to the outer suburbs, I was unexpectedly caught in a sudden downpour whose wet lash sent people scurrying for shelter in doorways and under awnings, and I too hastened to search for a refuge. Fortunately, Vienna has a coffee-house waiting on every corner, and so I fled into the one directly opposite, with my hat already dripping and my shoulders soaked. Inside it proved to be almost a textbook example of the kind of coffee-house traditional in the inner suburbs, without the modish pretensions of the inner-city dancing bars copied from Germany, but firmly in the old Viennese style and filled with ordinary people who were devouring more newspapers than pastries. Now that it was evening, the air, thick enough already, was veined with coils of blue smoke, yet this coffee-house felt clean and smart, with its evidently new velvet sofas and the gleaming aluminium of its cash-register; in my haste I had not taken the trouble to read its name outside, and why should I?—And now I was sitting in the warmth and looking impatiently through the streaming blue window-panes to see when the tiresome rain would be good enough to move on a couple of kilometres.

Sitting there with nothing to do, I was already beginning to succumb to that indolent passivity which emanates like an invisible drug from every genuine Viennese coffee-house. With this empty sensation I looked in turn at each of the customers, noting the unhealthy grey shadows cast round their eyes by the artificial light in this smoky room, watched the girl at the counter as she mechanically gave the waiter sugar and a spoon for each coffee-cup, dreamily and unconsciously read the unimportant posters on the walls, and found my stupor almost enjoyable. Suddenly, however, I was strangely shaken out of my dozing state, an inner motion began causing me vague unrest, like the beginning of a slight toothache when one cannot yet tell whether it comes from the left, the right, from the upper or the lower jaw; I felt only a faint tension, an unease of the spirit. For suddenly— I could not have said how—I realized that I must have been here years earlier and be attached by some memory to these walls, these chairs, these tables, this unfamiliar smoky room.

But the more I strove to grasp this memory, the more it withdrew, malicious and slippery—vaguely luminous, like a jellyfish, in the lowest depths of consciousness, and yet impossible to catch or seize. It was in vain that my eyes clung to every object of furniture: of course there was much that was new to me, like the counter, for example, with its rattling cash-register, and the brown wall-panelling of imitation rosewood; all that must have been installed at a later date. And yet, and yet, I had been here once, twenty and more years ago, here part of my own self, long since submerged, remained invisibly hidden like a nail in a log. I forced all my senses to probe and patrol the room and simultaneously to penetrate my inner world—

and yet, confound it, I could not reach that vanished memory buried inside myself.

I felt annoyed, as one always does when some failure draws attention to the inadequacy and imperfection of one's mental powers. But I did not abandon the hope that I might after all reach that memory. I knew that I needed only to lay my hand on a tiny hook, for my memory works curiously, both well and badly, being on the one hand stubborn and self-willed, yet also indescribably faithful. It often sucks the crucial element of events and faces, reading and experience, right down into its obscurities and releases nothing from this underworld without being compelled to do so: a mere summons from my will does not suffice. But I have only to grasp the slightest clue, a postcard, a scrap of writing on an envelope, a yellowing page from a newspaper, and at once whatever I have forgotten darts forth, like a fish on a hook, from the dark swirling surface, in all its bodily and sensuous presence. I then know every detail about a person, his mouth, and in his mouth the gap between his teeth on the left when he laughs, and the brittle tone of that laugh and how it makes his moustache start twitching and how a different, new countenance emerges from that laugh—I see all these things immediately in a complete vision and know every word of the story that person told me years ago. But to see and feel the sensuous presence of the past, I need some sensory stimulus, some assistance, however tiny, from reality. Hence I closed my eyes in order to concentrate better and to shape and seize that mysterious fish-hook. But nothing! Still nothing! Buried and forgotten! And I grew so angry with the bad, self-willed memory-machine between my temples that I could have struck my forehead with my fists, as one shakes a malfunctioning machine that ignores the rules and refuses to yield up what one wants. No, I could not sit quietly any longer, so much did this mental failure irritate me, and I rose from sheer annoyance to seek some fresh air. But how curious—scarcely had I taken the first steps through the premises when that first phosphorescent glow began to glimmer and sparkle within me. To the right of the till, I remembered, there must be a windowless room lit only by artificial light. And that turned out to be correct. There it was, with different wallpaper, but with exactly the same dimensions, this rectangular back room, the games room, with its blurred contours in my mind. I instinctively looked round at the individual objects, my nerves already in joyful vibration (I felt I was about to know everything). Two billiard tables lounged like green, silent, muddy ponds, card tables crouched in the corners, at one of which two civil servants or professors were playing chess. And in the corner, just beside the iron stove, on the way to the telephone booth, stood a small square table. And then a flash suddenly shot through me. I knew at once, at once, with a single hot shudder that thrilled me with happiness: good heavens, that was where Mendel used to sit, Jacob Mendel, Book-Mendel, and after twenty years I had stumbled into his headquarters, the Café Gluck in the upper Alserstrasse.* Jacob Mendel—how could I have forgotten him for such an inexplicable length of time, that most curious of people, that legendary man, that eccentric wonder of the world, famous in the University and in a small, awestruck circle—how could I lose the memory of him, the mage and broker of books, who would sit here continuously from morning to evening every day, a symbol of knowledge, the pride and glory of the Café Gluck!

And it was only for that second that I needed to turn my gaze inwards behind my eyelids, and already his vivid, unmistakable figure was rising from my image-creating blood. I at once saw him in his bodily presence, as he used to sit at the little square table with the dirty grey marble top, invariably piled with books and papers. He would sit continuously, imperturbably, his spectacled gaze fixed hypnotically on a book; he would sit, humming and murmuring as he read, and shaking his ill-polished, spotty bald head backwards and forwards, a habit he had brought from the *heder*,* the Jewish infant school of the East. Here at this table, and only here, he would read his catalogues and books as he had been taught to read in the Talmud school, softly singing and swaying, a black, rocking cradle. For as a child falls asleep and is lost to the world thanks to this hypnotic rising and falling rhythm, so, in the opinion of all the devout, the spirit enters more easily into the grace of mystical absorption thanks to the rocking and swaying of the idle body. And sure enough, Jacob Mendel saw and heard nothing that was going on around him. Alongside him the billiard-players were shouting and quarrelling, the waiters were running to and fro, the telephone was ringing; the floor was being cleaned, the stove was being stoked, but he noticed nothing. Once a red-hot coal fell out of the stove, and the floor two steps from him was already emitting smoke and a smell of burning,

when a customer, from the infernal stench, noticed the danger and
rushed forward to extinguish the fumes: but he himself, Jacob Mendel, only inches away and already surrounded by smoke, had perceived nothing. For he read as others pray, as gamblers gamble and as
drunkards stare stupidly into vacancy; he read with such touching
absorption that, since then, all the reading done by other people has
always struck me as profane. In that little Galician book-pedlar Jacob
Mendel I, as a young man, first saw the great secret of absolute
concentration that shapes the artist and the scholar, the true sage and
the complete lunatic, that tragic fortune and misfortune of complete
possession.

I was led to him by an older colleague at the University. At that
time I was studying the Paracelsian physician and magnetizer Mesmer,* a figure too little known even today, but I was having scant
success; for the relevant works proved inadequate, and the librarian,
whom as an innocent beginner I had asked for information, replied
in a surly tone that to track down secondary literature was my job,
not his. It was then that my colleague first mentioned his name. 'I'll
take you to Mendel,' he promised; 'he knows everything and can get
hold of anything, he'll get you the most far-fetched book from the
obscurest second-hand bookshop in Germany. The ablest man in
Vienna and, what's more, an original character, an antediluvian dino-
saur of books, one of a dying race.'

Thus the two of us went to the Café Gluck, and behold, there he
sat, Book-Mendel, black-clad, bespectacled, his beard billowing
round him, rocking as he read like a dark bush in the wind. We went
up to him, but he did not notice. He only sat and read and rocked his
torso, like a statue in a pagoda, backwards and forwards above the
table, and behind him, on a hook, dangled his threadbare black
greatcoat, likewise stuffed with periodicals and scraps of paper. To
announce our presence my friend gave a powerful cough. But Mendel, his thick spectacles pressed close to his book, still did not notice.
Finally my friend rapped on the tabletop, as loudly and forcibly as
one raps at a door—then at last Mendel lifted his stare, pushed his
awkward steel-rimmed spectacles up to his forehead with a swift
automatic movement, and beneath his bristling ash-grey eyebrows
we felt the piercing gaze of two peculiar eyes, small, dark, watchful
eyes, agile, sharp and flickering like the tongue of a snake. My friend
presented me, and I explained my problem, first of all—this was a

stratagem my friend had expressly recommended—complaining with a show of anger about the librarian who had refused to give me any information. Mendel leaned back and spat carefully. Then he gave a short laugh and said in strong Eastern dialect: 'He wouldn't? No—he couldn't! A *parch*,* that's what he is, a donkey with grey hair. I've known him, may God pity me, for a good twenty years, but in all that time he ain't learnt nothing. Pocketing their salary, that's all they're good for! They should be carrying bricks, them doctors, not sitting among books.'

This powerful effusion of feeling broke the ice, and a kindly gesture invited me to approach for the first time the square, marble-topped table covered with notes, and to make my first acquaintance with this altar of bibliophile revelations. I quickly explained what I wanted: eighteenth-century works on magnetism along with all the subsequent books and polemics for and against Mesmer; as soon as I had finished, Mendel screwed up his left eye for a second, just like a marksman taking aim. But truly, this gesture of concentrated attention lasted only a second, and then, as though reading from an invisible catalogue, he immediately reeled off the titles of two or three dozen books, each with place and date of publication and the approximate price. I was dumbfounded. Although I was prepared, I had not expected this. But he seemed to enjoy my astonishment, for he at once played the most wonderful bibliographical paraphrases of my theme on the keyboard of his memory. Did I also want to find out about the somnambulists and the first experiments with hypnotism, about Gassner and his exorcisms, Christian Science and Madame Blavatsky?* Another rapid fire of names, titles, and descriptions; and only now did I understand what a unique miracle of a memory I had stumbled across in Jacob Mendel—a veritable encyclopaedia, a universal catalogue on two legs. I gaped in stupefaction at this bibliographical phenomenon enfolded in the inconspicuous, indeed rather greasy garb of a little Galician book-pedlar, who, having rattled off some eighty names for my benefit, assumed an air of indifference, though inwardly well pleased at the trump cards he had played, and cleaned his spectacles with a handkerchief that might once have been white. To disguise my astonishment a little, I asked hesitantly which of those books he could obtain for me. 'Well, we'll see what can be done,' he growled. 'Come back tomorrow, Mendel will hunt up a few things for you in the meantime, and whatever can't be found, we'll find it elsewhere. If someone has *sechel*,* he's got luck too.' I thanked him politely, and, through sheer politeness, promptly committed an idiotic blunder by suggesting that I should write down the titles I wanted on a piece of paper. At the same moment I felt a warning nudge from my friend's elbow. But too late! Mendel had already given me a look—what a look!—a look that was simultaneously triumphant and offended, scornful and superior, a positively kingly glance, the Shakespearean glance of Macbeth when Macduff expects the invulnerable hero to surrender without a fight. Then he gave another short laugh, and the big Adam's apple in his throat staggered to and fro in a peculiar way; evidently he had choked back a coarse remark with some effort. And the coarsest rejoinder one could imagine would have been perfectly justified, coming from the good, worthy Book-Mendel; for only a stranger, an innocent (an '*amhorets*',* as he would say), could make such an insulting offer to write down book titles for him, Jacob Mendel, him, Jacob Mendel, as though he were an assistant in a bookshop or an attendant in a library, as though that incomparable, adamantine book-brain had ever needed such crude implements. Only later did I realize how much I must have wounded his eccentric genius with my polite suggestion; for this little, crumpled, beard-enfolded, and hunch-backed Galician Jew Jacob Mendel was a Titan of memory. Behind that chalky, dirty forehead, overgrown with grey moss, every name and title that had ever been printed on the title-page of a book was imprinted in invisible mental script as firmly as in hot-metal type. Whether a work had been published yesterday or two hundred years ago, he could instantly and exactly name its place of publication, its author, its price, new or second-hand, and with his infallible vision he also remembered the binding and illustrations and facsimile reproductions of every book; he saw every work, whether he had had it in his own hands or had once spied it from afar in a bookshop or a library, with the same optical clarity that the creative artist brings to an imagined structure that is still invisible to the world. If, say, a book was offered for six marks in the catalogue of a second-hand bookshop in Regensburg, he could remember instantly that the very same book had been available two years earlier for four crowns in an auction in Vienna, and also who had purchased it; no, Jacob Mendel never forgot a title or a figure, he knew every plant, every amoeba, every star in the ever-vibrating, ever-changing cosmos of the universe of books. In every field he knew more than the experts, he was more familiar with libraries than the librarians, he knew the warehouses of most firms by heart, better than their owners, although they had card-indexes while his only resource was the magic of recollection, that incomparable memory, which could be appreciated only by considering a hundred individual examples. Of course, that memory had been trained and formed with such demonic infallibility only through the eternal secret of all perfection: through concentration. Apart from books, this peculiar person knew nothing about the world; for all the phenomena of existence only began to be real for him when they were moulded into letters, gathered in a book, and, as it were, sterilized. He did not read even these books, however, for their meaning, for their intellectual and narrative content: it was only their names, their prices, their physical appearance, and their title-pages that attracted his passion. Ultimately unproductive and uncreative, a mere index to a hundred thousand names and titles, stamped into the soft brain-tissue of a mammal instead of being inscribed in a book catalogue, this specifically bookselling memory possessed by Jacob Mendel was nonetheless, in its unique perfection, no less a phenomenon than Napoleon's memory for faces, Mezzofanti's for languages, Lasker's for chess openings, Busoni's for music.* Installed in a university department, in a public position, that brain would have instructed and astounded thousands, hundreds of thousands of students and scholars, fruitful for learning, an incomparable acquisition for those public treasure-houses that we call libraries. But this higher world was forever closed to him, the uneducated little Galician book-pedlar, who had attended only a Talmud school; hence these fantastic abilities could only find employment as a secret science at that marble-topped table in the Café Gluck. Yet one day a great psychologist will come (this work is still lacking in our intellectual world) who will apply the persistence and patience with which Buffon* ordered and classified the varieties of animals to describing all the types, species, and genotypes of that magic power we call memory, both as individuals and in their variants; and he will need to recall Jacob Mendel, that genius of prices and titles, that nameless master of the science of bookselling.

By profession, and in the eyes of the ignorant, Jacob Mendel was of course only a petty huckster dealing in books. Every Sunday the *Neue Freie Presse* and the *Neues Wiener Tagblatt** carried the same stereotyped advertisements: 'Old books bought, best prices paid, prompt service, Mendel, upper Alserstrasse', and then a telephone number which in reality was that of the Café Gluck. He would rummage through warehouses and every week, together with an old porter sporting an imperial,* he would carry off new booty to his headquarters and then remove it again, for he lacked a licence to conduct a regular bookshop. Thus he was limited to petty trading, an activity that brought little profit. Students sold him their textbooks, which passed through his hands from each older generation to the younger, and in addition he sought and obtained any work he was asked for with a small additional charge. He was free with good advice. But money had no place in his world; for nobody had ever seen him save in the same shabby coat, consuming his milk and two rolls in the morning, afternoon, and evening, and at midday eating a snack which was brought to him from the inn. He did not smoke, he did not gamble, indeed one might say that he did not live, only his two eyes were alive behind his spectacles, feeding that enigmatic being, his brain, with an incessant supply of words, titles, and names. And the soft, fertile mass greedily absorbed this plenitude, as the meadow sucks in the many thousand droplets of rain. People did not interest him, and of all human passions he perhaps knew only one, admittedly the most human, that of vanity. If anyone came to him for information which had been wearily sought in a hundred other places, and he could provide it on the spot, that in itself gave him satisfaction and pleasure, as did perhaps the fact that in Vienna and elsewhere there lived a couple of dozen people who respected and needed his knowledge. In each of those vast, shapeless conglomerations that we call cities there are always some small facets, inserted at a few points, which reflect one and the same universe on a minute scale, invisible to most people but precious for the connoisseur who shares the same passion. And these connoisseurs of books all knew Jacob Mendel. Just as anyone seeking information about a sheet of music went to the Society of Music-Lovers to consult Eusebius Mandyczewski,* who would be seated amid his files and notes, a friendly presence in a grey skullcap, and would solve the most difficult problems with a smile the moment he raised his head; just as, even today, anyone needing information about old Viennese theatre and culture turns without fail to the omniscient Father Glossy,* so, whenever a particularly hard nut needed to be cracked, the few devoted Viennese bibliophiles would make their pilgrimage to the Café Gluck to see Jacob Mendel. For me, a young and inquisitive person, it afforded a special kind of delight to watch Mendel during such a consultation. Although normally, when presented with an inferior book, he would clap it shut and growl, 'Two crowns', a rare or unique volume would make him draw back respectfully; he would lay it on a sheet of paper, and one could see that he suddenly felt ashamed of his dirty, ink-stained, black-nailed fingers. Then he would begin to leaf through the rarity, page by page, carefully and tenderly, with enormous deference. In such moments nobody could disturb him, any more than one can interrupt a true believer at prayer, and indeed, as he scrutinized, fingered, smelt, and handled the book, each of these actions had something of the ceremonial, the liturgical sequence, of a religious act of worship. His crooked back would move to and fro as he growled and muttered, scratched his head, uttered peculiar and primitive sounds, a long-drawn-out, almost frightened 'Ah' and 'Oh' of ravished admiration and then a quick, alarmed 'Oy' or 'Oy vay' if a page proved to be missing or a leaf to be worm-eaten. Finally he would weigh the tome respectfully on his hand, sniffing and smelling the misshapen rectangle with half-shut eyes, no less carried away than a sentimental girl smelling a rose. During this time-consuming procedure, the owner, needless to say, was obliged to restrain his impatience. After concluding his inspection, however, Mendel would be ready, indeed eager, to provide information, to which he would unfailingly add a string of anecdotes and dramatic accounts of the prices placed on similar copies. At such moments he seemed to grow younger, clearer, more vital, and the only thing that could infuriate him beyond measure was the attempt by a newcomer to offer him money for such a valuation. He would then draw back, wounded, like a museum guide to whom an American tourist offers a tip in return for his explanations; for to hold a precious book in his hands meant as much to Mendel as the encounter with a woman does for others. These moments were his Platonic nights of love. It was only the book, never money, that had power over him. For that reason great collectors, including the founder of Princeton University, sought in vain to acquire his services as adviser and purchaser for their libraries—Jacob Mendel refused; it was impossible to imagine him anywhere but in the Café Gluck. Thirty-three years earlier, still with a soft, black, downy beard and curly ear-locks, he had come to Vienna from the East, a little crooked *yingele*,* to study for the rabbinate; but soon he abandoned the harsh single god Jehovah to devote himself to the sparkling and thousand-fold polytheism of books. At that time he first found his way to the Café Gluck, and gradually it became his workshop, his headquarters, his post office, his world. As an astronomer alone in his observatory contemplates the myriads of stars every night through the tiny round lens of his telescope, watching their mysterious pathways, their changing aggregations, their extinction and rebirth, so Jacob Mendel peered through his spectacles from that square table into the other universe of books, which likewise moves in continual circles of perpetual rebirth, that world above our world.

Naturally he was held in high esteem in the Café Gluck, whose fame we associated more with his invisible professorial chair than with the patronage of the great composer, the creator of *Alceste* and *Iphigenia*, Christoph Willibald Gluck.* He was as much part of its inventory as the old cherrywood counter, the two billiard tables with their much-patched cloths, the copper coffee urn, and his table was guarded like a sanctuary. For his numerous customers and inquirers were always urged by the staff in a friendly manner to order something, so that most of the profit accruing from his learning flowed into the wide leather pouch that Deubler, the head waiter, carried round his waist. In return, Book-Mendel enjoyed a variety of privileges. The telephone was at his disposal; his letters were kept and his orders placed; the fine old woman who looked after the cloakroom brushed his coat, sewed on buttons, and took a small bundle to the laundry for him every week. Only for him could lunch be brought from the nearby inn, and every morning the owner, Herr Standhartner, came in person to his table to greet him (mostly, indeed, without being noticed by Jacob Mendel, absorbed in his books). He entered in the morning on the stroke of half-past seven, and left the premises only when the lights were being extinguished. He never spoke to the other customers, did not read a newspaper, did not notice any changes, and when Herr Standhartner once asked him politely whether it was not easier to read by electric light than in the pale, flickering light of the old lamps, he stared up in astonishment at the electric bulbs: this change had completely escaped his attention, despite several days of noise and hammering during its installation. It was only through the two round holes of his spectacles, through these two gleaming and absorbent lenses, that the billions of black microbes of letters were filtered into his brain; all other happenings passed him by as empty noise. In fact, he spent more than thirty years, the entire wakeful part of his life, doing nothing but sitting at that square table, reading, comparing, calculating, in a prolonged dream that continued without intermission, interrupted only by sleep.

For that reason I was overcome by a kind of alarm when I saw the marble-topped table from which Jacob Mendel had dispensed his oracles standing empty like a tombstone in the dimly lit room. Only now, having grown older, did I understand how much disappears along with every such person, first because everything unique becomes daily more precious in our world which is hopelessly doomed to uniformity. And then, the young, inexperienced person in me had, from a deep intuition, been very fond of Jacob Mendel. And yet I had managed to forget—in the war years, admittedly, and in a devotion to my own work that resembled his. Now, however, in front of the empty table, I felt a kind of shame towards him, and at the same time a renewed curiosity.

For where had he gone, what had become of him? I called the waiter and asked. No, he was sorry, he didn't know any Herr Mendel, nobody of that name came to the café, but the head waiter might be able to tell me. The latter pushed his paunch weightily towards me, hesitated, pondered, and said: no, he didn't know any Herr Mendel either. But possibly I was thinking of Herr Mandl, who kept the haberdashery in the Florianigasse? I felt a bitter taste on my lips, the taste of transience: why do we live if the wind carries away our last traces just behind our shoes? For thirty years, forty perhaps, a human being had breathed, read, thought, spoken in those few square metres of space, and only three years, four years had to pass, a new Pharaoh had to come, and nothing more was known of Joseph,* nothing more was known in the Café Gluck about Jacob Mendel, Book-Mendel! I asked the head waiter, almost angrily, whether I could speak to Herr Standhartner, or whether anyone else from the old staff was still in the establishment. Oh, Herr Standhartner, came the reply, oh good heavens, he sold the café ages ago, he was dead, and the old head waiter was now living in his country cottage at Krems. No, there was nobody left... or was there? Yes, there was— Frau Sporschil was still there, the cloakroom attendant (*vulgo* chocolate-lady). But she certainly wouldn't be able to remember individual customers. I thought to myself that one does not forget a Jacob Mendel, and sent for her.

She came, Frau Sporschil, white-haired and tousled, with slightly dropsical steps from her obscure recesses, still hastily rubbing her red hands with a towel: evidently she had just been sweeping her gloomy chamber or cleaning the windows. From her uncertain manner I could at once see that she was ill at ease in being summoned so suddenly into the superior part of the coffee-house beneath the great electric bulbs. Thus she first looked at me distrustfully, squinting up at me with a very cautious, cowering look. What good intentions could I conceivably have? But hardly had I asked about Jacob Mendel when she stared me full in the face with positively liquid eyes and her shoulders straightened with a jerk. 'Good heavens, poor Herr Mendel, fancy anyone still remembering him! Yes, poor Herr Mendel'—she was almost weeping, she was so moved, as old people always are when reminded of their youth or of some shared happiness they have forgotten. I asked if he were still alive. 'Oh heavens, poor Herr Mendel, it must be five or six years, no, it's seven years since he died. Such a dear good soul, and when I think how long I knew him for, more than twenty-five years, he was there when I started working here. And it was a sin and a shame the way they let him die.' She grew more and more excited and asked if I were a relative. Nobody had ever bothered about him, nobody had enquired about him—and didn't I know what had happened to him?

No, I assured her, I knew nothing; she must tell me, tell me everything. The good woman assumed a bashful, embarrassed air, constantly wiping her wet hands. I understood: it was painful for her as the cloakroom attendant with her dirty apron and her dishevelled white hair to be standing here in the middle of the coffee-house, and she kept glancing anxiously to right and left in case one of the waiters might be listening. Hence I suggested that we should go into the games room to Mendel's old seat, and there she should tell me everything. Touched because I had understood, she gave a nod of gratitude and led the way, the old woman, already somewhat shaky on her feet, and I after her. The two waiters stared after us in astonishment, surmising some connection, and some customers also wondered at such a dissimilar couple. And at his table she told me (many details were later added by other accounts) about how Jacob Mendel, Book-Mendel, met his end.

Well, she began, he went on coming, even after the war had begun, day after day, at half-past seven every morning, and he sat and studied all day long as he always did; they all had a feeling, and often talked about it, that he had never realized there was a war on. After all, I knew that he never looked at a newspaper and never talked with anybody else; but even when the newspaper boys made such a noise with their extra editions and everyone else ran to see them, he never stood up or listened. He did not notice that Franz the waiter was missing (he was killed at Gorlice),* and did not know that Herr Standhartner's son had been taken prisoner at Przemysl,* and he never said a word when the bread got worse and worse and they had to give him a wretched coffee-substitute made from figs instead of milk. Just once he was surprised that so few students came to him, that was all. 'Heavens, the poor man, nothing gave him any pleasure or pain except his books.'

But then one day the disaster happened. At eleven in the morning, in broad daylight, a policeman came with a secret-service man; he showed the badge in his buttonhole and asked if a Jacob Mendel was in the habit of coming here. Then they went straight to Mendel's table, and he in his innocence thought they wanted to sell books or ask him something. But they immediately told him to come with them, and took him away. It was a scandal for the coffee-house, everyone gathered round poor Herr Mendel as he stood between the two policemen, his spectacles under his hair, looking from one to the other with no idea what they wanted from him. But she promptly told the policeman that it must be a mistake, for a man like Herr Mendel wouldn't hurt a fly; but the secret-service man shouted at her and told her not to meddle in official business. And then they took him away, and he did not come back for a long time, two whole years. She still did not know what they wanted from him. 'But I'll take my mortal oath', said the old woman in her excitement, 'Herr Mendel can't have done anything wrong. They made a mistake, I'd put my hand in the fire for him. It was a crime against that poor innocent man, a crime!'

And she was right, the good, moving Frau Sporschil. Our friend Jacob Mendel had indeed done nothing wrong, but merely committed (only later did I learn all the details) an act of terrible, touching stupidity, something barely imaginable even in those lunatic times, explicable only by the complete abstraction in which he lived, as though he were on the moon. What happened was this: the military censor's office, which was obliged to keep an eye on all correspondence with foreign countries, one day intercepted a postcard, written and signed by a certain Jacob Mendel, with the proper stamp for a foreign country, but—incredibly enough—directed to enemy territory: a postcard addressed to Jean Labourdaire, bookseller, Quai de Grenelle, Paris, in which a certain Jacob Mendel complained that despite paying his yearly subscription in advance, he had not received the last eight numbers of the monthly *Bulletin bibliographique de la France*. The deputy censor, in civilian life a schoolmaster with a private fondness for the Romance languages, was astounded when this document came into his hands. A silly joke, he thought. Among the two thousand letters that he rummaged through every week to examine them in search of suspicious messages and phrases that might imply espionage he had never encountered anything so absurd as this: someone in Austria had addressed a letter to France without a second thought, had cheerfully posted a card to the enemy's country, as though the frontiers had not been stitched together with barbed wire since 1914 and as though, on every day God made, France, Germany, Austria, and Russia had not reduced each other's male population by a couple of thousand people. First of all, therefore, he put the postcard in his desk drawer as a curiosity, without reporting this absurdity. But a few weeks later yet another card appeared from the same Jacob Mendel to the bookseller John Aldridge, Holborn Square, London, asking him to procure the most recent issues of *The Antiquarian*, and once again it was signed by the very same peculiar individual, Jacob Mendel, who had the touching naivety to add his full address. Now the schoolmaster who had been sewn into a uniform started feeling rather awkward under his tunic. Could this idiotic jest conceal some mysterious coded message? At any rate, he stood up, clicked his heels together, and laid both postcards on the Major's table. The latter shrugged his shoulders: a strange case! First of all he directed the police to investigate whether this Jacob Mendel really existed, and an hour later Jacob Mendel had already been taken into custody and was brought before the Major, still giddy from the shock. The Major showed him the mysterious postcards and asked whether he was the sender. Irritated by the Major's harsh tone and, above all, at being tracked down while reading an important catalogue, Mendel cried, almost rudely, that of course he had written these cards. Surely he had the right to demand a subscription for which he'd paid good money? The Major twisted round in his chair to speak to the lieutenant at the side-table. The two of them exchanged a wink of mutual understanding: an out-and-out madman! Then the Major considered whether to send the simpleton packing with a flea in his ear, or to treat the case seriously. When thus uncertain what to do, people in every kind of office almost always decide first to take notes. Note-taking is always good. If it does no good, it does no harm, and the notes just cover one more meaningless sheet of paper among millions.

Unfortunately, however, in this instance the note-taking did harm to a poor, innocent man, for the third question revealed something extremely ominous. First they asked his name: Jacob, *recte* Jainkeff Mendel. Profession: pedlar (for he did not have a bookseller's licence, only a pedlar's certificate). The third question was catastrophic: his place of birth. Jacob Mendel mentioned a village near Petrikau. The Major raised his eyebrows. Petrikau? Wasn't that in Russian Poland, near the frontier? Suspicious! Highly suspicious! And so he inquired more strictly when Mendel had acquired Austrian citizenship. Mendel's spectacles stared at him in dark astonishment: he did not understand. Damn it, did he have papers, documents, and where were they? He hadn't any, only his pedlar's certificate. The furrows in the Major's forehead climbed higher and higher. He'd have to explain his citizenship, once and for all. What had his father been? Austrian or Russian? Jacob Mendel answered with perfect calm: Russian, of course. And he himself? Oh, he'd smuggled himself across the Russian border thirty-three years ago and he'd lived in Vienna ever since. The Major grew more and more uneasy. When had he acquired Austrian citizenship? 'What for?' asked Mendel. He'd never bothered his head about such things. So was he still a Russian citizen? And Mendel, privately bored with these dreary questions, answered indifferently: 'Yes, I am.'

The Major, alarmed, threw himself back so brusquely that his chair creaked. Was this possible? In Vienna, in the capital of Austria, in the middle of the war, at the end of 1915, after Tarnow and the great offensive, a Russian was strolling about without let or hindrance, writing letters to France and England, and the police didn't turn a hair. And the blockheads in the newspapers were surprised that Conrad von Hötzendorf* hadn't advanced as far as Warsaw, the General Staff was astonished when all troop movements were reported to Russia by spies. The lieutenant also rose and stood at the table: the conversation was transformed abruptly into an interrogation. Why hadn't he reported himself as a foreigner right away? Mendel, still unsuspecting, answered in his sing-song Jewish dialect: 'What for should I report myself right away?' The question, thus turned round, was interpreted by the Major as a challenge, and he asked menacingly whether Mendel hadn't read the announcements. 'No!' Didn't he read any newspapers? 'No!'

The two of them stared at Mendel, who was already beginning to sweat with uncertainty, as though the moon had fallen into their office. Then the telephone rang, the typewriters rattled, the orderlies scurried, and Jacob Mendel was handed over to the garrison jail in order to accompany the next batch to the concentration camp. When he was told to follow the two soldiers, he stared in perplexity. He did not understand what was wanted, but he was not really worried. After all, what harm could the man with the gold collar and the coarse voice want to do him? In his higher world of books there was no war, no incomprehension, but only the eternal knowledge, and the desire to know more, about numbers and words, titles and names. So he trotted good-humouredly down the stairs between the two soldiers. Only in the police station, when all the books were removed from his coat pockets and he was told to surrender his wallet, stuffed with a hundred important notes and customers' addresses, did he begin to hit out in fury. They had to restrain him by force. But during this process, unfortunately, his spectacles clattered to the ground, and these, his magic telescope to the intellectual world, broke into several pieces. Two days later, in his thin summer coat, he was dispatched to a concentration camp for Russian civilian prisoners at Komorn.*

What psychic terror Jacob Mendel underwent in these two years in the concentration camp, without books, his beloved books, without money, amid the uncaring, coarse, mostly illiterate comrades in this huge dungeon, what he suffered there, cut off from his unique higher world of books like an eagle with clipped wings cut off from its ethereal element, no testimony reports. Gradually, however, as it recovers from its madness, the world is realizing that of all the cruelties and criminal abuses practised in this war, none was so senseless, so unnecessary, and hence so morally inexcusable as the rounding up of innocent civilians to coop them up behind barbed wire: most had reached retirement age, had lived in the foreign country for many years as though it were their home, and, trusting in the law of hospitality which is sacred even to Tungus* and Araucanians,* had neglected to flee in time—a crime against civilization, committed equally senselessly in France, Germany, and England, on every territory of a Europe gone insane. And perhaps, like a hundred other innocents, Jacob Mendel in this coop might have succumbed to madness or perished miserably of dysentery, malnutrition, psychic devastation, if an accident, a truly Austrian one, had not restored him to his world in the nick of time. For after his disappearance several letters from distinguished customers had come to his address; Count Schönberg, the former governor of Styria, a fanatical collector of works on heraldry; the former Dean of the theological faculty at Siegenfeld, who was working on a commentary on St Augustine; the eighty-year-old retired Admiral of the Fleet, von Pisek, who was still tinkering with his memoirs—all of them, his faithful clients, had written repeatedly to Jacob Mendel in the Café Gluck, and some of these letters were forwarded to their forgotten addressee in the concentration camp. There they fell into the hands of a captain who happened to be good-natured, and he was astonished to see what distinguished acquaintances that half-blind, dirty little Jew had, who, ever since his spectacles had been smashed (he had no money to buy new ones), had crouched in a corner, grey, eyeless, and silent like a mole. Anyone who had such friends must be something out of the ordinary. Hence he permitted Mendel to answer the letters and ask his patrons to put in a word for him. That did not fail. With the passionate solidarity of all collectors, the Count and the Dean vigorously activated their connections, and their combined guarantee ensured that in 1917, after more than two years' confinement, Book-Mendel was allowed back to Vienna, admittedly on condition that he reported daily to the police. But still, he was allowed back into the free world, into his old, small, poky attic room, he could again go past his beloved bookshelves and, above all, back to his Café Gluck.

Frau Sporschil, having seen it with her own eyes, was able to describe for me Mendel's return from his hellish underworld to the Café Gluck. 'One day—Mary, mother of God, I couldn't believe my eyes—the door opens, you know, in that sort of crooked way, only just a crack, the way he always used to come in, and there he is, poor Herr Mendel, stumbling into the café. He was wearing a tattered old army coat, darned all over, and something on his head that might once have been a hat that had been thrown out. He'd no collar on, and he looked like death, grey in the face and with grey hair and so skinny, it was pitiful. But in he comes, just as if nothing had happened, he never asks a question, he never says a word, he goes to that table and takes off his coat, but not quick and easy the way he used to, but breathing heavily. And he hadn't a book with him like he used to—he just sits down and doesn't say a thing, just stares straight ahead with empty blank eyes. Only little by little, when we brought him the big bundle of papers that had come for him from Germany, he started to read again. But he wasn't the same.'

No, he was no longer the same, no longer the *miraculum mundi*,* the magic registry of all books; all those who saw him at that time have sorrowfully told me the same thing. Something seemed to have been destroyed beyond repair in his gaze, which used to be quiet, as though he were reading in his sleep; something was wrecked; the hideous bloodstained comet in its furious course must also have wrought devastation in the peaceful, eccentric, halcyon star of his world of books. His eyes, accustomed for decades to the delicate, silent, insect-footed letters of print, must have seen terrible things in that human coop enclosed by barbed wire, for his eyelids cast a heavy shadow on his pupils that used to have such an agile, ironic sparkle; his eyes, once so lively, were now red-rimmed and brooded sleepily under his spectacles, now repaired and laboriously tied together with thin string. And more terrible still: in the fantastic, artificial edifice of his memory some pillar must have collapsed and thus brought the whole structure into disarray; for our brain, this mechanism shaped from the subtlest substance, this fine precision-instrument of our knowledge, is so delicately tuned that a blocked vein, a damaged nerve, a worn-out cell, a misplaced molecule is sufficient to silence the most magnificently wide-ranging harmony, the music of the intellectual spheres. And in Mendel's memory, that unique keyboard of knowledge, the keys were stuck when he returned. If anyone came, now and again, to ask for information, he would stare at him wearily, not quite understanding; he heard incorrectly and forgot what people told him—Mendel was no longer Mendel, as the world was no longer the world. No longer did he rock up and down, completely absorbed in reading, but he usually sat rigid, his spectacles only mechanically turned towards his book, and one could not tell whether he was reading or merely dozing. Sometimes, Frau Sporschil recounted, his head would fall heavily on to his book, and he would fall asleep in broad daylight, sometimes he would stare for hours into the alien, smelly light of the acetylene lamp that had been placed on his table in that period of coal shortages. No, Mendel was no longer Mendel, no longer a wonder of the world, but a useless bundle of beard and clothes, breathing wearily, a meaningless weight on what had once been his Pythian* seat, no longer the glory of the Café Gluck, but a disgrace, a stain, malodorous, repulsive to behold, a disagreeable, dispensable parasite.

That was the feeling he aroused in the new owner, Florian Gurtner from Retz, who, having grown rich from profiteering in flour and butter in the lean year 1919, had talked the honest Standhartner into selling him the Café Gluck for eighty thousand paper crowns which inflation soon turned into waste paper. With his peasant's hands he took a firm grip, hastily turned the venerable coffee-house into a smart modern establishment, bought new armchairs at the right moment for worthless paper money, installed a marble doorway, and was already negotiating for the premises next door so that he could turn them into a dance-hall. Hastily beautifying the café, he was naturally annoyed by that Galician parasite who occupied a table by himself all day long from morning to night and only drank two cups of coffee and ate five rolls of bread. Certainly Standhartner had urged him to take good care of his old customer and tried to explain what an important and significant man this Jacob Mendel was; you might say that in handing over the café he had included him in the inventory as a supplementary easement attached to the business. But along with the new furniture and the shiny aluminium cash-register Florian Gurtner had also acquired the capacious conscience of the entrepreneurial epoch, and he was only waiting for a pretext to sweep that last tiresome remnant of suburban shabbiness out of his distinguished premises. A good opportunity soon seemed to present itself; for Jacob Mendel was badly off. The last banknotes he had saved were ground down in the paper-mill of inflation, his customers had scattered. And the weary man no longer had the strength to be a little book-pedlar, climbing stairs and knocking on doors to gather books together. He was desperately poor, that was clear from a hundred little signs. He seldom had anything brought from the inn, and it took him longer and longer to pay the smallest sum for coffee and bread, as long as three weeks. Even then the head waiter wanted to put him out on the street. But the good Frau Sporschil, the cloakroom attendant, took pity on him and stood surety for him.

But the following month the disaster happened. The head waiter had already noticed several times that the bill for bread would not come out right. More and more rolls were undeclared and unpaid. Naturally his suspicions immediately fell upon Mendel; for the old tottering porter had already come several times to complain that Mendel owed him six months' payment and would not give him a penny. So the head waiter kept a sharp eye open, and two days later, hiding behind the fire-screen, he managed to catch Jacob Mendel surreptitiously rising from his table, going into the front room, seizing two rolls from a bread-basket and greedily devouring them. That explained the disappearances. The waiter promptly reported the incident to Herr Gurtner, and the latter, glad of the long-awaited pretext, bawled at Mendel in front of all the customers, accused him of theft, and even took credit for not summoning the police on the spot. But he ordered him to get lost, straight away and for ever. Jacob Mendel only trembled, said nothing, stumbled up from his seat, and went.

'It was a shame,' was how Frau Sporschil described his departure. 'I'll never forget how he stood up, with his spectacles pushed up to his forehead, white as a sheet. He didn't even take the time to put on his coat, though it was January, you know, in that bitter cold year. And he was so frightened he left his book lying on the table, I noticed it later and wanted to give it to him. But he'd already stumbled to the door. And I wouldn't have dared go into the street; for Herr Gurtner planted himself at the door and yelled after him, so that people stopped and gathered. Yes, it was a disgrace, I was ashamed to the depths of my soul! That couldn't have happened with old Herr Standhartner, to kick someone out just because of a few rolls, he'd have let him eat for nothing all the rest of his life. But people nowadays have no heart. To drive someone away who's sat somewhere day after day for thirty years—honestly, it was a disgrace, and I wouldn't like to have to answer for it to God—not me.'

She was quite excited, the good woman, and with the passionate loquacity of old age she kept repeating what a disgrace it had been and how Herr Standhartner couldn't have done such a thing. Hence I finally had to ask her what had become of our Mendel and whether she had seen him again. She pulled herself together and became even more excited. 'Every day when I passed his table, every time, believe me, it gave me a jolt. I couldn't help wondering where is he now, poor Herr Mendel, and if I'd known where he lived I'd have gone to bring him something warm; for where was he supposed to get money for heating and food? And so far as I know he hadn't a single relation in the world. But finally, when I never heard a thing, I thought it must all be over with him and I'd never see him again. And I was wondering whether I should have a mass said for him; for he was a good man, and after all we'd known each other for more than twenty-five years.

'But early one morning, at half-past seven, in February, I was cleaning the brass on the window-bars, and all of a sudden (I thought I'd drop dead with shock), all of a sudden the door opens and in comes Mendel. You know, he always pushed it open in such a funny crooked way, but this time it was different somehow. I could see right away there was something odd, his eyes were all glazed and heavens, how he looked, nothing but bones and beard! It felt creepy seeing him like that; I thought right away, he doesn't know what's going on, he's going about like a sleepwalker in broad daylight, he's forgotten all about the rolls and Herr Gurtner and how shamefully they threw him out, he doesn't know anything about himself. Thank God! Herr Gurtner wasn't there yet, and the head waiter had just drunk his coffee. So I ran over to explain to him he mustn't stay there and be thrown out again by that brute' (here she looked round timidly and quickly corrected herself) 'I mean, by Herr Gurtner. So I calls to him, "Herr Mendel". He looks up. And in that moment, heavens, it was awful, in that moment he must have remembered everything; for he gives a start and begins trembling, but not just with his fingers, no, he was shaking all over, you could see it in his shoulders, and he's already stumbling quickly towards the door. And there he collapsed. We phoned for an ambulance at once, and it took him away, feverish as he was. He died that evening, advanced pneumonia the doctor said it was, and that he didn't quite know what he was doing when he came to us once more. He was just driven, like a sleepwalker. Heavens, if you've sat there every day for thirty-six years, then a table like that is your home.'

We talked for much longer about him, the last two people who had known that strange person: I, to whom, as a young man, he had given, despite his tiny, microbe-like existence, my first intimation of a life wholly enclosed in the mind—she, the poor, put-upon cloak-room attendant, who had never read a book, who was attached to that comrade in her poor lower world only because she had brushed his coat and sewn on the buttons for twenty-five years. And yet we understood each other wonderfully well at his old abandoned table in the company of the shadow we had jointly conjured up; for recollection always links people, and loving recollection does so doubly. Suddenly, while chatting away, she remembered something: 'Lord, how forgetful I am—I've still got the book, the one that he left lying on the table that day. How was I to give it back to him? And after-wards, when nobody asked for it, I thought I could keep it in mem-ory of him. There's nothing wrong with that, is there?' She hastily fetched it from her cubby-hole at the back of the café. And I had difficulty in suppressing a gentle smile; for fate, always playful and sometimes ironic, likes to mingle something comical with the most shattering events. It was the second volume of Hayn's *Bibliotheca Germanorum erotica et curiosa*,* the compendium of erotic literature with which every book-collector is familiar. This scabrous catalogue, of all things—*habent sua fata libelli**—had fallen, as the last legacy of the departed mage, into these washed-out, red, cracked, ignorant hands, that had probably never held any book except the prayer-book. I had difficulty in sealing my lips tight against the smile that was forcing its way out against my will, and my slight hesitation confused the good woman. Was it something valuable, or did I think it was all right for her to keep it?

I shook her hand warmly. 'Of course you can keep it. Our old friend Mendel would be glad to know that at least one of the many thousands who owe him a book still remembers him.' And then I went, feeling ashamed in front of this good woman, who had remained faithful to that dead man with simplicity and yet in the most truly human way. For she, the uneducated woman, had at least kept a book in order to remember him better, but I—I had forgotten Book-Mendel for years, I of all people, who ought to know that one makes books only to attach people to oneself after one has breathed one's last and thus to defend oneself against the inexorable adversary of all life: transience and oblivion.

KARL KRAUS

From *Third Walpurgis Night*

The Viennese satirist Karl Kraus (1874–1936) founded in 1899 the periodical *The Torch* (*Die Fackel*), and wrote it single-handed from 1912 onwards. In a dense, compressed, and brilliant style, he campaigned against sexual hypocrisy and artistic ornamentation, inspired by a combination of moral honesty, aesthetic modernism, and social conservatism. He saw the degeneracy of the modern world as typified, and to an increasing extent caused, by journalism, which had replaced thoughts with opinions and artistic utterance with slogans and clichés. *The Torch* regularly reprinted, often without comment, statements in which journalists unwittingly gave themselves away: this, for example, from Kraus's favourite target, the Viennese liberal daily the *New Free Press*: 'What we reported yesterday has turned out to be true.' Hence journalists feature, alongside bloodthirsty officers and irresponsible politicians, among the villains in Kraus's immense semi-documentary drama about the First World War, *The Last Days of Mankind* (1922). Kraus was also widely known for his public readings from his own work and from Nestroy, Offenbach, Shakespeare, and German lyric poetry. They provided the linguistic standard by which modern verbal and hence imaginative and moral corruption could be condemned.

After the war Kraus initially supported the Social Democrats as the most enlightened party in the First Austrian Republic. However, when they seemed unable to counter the threat of Hitler, Kraus transferred his support to the Christian-Social Chancellor Dollfuss and his attempt to establish a Catholic corporate state as a bulwark against Nazism. Kraus also composed, but did not publish, the massive anti-Nazi polemic *Third Walpurgis Night*, from which the following extract is taken. He may have felt that Nazi atrocities defied satire; he may also have been afraid that Nazi agents would murder him, as they did the exiled Jewish journalist Theodor Lessing in Bohemia in August 1933. However, his polemic moves easily from the Nazis' offences against language to their crimes against humanity, all detailed by allowing large numbers of newspaper cuttings to speak for themselves. The title proclaims the Goethean framework. Having shown the German witches celebrating Walpurgis Night (30 April) in *Faust*, *Part I*, Goethe created a Classical Walpurgis Night, featuring all the strange monsters from Greek legend, in *Faust, Part II*. Nazism, however, goes beyond anything Goethe could have imagined.

In the present extract, Kraus first contrasts absurd attempts to attract tourists to the new Germany with the violence inflicted on unwary foreigners who annoy their hosts by looking Jewish or ignoring Nazi ceremonies. He then turns to the tasteless, indeed blasphemous attempts to Nazify the Oberammergau Passion Play by presenting an Aryan Christ, and from there to the sufferings, rivalling those of Christ, that the regime has already inflicted on many martyrs. He concludes by finding in Shakespeare, in the most desolate passages of *Macbeth* and *King Lear*, the only words adequate to describe the Nazis' barely imaginable orgy of bloodshed.

———

The national achievement, even if any scope remained for further progress, seems not to be fulfilling its promise. The discovery that the Jews, the Marxists, the cyclists,* not to mention the adherents of relativity theory, are to blame for the outcome of the war as well as all other evils, has if anything caused confusion. Though this constantly provides the main ground for the complaint that foreigners lack a sympathetic attitude to what is going on in Germany, the best of the Germans have lost their heads. Even a Hercules, obliged to choose between racial pride and promoting tourism, could not have accomplished both at once. On one hand a success can be recorded, in that an English paper was prepared to print words of love for money:

Germany cordially invites you to visit it this summer. The famous attractions that Germany offers to travellers *have now been enhanced by the enchanting spectacle of the rebirth of a nation*.

It adds, quite rightly, that Germany now enjoys the distinction of being the most interesting country in Europe. Apart from the fact that absolute order, of course, prevails everywhere and both safety and comfort are guaranteed, you will encounter new ideas and larger prospects than before, and these (as in those tours of the battlefields)*

will give you *indelible impressions* that will always *remain in your memory*.

The air is filled with music, and nowhere else is it easier for the cultivated traveller

to *become acquainted with the best and most beautiful aspects of life*. Germany *now enables young and old to complete a modern education on the highest level*.

It invites you to participate actively in the life of its *art*, its *scholarship*, its *philosophy*, its *history*, and, above all, in the *art of refined living* with which Germany now *imbues the existence of every individual*.

Germany today, *more than ever before, is your courteous and honest host....* For a modest sum, you can *make your life's dream come true* in Germany.

Where honesty speaks for itself, it cannot fail to make an impression on the world. If only the locals would see reason and be satisfied now that they have licked blood. The British, now—they're a much-travelled nation!* Then why don't they come here? Oh, there have been misunderstandings. The courteous and honest host won't beat strangers down; but as they sometimes look strange, he can't help beating them up. He announced 'Germany invites you', but when they arrived, it was 'How-Jew-do.' Sometimes the apology says that it was just a misunderstanding, a confusion because of the tourist's appearance, which was his own fault. The explanation is admitted to be correct, but somehow it's hard to feel at ease. The whole Orient has long had misgivings because of its Oriental appearance, but the West is also hesitant. The main difficulty is that the rest of the world is not familiar with the customs of the country and is afraid of infringing them. Ignoring the needs of German tourism, the outside world has spread reports that Americans, unaware that you have to stand for the Horst Wessel Song* and leap to attention* in front of flags, were knocked down and trampled on. Then it was the turn of English, French, Belgian, Dutch, Swiss visitors. A Romanian engineer had his hands put in the fire, 'to make him admit he's a Jew'. A British visitor, stopped and searched seven times in an hour, warns in *The Times* against going to Germany, and it would have been so helpful for all concerned if Thomas Cook had simply explained the rules of conduct beforehand. The locals would find them useful too: a landowner was misled into calling the Hitler salute childish; 'sections of the population stand with their hands in their pockets when storm troops march past with flags', obviously thinking that that too will pass; a girl in Neuruppin got a placard round her neck saying she was a shameless slut because she stayed in her seat for the Horst Wessel Song. The population find the ideals exciting but hard to live up to, at least outside the camps; nobody goes to the Schlageter exhibition and in a questionnaire by the Erfurt Theatre Offenbach received more votes than Johst.* A run of bad luck, a chapter of misunderstandings: the locals think the foreigners are Jews, the foreigners think the locals are barbarians, but that the latter cannot tell the difference is truly embarrassing. What will become of Oberammergau if Bayreuth itself needs a special consecration in which the government buys up all the free tickets? There a tragic conflict erupted between tourism and conviction. It seems that guest-house owners who dress up as apostles have become National Socialists and are suffering agonies of conscience because they have to play the part of Jewish types. So, to avoid the painful sense of being impostors, they promptly started growing the long beards and side-locks that they need for the Passion Play. And what happens? Fellow-Nazis come from the North, see it, and pull out their real beards in the false belief that the beards are real. Forced to participate so physically in the Passion they were meant to enact, they had to admit that it wasn't one any longer, and suggested reducing their beards to a minimum and, instead of the sufferings of Christ,

presenting the life of Hitler,

which, however, was rejected,

as it was thought unlikely that this subject would attract any foreigners.

Finally agreement was reached on the golden mean whereby the Play would be retained in its old form but enlivened by repeated choruses of the Horst Wessel Song. Regarding the performers, it was decreed that 'Christ can only be a blond, blue-eyed man with a swastika on his robe' and that the apostles faithful to him must display the Aryan-Germanic type, while Judas is to be shown as 'a markedly Jewish type', a reform which cost the Minister of Propaganda* arduous self-denial. The possibility of depicting the life of the Nazirene, however, is postponed until such time as suitable advertising shall have elicited a more sympathetic attitude from the outside world, unless indeed it emerges spontaneously, in accordance with Goebbels's conviction

that what we are doing today is breaking a path for the entire civilized world—for the National Socialist world. Even if such a world does not yet exist, in ten years it will be copying our laws. *What we are doing today will in ten years provide a model for the whole world.* What we are doing today will set the *standard for the whole of Europe.*

All we had to do, he continued, was to construct a system that would outlast future centuries and create an organization that would survive even 'if talent should be lacking'. We must provide for coming generations, and the change in Oberammergau's repertoire will happen naturally, for Kube* has said:

Adolf Hitler's mission is a divine one.

And would it be imaginable without the sufferings that so many had to undergo for the sake of the ultimate goal? Have we not read about martyrs, war veterans, and many a one whose body only recently became 'a single bloody pulp from the back to the knees'? To keep him aware of his high calling, he was drenched in cold water,

whereupon flesh was plucked from his chest with pincers.

And then the keeper of the faith took his burning cigar out of his jaws

and burned a wreath round the neck of the chained prisoner.

And spoke the words:

A red coral necklace to remember us by!

'We saw the man and his wounds', said someone in the refugee office in Saarbrücken. Those in protective custody try to escape such trials by thrusting safety-pins into their hearts or a pencil into their eyes, breaking their skulls against the iron bedsteads in their cells, and thus devising strange ways of putting an end to stranger forms of suffering. Yet the strict rites of protective custody outlast the feebleness of refugees from life, they are sustained by the firm belief of their adherents, and, still more, by the disbelief of those who sleep peacefully in their beds. Yet what humanity cannot grasp, because it serves deliverance to one of humankind's goals, should still be recorded. In memory of all the slaughtered saints who bit the bullet, those crushed underfoot and those carried off only by sickness: of the hero executed in Hamburg and of his mother who heard it on the radio and rushed screaming into the street; of the woman in Cologne who, as her husband was being tortured, jumped out of the window in mortal terror and was left lying with her legs broken; of the auxiliary police unit in Krems,* struck by the most cowardly of all murders; of those killed and mutilated in the Vienna jeweller's shop; of the aged rabbi in Oberwiesenfeld with whom they played at execution until the game turned serious; of the child—they told the story themselves—who ran crying after his mother as she was dragged through the back streets of Pirmasens as a hostage to make the runaway father go back to his murderers. And of this creature of God:

... and tried to set the wooden building on fire with rags soaked in petrol.

The fire-raisers were disturbed at their work by the barking of the nightwatchman's dog. Thereupon one of the Nazis fired a revolver at the animal and injured it severely. Nevertheless the dog was still able to reach the nightwatchman's house, some three hundred yards away, and rouse its master.

When the nightwatchman arrived at the clubhouse, the intruders had already fled. The man extinguished the fire with a few buckets of water.

Early in the morning the faithful dog which had discovered the fire-raisers and suffered severe injuries had to be killed by a merciful shot.

And in memory of this:

My husband was taken from me *through a misunderstanding*. No messages, please.

People go out and are returned to their families in a lead-sealed coffin.

> Alas, poor country,
> Almost afraid to know itself! It cannot
> Be call'd our mother, but our grave; where *nothing*,
> *But who knows nothing, is once seen to smile;*
> Where sighs, and groans, and shrieks, that rent the air,
> Are made, not mark'd; where violent sorrow seems
> A modern ecstasy; the dead man's knell
> Is there scarce ask'd for who; and good men's lives
> Expire before the flowers in their caps,
> *Dying or ere they sicken.**

The atmosphere in 'our suffering country under a hand accurs'd'* is painted by such terrific Shakespearean strokes ('some holy angel fly to the court of England and unfold his message!')*—but the suppressed groans were not those of indifferent baseness. They know nothing; they do not believe it. Yet there must be a meaning which people cannot perceive until the Führer opens their eyes. It was symbolic when a group of young inmates of the home for the blind in Halle appealed to him

to allow them to see in him their Führer and to name their room 'Adolf Hitler Room'. The Reich Chancellor granted this request in a special letter and sent the boys a magnificent photograph with his personal signature.

Gloster perceived the leadership principle: ''Tis the times' plague when madmen lead the blind.'* He was blind to the blessing, and not all are worthy of it. That is why the German League for the Blind expelled its Jewish members, but an Austrian one served as a communications centre. And outside an Israelite one it was a sighted person who spelt out the sign and said to his companion:

'Israe-lide Home—for—the—Blind—I'll scrub that out in two ticks. The blind can't see it anyway!'

While, to reach a Christian majority, one must stay well out of sight. For this fate operates without regard to denominations, and the more fulfilment eludes its grasp, the more insatiably it presses towards its obscure goal.

JOSEPH ROTH

The Leviathan

Joseph Roth (1894–1939) was born in Brody, a few miles from the border between the Austrian and Russian Empires. After studying German literature at Vienna University Roth volunteered for the army in 1916 and was assigned to the information service. This started him on the journalistic career which he pursued with great distinction in post-war Germany. Between 1923 and 1929 he worked for the outstanding liberal paper, the *Frankfurter Zeitung*, which sent him to France, Russia, Poland, and Albania. Later years were overshadowed by the insanity of his wife Friederike ('Friedl') Reichler, by exile from Nazi Germany, and by alcoholism and depression. His early emotional Socialism gradually mutated into an equally emotional, unrealistic devotion to the restoration of the Habsburg monarchy and a vehement condemnation of most aspects of modernity, especially the Hollywood film industry, seen at its most extreme in his apocalyptic polemic *The Antichrist* (1934). Unlike most Western Jews, he felt warm affection for the Eastern Jews among whom he had been brought up, and commemorated their way of life in a journalistic masterpiece, *Jews on their Travels* (1927), and in much of his fiction. Although he never converted, he loved to describe himself as both a Jew and a Catholic. Writing from Russia in 1926 to Benno Reifenberg, a fellow-journalist on the *Frankfurter Zeitung*, he stressed his European identity and listed its facets: 'I am a Frenchman from the East, a humanist, a rationalist with religion, a Catholic with a Jewish brain, a real revolutionary.'

While Roth's first novel, *The Spider's Web* (1923), is a thriller set among far-Right groups in contemporary Berlin, his next, *Hotel Savoy* (1924), not only presents the realities of post-war Europe in its Polish hotel crowded with refugees but introduces the symbolic overtones which are the hallmark of his best fiction. His acknowledged masterpieces are *Job: The Story of a Simple Man* (1930), where an Eastern Jewish schoolteacher suffers Job-like misfortunes, challenges God, but has his long-lost son restored to him in a strange fairy-tale ending; and *Radetzky March* (1932), where the inarticulate relationship between a father and a son, debarred by masculine codes from expressing their deep affection, is depicted against the background of a decaying Habsburg Empire and, by implication, the dissolution of an ordered world. The later fiction, written during

Roth's exile in Paris, has strong suggestions of religious and mythic imagery, drawn from both Jewish and Christian sources. *Tarabas* (1934) evokes the millennial suffering of the Jews but centres on a Russian soldier who eventually does penance for his anti-Semitic violence by becoming a beggar and dying in a monastery. *Weights and Measures* (1937), a discreet parable about the relations between law and love, ends with its dying protagonist, a corrupt Habsburg official, imagining a merciful judgement by the 'Great Inspector'. *The Legend of the Holy Drinker* (1939) adopts the genre of the Catholic saint's legend to show an alcoholic tramp becoming convinced of a divine grace that will pardon his infirmities.

Although part of 'The Leviathan' was published in a magazine in 1934, the story as a whole appeared only posthumously in 1940. Its setting, a small town lost among the plains and swamps stretching from Galicia across the Ukraine, is familiar from Roth's other works; indeed, Nissen Piczenik appears briefly elsewhere as a minor character. This is the Eastern landscape presented two generations earlier by Franzos as 'Half-Asia', a backward region in urgent need of modernization. Roth, by contrast, celebrates the simplicity of this world and shows modernization as a remorseless force of corruption. Its proponent, Jenö Lakatos, had already appeared as a tempter in the story 'A Murderer's Confession' (1936); here his lameness makes him clearly reminiscent of the Devil. His victim, Nissen Piczenik, leads an emotionally starved life which erupts in a sensitively described mid-life crisis. Roth shows, however, that Piczenik's psychological struggles are only the beginnings of a spiritual quest which focuses on the corals and on the sea from which they come. 'Yonder is the sea,' says Psalm 104, 'great and wide, wherein are things creeping innumerable, both small and great beasts. There go the ships; there is Leviathan, whom thou hast formed to take his pastime therein' (verses 25–6). Leviathan's strength is described in Job 41. Jewish mythology, preserved in the Talmud, further asserts that having created a pair of these monsters, God foresaw that if they bred their progeny would devour all other creatures, and therefore killed the female and pickled her, so that the just may eat her flesh as a delicacy in Paradise. Coral too has biblical associations: its Hebrew name, *almog*, is used in 1 Kings 10: 11 for the valuable trees, also called sandalwood, brought from Ophir. In Roth's story the corals, like the water in the swamps, connect Piczenik with the ocean which is the source of life and death, and the lurking power of Leviathan, 'the primal fish', enhances the maternal implications of the ocean which finally swallows up Piczenik, though the name of his ship, the *Phoenix*, supports the hope of resurrection with which the story ends.

———

I

In the little town of Progrody there once lived a coral-dealer who was well known throughout the region for his honesty and for his good and reliable wares. Peasant women came to him from distant villages when they needed finery for special occasions. They could easily have found other coral-dealers close by, but they knew that these could only supply ordinary trinkets and cheap frippery. For that reason they often travelled many versts* in their rattling little carts in order to reach Progrody and its famous coral-dealer Nissen Piczenik.

They usually came on the days when the fair was held. Monday was the horse-market, Thursday the pig-market. The men inspected the animals; the women, barefoot and with their boots hanging over their shoulders, and in colourful headscarves that shone even on dull days, went in irregular groups to the house of Nissen Piczenik. Their hard, naked soles made muffled, cheerful drumbeats on the hollow planks of the wooden sidewalk and in the broad, cool hall of the old house where the dealer lived. The vaulted hall led to a quiet courtyard where soft moss flourished among the irregular cobblestones and blades of grass sprouted in the warm season. Here the peasant women had a friendly reception from Piczenik's chickens, led by the cocks with their proud combs that were as red as the reddest corals.

It was necessary to knock three times on the iron door, where an iron knocker hung. Then Piczenik would open a small peephole that was cut into the door, look at the people who were demanding admission, push back the bolt, and let the women in. Beggars, wandering minstrels, gipsies, and men with dancing bears generally got alms which he handed through the peephole. He had to be extremely careful, for on all the tables in his spacious kitchen and in his living-room lay the noble corals, in large, small, and middle-sized heaps, various nations and races of coral jumbled together or already arranged by kind and colour. He didn't have ten eyes in his head, to keep one on every beggar, and Piczenik knew that poverty tempts one irresistibly into sin. Of course well-to-do peasant women also stole occasionally, for women readily succumb to the pleasure of acquiring surreptitiously and riskily the finery which they could easily afford to buy. But when customers were present the watchful dealer turned a blind eye, and he allowed for a few thefts in the prices he demanded for his wares.

He employed no fewer than ten threaders, pretty young girls with good sharp eyes and delicate hands. The girls sat in two rows at a long table and fished for the corals with fine pins. Thus they produced the beautiful, regular necklaces with the smallest corals at each end and the largest and shiniest in the middle. While working the girls would sing in chorus. And in summer, on hot, blue, sunny days, the long table at which the threading women sat was placed in the courtyard, and their summer song could be heard all over the town, and it drowned the warbling of the larks in the sky and the chirping of the crickets in the gardens.

There are far more kinds of coral than ordinary people, who know them only from shops and shop-windows, can realize. First of all they may be polished or unpolished; then some are faceted while others are spherical; some are pointed or cylindrical, and look like barbed wire; there are shiny yellow corals, almost with the pinkish-white shade that you sometimes see at the upper edges of rose petals, yellowish-pink, pink, brick-red, beetroot, cinnamon corals, and finally some that look like firm, round drops of blood. There are circular and semicircular corals; some look like little tubs, others like little top hats; there are straight, crooked, and even humpbacked corals. There are stars, spikes, cornets, flowers. For corals are the noblest plants of the world beneath the ocean, roses for the capricious goddesses of the seas, as rich in forms and colours as the caprices of the goddesses themselves.

As will be clear, Nissen Piczenik did not keep a shop. He ran his business in his home, that is, he lived with the corals, day and night, summer and winter, and since the windows of his parlour as well as his kitchen looked on to the courtyard and were moreover protected by thick iron bars, his home was steeped in a beautiful, mysterious twilight that recalled the seabed, and it was as though the corals grew there instead of just being sold. Indeed, thanks to a special, almost intentional caprice of nature, Nissen Piczenik, the coral-dealer, was a red-haired Jew whose copper-coloured goatee beard was like a sort of reddish seaweed and gave the whole man a striking resemblance to a sea-god. It was as though he himself created, or planted and picked, the corals in which he dealt. And his wares were so firmly linked to his appearance that people in the town of Progrody did not call him by his name; in time they even forgot his name and simply called him after his profession. They would say, for example, 'Here comes the coral-dealer,' as though he were the only one in the world.

Nissen Piczenik had in fact a familiar tenderness for corals. Remote from science, unable to read or write—for he had never been to school, and he could only sign his name clumsily—he lived in the conviction that corals were not plants but live animals, a kind of tiny red sea animal—and no professor of marine biology could have persuaded him otherwise. Indeed, for Nissen Piczenik the corals were still alive after they had been sawn, cut, polished, sorted, and threaded. And he may have been right. For he could see with his own eyes how his pink coral necklaces gradually lost their colour when placed on the bosoms of sick or sickly women, but kept their colour on the bosoms of healthy women. In the course of his long career as a coral-dealer he had often noticed how corals which, despite their pink hue, had got paler and paler when lying in his cupboards, suddenly began to shine when hung round the neck of a beautiful, young, and healthy peasant girl, as though they fed on women's blood. Sometimes people would sell coral necklaces back to the coral-dealer; he recognized the jewels that he himself had threaded and guarded—and he could tell at once whether they had been worn by healthy or sickly women.

He had his own special theory about corals. In his view they were, as has been said, marine animals which imitated trees and plants out of prudent modesty, in order not to be attacked or devoured by sharks. What corals longed for was to be picked by divers and taken to the surface of the earth, to be cut, polished, and threaded, in order finally to fulfil the true purpose of their existence by adorning beautiful peasant women. Only here, on the women's firm white necks, nestling up against the vital artery, the sister of the female heart, did they come to life, acquire radiance and beauty, and exercise their innate magical power of attracting men and arousing their desire. Of course the old God Jehovah had created everything Himself, the earth and its beasts, the sea and all its creatures. But for a while, until the advent of the Messiah, God had given the Leviathan, which lay coiled on the deepest bed of all the waters, rule over the animals and plants of the ocean, especially over the corals.

After hearing all this you might suppose that the dealer Nissen Piczenik was regarded as a kind of eccentric. This was far from the case. Piczenik lived in the town of Progrody as a quiet, unassuming person, whose stories about corals and the Leviathan were taken quite seriously as information from an expert who had to know his trade, just as the draper could distinguish between Manchester fabrics and German percale,* or the tea-merchant between Russian tea from the famous firm of Popoff and the English tea supplied by the equally famous Lipton's. All the inhabitants of Progrody and the surrounding district were convinced that corals were live animals and that their growth and conduct beneath the sea were watched over by the primal fish Leviathan. There could be no doubting it, for Nissen Piczenik himself had said so.

The beautiful threaders in Nissen Piczenik's house often worked late into the night and sometimes even till after midnight. After they had left the house, the dealer would begin to busy himself with his stones, or rather animals. First he would examine the strings that the girls had made, then he would count the little piles of corals that had been or were still to be arranged by kind and size, then he himself began to sort them, feeling every single coral, smoothing and stroking it, with his strong, sensitive fingers covered in reddish hair. There were worm-eaten corals. They had holes in the places where holes served no purpose. The careless Leviathan had let his attention wander. And as a rebuke to him, Nissen Piczenik lit a candle, held a piece of red wax over the flame until it was hot and liquid, dipped the tip of a fine pin in the wax, and used it to fill the wormholes in the stone. While doing this he shook his head as though wondering how such a powerful God as Jehovah could have put such a frivolous fish as Leviathan in charge of the corals.

Sometimes, from pure pleasure in the stones, he himself would thread corals until day broke and the time came to say the morning prayer. The work did not weary him at all, he felt not the slightest tiredness. His wife was still asleep under the blanket. He cast a brief, indifferent glance at her. He did not hate her, he did not love her, she was one of the many threaders who worked for him, less pretty and charming than most. He had been married to her for ten years; she had not given him any children—and that was her sole task. He needed a fertile woman, fertile as the sea on whose bed there grew so many corals. But his wife was like a dried-up pond. Let her sleep, by herself, as many nights as she wanted! The law would have permitted him to divorce her. But by now he no longer cared about children and women. He loved the corals. And there was a vague homesickness in his heart, though he would not have dared to call it by its name: Nissen Piczenik, born and brought up in the very heart of the continent, longed for the sea.

Yes, he longed for the sea on whose bed the corals grew, or rather, in his belief, romped. There was nobody far and wide with whom he could have talked about his longing; he had to bear it deep within himself, as the sea bore the corals. He had heard of ships, of divers, of captains, of sailors. His corals came in well-packed crates, still smelling of the sea, from Odessa, Hamburg, or Trieste. The public letter-writer in the post-office dealt with his business correspondence. Before throwing away the envelopes, he made a close inspection of the colourful stamps on the letters from his distant suppliers. He had never been away from Progrody in his life. There was no river in this little town, not even a pond, only marshes all round, and the water could be heard gurgling beneath the green surface, but it could never be seen. Nissen Piczenik fancied that there was a secret connection between the hidden waters of the marshes and the mighty waters of the great seas—and that deep down in the marshes there might also be corals. He knew that if he ever expressed this opinion he would become the town's laughing-stock. He therefore remained silent and kept his opinion to himself. He sometimes dreamed that one day the great sea—he did not know which one, he had never seen a map, and to him all the world's seas were *the* great sea—would inundate Russia, and just the half of Russia where he lived. Then the sea, which he never hoped to reach, would have come to him, the mighty, unknown sea with the immeasurable Leviathan on its bed and with all its sweet and bitter and salty mysteries.

The road from the town of Progrody to the little station, where the trains arrived only three times a week, led through the marshes. And every day, even when Nissen Piczenik was not expecting any corals to be delivered, and even on the days when no trains came, he would go to the station, that is, to the marshes. He would stand at the edge of the marsh for an hour or more, listening devoutly to the croaking of the frogs, as though they could tell him about life on the bed of the swamps, and sometimes he really did believe that he had received all sorts of information. In winter, when the swamps were frozen over, he even ventured to place his foot on them, and that gave him a strange pleasure. The putrid smell of the swamps gave him an intimation of the mighty, bitter scent of the great sea, and his keen ears transformed the soft, sorrowful gurgling of the subterranean waters into the roar of the gigantic blue-green waves. In the town of Progrody, however, nobody knew what was going on in the coral-dealer's soul. All the Jews took him for one of themselves. This man dealt in textiles and that man in petroleum; one sold prayer-shawls, another candles and soap, a third headscarves for peasant women and penknives; one taught the children to pray, another to count, and a third dealt in kvass* and maize and boiled beans. And to all of them Nissen Piczenik seemed to be one of themselves, except that he happened to deal in corals. And yet, as you can see, he was a very special person.

II

He had poor and rich customers, regular and occasional. His rich customers included two local peasants, one of whom, Timon Semyonovich, had planted hops and made a large number of profitable deals every year when the commissioners came from Nuremberg, Saaz,* and Judenburg.* The other peasant was called Nikita Ivanovich. He had no fewer than eight daughters, who got married one after the other, and each one needed corals. The married daughters—by now there were four of them—had children barely two months after their weddings—and the children were daughters too—and they also needed corals, even as babies, to ward off the evil eye. The members of these two families were the grandest visitors to Nissen Piczenik's house. For the daughters of both peasants, their grandchildren, and their sons-in-law, the dealer provided good schnaps which he kept in his chest, a home-made schnaps, spiced with ants, dried mushrooms, parsley, and centaury. Other, ordinary customers made do with ordinary vodka from a shop. For in that region no proper purchase could be made without a drink. Buyer and seller drank so that their transaction might bring benefits and blessings to both. There were also piles of tobacco in the coral-dealer's home, in front of the window, covered by sheets of damp blotting-paper to keep it fresh. For customers did not go to Nissen Piczenik as people go to a shop, merely to buy goods, pay for them, and go away again. Most of the customers had made a journey of many versts, and they were not just Nissen Piczenik's customers but also his guests. He gave them something to drink, to smoke, and often to eat. The dealer's wife would cook kasha* with onions, bortsch with cream, she would roast apples, potatoes, and in winter chestnuts. Thus the customers were not just customers but also guests in Piczenik's house. Sometimes, while they were looking for suitable corals, the peasant women would join in the singing of the threaders; they would all sing together, and even Nissen Piczenik would begin humming to himself; and his wife, stirring at the stove, would move the spoon in time to the singing. When the peasants came from the market or the tavern to fetch their wives and pay for their purchases, the coral-dealer had to drink schnapps or tea and smoke a cigarette with them as well. And every old customer exchanged kisses with the dealer as though he were a brother.

For when we have had a drink, all good and honest men are our brothers, and all dear women are our sisters—and there is no distinction between peasant and dealer, Jew and Christian; and don't let me hear anyone say otherwise!

III

Each new year Nissen Piczenik became more discontented with his peaceful life, though nobody in the town of Progrody noticed it. Like all the Jews, the coral-dealer went to the house of prayer twice daily, at morning and evening, kept the high holidays, fasted on the fast-days, put on phylacteries* and prayer-shawl, rocked his body, chatted to people, talked about politics, about the Russo-Japanese War, about everything that was in the papers and was moving the world. But the longing for the sea, the home of the corals, remained in his heart, and twice every week, when the newspapers reached Progrody, the first items he had read out to him, since he could not read himself, were such maritime news as there might be. He had a very peculiar notion about the sea, as he had about corals. He knew that there were many seas in the world, but the real, genuine sea was the one you had to cross in order to get to America.

Now one day it happened that the son of the fustian-dealer Alexander Komrower, who had been called up three years earlier and put in the navy, returned home for a short spell of leave. No sooner had the coral-dealer heard about young Komrower's return than he appeared in the latter's house and began to interrogate the sailor about all the mysteries of ships, water, and winds. While everyone else in Progrody was convinced that young Komrower had been taken on to the dangerous oceans because he was so stupid, the coral-dealer regarded the sailor as a supremely fortunate boy who had been granted the honour and happiness of becoming a kind of intimate of the corals, indeed a relative of the corals. And the forty-five-year-old Nissen Piczenik was seen roaming about arm in arm with the twenty-two-year-old Komrower on the town's market-place, for hours on end. 'What does he want from Komrower?' people wondered. 'What does he want from me?' wondered the boy.

During the whole spell of leave that the young man was allowed to spend in Progrody, the coral-dealer hardly left his side. The boy was puzzled by the older man's questions, such as the following:

'Can you see as far as the seabed with a telescope?'

'No,' said the sailor, 'a telescope is for looking into the distance, not into the depths.'

'When you're a sailor,' went on Nissen Piczenik, 'can you drop down to the seabed?'

'No,' said young Komrower, 'but if you get drowned, I expect you sink down to the seabed.'

'Can't even the captain do it?'

'No, even the captain can't do it.'

'Have you seen a diver?'

'Sometimes,' said the sailor.

'Do the animals and plants in the sea ever come up to the surface?'

'Only the fish and the whales, which aren't really fish.'

'Tell me', said Nissen Piczenik, 'what the sea looks like.'

'It's full of water,' said the sailor Komrower.

'And is it as wide as a big stretch of land, for example a big plain without any houses on it?'

'It's as wide as that—and even wider!' said the young sailor. 'And it's just as you say: a wide plain, and here and there you see a house, but very seldom, and it isn't a house, but a ship.'

'Where did you see divers?'

'We have divers in the navy,' said the boy. 'But they don't dive to fish for pearls or oysters or corals. It's a military exercise, in case a warship sinks, for example, because then people would have to fetch up valuable instruments or weapons.'

'How many seas are there in the world?'

'I can't tell you,' answered the sailor, 'we did learn it in our training course, but I wasn't listening. I know only the Baltic Sea, the Black Sea, and the great ocean.'

'Which sea is the deepest?'

'I don't know.'

'Where are the largest number of corals to be found?'

'I don't know that, either.'

'Hm, hm,' said the coral-dealer Piczenik, 'pity you don't know.'

On the edge of the town, where the houses of Progrody became more and more wretched till finally they ceased altogether, there stood Podgorzew's tavern, a house of ill repute, frequented by peasants, day-labourers, soldiers, wanton girls, and good-for-nothing fellows. One day the coral-dealer Piczenik was seen entering it with the sailor Komrower. They were served with strong, dark-red mead and salted peas. 'Drink, my boy! Drink and eat, my boy!' said Nissen Piczenik in a fatherly tone to the sailor. The latter drank and ate vigorously, for, young though he was, he had already learnt a few lessons in the ports, and after the mead he was given bad, sour wine and after the wine some ninety-proof schnaps. While drinking the mead he was so taciturn that the coral-dealer feared he would learn nothing more about the waters from the sailor because his knowledge was simply exhausted. After the wine, however, little Komrower began chatting to Podgorzew the landlord, and when the ninety-proof schnaps came, he sang one song after another in a loud voice, like a proper sailor. 'Are you from our dear town?' asked the land-lord. 'Certainly, I'm a child of your town—my—our dear town,' said the sailor, just as though he were a peasant boy and not the son of the stout Jew Komrower. A couple of idlers and tramps sat down at the table beside Nissen Piczenik and the sailor, and when the boy saw the audience, he felt full of an alien dignity, a dignity the like of which he had thought only naval officers could possess. And he encouraged the others: 'Ask away, lads, ask away! I can answer every question. Look, this dear uncle here, you must know him, he's the best coral-dealer in the whole province, I've already told him plenty!' Nissen Piczenik nodded. And as he did not feel comfortable in this alien company, he drank a glass of mead and then another. By and by he felt that the evil-looking faces, which he had seen only through a peephole, were just as human as his own. But since caution and distrust were deeply rooted in his breast, he went out into the courtyard and hid his bag of silver money in his cap. He kept only a few coins loose in his pocket. Satisfied with his idea and with the reassuring pressure on his skull made by the moneybag under the cap, he returned to the table.

Nevertheless he admitted to himself that he did not really know himself why he was sitting here in the tavern with the sailor and the sinister characters. After all, his whole life had been orderly and inconspicuous, and until the arrival of the sailor and indeed until this hour his mysterious love for corals and their home, the ocean, had never been revealed to anyone. And something else happened which alarmed Nissen Piczenik very deeply. Although he was not at all in the habit of thinking in images, he now found himself imagining that his secret longing for the waters and for all that lived and happened on and under them was suddenly reaching the surface of his own life, just as occasionally, for an unknown reason, a rare and valuable animal, used to being at home on the seabed, will shoot up to the surface. Probably the unaccustomed mead, and the nourishment given to the coral-dealer's imagination by the sailor's stories, had awakened this image in him. But he was alarmed and surprised that such crazy notions could come to him, even more than at the fact that for once he was capable of sitting at a tavern table with disreputable companions.

This surprise and alarm, however, made themselves felt, so to speak, beneath the surface of his consciousness. At the same time he listened attentively and with keen enjoyment to the fantastic tales the sailor Komrower was telling. 'Which ship do you serve on?' the other guests asked him. He pondered for a while—his ship was named after a well-known nineteenth-century admiral, but at this moment the name seemed to him as ordinary as his own, and Komrower was resolved to make a massive impression—so he said: 'My battleship is called *Little Mother Catherine*. And do you know who that was? Of course you don't—and that's why I'm going to tell you. Well, Catherine was the richest and most beautiful woman in all of Russia, and that's why the Tsar married her one day in Moscow and immediately took her on a sleigh drawn by six horses—it was forty degrees below freezing—straight to Tsarskoye Selo.* And after them came their whole train on sleighs—and there were so many of them that the whole highway was blocked for three days and three nights. A week after this magnificent wedding, the violent and unjust

King of Sweden entered Petersburg harbour with his silly little wooden boats, but with plenty of soldiers on their decks—for the Swedes are very brave on land—and this Swede intended nothing less than to conquer the whole of Russia. But the Empress Catherine promptly went aboard a ship, the very battleship I'm serving on, and with her own hands she fired on the Swedish king's stupid boats until they sank. And as for the king, she threw him a lifebelt and then took him prisoner. She had his eyes put out, ate them up, and thus became even cleverer than she was before. But the king without eyes was sent to Siberia.'

'Well now,' said a good-for-nothing, scratching his head, 'with the best will in the world, I can't believe all of that.'

'If you say that again,' answered the sailor Komrower, 'you'll have insulted the Imperial Russian Navy, and I shall have to kill you with my weapon. So let me tell you that I learnt this entire story in our training course, and it was His Excellency, our Captain Voroshenko himself, who told it.'

More mead was drunk, and several glasses of schnapps, and the coral-dealer Nissen Piczenik paid. He had drunk something too, though not so much as the others. But when he came out onto the street, arm in arm with the young sailor Komrower, it seemed to him that the middle of the street was a river, the waves were rising and falling, the scattered paraffin lamps were lighthouses, and he had to keep to the edge in order not to fall into the water. The boy was staggering terribly. Every evening all his life long, almost since childhood, Nissen Piczenik had said the prescribed evening prayers, the one that must be prayed at twilight, and the other that welcomes the fall of darkness. Today, for the first time, he had missed both. The stars glittered at him reproachfully from the sky; he dared not raise his eyes. At home his wife was waiting for him with the meagre supper, radish with gherkins and onions and bread covered with lard, a glass of kvass and hot tea. He was more ashamed for himself than he was of being seen by other people. As he went along in this way, arm in arm with the heavy, stumbling young man, he felt as though he were meeting himself, as though the coral-dealer Nissen Piczenik were meeting the coral-dealer Nissen Piczenik—and one were laughing at the other. Still, he avoided meeting other people. He managed that. He accompanied young Komrower home, took him into the room where the Komrower parents were sitting, and said: 'Don't be cross with him, I was with him in the tavern, he's had a drop or two.'

'You, Nissen Piczenik, the coral-dealer, were with him in the tavern?' asked old Komrower.

'Yes, I was!' said Piczenik. 'Goodnight!' And he went home.

All his beautiful threaders were still sitting at the four long tables, singing and fishing for corals with fine pins in their delicate hands.

'Give me some tea at once,' said Nissen Piczenik to his wife, 'I've got work to do.'

And he gulped the tea, and while his hot fingers burrowed in the piles of large corals that had not yet been sorted and rummaged in their pleasant rosy coolness, his poor heart was wandering over the wide, roaring streets of the mighty oceans.

And there was a burning and a roaring in his skull. Sensibly, however, he took off his cap, pulled out the moneybag, and hid it again in his breast.

IV

And the day approached when the sailor Komrower had to return to his battleship, which was at Odessa—and the coral-dealer felt sad at heart. Young Komrower is the only seaman in all of Progrody, and God knows when he'll get another spell of leave. Once he's gone, there will be nothing more to be heard about the waters of the world, unless there happens to be something in the papers.

It was late in the summer, a serene summer with no clouds, no rain, animated and cooled by the always-gentle wind of the Volhynian plain. Two more weeks—and the harvest would begin, and the peasants from the villages would no longer come on market-days to buy corals from Nissen Piczenik. These weeks were the coral season. In these weeks the customers came in flocks, the threaders could hardly keep up with the work, the corals had to be threaded and sorted all night long. On the fine evenings, when the setting sun sent its golden parting greeting through Piczenik's barred windows and the heaps of corals of every kind and shade, animated by its melancholy and yet consoling light, began to shine as if every single stone bore a tiny light in its delicate interior, the peasants came, cheerful and tipsy, to fetch their wives, with their blue and reddish handkerchiefs full of silver and copper coins, in heavy, nail-studded boots that grated on the cobbles of the courtyard. The peasants greeted Nissen Piczenik with embraces and kisses, amid laughter and tears, as though discovering in him a long-lost friend who had been missed for decades. They had nothing against him, they even loved him, this quiet, tall, red-haired Jew with sincere, sometimes dreamy little china-blue eyes in which there dwelt honesty, upright dealing, the cleverness of the expert, and at the same time the folly of someone who had never been away from the town of Progrody. The peasants were not easy to cope with. For although they knew the coral-dealer as one of the rare honest tradesmen in the district, they always remembered that he was a Jew. Besides, they rather enjoyed haggling. First they seated themselves comfortably on the chairs, the settee, the two broad wooden beds covered with high bolsters. Some also lay on the beds, on the sofa, and even on the floor in their boots, to which silver-grey mud was sticking. From the capacious pockets of their sackcloth trousers or from the supplies on the windowsill they fetched loose tobacco, tore off the white margins of old newspapers that were lying about in Piczenik's room, and rolled cigarettes—for even the prosperous ones among them considered cigarette-paper a luxury. Dense blue smoke from cheap tobacco and coarse paper filled the coral-dealer's home, blue smoke full of golden sunlight, floating slowly in small clouds through the square gaps between the bars of the opened windows and out into the street. On one of the tables in the middle of the room hot water was boiling in two copper samovars—they also reflected the setting sun—and no fewer than fifty cheap tumblers of greenish glass with double bottoms passed from hand to hand, filled with steaming, golden-brown tea and with schnapps. Long before, that morning, the peasant women had spent hours negotiating the price of the coral necklaces. Now their menfolk thought the finery was still too dear, and the haggling began afresh. It was a stubborn struggle which the lean Jew had to wage single-handed against the huge majority of stingy and distrustful, strong and sometimes dangerously drunk men. Beneath the black silk skullcap that Nissen Piczenik wore at home, the sweat ran down his freckled cheeks with their scanty hair, into his red goatee, and in the evening, after the battle, the hairs of his beard stuck together and had to be separated with his little iron comb. Yet in the end he defeated all his customers, despite his folly. For in the whole great world he knew only the corals and the peasants of his home—and he knew how to sort and thread the former and how to convince the latter. The absolutely obstinate ones received what he called a bonus—that is, once they had paid the price which he did not immediately name but secretly longed for, he gave them another tiny coral necklace made of cheap stones, intended for children to wear round their arms and necks and infallibly effective against the evil eye of envious neighbours and evil-minded witches. When doing this, he had to keep a close eye on his customers' hands and judge the height and size of the piles of corals. Oh, it wasn't an easy struggle!

This summer, however, Nissen Piczenik appeared absent-minded, almost inattentive, with no interest in his customers and his business. His good wife, accustomed for years to his silence and his peculiar character, noticed his absent-mindedness and took him to task. Here he had sold a string of corals too cheap, there he had overlooked a petty theft, today he had failed to give an old customer a bonus, while yesterday he had given quite a valuable necklace to a new and unimportant customer. During these days, however, the coral-dealer lost his composure, and he himself felt his indifference, the normal indifference towards his wife, abruptly changing into anger against her. Indeed, although he had never been able to drown any of the many mice that were caught each night in his traps with his own hands—as everyone in Progrody did—but handed the captured animals over to his water-carrier Saul, to be disposed of in return for a tip: on one of these days he, the peaceful Nissen Piczenik, threw a heavy string of corals at his wife's head when she was uttering her customary reproaches, slammed the door, left the house, and went to the edge of the great marsh, the distant cousin of the great oceans.

Just two days before the sailor's departure the coral-dealer suddenly felt the desire to accompany young Komrower to Odessa. Such a desire comes suddenly, far quicker than an ordinary flash of lightning, and it strikes the very place it came from—the human heart. It strikes its own birthplace, you might say. Nissen Piczenik's desire was like that. And it is not far from such a desire to a decision.

And on the morning of the day when the young sailor Komrower was to depart, Nissen Piczenik said to his wife: 'I have to go away for a couple of days.'

His wife was still lying in bed. It was eight in the morning, the coral-dealer had just come from the house of prayer, where he had said his morning prayer.

She sat up. With her scanty, tousled hair, without her wig, and with yellowish scraps of sleep in the corners of her eyes, she seemed to him a stranger, even an enemy. Her appearance, her surprise, her fright seemed perfectly to justify the decision which he himself had considered foolhardy.

'I'm going to Odessa!' he said with sincere malice. 'I'll be back in a week, God willing!'

'Now? Now?' stammered his wife among the pillows. 'Now, when the peasants are coming?'

'This very minute!' said the coral-dealer. 'I've important things to do. Pack my things!'

And with an angry and malicious pleasure that he had never known before, he saw his wife getting out of bed, saw her ugly toes, her fat legs under her long nightshirt on which a few black, irregular dots were scattered, the marks of flea-bites, and heard her familiar sigh, the customary and constant song with which this woman greeted the morning; nothing linked him with her except the distant memory of a few tender moments at night and the traditional fear of divorce.

At the same time, however, a strange and yet familiar voice inside Nissen Piczenik was rejoicing: 'Piczenik is going to the corals! He's going to the corals! Nissen Piczenik is going to the home of the corals!...'

V

And so he got on the train with the sailor Komrower and went to Odessa. It was rather a long and complicated journey; they had to change in Kiev. The coral-dealer was travelling by railway for the first time in his life, but he did not feel as many people do when they make their first railway journey. Engines, signals, bells, telegraph posts, rails, conductors, and the landscape flying past the windows did not interest him. He was thinking about the water and the harbour towards which he was travelling, and if he noticed anything about the character and circumstances of railway travel, it was only in relation to the still-unknown character and circumstances of travel by sea. 'Do you have bells too?' he asked the sailor. 'Do they ring three times before a ship leaves? Do the ships whistle and toot like engines? Does the ship have to turn round when it wants to go back, or can it simply swim backwards?'

Of course, as always happens on journeys, they met other passengers who wanted to chat and with whom they had to discuss this and that. 'I'm a coral-dealer,' said Nissen Piczenik truthfully, when he was asked about his business. But if he was then asked: 'What are you going to do in Odessa?' he began telling lies. 'I'm planning some large-scale business deals there,' he said.

'That's interesting,' put in a fellow-traveller who had hitherto been silent. 'I'm also planning some large-scale business deals in Odessa, and the wares I deal in are related to corals, though much finer and more expensive than corals!'

'More expensive, maybe,' said Nissen Piczenik, 'but certainly not finer.'

'What do you bet?' exclaimed the other.

'It's impossible, I tell you. No need to bet!'

'Well then,' said the other triumphantly, 'I deal in pearls!'

'Pearls aren't finer at all,' said Nissen Piczenik. 'What's more, they bring misfortune.'

'Yes, if you lose them,' said the pearl-dealer.

All the others began listening attentively to this strange dispute. Finally the pearl-dealer unbelted his trousers and drew out a bag full of flawless, shimmering pearls. He shook some on to the palm of his hand and showed them to all the other passengers.

'Hundreds of oysters have to be opened', he said, 'before a pearl is found. The divers are well paid. Pearl-dealers are among the most respected merchants anywhere in the world. You could say that we form a special race. Look at me, for example. I'm a merchant of the first guild, I live in Petersburg, I have the most distinguished customers, two grand princes for example, their names are a matter of professional confidence, I travel through half the world, every year I'm in Paris, Brussels, Amsterdam. Ask anywhere about the pearl-dealer Gorodotsky, children will be able to tell you about me.'

'And I', said Nissen Piczenik, 'have never been outside our town of Progrody—and only peasants buy my corals. But all of you here will admit that a simple peasant woman, adorned with a couple of strings of beautiful, spotless corals, looks better than a grand princess. What's more, corals are worn by high and low, they dignify the low and adorn the high. You can wear corals morning, noon, and night, at balls for example, summer and winter, Sundays and weekdays, at work and at rest, in happy times and in mourning. There are many kinds of red in the world, my dear travelling companions, and it is written that our Jewish King Solomon had a very special red for his royal robe, for the Phoenicians, who honoured him, had given him a very special worm whose nature was to emit red dye as urine. It was a dye that doesn't exist nowadays, the Tsar's purple is not the same, for the worm became extinct after Solomon's death, that whole species of worm. And, you see, it's only in deep red corals that this colour is still to be found. But where in the world has anyone seen red pearls?'

Never before had the taciturn coral-dealer made such a long and energetic speech in front of complete strangers. He pushed his cap back from his forehead and wiped away the sweat. He smiled at each of his travelling companions in turn, and all bestowed the approval he deserved. 'He's quite right!' they all cried at once.

And even the pearl-dealer had to admit that, though Nissen Piczenik was wrong about the facts, as an orator on behalf of corals he was excellent.

Finally they reached Odessa, the radiant harbour with the blue water and the many ships as white as bridal dresses. Here the battleship was already waiting for the sailor Komrower, like a paternal house waiting for its son. Nissen Piczenik also wanted a closer look at the ship. And he went with the boy as far as the sentry-post and said: 'I'm his uncle, I'd like to see the ship.' He was astonished at his own audacity. No indeed, this was no longer the old continental Nissen Piczenik who was speaking to an armed sailor, it was not Nissen Piczenik from continental Progrody, but a new man altogether, like somebody who has been turned inside out as you might turn a glove or a coat, an oceanic Nissen Piczenik. He himself felt as though he had emerged, not from the train, but straight out of the sea, from the depths of the Black Sea. He was more familiar with the water than he had ever been with the town of Progrody where he had lived since birth. Wherever he looks, there are ships and water, water and ships. The ever-splashing water is lapping tenderly against the snow-white, coal-black, coral-red—yes, coral-red—sides of the ships, the boats, the dinghies, the yachts, the motor-boats, no, it isn't lapping, it's caressing the ships with a hundred thousand little waves that are long tongues and hands at once, tonguelets combined with little hands. The Black Sea isn't black at all. Seen from the distance, it is bluer than the sky, close up it is as green as a meadow. If you throw a scrap of bread into the water, thousands of nimble little fish come leaping, tripping, slipping, snaking, darting, and flying up to seize it. The cloudless blue sky stretches over the harbour. The ships' masts and chimneys rise towards it. 'What's this?—What's that called?' asks Nissen Piczenik incessantly. This is called a mast, that's the bow, here are some lifebelts, there are differences between boats and dinghies, sailboats and steamers, masts and funnels, battle-ships and merchant vessels, deck and stern, bow and keel. A hundred new words assail Nissen Piczenik's poor, but happy, head. After a long wait, he is given permission (as an exception, says the Chief Mate) to inspect the battleship and accompany his nephew. The First Lieutenant appears in person, in order to look at a Jewish tradesman aboard a battleship of the Imperial Russian Navy. His Excellency the First Lieutenant smiles. The gentle wind swells the long black skirts of the skinny red Jew's coat, revealing his thread-bare, much-patched, striped trousers in his muddy, knee-length boots. The Jew Nissen Piczenik even forgets the commandments of his religion. In front of the officer's radiant white-and-gold magnifi-cence he takes off his black cap, and his red curls flutter in the wind. 'Your nephew is a fine sailor!' says His Excellency, the officer. Nissen Piczenik cannot think of a suitable answer, he only smiles, he does not laugh, he smiles silently. His mouth is open, revealing his big yellow horse-teeth and his pink gums, and his copper-coloured goatee hangs almost over his chest. He looks at the helm, at the cannon, he is allowed to peep through the telescope—and God knows that the distance comes close, things that are nowhere near are near all the same, behind the glass. God gave people eyes, that's true, but what are ordinary eyes compared to eyes that look through a telescope? God gave people eyes, but also the intelligence to invent telescopes and increase the strength of those eyes!—And the sun shines on the deck, its rays touch Nissen Piczenik's back, and yet he doesn't feel hot. For the everlasting wind is blowing over the sea, indeed it seems as though a wind is coming from the sea itself, a wind from the depths of the water.

At last the moment of parting came. Nissen Piczenik embraced young Komrower, bowed to the lieutenant and then to the sailors, and left the battleship.

He had resolved to return to Progrody immediately after parting from young Komrower. Yet he remained in Odessa. He saw the battleship leave, the sailors hailed him as he stood on the harbour waving his blue handkerchief with its red stripes. He saw many other ships leave, and he waved to all their unknown passengers. For he went to the harbour every day. And every day he learnt something new. He heard, for example, what it means to 'lift anchor', or 'take in sail', or 'discharge cargo', or 'make the ropes fast', and so on.

Every day he saw many young men in sailor suits working on the ships, climbing up the masts, he saw the young men walking through the streets of Odessa arm in arm, a whole chain of sailors taking up the whole width of the street—and he felt sad at heart that he had no children. At such moments he wished he had sons and grandsons—and there was no doubt—he would have sent them all to sea, they would have been sailors. Meanwhile his wife, infertile and ugly, was lying at home in Progrody. Today she was selling corals in his place. Could she? Did she know the meaning of corals?

And in the harbour of Odessa Nissen Piczenik rapidly forgot the duties of an ordinary Jew from Progrody. And he did not go to the house of prayer morning and evening to utter the prescribed prayers, but he prayed at home, very hastily and without truly thinking about God; he merely prayed like a gramophone, his tongue repeated mechanically the sounds that were inscribed in his brain. Had the world ever seen such a Jew?

At home in Progrody, meanwhile, it was the coral season. Nissen Piczenik knew this very well, but he was no longer the old continental Nissen Piczenik, but the new, the newborn oceanic one.

'I have time enough', he said to himself, 'to return to Progrody! What have I to lose there! And how much I still have to gain here!'

And he stayed three weeks in Odessa, and every day he spent happy hours with the sea, the ships, and the little fish.

This was the first holiday Nissen Piczenik had had in his life.

VI

When he arrived back home in Progrody, he noticed that he had lost no less than one hundred and sixty roubles, including travel expenses. However, he told his wife, and everyone else who asked him what he had been doing for so long in foreign parts, that he had concluded 'important business deals' in Odessa.

At that time the harvest was beginning, and the peasants no longer came to market so much. The coral-dealer's house became quieter, as it did every year during these weeks. The threaders left his house in the late afternoon. And at night, when Nissen Piczenik came home from the house of prayer, he no longer found the clear song of the beautiful girls awaiting him, but only his wife, the usual plate of onions and radishes, and the copper samovar.

Nevertheless—remembering the days in Odessa, of which nobody but himself had any idea how fruitless they had been commercially—the coral-dealer Piczenik accepted the usual laws of his autumn days. He was already thinking how, in a few months' time, he might again pretend to have important business and go to another port, such as Petersburg.

He did not need to fear material hardship. All the money he had put by during his many years of dealing in corals lay, incessantly gathering interest, with the moneylender Pinkas Warshawsky, a respected local usurer, who was merciless in collecting debts but punctual in paying interest. Nissen Piczenik did not need to fear physical hardship; and he was childless and had no descendants to provide for. So why shouldn't he go to one of the many harbours?

And the coral-dealer was already beginning to devise plans for next spring, when something unusual happened in the neighbouring town of Suchky.

In this town, which was just as small as Nissen Piczenik's home, the town of Progrody, a man who was not known to anyone in the district one day opened a coral shop. This man was called Jenö Lakatos, and came, as people soon learnt, from the distant land of Hungary. He spoke Russian, German, Hungarian, Polish, and if the need had arisen, and if anyone had happened to want it, Herr Lakatos would also have spoken French, English, and Chinese. He was a young man with smooth, blue-black, oiled hair—and by the way, he was the only man far and wide who wore a shining stiff collar and a tie, and carried a cane with a golden knob. This young man had arrived in Suchky a couple of weeks earlier, had struck up a friendship with the slaughterer Nikita Kolkhin, and worked on the latter until he decided to start trading in corals jointly with Lakatos. The firm with the bright red sign was called N. Kolkhin & Company.

In the window of this shop there gleamed flawless red corals, lighter in weight than Nissen Piczenik's stones, but also cheaper. A very large coral necklace cost one rouble fifty, smaller necklaces could be had for twenty, fifty, eighty kopecks. The prices were in the shop window. And to make sure that nobody went past the shop, inside it a phonograph played merry howling songs all day long. They could be heard all over the town and further away—in the surrounding villages. Admittedly, Suchky did not have a big market like Progrody. Nevertheless—even though it was harvest-time—the peasants came to Herr Lakatos's shop to listen to the songs and to buy the cheap corals.

After this Herr Lakatos had been carrying on his attractive business for a couple of weeks, a prosperous peasant called on Nissen Piczenik one day and said: 'Nissen Semyonovich, I can't believe that you have been cheating me and others for twenty years. But now there is a man in Suchky who sells the most beautiful strings of coral for fifty kopecks each. My wife wanted to go there—but I thought we'd better ask you first, Nissen Semyonovich.'

'This Lakatos', said Nissen Piczenik, 'must be a thief and a swindler. That's the only way I can account for his prices. But I'll go there myself, if you'll take me on your cart.'

'Very well!' said the peasant. 'See for yourself.'

So the coral-dealer went to Suchky, stood for a while in front of the shop window, heard the howling songs coming from inside the shop, and finally went in and began talking to Herr Lakatos.

'I'm a coral-dealer myself,' said Nissen Piczenik. 'My wares come from Hamburg, Odessa, Trieste, Amsterdam. I don't understand how you can sell such beautiful corals so cheaply.'

'You belong to the older generation,' answered Lakatos, 'and, pardon the expression, you're a bit behind the times.'

Meanwhile Lakatos came out from behind the counter—and Nissen Piczenik saw that he limped a little. Evidently his left leg was shorter, for the sole of his left boot was twice as high as that of the right. He gave off a powerful, heavy scent—and you could not tell where on his meagre body the source of all his scents was located. His hair was blue-black as night. And his dark eyes, which could have looked gentle at first glance, glowed so intensely from second to second that amid their blackness there flamed a curious fiery glow. Under his black curled moustache, Lakatos's mouse-like teeth smiled white and shimmering.

'Well?' asked the coral-dealer Nissen Piczenik.

'Well,' said Lakatos, 'we aren't crazy. We don't dive down to the seabed. We simply produce artificial corals. My firm is called Lowncastle Brothers, New York. I've worked successfully for two years in Budapest. The peasants don't notice. Not the peasants in Hungary, and certainly not the peasants in Russia. They want beautiful, red, flawless corals. Here they are. Cheap, a bargain, beautiful, ornamental. What more could you want? Real corals couldn't be so beautiful!'

'What are the corals made of?' asked Nissen Piczenik.

'Celluloid, my dear fellow, celluloid!' cried Lakatos in delight. 'I won't hear a word against technology! Look: rubber trees grow in Africa, rubber is used for making indiarubber and celluloid. Is that unnatural? Are rubber-trees any less natural than corals? Is a tree in Africa any less natural than a coral tree on the seabed?—Well now, what do you say now?—What about doing business together?—Make up your mind!—A year from today you'll have lost all your customers to my competition—and you can take all your real corals back to the seabed, where the beautiful stones come from. Tell me: yes or no?'

'Give me two days,' said Nissen Piczenik. And he went home.

VII

In this way the Devil tempted the coral-dealer Nissen Piczenik for the first time. The Devil was called Jenö Lakatos from Budapest, and he introduced false corals into Russia, the celluloid corals that burn, when you set fire to them, as blue as the fiery hedge surrounding Hell.

When Nissen Piczenik got home, he kissed his wife casually on both cheeks, greeted the threaders, and began to look at his corals with rather bewildered eyes—bewildered by the Devil: the living corals that did not look nearly so flawless as the false celluloid stones of his competitor Jenö Lakatos. And the Devil put into the head of the honest coral-dealer Nissen Piczenik the idea of mixing false corals with the real ones.

So one day he went to the post office and dictated to the public letter-writer a letter to Jenö Lakatos in Suchky, so that in a couple of days the latter sent him no less than twenty poods* of false corals. Now we all know that celluloid is a light material, and with twenty poods of false corals you can make a lot of necklaces, large and small. Nissen Piczenik, seduced and deluded by the Devil, mixed the false corals with the real ones, thereby betraying both himself and the real corals.

Harvest had already begun in all the country round, and hardly any peasants now came to buy corals. But from the few who appeared now and again Nissen Piczenik now made more money than he had from his numerous customers in the past. He mixed the genuine with the false—and that was even worse than selling nothing but false wares. For that is what happens to people when they are seduced by the Devil: they surpass even the Devil in devilish devices. In this way Nissen Piczenik surpassed Jenö Lakatos from Budapest. And all the money that Nissen Piczenik made was conscientiously taken to Pinkas Warshawsky. And the Devil had seduced the coral-dealer so thoroughly that he took real delight in the idea that his money was growing and bearing interest.

Then, on one of these days, the usurer Pinkas Warshawsky suddenly died, and Nissen Piczenik was alarmed and promptly went to the usurer's heirs and demanded his money with interest. He got it on the spot, no less than five thousand four hundred and fifty roubles and sixty kopecks. With this money he paid his debts to Lakatos, and he asked for another twenty poods of false corals.

One day the rich hop-farmer came to Nissen Piczenik and asked for a coral necklace for one of his grandchildren, to keep off the evil eye.

The coral-dealer threaded a string with nothing but false corals, celluloid corals, and he also said: 'These are the most beautiful corals I have.'

The farmer paid the price that was proper for genuine corals, and went to his village.

A week after his grandchild had had the false corals put round his neck, he died of diphtheria, a terrible death by suffocation. And in the village of Solovetsk, where the rich hop-farmer lived (but also in the surrounding villages), the news spread that the corals of Nissen Piczenik from Progrody brought misfortune and sickness—and not only to those who had bought from him. For diphtheria began to rage in the neighbouring villages, it snatched many children away, and the rumour spread that Nissen Piczenik's corals brought sickness and death.

Because of this, no more customers came to Nissen Piczenik all winter. It was a hard winter: it had set in by November, it lasted till late March. Every day brought a merciless frost, snow fell rarely, even the ravens seemed to shiver as they perched on the bare boughs of the chestnut trees. Nissen Piczenik's house was very quiet. He dismissed one threader after another. On market-days he sometimes met one or other of his old customers. But they gave him no greeting.

Indeed, the peasants who had kissed him in summer now behaved as if they no longer knew the coral-dealer.

The temperature sank to forty degrees. The water in the water-carriers' pitchers froze on the way from the well to the house. A thick layer of ice covered Nissen Piczenik's window-panes, so that he could no longer see what was happening in the street. Large, heavy icicles hung from the iron bars and sealed the windows even more firmly. And when no more customers came to Nissen Piczenik, he put the blame not on the false corals but on the severe winter. Yet Herr Lakatos's shop in Suchky was always crowded. And the peasants bought his flawless and cheap celluloid corals and not Nissen Piczenik's genuine ones.

The streets and alleys of the town of Progrody were covered with ice and as smooth as mirrors. All the inhabitants felt their way with iron-tipped sticks. Nevertheless quite a few slipped and broke their necks or their legs.

One evening Nissen Piczenik's wife also slipped. She lay unconscious for a long time until compassionate neighbours picked her up and carried her indoors.

She soon began to vomit violently; the Progrody physician said it was concussion of the brain. She was taken to hospital, where the doctor confirmed the physician's diagnosis.

The coral-dealer went to the hospital every morning. He sat at his wife's bedside, listened to her ramblings for half an hour, looked into her fevered eyes and at her thin hair, remembered the few hours of tenderness he had given her, smelt the pungent smell of camphor and iodoform, and went back home and himself cooked bortsch and kasha and cut bread for himself and peeled the radishes for himself and made tea for himself and stoked the stove for himself. Then he shook all the corals from the many bags on to one of his four tables and began sorting them. Herr Lakatos's celluloid corals were kept separately in the cupboard. It was a long time now since Nissen Piczenik had taken the genuine corals for live animals. Since that Lakatos had come into the district and he himself, the coral-dealer Nissen Piczenik, had begun to mix the light celluloid things with the heavy genuine stones, the corals stored in his house were dead. Now corals were made of celluloid! A dead material was used to make corals that looked as though they were alive and were even more beautiful and more perfect than genuine live ones! What was his wife's concussion, compared to that?

A week later she died, doubtless because of the concussion. But Nissen Piczenik was not far wrong in saying to himself that his wife had died not just from the concussion but also because her life had not depended on the life of any other person in the world. Nobody had wanted her to stay alive, and so she had died.

Now the coral-dealer Nissen Piczenik was a widower. He mourned his wife in the prescribed manner. He bought one of the most durable gravestones for her and had complimentary words carved on it. And he spoke the prayer for the dead every morning and evening on her behalf. But he did not miss her at all. He could make his own meals and his own tea. He did not feel lonely once he was alone with the corals. And he was saddened only by the fact that he had betrayed them to their false sisters, the celluloid corals, and had betrayed himself to the dealer Lakatos.

He longed for spring. And when at last it came, Nissen Piczenik realized that his longing had been futile. In every other year, even before Easter, when the icicles began to melt at midday, customers used to arrive in creaking carts or tinkling sleighs. They needed corals for Easter. But now it was spring, the sun was brooding with more and more warmth, the icicles hanging from the roofs grew shorter each day and the piles of melting snow at the edge of the street grew smaller—and no customers came to Nissen Piczenik. In his oakwood cupboard, in his portable trunk, which stood on its four wheels, mighty and iron-bound, beside the stove, lay the noblest corals in piles and in large and small necklaces. But not one customer came. It kept getting warmer, the snow disappeared, the mild rain fell, the violets flowered in the woods, and in the marshes the frogs croaked; but not one customer came.

About this time people in Progrody first noticed a certain curious change in Nissen Piczenik's manner and character. Indeed, the inhabitants of Progrody began for the first time to surmise that the coral-dealer was an odd person, an eccentric even—and some lost their traditional respect for him, and some even mocked him in public. Many good people of Progrody no longer said: 'The coral-dealer is going past,' but 'That's Nissen Piczenik going past—he used to be a great coral-dealer.'

It was his own fault. For he did not behave in at all the way that the laws and the dignity of mourning prescribe for a widower. Although people had turned a blind eye to his odd friendship with the sailor Komrower and their visit to Podgorzew's notorious tavern, they could not observe his visits to the tavern without becoming gravely suspicious. For since his wife's death Nissen Piczenik went to Podgorzew's tavern almost every day. He began passionately drinking mead. And as the mead presently came to taste too sweet, he had it laced with vodka. Sometimes one of the wanton girls would sit beside him. And though he had never in his life known any other woman besides his late wife, had never known any other desire than to caress his real wives, the corals, and to sort and thread them, sometimes in Podgorzew's sordid tavern he felt himself succumbing to the women's cheap white flesh, to his own blood, which jeered at the dignity of his life as a respected citizen, and to the wonderful hot oblivion that streamed from the girls' bodies. And he drank, and he caressed the girls who sat beside him and who sometimes sat on his knee. He felt desire, the same desire as when playing with his corals. And with his strong, reddish-haired fingers he felt, less adroitly, indeed with absurd clumsiness, for the girls' nipples, which were as red as many corals. And he went downhill, as they say, quickly, quicker and quicker, almost daily. He felt it himself. His face became thinner, his lean back was bent, he no longer cleaned his coat and his boots, he no longer combed his beard. Every morning and evening he spoke his prayers mechanically. He felt it himself: he was no longer *the* coral-dealer, he was Nissen Piczenik, who used to be a great coral-dealer.

He was aware that in a year or six months he would be the town's laughing-stock—and what did he really care? His home was not Progrody, but the ocean.

So one day he made the fatal decision of his life.

First, however, he set off one day for Suchky—and lo and behold, in the shop of Jenö Lakatos from Budapest he saw all his old customers, listening devoutly to the howling songs on the phono-graph and buying celluloid corals at fifty kopecks a necklace.

'Well, what did I tell you a year ago?' called Lakatos to Nissen Piczenik. 'Do you want another ten poods, twenty, thirty?'

Nissen Piczenik said: 'I don't want any more false corals. As far as I'm concerned, I deal only in the genuine article.'

VIII

And he went home to Progrody and went in stillness and secrecy to Benjamin Broczyner, who kept a travel bureau and dealt in passenger tickets for emigrants. It was particularly from deserters, and from the very poorest Jews who had to emigrate to Canada and America, that Broczyner made his living. He was the Progrody agent for a Hamburg steamship company.

'I want to go to Canada!' said the coral-dealer Nissen Piczenik, 'and as soon as possible.'

'The next boat is called *Phoenix* and leaves from Hamburg in two weeks. We can get your papers ready by then,' said Broczyner.

'Fine, fine!' answered Piczenik. 'Don't say a word to anyone.' And he went home and packed all the corals, the genuine ones, in his portable trunk.

As for the celluloid corals, however, he placed them on the copper base of the samovar, set fire to them, and saw how they burned with a stinking bluish flame. It took a long time; there were more than fifteen poods of false corals. They left a large heap of curly, grey-black ash. And the greyish-blue smoke from the celluloid coiled and curled round the paraffin lamp in the middle of the room. That was how Nissen Piczenik took leave of his home.

On 21 April he boarded the steamship *Phoenix* in Hamburg as a steerage passenger.

The ship had been at sea for four days when the catastrophe came; some people may still remember it.

More than two hundred passengers went down with the *Phoenix*. They were drowned, of course.

But as for Nissen Piczenik, who also went down with the ship, one cannot say that he was simply drowned like the others. Rather—this can be said with a good conscience—he went home to the corals, to the bed of the ocean, where the mighty Leviathan coils.

And if we are to believe the report of a man who escaped death, as they say, by a miracle, then we must add that long before the lifeboats were full, Nissen Piczenik plunged overboard into the water to join his corals, his genuine corals.

For my part, I am willing to believe it. For I knew Nissen Piczenik, and I can testify that he belonged to the corals and that his only home was the ocean bed.

May he rest in peace there alongside the Leviathan until the coming of the Messiah.

NELLY SACHS

Four Poems

(translated by Michael Hamburger and others)

Nelly (originally Leonie) Sachs (1891–1970), daughter of a well-to-do factory-owner, was brought up (like Mann's fictional Aarenholds) in the exclusive Tiergarten district of Berlin in an assimilated family which had largely abandoned Jewish traditions. Her first book, *Legends and Stories* (1921), was inspired by the figures of Jesus and St Francis, especially as treated by Rilke and the Swedish writer Selma Lagerlöf. Sending Lagerlöf a copy, Sachs described herself as 'a young German'. Sachs's life was overshadowed by an unfulfilled love conceived in her teens for a man whose identity remains unknown but who appears to have fallen victim to the Nazis. She did not marry, and after her father's death in 1930 she lived in seclusion, tending her frail mother, until, after harassment by the Gestapo, they escaped from Nazi Germany in May 1940 by the last passenger flight to leave Berlin for Stockholm. They owed their survival to a Gentile friend, Gudrun Harlan, who visited Sweden and asked the aged Lagerlöf and the King's brother to help them obtain an immigration permit; the permit arrived a few days before Nelly Sachs was due for deportation to a labour camp.

In Sweden, Sachs was supported by the Jewish community and scraped a living by translating Swedish poetry while publishing successive volumes of her own, including *In the Habitations of Death* (1947), *Eclipse of the Stars* (1951), *And no one knows how to go on* (1958), *Flight and Metamorphosis* (1959), and the verse play *Eli* (1951). She became a Swedish citizen in 1952. Eventually she received international recognition, with many literary prizes including the Nobel Prize for Literature, which she shared with the Hebrew novelist Samuel Joseph Agnon in 1966. Since her later poetry addressed not only Jewish but universal questions, however, she was not altogether pleased to be labelled a Jewish writer, and described herself in her acceptance speech as a 'German poet'. She revisited Germany only briefly to receive the Droste-Hülshoff Prize in 1960, but the more rewarding parts of her journey seem to have been a stopover in Zurich, where she had a long talk with Paul Celan (commemorated in his poem 'Zurich, at the Stork', pp. 304–6 below), and a later visit to Paris, where she and Celan laid flowers on Heine's grave.

Terror and exile led Nelly Sachs to identify with a Judaism that had not been part of her life before 1933. She took little interest in Jewish religious practice. Her understanding of Judaism came from Martin Buber's books of Hasidic tales, with their introductions setting out the main principles of Hasidic thought, and from the mystical traditions of the Kabbalah. Such Kabbalistic texts as the *Zohar*, of which she read extracts in Gershom Scholem's translation, enabled her to conceive life as a state of exile from God which could be overcome only in moments of mystical exaltation. Most of the following poems come from *In the Habitations of Death*, where she wrote directly about the death-camps, contrasting the abuse of rationality in these 'ingeniously constructed dwellings of death' with the mystical hope that is present even when 'the body of Israel passes as smoke through the air'. She identifies herself with the scribe of the *Zohar* in continuing the Jewish mystical tradition, and displays a confidence in the expressive power of language that contrasts with Celan's conviction that poetry is close to silence. While she sees Job as the central image of Jewish existence, her eclecticism is shown by her conception of Christ as the last of the Jewish prophets, by her interest in the Christian theosophy of Jakob Böhme and in the mysticism of Simone Weil, and by several poems which try to fuse Christian and Hasidic traditions.

———

O the chimneys

And though after my skin worms destroy this
body, yet in my flesh shall I see God. – JOB 19: 26

O the chimneys
On the ingeniously devised habitations of death
When Israel's body drifted as smoke
Through the air—
Was welcomed by a star, a chimney sweep,
A star that turned black
Or was it a ray of sun?

O the chimneys!
Freedomway for Jeremiah and Job's dust—
Who devised you and laid stone upon stone
The road for refugees of smoke?

O the habitations of death,
Invitingly appointed
For the host who used to be a guest—

O you fingers
Laying the threshold
Like a knife between life and death—

O you chimneys,
O you fingers
And Israel's body as smoke through the air!

But who emptied your shoes of sand

But who emptied your shoes of sand
When you had to get up, to die?
The sand which Israel gathered,
Its nomad sand?
Burning Sinai sand,
Mingled with throats of nightingales,
Mingled with wings of butterflies,
Mingled with the hungry dust of serpents;
Mingled with all that fell from the wisdom of Solomon,
Mingled with what is bitter in the mystery of wormwood—

O you fingers
That emptied the deathly shoes of sand.
Tomorrow you will be dust
In the shoes of those to come.

The voice of the Holy Land

O my children,
Death has run through your hearts
As through a vineyard—
Painted *Israel* red on all the walls of the world.

What shall be the end of the little holiness
Which still dwells in my sand?
The voices of the dead
Speak through reed pipes of seclusion.

Lay the weapons of revenge in the field

That they grow gentle—
For even iron and grain are akin
In the womb of earth—

But what shall be the end of the little holiness
Which still dwells in my sand?

The child murdered in sleep
Arises; bends down the tree of ages
And pins the white breathing star
That was once called Israel
To its topmost bough.
Spring upright again, says the child,
To where tears mean eternity.

Job

O you windrose of agonies!
Swept by primordial storms
always into other directions of inclemency;
even your South is called loneliness.
Where you stand is the navel of pain.

Your eyes have sunk deep into your skull
like cave doves which the hunter
fetches blindly at night.
Your voice has gone dumb,
having too often asked *why*.

Your voice has joined the worms and fishes.
Job, you have cried through all vigils
but one day the constellation of your blood
shall make all rising suns blanch.

PAUL CELAN

Selected Poems

(translated by John Felstiner)

Paul Celan (1920–70), originally Paul Anczel, was born in Cernauti, then in Romania; previously it was known as Czernowitz, the capital of the Bukovina province of the Austrian Empire; it is now Chernovtsy in Ukraine. His parents were German-speaking Orthodox Jews for whom German was the supreme language of culture. Like many others, they suffered the hideous irony of being deported by the German forces in 1942 to a concentration camp across the River Dniester, where they died. Paul survived by luck, doing forced labour until the Soviets occupied his home town in 1943. After the war he lived in Bucharest, translating from Russian into Romanian, but in 1947, to avoid the Communists, he went first to Vienna, then in 1948 to Paris, where in 1952 he married the artist Gisèle Lestrange (1927–91) and lived as a translator and language teacher, later a lecturer at the École Normale Supérieur, until his suicide.

Celan is now recognized as the greatest German poet since Rilke. Yet he was sharply conscious of the problems, not only of writing poetry after the Holocaust, but of writing it in the language employed and arguably tainted in the administration of mass murder. The long, surging, dactylic lines of his early poems soon became compressed into concise, emotionally restrained, mostly rhymeless verse, fragmentary in syntax, tentative and questioning in tone. 'The poem today tends towards silence,' he said in 1960; 'the poem survives on the edge of itself.' He called the poem a 'crystal' from which all clichés, 'the garish talk of rubbed-off experience', have been 'etched away'. But he also described his poems as 'messages in bottles, dispatched in the hope that they will be washed up on land, somewhere and some time'. Despite their obscurity, they are dialogic poems, in which the pronoun 'you', addressed to the reader, to God, or to the poet himself, occurs much more often than the familiar lyric 'I'. His few prose writings include the story 'Conversation in the Mountains' (1959), a dialogue between two Jewish voices, and his speech 'The Meridian', acknowledging the award of the distinguished Büchner Prize in 1960.

The poems here were selected, and the translations made, by the Celan scholar John Felstiner. Most have already appeared in his book *Paul Celan: Poet, Survivor, Jew* (1995), but some have undergone slight revisions, and two, which were only partially translated in his book, are given here complete. The annnotations also depend heavily on Felstiner's book, to which the reader is referred for an exploration of the net of associations—not reducible to any cut-and-dried interpretation—that the poems evoke.

The first poem, 'Black Flakes', dates from 1943, when Celan learnt that his mother had been found unfit for work and shot. It was originally entitled 'Mother'. 'Deathfugue', Celan's first published poem, returns on a more universal plane to the experience of death-camp inmates. It is a fugue-like composition in which the same recurring phrases are varied and interwoven. Felstiner's translation adds to the texture by gradually introducing German phrases, thus suggesting, as he puts it, 'the darkness of deathbringing speech', and bringing home the paradox that Celan felt obliged to write poetry commemorating the death-camps in the language of the perpetrators, which was also that of Goethe and Heine. The poem was first published in Romanian as 'Tango of Death', apparently alluding to the fact that at a camp in Galicia an SS lieutenant ordered Jewish violinists to accompany marches, gravedigging, and executions with a tango. This allusion survives in the phrase 'play on for the dancing'.

After moving to France in 1948, Celan evoked biblical exile with 'In Egypt', whose title alludes to the captivity of the Hebrews in the land of the Pharaohs. 'Tenebrae', written in March 1957, associates the suffering of the Jews in the Holocaust with that of Christ on the Cross, addressing God in a tone of restrained reproach, alluding both to the tortured body on the Cross and to the body received in the Eucharist, and implying an immense scepticism with the phrase 'open and void'.

The remaining poems come from the 1963 collection *Die Niemandsrose* ('The No One's Rose' or 'The No-Man's-Rose', by analogy with 'no-man's-land'). It is here that Celan explores his Jewish heritage most extensively. The book is dedicated to the memory of another Jewish poet, Osip Mandelstam (1891–1938?), who perished in the Gulag; Celan translated many of his poems from Russian into German. The untitled poem beginning 'There was earth inside them', a kind of inverted psalm which stubbornly refuses to praise the Lord, recalls the forced labour of 'Deathfugue' and the reproachful tone of 'Tenebrae', but ends with the hope of communication and a suggestion of fidelity in the shared ring 'on our finger'. Similarly, 'Zurich, at the Stork' reports that in his conversation with Nelly Sachs on Ascension Day, 26 May 1960, Celan 'spoke against' the God in whom Sachs believed, and records her gentle and enigmatic rejoinder. Sachs is also the 'sister' addressed in 'The Sluice', a poem which sets Jewish memory against the devastation wrought by

German barbarism. 'Psalm' is an anti-psalm, negating in its first line the act of creation by which God 'formed man of the dust of the ground' (Genesis 2: 7), and opposing God with the defiantly humanistic and vitalist rose. The 'purpleword' and the 'thorn' suggest the crown of thorns and purple robe which accompanied Christ's crucifixion, but the word here seems to be the poetic word of man set against the creative and destructive word of God.

Celan displays his versatility with the ballad 'A Rogues' and Gonifs' Ditty . . .', written early in 1961. Satirically adopting the supposed view of anti-Semites, he casts himself as a hook-nosed Jew, a member of the underworld, who will end up on the gallows, and associates himself with the medieval poet of low-life Paris, François Villon, and with the traditional view of Yiddish as a secret language used by thieves. But the low is also the high: Sadagora, a small town near Celan's birthplace Czernowitz (the poem reverses their usual relations), was the seat of a famous dynasty of Hasidic rabbis. The poem continues into word-play which is more meaningful than it looks at first sight, for 'almond-tree' is the literal meaning of 'Mandelstam', and Celan mutates it into 'Machandelbaum', 'juniper-tree', the title of one of the Grimms' fairy-tales; the translator has ingeniously substituted 'Allemandtree' (from French *allemand*, 'German').

'Radix, Matrix' returns to the Bible, asking how the prophecy that the descendants of Abraham would bring forth the Messiah can be related to the mass murder of the Jews, introducing aggressively phallic imagery, but also incorporating into this history Celan's own family and addressing his mother as 'you'. Like 'Psalm', it ends with strange, defiant hope: the way down may lead to 'one of the wild- | blooming crowns', recalling the motif of kingship and the rose of the earlier poem. 'Mandorla' indicates Celan's increasing interest in Jewish mysticism. When he wrote it, he had moved on from reading Buber to studying Scholem. Hence the stress on 'Nothing', supported by an aural Hebrew pun on *ayin* meaning both 'nothing' and 'eye'. The 'almond', which is the literal meaning of the Italian *mandorla*, also evokes Mandelstam again (German *Mandel*, almond), while the 'King' suggests the royal title so often used in the Bible (e.g. Psalm 24). Finally, a Jewish legend is evoked in 'To one who stood before the door', begun on the same day that Celan wrote 'Mandorla'. The being addressed is the Golem, the speechless man made out of clay by the sixteenth-century Rabbi Löw of Prague to defend the Jews. Legend often depicts him as a dangerous figure who gets out of control, but here he is the object of prayer, described as a 'brother' and a 'chittering manikin', who evokes not fear but pity.

Black Flakes

Snow has fallen, with no light. A month
has gone by now or two, since autumn in its monkish cowl
brought tidings my way, a leaf from Ukrainian slopes:

'Remember, it's winter here too, for the thousandth time now
in the land where the broadest torrent flows:
Ya'akov's* heavenly blood, blessed by axes...
Oh ice of unearthly red—their Hetman* wades with all
his troop into darkening suns... Oh for a cloth, child,
to wrap myself when it's flashing with helmets,
when the rosy floe bursts, when snowdrift sifts your father's
bones, hooves crushing
the Song of the Cedar*...
A shawl, just a thin little shawl, so I have
by my side, now you're learning to weep,
this hard world that will never turn green, my child, for your child!'

Autumn bled all away, Mother, snow burned me through:
I sought out my heart so it might weep, I found—oh the summer's
    breath,
it was like you.
Then came my tears. I wove the shawl.

Deathfugue

Black milk of daybreak we drink it at evening
we drink it at midday and morning we drink it at night
we drink and we drink
we shovel a grave in the air there you won't lie too cramped
A man lives in the house he plays with his vipers he writes
he writes when it grows dark to Deutschland your golden hair
    Margareta*
he writes it and steps out of doors and the stars are all sparkling he
    whistles his hounds to come close
he whistles his Jews into rows has them shovel a grave in the ground
he commands us play up for the dance

Black milk of daybreak we drink you at night
we drink you at morning and midday we drink you at evening
we drink and we drink
A man lives in the house he plays with his vipers he writes
he writes when it grows dark to Deutschland your golden hair
    Margareta
Your ashen hair Shulamith* we shovel a grave in the air there you
    won't lie too cramped

He shouts jab this earth deeper you lot there you others sing up and
    play
he grabs for the rod in his belt he swings it his eyes they are blue
jab your spades deeper you lot there you others play on for the
    dancing

Black milk of daybreak we drink you at night
we drink you at midday and morning we drink you at evening
we drink and we drink
A man lives in the house your goldenes Haar Margareta
your aschenes Haar Shulamith he plays with his vipers

He shouts play death more sweetly this Death is a master from
    Deutschland
he shouts scrape your strings darker you'll rise then as smoke to the
    sky
you'll have a grave then in the clouds there you won't lie too
    cramped

Black milk of daybreak we drink you at night
we drink you at midday Death is a master aus Deutschland
we drink you at evening and morning we drink and we drink
this Death is ein Meister aus Deutschland his eye it is blue
he shoots you with shot made of lead shoots you level and true
a man lives in the house your goldenes Haar Margarete
he looses his hounds on us grants us a grave in the air
he plays with his vipers and daydreams der Tod ist ein Meister aus
    Deutschland

dein goldenes Haar Margarete
dein aschenes Haar Sulamith

In Egypt

Thou shalt say to the eye of the woman stranger: Be the water.
Thou shalt seek in the stranger's eye those thou knowest are in the
    water.
Thou shalt call them up from the water: Ruth! Naomi! Miriam!*
Thou shalt adorn them when thou liest with the stranger.
Thou shalt adorn them with the stranger's cloud-hair.
Thou shalt say to Ruth and Miriam and Naomi:
Behold, I sleep with her!
Thou shalt most beautifully adorn the woman stranger near thee.
Thou shalt adorn her with sorrow for Ruth, for Miriam and Naomi.
Thou shalt say to the stranger:
Behold, I slept with them!

Tenebrae*

Near are we,* Lord,
near and graspable.

Grasped already, Lord,
clawed into each other,* as if
each of our bodies were
your body, Lord.

Pray, Lord,
pray to us,
we are near.

Wind-skewed we went there,
went there, to bend
over pit and crater.

Went to the water-trough, Lord.

It was blood, it was
what you shed, Lord.

It shone.

It cast your image into our eyes, Lord.

Eyes and mouth stand so open and void, Lord.
We have drunk, Lord.
The blood and the image that was in the blood, Lord.

Pray, Lord.
We are near.

THERE WAS EARTH INSIDE THEM, and
they dug.

They dug and dug, and so
their day went past, their night. And they did not praise God,*
who, so they heard, wanted all this,
who, so they heard, witnessed all this.

They dug and heard nothing more;
they did not grow wise, invented no song,
devised for themselves no sort of language.
They dug.

There came then a stillness, there came also storm,
all of the oceans came.
I dig, you dig, and the worm also digs,
and the singing there says: They dig.

O one, o none, o no one, o you.
Where did it go, when it went nowhere at all?
O you dig and I dig, and I dig through to you,
and the ring on our finger awakens.

Zurich, at the Stork*

For Nelly Sachs

Our talk was of Too Much, of
Too Little. Of Thou
and Yet-Thou, of
clouding through brightness, of
Jewishness, of
your God.

Of—
that.
On the day of an ascension, the

Minster stood over there, it came
with some gold across the water.

Our talk was of your God, I spoke
against him, I
let the heart that I had
hope:
for
his highest, death-rattled, his
wrangling word—

Your eye looked at me, looked away,
your mouth
spoke toward the eye, I heard:

We
really don't know, you know,
we
really don't know
what
counts.

The Sluice

Over all this
grief of yours: no
second heaven.

....

To a mouth
for which it was a thousandword,*
lost—
I lost a word
that was left to me:
Sister.

To
polygoddedness*
I lost a word that sought me:
*Kaddish.**

Through
the sluice I had to go,
to salvage the word back into

and out of and across the salt flood:
*Yizkor.**

Psalm

No one kneads us again out of earth and clay,
no one incants our dust
No one.

Blessèd art thou, No One.
In thy sight would
we bloom.
In thy
spite.

A Nothing
we were, are now, and ever
shall be, blooming:
the Nothing-, the
No-One's-Rose.

With
our pistil soul-bright,
our stamen heaven-waste,
our corolla red
from the purpleword we sang
over, O over
the thorn.

A ROGUES' AND GONIFS'* DITTY
SUNG AT PARIS EMPRÈS PONTOISE*
BY PAUL CELAN
FROM CZERNOWITZ NEAR SADAGORA

> Now and then only, in dark times.
>
> (HEINRICH HEINE, 'To Edom')*

Back then, when they still had gallows,
then—right?—they had
an On High.

Wind, where's my beard got to, where's
my Jew-patch,* where's

my beard that you pluck?

Crooked, the path I took was
crooked, yes,
for yes
it was straight.*

Hey-ho.

Crooked, so goes my nose.
Nose.

And we made for *Friuli*.*
There we would have, there we would have.
For the almond tree was blossoming.
Almondtree, Talmundree.
Almonddream, Dralmondream.
And the Allemandtree too.
Lemandtree.

Hey-ho.
Aum.

*Envoi**

But,
but it rears up,* that tree. It,
it too
stands against
the Plague.

Radix, Matrix*

As one speaks to stone, as
you,
to me from the abyss, from
a homeland con-
sanguined, up-
hurled, you,
you of old to me,
you to me in the nix of a night,
you in Yet-Night en-
countered, you
Yet-You—:

Back then, when I wasn't there,
back then, when you
paced along the field, alone:*

Who,
who was it, that
stock, that murdered one, that one
standing black into heaven:
rod and testis—?

(Root.
Root of Abraham. Root of Jesse.* No One's
root—O
ours.)

Yes,
as one speaks to the stone, as
you
thrust with my hands
there and into Nothingness, so
it is with what's here:

even this
spore bed splits,
this
Downward
is one of the wild-
blooming crowns.

Mandorla*

In the almond—what stands in the almond?
The Nothing.
The Nothing stands in the almond.
There it stands and stands.

In the Nothing—who stands there? The King.
There stands the King, the King.
There he stands and stands.

Jewish curls, no grey for you.

And your eye—whereto stands your eye?
Your eye stands opposite the almond.
Your eye, the Nothing it stands opposite.
It stands behind the King.
So it stands and stands.

Human curls, no grey for you.
Empty almond, royal blue.

TO ONE WHO STOOD BEFORE THE DOOR, one
evening:
to him
I opened my word—: toward the
clod I saw him trot, toward
the half-
baked
brother born in a
doughboy's dung-caked boot,
him with his god-
like loins all bloody, the
chittering manikin.

Rabbi, I gnashed, Rabbi
Löw:*

For this one
circumcise his word,
for this one
scribe the living
Nothing on his soul,
for this one
spread your two
cripplefingers in the hale-
making prayer.
For this one.

....

Slam the evening door* shut, Rabbi.

....

Fling the morning door open, Ra- —

FRANZ FÜHMANN

The Jews' Car

Franz Fühmann (1922–84), an important East German writer, born into the Sudeten German community of what was then Czechoslovakia, passed through several ideological phases: a Nazi under the Third Reich, and a Stalinist in the newly founded GDR, he shared the general disillusionment after Stalin's official denunciation by Khrushchev in 1956; when East German forces helped to suppress the Prague Spring in 1968 Fühmann turned from politics to self-exploration and myth. The latter interest is foreshadowed in 'The Jews' Car', the first of a series of semi-autobiographical, self-contained snapshots of historical moments which, taken together, recount the protagonist's progression towards Communism. It documents the persistence in popular memory of the 'blood libel': the claim, traceable to the eleventh century, that Jews kidnapped Christian children in order to drink their blood as part of the Passover ceremonies. This fantasy gained credibility by appearing as a demonic parody of the Eucharist. The late nineteenth and early twentieth centuries saw a resurgence of the blood libel, especially in Eastern Europe: three famous cases were at Tisza-Eszlar (Hungary) in 1882, at Polna (Bohemia) in 1899, and at Kiev in 1911; the last forms the basis of Bernard Malamud's novel *The Fixer* (1966).

In Fühmann's version, likewise set in Bohemia, the legend has been modernized: the Jews are now supposed to cruise about in a car—yellow, like the medieval Jewish badge—looking for victims. Their imagined ownership of a car, something still unusual in rural Bohemia in 1931, fuses the image of the Jew as child-murderer with that of the Jew as unscrupulous capitalist, and stresses also the mobility ascribed to the Jews by contrast with the stable lives of the country people. The narrator's credulity also illustrates how superstitious anti-Semitism is sustained by emotional processes: when the legend of the Jews' car has been factually disproved, the narrator more than ever needs a scapegoat to blame for his humiliation, and perversely finds it in the Jews. In the context of Fühmann's book as a whole, this childish projection helps to explain the protagonist's temporary but intense commitment to National Socialism, but it also shows how the Nazis could terrify their adherents by appealing to pre-existent fantasies about an omnipresent enemy.

How far down does recollection reach? A warm green, that seems to be the earliest image in my memory: the green of a tiled stove, with a relief of a gipsy camp running round its upper rim; but I know that only from my mother's stories, no mental effort can bring this image back. But I have kept the green: a warm green, like a wine bottle, with a dull sheen. Whenever I see this green before my eyes, I feel myself floating gently in the air above the floorboards: Mother told me I could only see the gipsies when my father took me, a two-year-old whippersnapper, and lifted me up.

The next thing in my memory is something soft and white, on which I had to sit still for an eternity while staring into a blackness that kept curving up and down, and then a cavern of elder-blossom with a bench and a man sitting on it who smelt of adventures and let me ride on his knee and pushed into my mouth a piece of wonderfully sweet sausage, which I chewed greedily, and this recollection is linked with a scream and a gale that suddenly tore the man and the bower away from me to whirl them abruptly into nothingness. It wasn't a gust of wind, of course, it was my mother's arm, for she had torn me out of the green cavern, and the scream was her scream of horror. The man whose knee had rocked me was one of the village laughing-stocks, a farmer who had gone to the dogs; staggering on legs as bent as sabres, he used to go round the villages begging for bread and schnapps, and the smell of wild adventures was the raw alcohol on his breath and the sausage was a scrap from the horse abattoir. Anyway, it must have been splendid to ride on his knees: this is the first image that I can still see quite distinctly, and I was three years old at the time.

From then on the images come thick and fast: the mountains, the forest, the well, the house, the stream and the meadow; the quarry with its caves inhabited by imaginary ghosts; toad, hornets, the hooting of the owl, the avenue of rowan trees outside the grey factory, the fair with its fragrance of Turkish honey and the barrel-organ noise of the barkers outside the booths, and finally the school with its whitewashed corridor, always gloomy despite its high windows, with fear coming from all the classrooms and creeping along it like drifting fog. I have forgotten the teachers' faces; I can see only two grey eyes squinting over a long sharp nose and a bamboo cane with round notches in it, and the faces of the other pupils have paled and faded too, except for a girl's face with brown eyes, a narrow mouth that hardly curved at all, and short, light hair above her high forehead: the face whose eyes made you drop yours, confused for the first time by a mysterious power, you never forget it, even if something bitter happened afterwards...

One morning in the summer of 1931, when I was nine, Gudrun K., the class gossip, swinging her black pigtails and gabbling like a pondful of frogs, rushed into the classroom, a few minutes before the bell, as always, and shrieked: 'Listen, listen, all of you, have you heard the latest?' As she shrieked, she was panting and waving her arms wildly; but though she was gasping for breath, she still shrieked: 'Listen, all of you!' while gulping for air. The girls raced towards her, as always, and thronged round her as rapidly as a swarm of bees round their queen; but we boys hardly noticed her fuss, for the gossip had often proclaimed as a sensation something that turned out to be trivial. So we went on with what we were doing: we happened to be discussing the latest adventures of our idol Tom Shark, and Karli, our leader, was demonstrating how by his method the most dangerous wolfhound could be dealt with in a matter of seconds: you gripped it firmly at the place in its mouth where its teeth were sharpest, grasped the upper jaw, pulled down the lower jaw, turned the skull right round, and kicked the beast in the gullet—just then we heard a shrill scream from the crowd of girls. 'Eek, how horrid!' one of them had screamed, a sharp squeaking 'Eek' of panic; we spun round and saw the girl standing with her hand in front of her gaping mouth and sheer terror in her eyes, and the group of girls was bent over in horror. 'And then they stir flour into the blood and bake it into bread!' we heard Gudrun hastily recounting, and we saw the girls shaking. 'What rubbish are you telling them?' shouted Karli. The girls weren't listening. We went hesitantly over to them. 'And then they eat it?' asked one in a hoarse voice. 'They eat it at their feast, they all meet together at midnight and light candles, and then they say a spell, and then they eat it!' declared Gudrun, panting with eagerness. Her eyes were burning. 'What sort of spell?' asked Karli, laughing, but his laugh didn't sound genuine. Suddenly I felt a strange fear. 'Come on, tell us!' I shouted at Gudrun, and the other boys shouted too, and we thronged round the girls who surrounded Gudrun, and Gudrun repeated her story in hasty sentences, almost shouting. It all came bubbling out: a Jews' car had appeared in the mountains and travelled in the evenings on lonely roads to catch girls and slaughter them and bake magic bread with their blood; it was a yellow car, all yellow, she went on, her mouth and eyes distorted with horror; a yellow car with four Jews in it, four black murderous Jews with long knives, and all the knives were bloodstained, and blood was dripping from the footboard, people had seen it distinctly, and they had already slaughtered four girls, two from Witkowitz and two from Böhmisch-Krumma; they had hung them up by the feet and cut off their heads and caught the blood in frying-pans, and we huddled closer together, a lump of shrieking, trembling horror, and Gudrun outshrieked our horror with a shrill owl's voice and insisted greedily, though nobody doubted her story, that it was all absolutely true. If she'd gone to Böhmisch-Krumma yesterday to deliver some home-made goods, she'd have been able to see the Jews' car with her own eyes: yellow, all yellow, and the blood dripping from the footboard, and I stared into Gudrun's red face and thought admiringly how lucky she was not to have been slaughtered, for the Jews' car driving through the fields and catching girls was something I didn't doubt for a single moment.

Although I had never seen a Jew, I had learnt a lot about them from grown-ups' stories. The Jews all had hooked noses and black hair and were to blame for everything that was wrong with the world. They drew money out of honest people's pockets with dirty dodges and had created the crisis that threatened to strangle my father's pharmacy; they took away the farmers' crops and cattle and bought up corn from all over the place, poured alcohol over it, and threw it into the sea in order to make the Germans starve, for they hated us Germans with deadly hatred and wanted to destroy us all—so why shouldn't they lurk on country roads in a yellow car to catch and slaughter German girls? No, I didn't doubt the existence of the Jews' car for a moment, and even the words of the teacher, who in the meantime had entered the classroom and asserted that the story of the Jews' car, which all our mouths had screamed at him, was unlikely to be true, made no difference. I believed in the Jews' car; I could see it, all yellow, driving between cornfield and cornfield, four black Jews with long sharp knives, and suddenly I saw the car stop and two of the Jews jump into the cornfield beside which a brown-eyed girl was sitting and making a wreath of blue cornflowers, and the Jews, with knives between their teeth, grabbed the girl and dragged her to the car, and the girl screamed, and I heard her screaming, and I was in seventh heaven, for it was my name that she screamed. Loudly and despairingly she screamed my name; I looked for my Colt, but I couldn't find it, and so I rushed with bare hands out of my ambush and leapt at the Jews. I knocked the first to the ground with a blow to his chin; just as the second lifted the girl to roll her into the car, I hit him in the nape of the neck with the side of my hand, so that he collapsed too; the Jew at the wheel stamped on the accelerator, and the car shot towards me. But of course I was waiting for that, so I sprang aside; the car shot past, I jumped onto the boot, smashed the roof with a blow of my fist, wrested the knife from the hand of the Jew in the passenger seat just as he was about to stab, threw him out of the car, overcame the Jew at the wheel, braked, jumped out and saw the girl lying unconscious in the grass beside the cornfield, and I saw her face, lying motionless in front of me in the grass, and suddenly I could see only her face: brown eyes, a narrow mouth that hardly curved at all, and short, light hair above her high forehead. I saw her cheeks and eyes and lips and forehead and hair, and I felt as though this face had always been veiled and I was seeing it naked for the first time. Shyness seized me; I wanted to look away but couldn't and bent over the girl lying motionless in the grass and touched her cheek, a breath, with my hand, and I felt flaming hot, and suddenly my hand burnt: a sudden pain; my name rang in my ears; I sat up with a jerk, and the teacher gave me a second blow with the ruler on the back of my hand. 'Two hours' detention,' he snorted, 'I'll stop you sleeping in lessons!' The class laughed. The teacher struck a third time; my hand swelled up, but I gritted my teeth. Two rows in front of me, the girl was sitting whose face I had seen in the grass, and I thought that she would now be the only one not to laugh at me. 'Sleeping in the lesson—does the fellow think his desk is his bed?' The teacher had said that as a joke, and the class roared with laughter. I knew she would never laugh at me. 'Quiet,' shouted the teacher. The laughter died away. The weals on my hand turned blue.

After my detention I dared not go home; as I walked slowly up the village street, I pondered a plausible excuse and finally hit on the idea of telling my parents I had been looking for the Jews' car, and so, in order to arrive home not via the main street but via the fields, I turned away from the street and went along a path towards the mountains: cornfields on the right, meadows on the left, and corn and grass waved above my head. I was no longer thinking about detention or about the Jews' car; in the waves of grass I saw the girl's face, and I saw her light hair in the corn. The scent of the meadows was bewildering, the firm flesh of the harebells waved blue at the level of my chest; the thyme sent out wild waves of intoxicating scent, swarms of wasps buzzed angrily, and the poppies next to the blue cornflowers glowed, a burning poison, in hot red. The wasps whirred wildly round my face, the sun was steaming; the crickets shrieked a mad message at me, large birds shot abruptly out of the corn; the poppies next to the cornflowers flamed menacingly, and I was confused. Until now I had stood amid nature as innocently as one of its creatures, a dragonfly or a blade of grass, but now I felt as if it were rejecting me and a crack were opening up between my environment and myself. I was no longer earth and no longer grass and tree and animal; the crickets shrieked, and I could not help thinking how they rubbed their wings together when chirping, and suddenly that seemed shameless, and suddenly everything was different, as though I were seeing it for the first time: the ears of corn jingled in the wind, the grasses nestled softly together, the poppies glowed, a mouth, a thousand mouths of the earth, the thyme brewed bitter steam, and I felt my body as something alien, something that wasn't me; I trembled and drew my fingernails over the skin of my chest and tugged at it; I no longer knew what was happening to me, and then, pushing corn and grass aside, a brown car came slowly down the path.

On catching sight of it, I shuddered as though I had been caught committing a crime; I pulled my hands away from my chest, and the blood shot abruptly into my face. I laboriously collected my thoughts. A car? 'What's a car doing here?' I thought, stammering; then suddenly I understood: the Jews' car! A shiver ran down my spine; I stood paralysed. In the first instant the car had seemed to be brown, but now, as I took a second look, horrified and spurred on by shivering curiosity, I saw that it was more yellow than brown, actually yellow, all yellow, bright yellow. If at first I had seen only three people in it, then I must have been mistaken, or perhaps one had been crouching down, yes, he must have crouched down, there were four of them in the car and one was crouching in order to leap at me, and I felt deadly fear. It was deadly fear; my heart stopped beating; I had never noticed its beating, but now it was no longer beating, I felt it: a dead pain in my flesh, an empty space, tightening, that was sucking out my life. I stood paralysed and stared at the car, and the car came slowly down the path, a yellow car, all yellow, and it was coming towards me, and then, as though a mechanism had been set in motion, my heart suddenly started beating again, and now it was beating furiously, and my thoughts were furiously racing: scream, run away, hide in the corn, jump into the grass, but in the last second it occurred to me that I mustn't arouse suspicion. I mustn't let anyone see that I knew it was the Jews' car, and so, racked with horror, I went down the path fairly slowly towards the car, which was driving at walking pace, and the sweat was dripping from my forehead, and at the same time I was freezing, and so I walked for nearly an hour, although the village was only a couple of steps away. My knees were trembling; just as I thought I would keel over, I heard a voice from the car, like the cracking of a whip: a summons, perhaps, or an order, and everything went black in front of my eyes; I could only feel my legs running and taking me with them; I saw and heard nothing more, and ran and screamed, and only when I was standing in the middle of the village street, among houses and people, did I dare, panting, to look round, and then I saw that the Jews' car had vanished without a trace.

Naturally I told the class next morning that the Jews' car had chased me for hours and almost caught me, and that I had only escaped by daringly doubling back, and I described the Jews' car: yellow, all yellow, and with four Jews in it brandishing bloodstained knives, and I wasn't lying, for I had seen it all for myself. The class listened breathlessly; they crowded round me and looked at me with admiration and also with envy; I was a hero, and could now have become leader instead of Karli, but I didn't want to; I only wanted a look from one person, and didn't dare search for it. Then the teacher came; we yelled the monstrous news at him. I described feverishly what I had seen, and the teacher asked about the time and the place and the circumstances, and I was able to answer every question precisely, with no evasions or contradictions, nothing but irrefutable facts: the yellow car, all yellow, the four black people in it, the knives, the blood on the footboard, the path, the order to catch me, the flight, the pursuit; and the class listened breathlessly.

Then the girl with the short, light hair looked up, and now I ventured to look her in the face, and she turned half round on her

seat and looked at me and smiled, and my heart floated away. That
was bliss; I heard the crickets screaming and saw the poppies glowing
and smelt the scent of thyme, but now all that no longer confused
me, the world was intact once more, and I was a hero who had got
away from the Jews' car, and the girl looked at me and smiled and
said in her quiet, almost pensive voice that yesterday her uncle and
two friends had come on a visit; they had come by car, she said
slowly, and the word 'car' plunged into my heart like an arrow; they
had come in a brown car, she said, and she said in reply to the
teacher's hasty question that at the same time as I had claimed to see
the Jews' car they had driven down the same path, and her uncle had
asked directions from a boy standing on the edge of a field, and the
boy had run away screaming, and she ran her tongue over her thin
lips and said, very slowly, that the boy by the path had been wearing
green leather shorts just like mine, and she looked at me with a
friendly smile, and I could feel everyone looking at me, and I felt
their eyes darting like angry wasps, swarms of wasps over thyme
bushes, and the girl smiled with that quiet cruelty of which only
children are capable. When a voice came out of me, yelling that the
stupid cow was talking rubbish, it *was* the Jews' car, yellow, all yellow,
and four black Jews in it with bloodstained knives, I could hear her
quiet voice coming through my yelling as though from another world
and saying that she herself had seen me running away from the car.
She said it quite quietly, and I heard my yelling abruptly stop; I shut
my eyes, it was deathly still, then suddenly I heard a laugh, a sharp,
giggling girl's laugh as shrill as the chirping of crickets, and then a
great roar of laughter surged through the room and washed me away.
I rushed out of the class and ran to the lavatory and locked the door
behind me; tears gushed from my eyes, I stood dazed for a while in
the acrid smell of chlorine and had no thoughts and stared at the
stinking black tarred wall, and suddenly I knew: It was all their fault!
It was their fault, and theirs alone: they had caused everything that
was wrong with the world, they had ruined my father's business,
they had made the crisis and thrown the wheat into the sea, they
drew money out of honest people's pockets with dirty dodges, and
they had even played one of their filthy tricks on me in order to make
me look a fool in front of the class. They were to blame for everything; them, nobody else, just them! I ground my teeth: it was their
fault! I uttered their name, howling; I beat on my eyes with my fists

and stood in the black-tarred boys' lavatory steaming with chlorine and screamed their name: 'Jews!' I screamed, and again, 'Jews!'— what a sound: 'Jews, Jews!'—and I stood howling in the lavatory compartment and screamed, and then I was sick. Jews. It was their fault. I choked and clenched my fists. Jews. Jewsjewsjews. It was their fault. I hated them.

JUREK BECKER

The Wall

Jurek Becker (1937–97) was born in Łódź in Poland. When the Germans conquered the city in 1940, its Jews were confined to a ghetto in a slum area. Becker accordingly spent his early childhood first in the Łódź ghetto with his parents, then, after their deportation in 1943, in the concentration camps at Ravensbrück and Sachsenhausen with his mother. She died during this time, but Becker's father, who had been taken to Auschwitz but survived, found him in 1945 and brought him up in East Berlin with minimal awareness of being Jewish. Becker objected to the official conformism of the GDR: he was expelled from the Humboldt University in 1960, and although he was a member of the Socialist Party, he ran into trouble during his career as a scriptwriter and novelist for opposing pressure on writers to depict the GDR positively and for protesting against the expatriation in 1976 of the poet Wolf Biermann. Expelled from the Party, Becker left the GDR in 1977 and lived mainly in West Berlin, avoiding pronouncements about politics.

Becker did not consider himself a Jew, except insofar as others forced him to do so; he was in the habit of saying: 'My parents were Jews.' Nevertheless, Becker repeatedly explored the implications of his own past through the experiences of Jewish characters. 'The Wall' is unlikely to be autobiographical, since Becker said that his childhood years in ghetto and camps were buried by amnesia. As in *Jacob the Liar* (1969), Becker makes the Łódź ghetto sound slightly less harsh than it was. While in reality people lived crowded together, here old Tenzer has a sizeable room to himself and is able to conceal a potted plant. Nor was there a transit camp in the Łódź ghetto. However, as David Rock points out in his edition of the story, many details are accurate: there was a ban on keeping plants; toilet facilities did consist of a bucket that had to be emptied daily (the boys smell another that has been left in a deserted house). In most ghettos the Jews were evacuated in entire families, street by street, though in the Łódź ghetto adults able to work were kept and old people, invalids, and children were deported to the Chelmno death-camp or killed on the spot. Members of different social classes, and Jews from Germany, were all bundled together: thus, in the story, the enterprising boy Julian, the son of a doctor, evidently comes from a higher social class than the narrator, while we hear also of a German-sounding Dr Engländer in confinement. The reference to the boy getting a piece of bread and half an onion for his supper indicates the harsh rationing imposed on the inmates of the ghetto.

Becker's gift for storytelling has often been associated with the tradition of Yiddish narrative represented by Sholem Aleichem and Isaac Bashevis Singer, though Becker himself protested that he never read Singer and encountered Sholem Aleichem's work only after writing *Jacob*. With 'The Wall' we are in the hands of a master storyteller like Mark Twain. The rivalry between the narrator and Julian recalls the relationship between Huckleberry Finn and Tom Sawyer. Huck Finn in the ghetto... The essential solitude of the narrator is that of all Becker's fictional protagonists. Just as the boy will never tell what happened during the night (except possibly to his mother), so Jacob is unable to tell his fellow-inmates *how* he learnt that the Soviet army is approaching and is cut off from them by a network of lies.

By writing about the past from a child's perspective, Becker is adopting a favourite technique of German writers since 1945. Alfred Andersch in *Zanzibar* (1957), Günter Grass in *The Tin Drum* (1959), and Christa Wolf in *A Model Childhood* (1976) all present the Third Reich through the eyes of uncomprehending children. Through the boy narrator's tragicomic naivety—as when he regrets the murder of the cobbler Muntek because his family's shoes were lost—Becker makes the reader more aware of the atrocities going on all round, and the moving depiction of parental solicitude acquires additional poignancy from the vast inhumanity surrounding it. The child's imagination fills the hut with invisible elves, makes him see a devil through a window, and turns the German soldier into a giant. Like the child narrators deployed by Grass and Wolf, however, Becker's narrator also has some complicity in the crimes being committed: by talking about the potted plant illicitly kept by Tenzer, he may well have caused the old man to be killed. And, unwittingly, he reveals to the alert reader tensions in the adult world. Through him, for example, we can make out the mixture of love and antagonism between his parents. We are also reminded that parents are not really the reliable protectors the child thinks them. After all, the boy's parents will not be able to save him from annihilation. His father may say reproachfully: 'Does your father tell lies?' but at the end he does lie to the boy in pretending that the iodine will not hurt his wounds, and in the last sentence we see the lie, and the father's trustworthiness, about to be exposed.

———

My God, I'm five years old, we Jews are once more quietly happy. Our neighbour is called Olmo again, and he spends half the day yelling at his wife, and anyone with nothing better to do can stand behind the door and listen to every word. And the street has its houses again, and something happened to me in every one of them. I mustn't leave the street, my father has strictly forbidden it. Often I don't believe the reason he gives for forbidding it, but sometimes I do: that there's a boundary, an invisible one, beyond which children are caught and taken away. Nobody knows where the boundary runs, that's the crafty thing about it, it probably keeps changing, and before you know where you are you're on the wrong side of it. It's only in their own street, as my father knows, that children are fairly safe, safest of all outside their own house. My friends with whom I talk about these monstrous things have different opinions. The know-alls laugh, but some have heard the same thing.

I ask: 'What will happen to me if they catch me?' My father answers: 'It's better if you don't find out.' I say: 'Come on, tell me, what will happen?' He just makes his vague gesture and stops the conversation. Once I say: 'Who is it who catches children, anyway?' He asks: 'Why do you need to know that?' I say: 'It's the German soldiers.' He asks: 'The Germans, our own police, what difference does it make if they catch you?' I say: 'But there's a boy who plays with us every day, and his home is many streets away.' He asks me: 'Does your father tell lies?'

I'm five years old and can't keep still. The words jump out of my mouth, I can't keep it shut, I've tried. They push against the inside of my cheeks, they multiply at a furious rate and hurt my mouth till I open the cage. 'That child,' says my mother, who has no face any more, only a voice, 'just listen to that child, he's crazy.'

What happened has got to be strange and unheard-of, otherwise it's not worth recounting. I may have killed Tenzer the shopkeeper, I'll never know for sure. He lives in our street and has a little black cap on his head and wears a little white beard, he's a tiny little man. If it's cold or rainy you can go to him, he knows stories. The most hard-boiled fellows sit quietly in front of him and stay silent and keep their mouths shut and stay quite still, even if they make jokes afterwards. But he never lets in more than four at once. I'm his favourite: I like thinking that. Once when he picked me up and put me on top of the cupboard he turned out to be very strong, we were all surprised.

My father says: 'Who'd put a child on top of a cupboard? And anyway, why are you always sitting listening to old Tenzer, he's probably not right in the head.' I say: 'You're not right in the head.' Then he lifts his arm, but I run away; and when I come back later, he's forgotten about it. My father often lifts his arm, but never hits anyone.

One day I quarrel with everyone else and go to Tenzer, I've never been alone with him before. When he opens the door and finds nobody outside except me, he's surprised and says: 'Only a little visit today?' He's busy, he's doing his laundry, but he doesn't send me away. I can watch him. He doesn't wash laundry the way my mother does, with water spraying into every corner. He takes hold of the underpants and the shirts gently, so that they don't get even more holes, and sometimes he sighs when he sees a particularly big hole. He holds a shirt high above the basin, and while it drips, he talks: 'It's thirty years old by now. Do you know what thirty years mean for a shirt?' I look round the room, there isn't much to see, there's only one thing that is new to me: behind the high headboard of the bed, on the floor beside the window, there's a pot. A blanket hangs in front of it so that you can't see it. I couldn't have discovered it if I hadn't lain down on the floor and looked exactly in that direction because I was bored. I go round the bed to reach the thing, I push aside the blanket, which would block the view of someone twice my height. There's a green plant growing in the pot, a peculiar plant that pricks you the moment you touch it. 'What are you doing?' yells Tenzer the shopkeeper, hearing me scream. There's a drop of blood on my index finger, I show him my thick blood. I put my finger in my mouth and suck, then I see tears in his eyes and I get even more of a fright. I ask: 'What have I done?' 'Nothing,' he says, 'nothing at all, it's my fault.' He explains to me how the plant works and how many animals would eat it up if it didn't have prickles. He says: 'You mustn't tell anyone about it.' I say: 'Of course I won't tell anyone.' He says: 'You know that nobody's allowed to have a plant?' I say: 'Of course.' He asks me: 'Well, what would they do to him?' I don't answer and just look at him, because he's about to tell me. We stare into each other's eyes for a bit, then Tenzer grabs a piece of laundry from the basin and wrings it violently. He says: 'That's what they'd do to him.' Of course I tell millions of people about it, not my parents, but all my friends.

I go back to Tenzer the shopkeeper, because since that day he's let me play with his plant as if we were brothers. A horribly ugly old woman opens the door, so ugly that anyone else in my place would have been terrified too. She asks in her vulgar voice: 'What d'you want here?' I know that Tenzer was always alone, and he'd never have let in somebody like her; her presence in his flat is even more alarming than her appearance. I run away from the old witch and pay no attention to the magic spell she shouts after me. The street hardly sees me, I run so fast. I ask my mother where Tenzer the shopkeeper is. She cries, she's just been embroidering the blanket which is part of her. I ask: 'Where is he? Tell me.' But it's my father who tells me when he comes home that night: 'They've taken him away.' By now I'm no longer surprised, hours have passed since I asked my question, and they've often taken people away who suddenly weren't there any more. I ask: 'Whatever did he do?' My father says: 'He was meschugge.'* I ask: 'What did he really do?' My father rolls his eyes and says to my mother: 'You tell him, if he insists on knowing.' And finally she says, though in a very low voice: 'He had a flowerpot. Just imagine, they found a flowerpot in his flat.' It's rather quiet, I'm in pain because I can't say that that flowerpot and I are acquainted. Tears fall on to my mother's handkerchief, she's never had a good word to say for Tenzer before. My father eats his slice of bread as he does every night after work, I'm the one who's really concerned, and nobody pays any attention to me. My father says: 'Like I always said, he isn't right in the head. To get taken away because of a flowerpot, that's the most ridiculous reason there could be.' My mother isn't crying any more, but she says: 'Perhaps he was very fond of the flower. Perhaps it reminded him of someone, you never know.' My father says loudly, eating his bread: 'But you don't put a flowerpot in your room. If you insist on living dangerously you plant tomatoes in the pot. Tomatoes are a far better way of remembering someone.' I can't control myself any more, I don't like my father very much at that moment. I shout: 'It wasn't a flower, it was a cactus!' Then I run outside and that's all I know.

My father wakes me in the middle of the night; the curtain in front of my bed is open. He says: 'Come along, old chap.' He bends over me and cuddles me, and this night my mother is already dressed as well. There's a lot of movement in the building, sounds of footsteps and rattling behind the walls. He lifts me out of my bed and stands me on my feet. To stop me collapsing with tiredness, he supports my back with his hand. It's good that he isn't in any hurry. My mother arrives with my shirt, but I sit down on the bucket that is our toilet. The moon is lying on the window-bars, suddenly there are two fully packed suitcases in the room. If you look at the moon for long enough, it doesn't keep its face still, it blinks at you. Then my mother puts my shirt over my head. 'Come along, old chap,' says my father. They both try to think what they might have forgotten; my father finds a pack of cards and stuffs it into his pocket. I too have luggage to take, I put the ball that my mother sewed from old rags beside the suitcases; but they say there's no room for it. Then we go down the dark staircase, across the whispering courtyard, into the street.

Many people are there already, but not my friends. 'Where are the others?' I ask my father. He frees himself from my mother and says: 'It's only our side of the street. Don't ask what's behind it, these are our orders.' This is a misfortune, for my friends all live on the other side of the street tonight. I ask: 'When are we coming back?' They stroke my head again but don't explain anything. Then we clatter away in response to a command given by someone I can't see. The walk gets more boring with every step; we probably cross the invisible boundary ten times, but if you've been given orders, then of course the prohibition is suspended.

A small part of the ghetto—and this has nothing to do with recollection, this is the truth—a small part of the ghetto is like a camp. There are some long stone huts, grouped with no symmetry, and round them goes a wall. It hasn't been built all that high, its height seems different from one day to the next, but anyway, if there were two men, one could look over it by standing on the other's shoulders. And anyone who stands back far enough can see broken glass glittering on top. But one wonders what's the point of a camp in the middle of the ghetto, which is already enough of a camp. I can answer that, though nobody explained it to me at the time: people are assembled in this camp before being sent to another camp, or to a place where they are needed more urgently than in the ghetto. In short, the camp is for waiting. Whether being here is a good sign or a bad one is discussed day and night in the long stone huts. I can't stand hearing any more about it.

The three of us are assigned a bed, a hard wooden thing. Although it is a little wider than the one I used to have, the narrow space causes us torments. There are also empty beds in the hut. After the very first night I lie on one of them and announce that from now on I'm always going to sleep here. My father shakes his head, I shake my head back and want to hear reasons, then he lifts his arm again. I have to give way, it's a victory for unreason. We try out various positions: me on the left or the right, then with my head between my parents' feet. 'That gives us the most space', says my father, but my mother is afraid one of their four feet could hurt me. 'Sometimes people kick out when they're dreaming. You don't realize it, but you do it.' My father can't argue with that. 'Pity, though,' he says. Finally I lie in the middle, without being asked, and have to promise to move as little as possible.

Every morning there's a roll-call, that's the first word I learn in the foreign language. We stand in a long row in front of the hut, and we have to be very quick about it, for a German is already standing there waiting. Our toes mustn't be too far forward and our heels mustn't be too far back, my father moves me into the right position. The first person in the row has to shout 'One!' then the counting continues till the end, the numbers roll towards me and pass over my head. My mother shouts her number, then my father shouts first his and then mine, then it's the next person's turn. That annoys me, I ask: 'Why can't I shout my number myself?' My father answers: 'Because you can't count.' 'Then you should whisper my number to me,' I say, 'and I'll shout it out.' He says: 'First of all there isn't enough time, and second, whispering isn't allowed.' I say: 'Why don't we stand in the same place every morning? Then we'd always have the same number, and I could learn it.' He says: 'Listen, old chap, this isn't a game.' There are two people in our row who aren't much older than me, one of them shouts his number himself, the other is counted by his father. I ask the first: 'How old are you?' He spits past my head and walks away, he must be from the upper end of our street which I've only seldom been to. After the counting, the German shouts: 'Dismiss!' and that's a roll-call.

By the second day I'm bored stiff. There are a few younger boys, but when I approach, their leader says to me: 'Hop it, sharpish.' Then they all give me a dirty look, the idiots, just because their leader wants to show off by using that word. I ask my mother what 'sharpish' means, she doesn't know. I say: 'It must mean the same as "quickly".' My father says: 'Big deal.' The camp is dead, and I can't

bring it to life. I cry, but it doesn't help; in a corner of the camp I find
a patch of grass. I mustn't go too far away, says my mother; my father
says: 'Where can he go in this place?' I discover the gate, the only
place where anything is moving, sometimes a German arrives, sometimes one goes. A soldier who's a sentry is walking up and down,
until he sees me standing. Then he jerks up his chin, I can't say why
I'm so little afraid of him; I step back a couple of paces, but when he
starts walking up and down again, I take the paces back. He moves
his head that way once more, I do him a favour once more, then he
leaves me in peace.

In the afternoon there's another soldier standing by the gate. He
shouts something at me that sounds dangerous. I go into a hut that
isn't ours. I'm frightened, but it's the only thing I can do. It contains
the same beds, and also a stench that I've never smelt before. I see a
rat running, it dodges me, I crawl on all fours but can't find its hole.
Someone grabs me by the scruff of the neck. He asks me: 'What are
you doing here?', he's blind in one eye. I say: 'I'm not doing anything.' He puts me where the others can see me. Then he says: 'Tell
the truth.' I say again: 'I'm not doing anything here. I'm just looking.' But he says loudly: 'He wanted to nick things, the little bastard,
I caught him at it.' I shout: 'That's not true at all.' He says: 'It's true
all right. I've been watching him half the day. He's been here for
hours, waiting for a chance.' Someone asks: 'What are you going to
do to him?' The liar says: 'Shall I give him a thrashing?' Someone
says: 'Better boil him.' I scream: 'I didn't want to nick anything,
really I didn't!' His hand won't let me go, and the liar squeezes me
tighter and tighter. Fortunately someone shouts: 'Let him go, he's
the son of someone I know.' But he keeps hold of me a bit longer and
says I'd better not get caught again. I don't tell my father anything
about this, he'd probably punish the brute, but I might have to stay
in our hut in future, so it wouldn't be worth it.

The next day everything is all right: early in the morning the other
side of the street moves into the camp. I haven't taken five steps
outside when someone who sounds like Julian calls to me and then
hides. I don't have far to look, he's standing round the next corner,
pressed against the wall and waiting for me to find him. Julian is a
good friend of mine. We haven't seen each other for ages, it could be
a week. His father was a doctor, that's why he wears good clothes,
and he still does. He says: 'Damn and blast.' I say: 'Julian.' I show

him the camp, there isn't much to show, his hut is the one furthest from ours. We look for a place where we can always meet from now on; he ends up choosing it, though he's only been here for a few minutes and I've been here probably for a week.

He asks: 'Did you know Itzek is here too?' He takes me to Itzek's hut, Itzek is another good friend of mine. He's sitting on his bed and has to stay with his parents, so he can't be pleased at my presence. We ask his father: 'Can't he at least come outside with us for a bit?' He says: 'He doesn't know his way around here yet.' 'But I know my way around,' I say, 'I've been here for days and days. I'll definitely bring him back.' He says: 'Certainly not.' It's only when Itzek starts crying that his mother, who's usually strict, allows him to go out. We show Itzek our place, we sit on the stones. The wonderful thing about Itzek is his pocket-watch, I look at his trouser pocket where it always ticks. Twice now I've been allowed to hold it to my ear and once to wind it up, because I won a bet. His grandfather gave it to him, because he was so fond of him, and told him to keep it well hidden, otherwise the first thief would take it. Julian has something wonderful too, a wonderfully beautiful girlfriend. Nobody but him has ever seen her, she's got fair hair and green eyes and is madly in love with him. Once he told us that they sometimes kiss, we wouldn't believe him, then he showed us how she holds her mouth when she kisses him. I'm the only one with nothing wonderful. My father has a torch with a dynamo, you have to move a switch to make it light up. But if he finds it missing, you can guess who'll be suspected.

I say to Itzek: 'Show me your watch.' But his wretched parents found it and bartered it for potatoes. Julian still has his girlfriend. Itzek cries about the watch, I don't make fun of him; I'd comfort him a bit if I weren't ashamed. Julian says: 'Stop blubbing, kid.' Itzek runs off, Julian says: 'Just leave him,' and the beautiful watch has been bartered for potatoes, what's the sense in that? I tell Julian what a day in this camp is like, so that he won't expect too much. He tells me about his girlfriend, whose name is Marianka, until Itzek comes back.

Not much has happened in our street since I stopped living there, only Muntek the cobbler has killed himself. He used always to come out of his dirty shop when we sat on his steps and kicked us, and now he's dead. It's a funny feeling, because it's not long since he was alive. I ask: 'How did he do it?' Julian says that he slashed his wrists with broken glass and bled to death. But Itzek, who lived three doors closer to the cobbler than Julian did, knows that Muntek plunged his cobbler's knife into his heart and twisted it three times. Julian says: 'I never heard such nonsense.' They quarrel for a while, till I say: 'It doesn't matter.' But the story has a sad end, for Itzek's mother had left some shoes with Muntek to be repaired. When she heard about his death, she rushed there, but the shoes were gone, the shop had already been looted.

Sitting down, Julian pees between me and Itzek, he can do that better than anyone else, in a magnificent arch. Then he has a plan and looks important to show that we've got to huddle together. He whispers: 'We must go back to our street, we'd better do it at night.' Julian has never made such a crazy suggestion before. Itzek asks him: 'Why?' Julian looks at me to make me tell the dope why, but I don't understand it myself. Julian says: 'The whole street is empty now, right?' We answer: 'Yes.' He asks: 'And what about the houses?' We answer: 'They're empty too.' 'The houses aren't empty at all,' he says, and all of a sudden he knows something we don't. We ask: 'How do you mean, the houses aren't empty?' He says: 'Because they're full, kid.' He spends a little time despising us, then he has to explain the matter because otherwise we'd go away. So: the street was cleared, house by house, but the people couldn't take much with them, we know that perfectly well ourselves, at most half their belongings. The other half is still in the houses, Julian reckons there must be mountains of stuff left. He tells us that for example he wasn't allowed to take his big tin car, because his stupid mother trampled on it and gave him a bag of laundry to carry instead. I think of my grey rag ball. Only Itzek didn't have to leave anything behind, he had nothing anyway. 'You'll never get over the wall,' I say. Julian throws a stone at the wall, so close to my hand that I can feel the wind it makes. He asks me: 'Over that?' I say: 'Yes, over that.' He asks: 'Why not?' I say: 'The Germans watch like hawks.' Julian looks round grandly and then says: 'Where do you see any Germans? Besides, they sleep at night. Didn't you hear what I said? That we'd have to try it at night?' Itzek says: 'He's got wax in his ears.' I say: 'Besides, the wall is much too high.' Itzek says to his friend Julian: 'See how scared he is.' Julian only says: 'We'll have to look for a good spot.' Julian says to me: 'Coward.'

We look for the spot, and of course Julian is right, there is one.

Metal buttresses are set in the wall like steps. 'What did I tell you', says Julian. My heart is pounding, because now I've got to go along or be a coward. This spot has another advantage: it's a long way from the camp entrance and therefore also from the guard. There is another guard who goes around and passes every place at some time or other, but most of the time he stays in his little German hut, sitting and smoking, or lying asleep. Julian says: 'I tell you again, the Germans all sleep at night.' I ask: 'How do you know?' He answers: 'Everyone knows that.' And Itzek points to me and says: 'He's the only one who doesn't know that.' 'Shall we go tomorrow night?' asks Julian, looking at me.

I think how easy it would be to agree to everything now and later simply not show up. I peer at the buttresses and shake the lowest one, I say: 'The Germans must be crazy.' 'So what about it?' Julian asks me again. I say: 'Ask him too.' Julian asks Itzek: 'Shall we go tomorrow night?' Itzek is silent for a bit, then he says: 'Better the night after.' 'Why only the night after?' Itzek says: 'There's no point in hurrying.' That's what his father is always saying; he's a lawyer by profession, whatever that is.

My preparations begin this evening. If I'm ever to manage to slip out of bed without being noticed, then I can't sleep between my parents, I must be at the edge. I start coughing until my father asks what the matter is. My mother puts her hand on my forehead, the coughing doesn't stop, I see them whispering together. When we lie down, I say: 'I can't breathe in the middle. I won't fall out.' And I cough so hard that I really can't breathe and they have no choice but to let me lie at the side. Every night someone shouts: 'Lights out!' then the light goes out and people whisper for a bit longer. The elves fly in the dark, they are a secret you mustn't talk about; once when I wanted to talk about elves with my mother, she only put her finger on her lips, shook her head, and didn't say anything. The hut roof opens for the elves, the walls bow to the ground, but you can't see them, you only feel the breath. They float in and out as they please, sometimes one touches you with its veil or with the wind. Sometimes they speak to you, too, but always in the elves' language which human beings don't understand; besides, elves speak very very softly, they're gentler and more delicate than humans in every way. They don't come every night, but quite often, and then there's a hidden, cheerful movement on the air until you fall asleep, and probably longer. The least light makes them disappear.

This night I want to practise getting up, I've said to myself: 'If I can once manage to get out of bed without waking them, then I'll manage when it matters. Just so long as they've gone to sleep.'

Usually my father goes to sleep so fast that he's already snoring before the elves arrive. Sometimes I deliberately poke him in the side, without disturbing him. But today of all days they whisper together and embrace like children and kiss as if they hadn't had the whole day for it. I can't do anything, they've never kissed each other like that in the hut. I hear my father whispering: 'Why are you crying?' Then I feel tired, I think the first elves have arrived. I hear my mother whispering: 'He isn't coughing any more, can you hear?' Then she wakes me and says: 'Come on, the roll-call won't wait for you.'

My mother says to my father: 'Leave him in peace, he hasn't slept properly.' Such a misfortune will never happen to me again, I swear it, even if I have to prop my eyes open with pieces of wood. The next night I'll have to leave the bed and the hut without a rehearsal; but the good thing is that now I know how easily you can fall asleep even if you don't want to. My father nudges me as we wait in line, I look up and hear him saying softly: 'Twenty-five!' Although my mind is already on the next night, my heart pounds, now I've the chance to show what I can do. The numbers race towards me, the German in front of us always keeps his eyes on the number. I'm frightened; my father has no idea what sort of moment he's picked. I have to clamp my lips together so as not to shout too soon, then I scream: 'Twenty-five!' It must have been just the right moment, after the woman before me and before my father, the numbers run away from me like wildfire, it's a good feeling. After the roll-call my father says: 'You did that really well. Only you mustn't scream so loud next time.' I promise not to, he lifts me on to his arm, that isn't pleasant in front of so many people.

We meet, Julian, Itzek, and myself, and wait for the next night. Julian has observed that at our spot there is no broken glass on top of the wall, that's a bit of luck. Itzek says he saw that too. Julian says: 'I don't even need to go into our room, I'll go somewhere else. Will you go into your rooms?' I wonder whether our room is worth it: the rag ball is still there, perhaps the torch, which hasn't yet shown up in the camp. Itzek asks: 'Be honest, who's scared?' 'Not me,' says Julian, 'not me either,' says Itzek, 'not me either,' I say. I ask Julian if he wouldn't like to visit his girlfriend when we're outside. He answers: 'Not at night.'

A cold rain drives us away, Julian is the only one who knows where to go. He knows an empty hut, and we run to it. Even if I don't like to admit it, Julian is our leader. The door is missing, we enter the dark space with nothing in it; only bunk beds stand pushed together at the walls, I never saw them like that before. Itzek clambers about, jumping from one to another like a cat, and Julian puts on an air as if everything here belonged to him. Then someone says: 'Get out of here, and look slippy.' Itzek is so frightened he falls off a bed and picks himself up and dashes out. Julian has already disappeared, leaving me standing in the middle of the room. The voice, which sounds tired and at the same time seems to belong to someone strong, says: 'What's the matter with you?' I'm standing still out of curiosity, and besides, that will show Julian who's a coward. I say: 'With me?' Then something white slowly emerges from a bed, way back in the pile of beds, I've seen enough. I rush out into the open air, where Julian and Itzek are standing at a safe distance and waiting, perhaps they're glad, perhaps disappointed, that I've escaped from the danger safe and sound. I say: 'Gosh, that's really something!' But they don't want to hear my story, the rain has almost stopped.

We plan to meet that night at our usual place and then go to the wall together. Julian asks why we don't meet directly at the wall, and I know a reason: if one of us isn't punctual, it wouldn't be wise to wait for him at the wall. After we've agreed, Julian says: 'I think we should meet at the wall.' I ask, without thinking: 'What time are we meeting, anyway?' We consider for a bit, then Julian gives me a nasty look, as if I'd created the problem by asking my question. He always needs someone to blame, and says to Itzek: 'If you weren't so dopey and still had your watch, it would be all right.' None of us knows any sign at night that could guide us, till Itzek says: 'Lights out is at the same time everywhere, isn't it?' That's the best idea, even Julian can't argue with it, lights out could be the sign we need. 'After lights out,' says Itzek, 'wait for an hour, then everyone will be asleep, then we can meet.' 'And how long is an hour?' asks Julian, but he can't think of any better suggestion. We agree on the length of an hour: it's the time that the last person in the hut needs to fall asleep, and then a bit longer. We place our hands on one another's and swear an oath and separate till night. Then I'm with my parents, lying on our bed. My mother gets up from her sewing and says I'm wet through, she takes my shirt off and dries my hair. Many people are walking about in the hut with their hands behind their backs, one of them is my father. Somebody is singing a song about cherries that a pretty girl is always eating, about bright clothes she always wears and the little song she always sings.

For the first time in my life I can hardly wait for night to come. My fear has gone, that is, it's still there, but with expectation on top of it. If only I don't fall asleep again, I think, I mustn't fall asleep. I say to my mother: 'I'm tired.' It's still afternoon, she puts her hand on my forehead and then calls to my father. 'Just imagine, he's tired and wants to sleep.' My father says: 'No wonder someone's tired when he spends the whole day running around.' My mother looks at him with annoyance. He says: 'Let him lie down and sleep, if he wants to and can,' then he starts walking about again. I lie down, my mother covers me up. She asks if anything is hurting, she presses one or two places. I say impatiently: 'There's nothing hurting.' She says: 'Don't be so cheeky.' She leaves her hand lying on me under the blanket, I don't mind that, it's very pleasant. I really am getting tired as time goes by, as the rain beats on the roof, as they walk in long circles, and as she holds my stomach. I think about what I'd like to find in the empty houses at night, it mustn't be too heavy because of the need to carry it, and not too big either; I don't decide, but the word 'splendid' keeps going through my mind. I expect I'll find something that will make lots of people stare and ask: 'Good heavens, where did you get that?' Then I'll smile and keep my secret nicely to myself, and they'll all rack their brains and be envious. I can feel that I'm about to go to sleep, there's always a buzzing in my ears before sleeping. I can't possibly stay asleep, I think, however tired I might be: in the evening 'lights out!' is always bawled out so loudly that it would waken a bear. I'm pretty smart.

I sleep, then I'm awake again, it's nearly time to lie down. I get my piece of bread and half an onion. It surprises me a little that nobody seems to notice what special things are going on. Only my mother persists in saying that there's something the matter with me; her hand keeps dancing on my forehead, and she reminds my father how I've been coughing. I'm about to jump up and show her how healthy I am, but I remember just in time how wrong that would be. I mustn't be too healthy, I must keep coughing, or else they'll put me back between them for the night. 'There you are,' says my mother. She wants to fetch Herr Engländer, the famous doctor from the next hut, but my father says: 'That's right, just go and fetch him. He'll come and examine him, and next time, when something really serious is wrong, then he won't come.'

The voice shouts: 'Lights out!' Another hour, I think in alarm. Itzek is lying there now, Julian is lying there now, I think, another hour for each of them. I'm afraid my parents may notice my inner trembling, but they're already beginning to kiss and whisper again. I've never felt so wide awake in my life. Ignoring the distraction beside me, I notice absolutely everything that's going on in the hut: the whispering in the next bed, the first snore, a groan that doesn't come from sleep but from unhappiness, the second snore, a symphony of snores, light from the sky coming through a crack in the wall. I notice the rain stopping, it's still dripping on to the floor somewhere, but not on the roof. Two beds away there's a very old lady who talks in her sleep. Sometimes it wakes me up, I wait for her to start again, my father says you can be a different person in your sleep. She's silent, but someone is crying, that doesn't matter, crying tires you out and makes you fall asleep. Then I hear snoring that delights me, because it's my mother's snoring. It sounds very soft and irregular, with little pauses, as though it had run into obstacles on its way. None of the elves has yet shown itself, perhaps the rain today has kept them away. A good part of the hour is past, I shouldn't like to be the first at the rendezvous. The hour will be over, I decide, when my father is asleep too. I sit up and let my legs hang over the side. If he asks me what's the matter, then he isn't asleep. Itzek too is sitting up in bed, that helps me, Julian's heart is pounding now as well. The crying has stopped, and there hasn't been any whispering to be heard for quite a while. So my hour must be up.

I stand beside the bed and nothing happens. This morning I twice walked from here to the door with my eyes shut, to make up for the failed rehearsal during the night, and didn't bump into anything. I only trod on the foot of an old granddad who was in my way, and he grumbled. I lift up my shoes, the hour is up. I take a step, then another, the floor creaks a little, you don't hear that by day. The darkness is so black that there is no difference between having your eyes closed and open. My steps get brisk, but suddenly everything stops, I nearly drop with fright, because somebody screams. It's the terribly old woman. I stand still until she's silent again; what will happen if she wakes my parents and then: 'Where's the child?' But they remain asleep, because the woman's screaming is part of the night. My legs find the corner by themselves, then I see a grey shimmer coming from the door, the night light. The last steps are rash and quick, because I suddenly think: 'What if the doors are locked at night!' The door opens wonderfully easily and closes quickly, oh, I'm outside in the camp. I sit down, put on my shoes and curse myself, I've forgotten my trousers. I always keep my shirt on when sleeping, only take off my trousers, that's a rule my mother has introduced here; the trousers lie folded on the bed as a pillow, so that nobody steals them. Now I've got to climb over the wall in my shirt and underpants; Itzek and Julian will crack jokes.

I can't find the moon. Yesterday I asked Julian: 'What will they do to us if they catch us?' He answered: 'They won't catch us', that reassured me very much. There are puddles on the ground, I find the moon in one of them. Of course I stop in front of every corner and don't take risks. I think: 'Even if my father wakes up now, it won't do him any good.'

Behind the last corner Julian is squatting by the wall. He laughs, naturally, and points his finger at me. I sit down on the ground beside him. He's still amused, I ask: 'Isn't Itzek here yet?' He says: 'Where do you think he is, kid.' The bottom buttress is so low that I can grab it while seated, it wobbles a little. 'Perhaps he's gone to sleep,' I say. Julian says nothing, he strikes me as very serious now that he's finished laughing. I never felt his superior powers so much as I do now. I ask: 'How long shall we wait?' He says: 'Shut up.' I imagine Itzek's horror when he wakes up in the morning and every-thing's over. But this is no time for compassion, I await Julian's orders and start feeling afraid of the wall. It is much higher than by day, it's getting higher by the minute. When a raven croaks over our heads, Julian stands up; perhaps the bird's cry was the sign he was waiting for. He says: 'Your Itzek is a coward.'

Later, when we're back with our booty, I'll be just as big a hero as he is, then it won't matter who gives orders now and who obeys. But Julian is silent for so long that I'm afraid something may be wrong. I ask: 'Do you want to put it off?' He says: 'Rubbish.' I admit there was a little hope in my question, but now I know that tonight we're going out of the camp. 'What are we waiting for?' He says: 'Nothing.' He pushes me aside because I'm in the way, he tests the first buttress, then the second and the third, he can't reach the fourth from the ground. He climbs on to the first buttress and is now high enough to touch the fourth, then he jumps back to the ground. He says: 'You go first.' I ask: 'Why me?' He says: 'Because I say so,' and I feel how right he is. All the same, I ask: 'Can't we draw lots?' 'No,' he says impatiently, 'go on, or else I'll go by myself.' That's the firmest proof that Julian isn't frightened like me; he gives me a little nudge, he helps me to master myself. A couple of questions occur to me that I could ask him; but if Julian is serious and goes by himself, then I'll be left standing here. I step up to the wall, he says: 'You must grab hold of the third and climb on to the first.' He pushes me from below so that it looks as if I couldn't have done it without his help. I stand on the bottom buttress and am no longer afraid of the wall, only of its height. I'm helped by the thought that I'll have conquered the wall when Julian still has to climb it. As though on a ladder for giants, one has to take a big step and grab a higher buttress, that isn't much effort. Beside me on my right is the cold wall, under me on my left Julian is getting further and further back, he has raised his face to the sky and is looking at me. He asks me: 'How's it going?' For the first time in my life I despise him, and I say from my height: 'Don't make such a noise.' I won't tell him how easy it is, he just sent me on ahead because he was scared. All of a sudden the top of the wall is in front of my eyes.

I can see a street. I see dark houses, the damp stones on the square, nothing's moving, the Germans really are asleep. He calls softly: 'What can you see?' I call back in excitement: 'A long way off I can see a cart drawn by horses. I think they're white.' He calls in surprise: 'You're making that up.' I say: 'Now it's turned a corner.' I prop my arms on the top of the wall, there's a bit of broken glass there. They're small pieces, you can't see every one, I feel the wall with my hands. The biggest piece can be broken off, and with it I scrape over the other splinters. 'What are you doing?' asks Julian from below. I carefully wipe the glass away with my sleeve and puff. Then I roll on to the wall, my fear starts up again, fear is what I'm most afraid of. I have to get my knees under my stomach, that's the hardest job. For a moment I place my knee on glass. I can't scream, I find a better place for my knee, it'll just have to bleed; and Julian, the idiot, calls: 'Why can't you go on?'

I have to turn round, I'm horribly afraid of losing my balance. Julian had better not say anything more, or I'll spit on his head. Then, after turning, I see him standing there and only realize now how high up I am. I lie down on my belly again, my legs are already outside, I can't pay any heed to particular pains. I let myself down as far as my arms can reach, I can't find a foothold because there are no buttresses here. I hang there and can't get up again, I hear Julian calling: 'What's the matter? Say something.' I close my eyes and see the wall from below, thinking how small it looks when you're strolling about in the camp. What can happen, I'll fall down and hurt myself a little, I've fallen down thousands of times. I'll stand up and wipe my hands clean, while Julian still has to make the crossing. What if he doesn't come? At the thought I go cold, I'm hanging here and Julian will disappear and go to bed. I can't go into the houses all by myself, it was Julian's idea all along. I call: 'Julian, are you still there?' Then I'm flying, even though I didn't decide to do anything, the top of the wall slipped out of my hands. It's a long time before the ground arrives, I fall slowly, landing on my head, the wall scrapes along my stomach the whole steep way. I lie comfortably on my back, I keep my eyes shut for a bit before I take a good look at the sky, which is right above me. Then I see Julian's face on top of the wall, he's a good fellow, and brave too. He calls: 'Where on earth are you?' Then I have to move, two sore spots are troubling me, one on my right hip, the other on my head. I say: 'Here, Julian.' I feel dizzy too, I must step aside so that he doesn't land on my head, I think: 'I've made it, anyway.' Julian's method is different, he sits on the wall. He slides forwards, he seems to be hurrying, he supports himself on either side, his arms soon look like wings. No, he isn't a coward, he flies to the ground, he falls on his back beside me, he gets up much quicker than I did. Since I'm behind him, I walk round him, but he turns so that I can't see his face, and he takes a few steps away. I'd like to look at him and grab him by the shoulder, then he pushes me back, because he's crying. He's brave all the same, my headache comes and goes, my hip hurts with every step I take. I ask: 'Are your hands bleeding too?' As though he had only just thought of this possibility, Julian looks at his hands, turns them towards the moon, they aren't bleeding. To comfort him I show him mine, he says:

'What on earth have you done, you ass?' I say: 'The glass.' He says: 'You shouldn't touch it.'

I'm cold, how many jackets does a burglar need? Now we're characters from a story, Julian especially; he asks: 'Are you still there?' That means he can't hear me, I'm creeping softly like an old hand. As I take more steps I get used to my sore hip, but the headache gets worse. It's all right so long as I don't turn my head. A dog barks somewhere, it's a long way off and has nothing to do with us. I say: 'Let's go into this house.' We go to the nearest house, but the front door is locked. We don't leave out a single door, but it's the same with all of them. I cry a little, partly because of my sore head and the cold, Julian doesn't laugh. He tugs me by the sleeve and says: 'Come on,' that makes me feel better. He says: 'Do you know what I think?' And when I shake my head, so that it hurts again, he says: 'I think people are still living here. That's why the houses are locked. It's only our street that's empty.' I stop in front of a window, anxious to know if Julian is right. I stand on tiptoe to see if there are people sleeping in the room. Then a devil's face looks at me, with only the pane of glass between us. I run away so fast, even with my hip, that Julian doesn't catch me up until the next street corner. I say: 'There was a devil behind that window.' Julian says: 'There are people living there, you idiot.'

He finds our street, I hardly recognize it at night. We go past a fence that I know has two loose posts. I tap one of them and I'm right, in my street I could display lots of tricks. I ask Julian why he doesn't just take the nearest house, knowing he's afraid it could be locked too. He says: 'I know what I'm doing.'

Then I feel good, because my head isn't so sore. We'd be inside a house long before now if Julian were as cold as I am. I think: 'I hope he won't feel warm for much longer.' Some day I'll be the leader, then I'll wear warm clothes. He asks: 'Are you still there?' We go past my house, he's only thinking of his own; without him I could go in if I liked. I think of father's torch, I must be tired. We don't waste a word on the workshop of the dead cobbler Muntek, in my time, at least, he lived here and would chase us away. I've never felt so cold in our street, the wind blows against my bare legs, but Julian is the first to sneeze. He's standing at his house and can't get through the door. He shakes a bit and kicks a bit, but the door stays shut. I say: 'Don't make such a row.' He answers: 'Shut your face.' As it's a long way to my house, I only go to the next one, and it's open. I call Julian, we're very close to our good fortune. The house has three storeys, we start at the top, because that's how Julian wants it. The landing is all black, a door opens, a dark grey hole. My heart pounds, because I don't know if it was Julian or a stranger who opened the door, till Julian says: 'Do come on.' There's hardly anything in the room except a mess: chairs lying on the floor, a table, an open cupboard, in which our hands can't find anything. I ask: 'What's the stink here?' Julian says: 'You stink.' I sit on a smashed bed. Julian goes to the window and opens it. There's more light, he leans far out and asks: 'Do you know where our camp is?' I stand beside him and say: 'No.' He shuts the window again and says: 'But I know,' that's what Julian is like. On the way back to the door we bump against a bucket from which the stench comes.

The rooms in the house are all empty in the same way. In one there's a machine, much too heavy to take away. Julian says: 'That's a sewing-machine.' In one we find a chest half full of coal, what can we do with coal in the camp? In one the latch falls off the door, I pick it up and decide to take it with me, at least for now. Julian takes the latch away from me and puts it back in its place. In the next house, in the very first room, Julian finds something. He examines it and soon exclaims: 'Gosh, it's a pair of binoculars!' I've never heard the word before, he says: 'Come here and look through them.' I go over to him at the window, he holds the find in front of my face, sure enough, you can see things in it that nobody can see with the naked eye, even at night. Julian shows me how to turn the little wheel so that the images become blurred or distinct, but I can't see anything anyway because suddenly there are tears in my eyes. I give him back his binoculars, it's rotten luck that he was the one who found them. In the next room Julian comes up to me and says: 'We've got to go back.' I say: 'I'm not going until I find something too.' He says again that I'd better hurry, as though it depended on my abilities whether I find something or not. He stays with me in every room as long as I want, he opens every window and looks at everything through his damned binoculars.

I can feel that I'd settle for less and less, but there's nothing there. Julian says: 'We've got to go. Or do you want it all to come out?' I say I'd like to go into just one more flat, where the rag ball is lying under my bed, then we'll run back to the camp. 'Fine,' says Julian, since finding the binoculars he's been a generous friend. As we walk down the street, I can't answer the question what will happen if my house happens to be locked. Julian sees it through his thing long before I can, and says: 'The door's open.' There's no ball under the bed, I crawl into every corner. It was here when we left the room, there's no doubt about it, so someone's come later and stolen the ball, it was all a waste of time.

Julian asks: 'What's the matter?' because I'm sitting on the bed and crying. He puts his hand on my shoulder, even though he might have grinned, he's quite a good friend. Now he ought to ask me if I want his binoculars; naturally I wouldn't take them, but that would help a lot. Then I think of my father's torch. It hasn't shown up in the camp so far, perhaps it'll show up here, provided the thief who took the rag ball didn't find it. I don't know where my father kept it hidden, I don't think there was any regular place for it, sometimes it lay on the table, sometimes elsewhere. I stand up and ask Julian: 'If you had a lamp the size of your hand, where would you hide it here?' He looks round three times, then he asks: 'Are you sure it's here?' I say: 'It must be here.' Julian puts his binoculars on our table and starts searching, I like that and then again I don't like it. I search as hard as I can, I've got to find the torch before he does. There are a couple of places I know and he doesn't, a hole in the floor, a little space under the window-ledge, a loose board in the top of the wardrobe. My knowledge does me no good, I crawl through the room on my stomach, I climb on to the chair, the torch doesn't show up. If Julian says again that we've got to go, then we've got to go. I get under the bed for the last time, then I hear him say: 'Do you mean this one?' He's quite calm, he's put the torch on the table and isn't waiting for gratitude. I ask: 'Where did you find it?' He says: 'In the drawer.' He says that like someone who can't understand how I can almost lose my mind over such a ridiculous torch. He takes his important binoculars and goes to the door. I might never have thought of the drawer, you don't need to crawl on your stomach to get to it, you don't need to climb on to the chair; the thief who took the ball wasn't clever enough either.

I'll shine the light when we're in the camp, Julian is now impatient. I run after him to the stairs, though I'm the one who knows every step here. 'Thanks, Julian,' I say, or else I just think it,

suddenly I feel sorry for Itzek. Julian forbids me to try out my torch
in the street. I do as he says, pay no heed to the way and follow him,
I'm not feeling cold yet. I have to hold the torch in my hand because
I forgot my trouser pockets as well. I ask: 'Do you remember the
way?' 'Go by yourself if you want,' says Julian, that means he knows
the way. I've no idea why he's cross, I'd like to be friendly to him. I
say: 'If you need the torch, you can always borrow it.' He says: 'I
don't need your torch.' I think he wants to be back home as much as
I do, and that puts him in a bad temper; he's as nervous as I am of
standing in front of the wall and climbing up and having to jump
down. I say: 'If the Germans are all asleep, we don't need to climb
up. Why don't we just go through the gate?' 'Because it's locked, you
idiot,' says Julian.

The way is getting colder. Naturally Julian finds the camp, and
because I never doubted that he would, I don't feel relieved. He also
finds our spot. He whispers: 'Kid, do you know what's wrong?' I
whisper: 'What is it?' 'The iron bars,' he whispers, 'there aren't any
on this side.' I'd like to have an idea too and I whisper: 'We must
walk round the camp, there'll be such things somewhere or other.'
'But there's glass everywhere on top of the wall, except at this one
spot', whispers Julian. I look at my hands, which I'd forgotten about,
at my knee. I whisper: 'If we find a spot somewhere else, then we'll
take a stone and smash the glass first.' I can see how good my idea is,
because Julian now says nothing and looks for a stone. He puts the
stone in his trouser pocket and leads the way; if we find buttresses on
this side of the wall, I'll be the one who rescued us. Julian says as he
goes ahead: 'Stop making a fuss about your stupid torch, or I'll take
it away from you.' He always shows off most when he's right; I'd be a
better leader than he is, if I were the leader. We have to go in a curve,
a big curve leading away from the wall and past the camp entrance,
where there's nobody to be seen, but that's how Julian wants it. He
takes my torch away, although I didn't do anything with it, it's for
safety, I don't protest; a leader has to think of everything and doesn't
need to explain everything. We creep across the street that leads
directly to the camp gate, there's still nobody there who might be
watching us. We come back to the wall, Julian gives me back my
torch, I expected nothing else. We walk and walk and don't find any
buttresses. I say: 'Julian, there won't be any.' 'I know that myself,' he
says, but keeps on walking. Then I ask: 'How much longer do we

have to walk?' He answers by standing still, he sits down and rests his back against the wall. I sit down too and don't ask any questions, I look at Julian and see something awful: he's crying. Now we really are without help, he's crying because he doesn't know what to do. His crying earlier on, when he jumped off the wall and fell down, was nothing compared with this. We move closer together, he's probably just as cold as I am. He's probably a few months older. I ask: 'Shall we go into an empty house and lie down?' He says: 'Are you crazy?' A couple of times my eyes close. I think what a pity it is that Julian didn't have the idea about the empty house. My torch hardly makes a circle of light on the ground, the sky is so light by now. I think of my father, who ought to come and fetch us, first me, then Julian, or both together, one under each arm, he ought to put me to bed and cover me up warmly, gosh, that would be good. He ought to hold my mother by the hand, they should both stand by my bed and look down at me and smile till I wake up.

Then something hurts. In front of us stands a huge German, he's prodded me with his foot, he does it again, but not like someone who wants to kick. With his burning eyes he says a few unintelligible words; I'm so scared I don't want to stand up. The disaster will really start when I stand up, I stay seated. But Julian is standing beside me, held up by his collar. The giant says in funny Polish: 'What are you doing here?' I look at my friend, the giant shakes him a bit. Julian points to the wall and says: 'We're from the camp.' I admire him for a long time because of the calm way he says that; the giant says: 'And how did you get out?' Julian tells him the truth, meanwhile I look at the helmet and the rifle that towers over the giant shoulder, the giant shoe on my stomach that keeps me prisoner. I've not the least doubt that we're about to get shot, that was clear to us from the outset. The giant asks why the dickens we didn't go back into the camp. Julian explains that too, he's never been such a hero as he is now. The giant looks up at the wall and seems to understand the matter. He takes his foot off my stomach, it's like an order to get up, and as soon as I'm upright he grips me by the collar. The torch is still lying on the ground, I must get it somehow before we're taken away.

The giant lets us both go and says: 'Come with me to the guard-room.' But he stands still and doesn't move, we naturally stand still as well, he's the one who should start. 'Come on, off you go,' he says, giving us a shove. I turn to the wall and pick up my torch, it's the last chance. The giant asks: 'What have you got there?' and grabs my hands which are behind my back. He sees the torch, he takes it and tries it out and puts it away in his pocket, as if everything here belongs to him. All the bad things I've ever heard about the Germans are suddenly true, I hate him like poison. If it had been anyone else I'd have tried to persuade him to give me back the torch, even if it meant a quarrel, even with my father, but nothing has any point with this giant German. I see Julian stuffing his shirt far into his trousers, apart from the two of us nobody knows what he's hiding under his shirt. I hope he'll get away with the binoculars, the giant mustn't get the binoculars. He says: 'Off you go now.' He gives us another shove, we walk in front of him, I see Julian moving his booty from his back on to his stomach. If we're shot, I think, the binoculars won't be much use to him. The giant tells us to stop.

He turns us round with his giant hands and makes us face him. He looks at us for a long time as though he's preoccupied, I hope his worries are the very worst kind. He says: 'Do you know what will happen to me if I don't take you to the guardroom?' As if that's any concern of ours, he isn't just a thief, he's an idiot too. I think: 'What happens to you can't possibly be bad enough.' Julian says: 'I don't know.' I'd like to answer that I'm not interested, that would be a good answer; but I can see his great paws dangling, I wish I were a giant. Suddenly he grabs us by the scruff of the neck and throws himself down so that we have to fall to the ground with him. He's still holding me by the scruff as though I were made of wood. He says: 'Not a word.' I see a light far behind us at the wall, a motor-cycle. Soon its noise can be heard as well, I imagine I can hear the giant's heart beating; by now his heart even drowns the noise of the motor-cycle. He says 'Not a word,' though nobody's speaking except him. He's a thief, a fool, a coward, I'm not scared of someone like that. I can't see Julian because the giant body is lying between us. A long way from us, the motor-cycle turns a corner, but we have to lie for a while longer.

'Stand up,' says the giant. He lets us go and dusts off his uniform. I look at my underpants and know that my mother will give me a hard time if I survive this. The giant takes off his helmet and wipes his brow, like all Germans he's got fair hair. He takes his time, as though the cold was only for me and not for him. His helmet's back on his head, he takes his rifle; now it must be time to take us away and shoot us, they can do that. Julian asks: 'Are you going to shoot us now?'

The giant says nothing, he probably doesn't think Julian's question important. He looks up and down the street, nobody's meant to see what he's about to do to us. He says to Julian: 'Just don't try to run away', and wags his finger threateningly. Why did he take his rifle in his hand if it wasn't to shoot us? But he leans it against the wall. He probably doesn't know himself what he wants, the torch is a little lump under his jacket, I should simply have left it lying by the wall, then some lucky person would have found it eventually. He points to me and just says: 'You,' and I must go up to him. He says: 'I'll lift you on to the wall. But jump quickly and run to your huts as fast as you can, it mustn't take long. Understood?' So that's it, I don't know if I'm relieved now, I'll have to jump again in a minute. 'We've got a spot,' says Julian, 'where there isn't any glass. It's not far from here. The giant says: 'There's no glass around here,' and lifts me up with no further ado. I've no time to think, it hurts, because he's holding my by the hips. He says: 'Stand on my shoulders.' I lean against the wall and do what he orders, I still can't reach the top. He says: 'Now climb on to my head.' He holds me by my ankles, I pay him back for the torch: I make myself heavy and am not careful with his head. He's lucky to have a helmet, without his helmet he'd get a shock. He says: 'Hurry up.' I'm standing on one leg, there's no more room on the helmet, now I can grab hold of the top of the wall. He asks: 'Can you hold on?' I lift my foot carefully off his head and then he goes away from under me. I'm hanging on and I'll never get on to the wall; that's how I hung on earlier, only then I wanted to get to the ground, not on top. I look down over my shoulder and see him picking up his rifle.

That's the worst fright of all, you can't possibly imagine it: to be hanging high in the air to be shot after all, despite his fine words. I can't hold on to the wall any longer, I fall off. The fall gets longer as the years go by, no wall can be as high as that, then I'm caught by the giant. It's as though I'd never fallen. The giant puts his hand on my mouth before I can scream. He says: 'Whatever are you doing?' He puts me on my feet, picks his rifle off the ground, and leans it against the wall again. Then he says: 'Try again, on you go.' He takes me again, I'm now getting used to his shoulders, this time I leave his head alone. When I see Julian standing down below, I feel envious: I have to fight for my life, I fall down and get shot or don't get shot, and he's standing there watching it all peacefully. And he's even allowed to keep his binoculars, we'll have a word about that when we get the chance.

I clutch the top of the wall once more. The giant lets one of my ankles go, the other stays in his hand. He says to Julian: 'Give me the rifle.' He props the rifle-butt against my bottom and pushes me up, I can almost sit on it, I get on top of the wall without difficulty. I lie on my stomach and see how right he is, I can't find the smallest piece of glass, the glass is a mystery. I can see into our camp, which is still quiet and empty as at night, but already bright as day. From below the giant calls: 'Down you go.'

I turn on the wall and hang on the other side and fall till I can't fall any further. I lie there crying, I'm back and have brought nothing but aches. I'm not interested in Julian any more, in future he can find other people to carry out his bright ideas. I stand up, my parents come closer. My father must be glad that I'm still alive, my mother will cry when she sees me and then wash all my wounds clean; I can't tell them the truth. My hands are bleeding again, my knees are bleeding, my elbow seems to have been dipped in dirt and blood. One comfort is that they'll probably be so sorry for me they'll cuddle me. I'm off, tomorrow I'll say to Julian: 'Oh sure, all Germans sleep at night.'

As I turn round, he jumps off the wall in his way. He doesn't fall badly, but he lies there without getting up. I go back to him, because he's my friend, because he's lying on his stomach like that. He's crying, he cries and cries as I've never seen anyone cry before. I'd already finished crying, but now I start again myself. I ask: 'Did he take your binoculars away?' It takes some time before he pushes my hand away and stands up. I see the binoculars under his shirt. He hobbles away and doesn't stop crying, I run after him, at last I'm better off than he is. I ask: 'Shall we see each other tomorrow?' I can't see anything wrong with this question, but what does Julian do? He hits me on the head. He looks at me as if his fists were ready to hit me again, then he hobbles off. I stand still and hear him still crying; I needn't be so compassionate as to run after him. I'm looking forward to the hut where I won't be cold any more.

Behind the door it's dark. I close it so quietly that I don't hear anything; anyone who wasn't awake already will still be sleeping. My parents are sitting on the bed, looking at me with wide eyes. Some-one whispers: 'Heavens above, what have they done to you?' At that moment nothing is sore any more, and yet I feel as if the worst is still to come. My mother holds both hands in front of her mouth, my father doesn't move, I stop between his knees. He puts a hand on my head and turns me right round once. Then he holds me tight by both shoulders and asks: 'Where have you been?' I say: 'I was outside and fell down.' My father says: 'Nobody falls like that.' My mother has got up and is looking in our brown case. My father shakes me so hard that my head, which has been quiet for a long time, starts hurting again. I say: 'We met outside and we quarrelled and had a fight. That's true.' He says: 'Who's "we"?' I say: 'You don't know him', suddenly it's easy to tell lies again. My mother is holding a dripping towel, she takes me from my father and leads me to the light at the window. My father follows us and looks on. 'Go to Professor Engländer and ask if he can take a look at him,' says my mother. My father asks: 'Can't we wait till after the roll-call?' 'No,' she says crossly, 'or is it too dangerous for you?' Then off he goes on tiptoe, and at last my mother cuddles me. She says: 'You've got to under-stand how excited he is.'

She puts me on the bed and takes my head in her lap. I think that maybe I'll tell her the truth later on, nobody but her. She says: 'You're so tired, my little one.' It's happiness to lie beside her, though she won't let me sleep because she's examining my cuts with her finger. She speaks to someone, a couple of times I hear the word 'probably'. I open my eyes, and she's smiling down at me as if I were something funny.

My father is holding a small dark bottle in his hand. 'Engländer gave me iodine,' he says. I ask: 'Will it hurt?' My mother says: 'Yes, but there's no other way.' Then I stand up and take a few steps back, because I think I've been hurt quite enough tonight. My father says: 'Don't listen to her, it doesn't hurt. It just cleans the wound.' That sounds better. He says: 'I can prove it.' I watch very closely, after all it's my pain, I look at his outstretched arm. He lets a few drops trickle out of the bottle on to his arm, they form a small black lake and slowly separate. Then he says: 'Is that supposed to hurt? Do you think I'd pour the stuff on my arm of my own free will if it hurt?' I look at his eyes from close to and don't see the slightest trace of pain. Another proof is that my mother goes away from us; she was wrong and won't admit it, so she's just going away. My father says: 'Now come here.' I hold out my elbow, he twists my arm a little, so that the drops will land precisely on the wound.

MAXIM BILLER

Robots

Maxim Biller was born in Prague in 1960. His family moved to West Germany in 1970. He has published two collections of short stories, *When at last I'm rich and dead* (1990) and *Land of the Fathers and Traitors* (1992). He shows the strong influence of American fiction: Joseph Heller (who appears as a character in one of the stories from the first collection) and above all Philip Roth, who in *Portnoy's Complaint* broke taboos on writing about teenage sexuality and, more importantly, about discomfort with one's Jewish identity. Like several other authors, especially the polemical essayist Henryk M. Broder and the bitterly comic novelist Rafael Seligmann, Biller wants to break down well-established conventions of regarding Germans as guilty and contrite and Jews as pitiable and therefore virtuous victims. A philo-Semitism based on such premises is hypocritical: it conceals the resentment that the guilty feel towards their victims—as Broder has put it, 'the Germans will never forgive the Jews for Auschwitz'—and it assigns to Jews a moral superiority which is insufferable, especially since Jews in fact share the failings of other people. Several of Biller's stories, like the one translated here, stress Jews' hard struggle for economic survival, their corrupt business methods (shared with Gentile businessmen), and their prominence in the building programme which turned the west side of Frankfurt into a wasteland of skyscrapers, and which led Rainer Werner Fassbinder to demonize the figure of 'the rich Jew' in his crudely anti-Semitic play *Garbage, the City, and Death* (1975). Biller invites us to look hard at recent history and discard the sentimental illusion that any one group of people is morally privileged.

In questioning post-Holocaust philo-Semitism, Biller draws on Jewish history before emancipation for analogies. He compares Jewish businessmen in West Germany to the 'court Jews' who raised revenue for princes in early modern Germany and in return enjoyed legal protection. In referring to Spinoza's excommunication by the Jewish community, he implies that a conception of Jewish identity based on the Holocaust, in which the Jews are morally privileged victims, has taken the place of orthodox Judaism and is maintained by equally oppressive sanctions. And he touches a sore point by referring to the revelation that Werner Nachmann, once a leading public spokesman for West German Jews, systematically misappropriated money paid to the Jewish community in reparation for their sufferings in the Holocaust.

'Robots' asks to be read as a grim comedy of cynicism, illustrating the power of greed and showing what dubious motives can underlie moral indignation. The blackness into which the Auschwitz victims disappear near the beginning is repeated when the light on the staircase goes out after Pucher and Aszkowicz have struck their bargain. Not all the characters, though, are robots controlled by money. Jurek breaks free from automatism when he saves the life of the child Salek Pucher; but an automatism resulting from fear destroys Jael's unborn child fifty-five years later. If self-sacrifice is one way of escaping automatism, sexual love can be another: ought we really to disapprove of the teenagers who enjoy making love on what should be a solemn trip to Poland?

In Poland the sky is white, and under this sky there lies a vast plain with towns, meadows and dry fields. An area where everything is visible. Anyone who wants to hide will run far to the south, where he will be able to find a refuge in the Beszczady swamps, the Tatra mountains, or the Carpathians. Of course there is also the possibility of pretending to be invisible in a cellar, an attic, or a cupboard, but in this country there are simply too many people who despise such magic—old acquaintances, neighbours, or professional lickspittles, all of them goyim, with no sympathy for the problems of their Jewish compatriots who are having swastikas and SS-runes burnt into their arses by the Nazis. But in 1941 you've got to look after yourself, and the cruel insight evoked by the German festival of blood frightens only the timid bourgeoisie. Everyone else knows that the Nazis' guns have created a situation where no one can even think of judging anyone else. The violent anarchy that has gripped Europe and Asia excuses anything you do, all value-systems seem suspended, including that of National Socialism. Ideologies and ethics aren't even utopian blueprints any longer; instead the earth is cold, and the bodies lying on this earth are colder still.

It is then that Salomon Pucher meets us for the first time. He is eleven, a fair-haired little boy with thin arms, good intentions, and a distrustful glance. In Lodz, in the ghetto, Salomon was entrusted by his parents to the Bronner family, but after the Bronners were taken away in their turn, he stayed on his own until Jurek started looking after him. Jurek was a medical student, but it was a long time since he had seen the inside of the university. He sometimes helped the people who collapsed from weakness or starvation on the pavements of the ghetto. When Salek,* roaming about, ran into him one evening, he decided to devote himself only to the boy. They stayed together, Jurek supplied Salek with food, he played dominoes and mikado with him and taught him Polish, mathematics, and geography. At last Jurek's turn came, and Salek, who had fallen through the grid of SS bureaucracy and in principle no longer existed, went with his older friend. Jurek wanted to have the boy's company, he had got used to him, and besides he thought that Salek wouldn't be able to survive alone, so that the death in store for him would be a merciful release, like putting a puppy to sleep when no one wants it.

At that time the deportees arriving in Auschwitz were forced to walk from the main camp to Birkenau, and so one night we see Salek and Jurek marching side by side on the edge of a column crawling forward like oil. Jurek was still clutching Salek's small hand in his slender fingers, absorbed in the thought of their imminent shared death. But just afterwards he was swept away by the realization that, in honesty, he wanted to sacrifice the boy not out of compassion but out of egoism. Jurek looked for the moon in the night sky, but it had slipped behind the gigantic steely Polish clouds, the darkness had gripped everything and everyone, the procession was permanently plodding into a black wall, and the watchmen's lamps gave only an occasional flicker. 'Let yourself drop and lie there until you can't hear anything', said Jurek to the boy, and the next moment he broke out of the crowd and ran away with loud yells. Salek stuck his nose between the sand and the stones, he pressed his stomach against the ground, and the Jews stepped over him as if he were King David. Cries rang out, a couple of shots cracked, a penetrating groan went through the ranks, and soon all was quiet around Salek Pucher. In the distance he could hear steps scraping and crackling, then he could hear nothing more, and when, after another shot, Jurek's death-shriek again divided the sky into a white and a black half, this eleven-year-old monster of survival knew that he had got away.

Salek got up and ran off. Before him was the Polish pampa, that endless space, and there was only the earth for him to burrow into if he wanted to hide. Of course there were some Poles who would not betray a Jewish child. But the peasants' patience with Salek never lasted very long, he wasn't humble and grateful enough. He would

take bread, milk, and a sleeping-place for granted like a spoilt child
returning home, and so they kept throwing Salek out, and then he
would run off again to look for other protectors. So Salek ran and
ran till the war was over, and then he ran a bit further to get to
Germany, to Frankfurt, where first of all the Joint* looked after him.
In autumn 1946 he was given a home by the resurrected Slavka
Bronner, who had seen her first husband for the last time on the
ramp at Birkenau; her second, whom she married in the seventh
month of peace, was soon afterwards crushed against the wall of a
bombed-out house in the centre of Frankfurt by an American army
jeep. Every evening she would tell Salek about his parents and about
her own past life; she would explain the simplest things to him two
or three times, asking whether he had understood everything, using
primitive images and absurd comparisons, for she still considered
him a child, though it was already some time since he'd started
shaving, having girlfriends, and drinking whisky. She would lie right
on the edge of the heavy German double bed they shared, holding
Salek's hand and staring through barely opened eyes at the opposite
wall. Later, when she was asleep, she would mutter and call out sharp
German words, but Salek caught hardly any of that, because,
unknown to Slavka, he was out night after night.

On one of these tours Salek got to know an elderly German
woman who was not very pleasant but always did what he wanted.
Salomon, almost eighteen by now, entrusted himself directly to the
care of Annemarie Abergast, whose husband, a Russian prisoner
of war somewhere in Uzbekistan, was personally atoning for the
collective guilt. Meanwhile Annemarie restored new life to the glass-
cutting works until there was enough profit to reward Salek Pucher
for his charm and the sweet down on his bottom with a substantial
credit, which not only founded his lightning economic career but
also gave Annemarie the feeling that she had personally made reparation. It is understandable that in Salek's memory the sad, all-
knowing orgasms of her Indian summer counted for more than those
few thousand marks, which he could have got elsewhere. His
relationship with Annemarie corresponded, while it lasted, to the
whole relationship between Jews and Germans, in which a historic
urge for overcompensation kept shoving material things in front of
ideas, although these two nations are so dreadfully sensitive about
their souls.

It was clear that someone like Saleczek Pucher, who was already wondering why the Germans' and Jews' common task of coming to terms with the past had to end in two separate rubber cells, was not going to sit idly waiting for such an economic downturn, but preferred to mount a frontal attack. He took the same path as many other Jewish immigrants in post-war Germany: he made deals, he made them without regard to honour and morality, and if he was able to write his own hunting permit, that was because of his open hatred and the self-pitying helplessness of someone who has got off. Having buried half the Jewish people alive, the Germans deserved to be shat on, there was no need to bother about them, and so young Salomon Pucher set to work to occupy every commercial niche that he could find in enemy territory and invest in without risk. He began at the age of seventeen with wholesale trade in spirits. Then the bars and the girls came along, and Salomon ate his way enjoyably through the fifties, which he liked because in that period the Germans still thought, talked, and looked just as they had done under Hitler. At the beginning of the sixties he at last joined the Frankfurt Social Democrats; this brought him lots of interesting building projects and many new friends, with the sole drawback that, being Germans, they loved their court Jew because they were sorry for themselves and afraid of Jewish retaliation with Zyklon B.*

In this phase of his life Salomon Pucher gradually began to realize that he would never leave Germany. Along with a couple of Frankfurt associates he had bought up half the beach near Ha-Yarkon Street in Tel Aviv, and there they built one hotel after another. They couldn't do more for Zionism than that. That was just as clear to Salomon Pucher as to his associates, but he was one of the few who dared to say so out loud. No, Salomon Pucher would never let his two sons Ari and Danni put on Israeli uniforms and run into Arab guns, he knew how precious life is, and it's best, he thought, to lose it while asleep in your own bed, but certainly not on some dusty Oriental battlefield. But he wasn't concerned only about his sons. Quite simply, he hated the idea of making aliyah.* Salomon Pucher didn't feel like ending up among the sabra* barbarians; he had become a Central European, albeit belatedly, equipped with a fondness for pop art, Mercedes Benz, jacuzzis, and Günter Grass, devoured by loathing for his own wife, who had had a nose job and spent every afternoon in the Mövenpick restaurant in the Fressgasse* with her tarted-up girlfriends.

The years passed, and one day was like the next. Salomon Pucher was no longer his own master: he moved like a microscopic pencil dot between the prescribed co-ordinates of his villa in Lerchenberg, the city planning office, the community restaurant, 27 Bockenheimer Landstrasse, Café Schwille, the Frankfurter Hof,* St Moritz, Cannes, and Bad Homburg. The prosperity he had built up together with the scum of Germany meant less and less to him; he suddenly realized that the kind of revenge he had chosen was terribly blinkered. Salek, normally so eloquent, kept this embarrassing insight to himself; he thought day and night about himself and his Jewish friends, about the crazy provisional arrangement they had set up between Berlin, Munich, and Cologne, about fear, silence, and his own baseness—he rolled this stone to and fro until it was only a grain of sand, and that in turn slipped through the sieve of his memory.

For over ten years Salomon Pucher had been on the Jewish Community Council. He had been made its chairman immediately in the first election. He dreamed of a self-respecting German Diaspora Jewry, he did all he could to create it, and so he sought above all to remind the people of Frankfurt again and again that their Jews existed. The reactions of the goyim, hostile or sentimental, were to be the mirrors in which the Jews recognized themselves—that was Salomon Pucher's plan. He exploited every opportunity, no matter whether he had the West End Synagogue restored, made after-dinner speeches at receptions funded by the Deutsche Bank, laid on Israeli Culture Weeks, or charged his cultural advisers to organize a lecture-circus on Jews in literature. During the controversy over the Fassbinder play he even said in an interview: 'Yes, of course, Fass-binder's dirty Jewish speculator B. was modelled on me. I'm grateful to him, because he's thus enabled us to have a fruitful discussion on the relationship between the Germans and their Jewish fellow-citizens, with the stress on "fellow-citizens", because it refers to the living Jews, not to the dead; you can be nice to the dead in retrospect, and it doesn't hurt.'

People said that on the Community Council Salomon Pucher held the reins as no one else could. That was no doubt right. He was a gentle autocrat, but when he thought it necessary, he could frighten the living daylights out of any attacker by coarse remarks and personal abuse. So what was the matter with him at the Community's last general assembly, when the young journalist Henry Aszkowicz managed to inflict grave embarrassment on him with a couple of words? The words were spoken, and the eighteen councillors sitting beside Pucher on the podium were as silent as a dead dog. Salomon Pucher bared his teeth, breathed heavily through his nose, and the loud puffing that resulted gave dignity to a mysterious sentence: 'Pah—hundreds of millions!'

Pucher added angrily: 'Have you counted them, Herr Aszkowicz?' Then he pushed the microphone aside with an offended air, but not quickly enough, and so those assembled in the Community Centre's auditorium could hear in the loudspeakers the echo of Pucher smacking his powerful lips.

Puffing and smacking his lips were as much part of Pucher as the Oriental sums of money of which Henry Aszkowicz had spoken. A little earlier he had stepped up to one of the public mikes and purred in a tearful staccato: 'You should have put a stop to his activities, Herr Salomon Pucher! You with your influence! You with your political contacts! You with your friends from the Deutsche Bank! You with your hundreds of millions!'

The assembly was concerned with Werner Nachmann, the former chairman of the Central Council of German Jews, whose demise was followed by the realization that two centuries earlier this man could never have died a peaceful, natural death: in times of medieval cruelty and vengefulness he would have been burnt on a pyre with loud screams... Nachmann had stolen over thirty million marks of reparation money,* and Salomon Pucher shared the political responsibility with every other member of the Central Council. Some members of the Jewish community accordingly demanded that Pucher should resign from all his official posts and also vacate that of Community Chairman. In view of Pucher's superior standing, it was of course ludicrous to expect any such thing, and if one examined the biographies and business dealings of those attempting the putsch, it revealed the blue colour of self-righteous moralism. And yet Salomon Pucher was fighting against his opponents' charges with an old-maidish mixture of passion, exhaustion, and arrogance, although he really took none of them seriously except for the strangely indignant Henry Aszkowicz. The latter, having ended his first diatribe, began a second almost before the previous speaker had finished. 'You've got your hands just as dirty as the other swine on the Central Council who protected Nachmann's arsehole!' bawled Henry Aszkowicz suddenly and with so much aplomb that the meeting fell silent in awe—less from alarm at his mode of expression than from cheap respect for someone who obviously had honest motives. 'And you're just as big a swine, Herr Salomon Pucher!' cried Henry Aszkowicz once more at the top of his voice, and then he crowned these words with the last idea he would have that day: 'You're a dirty Nachmann Jew, Pucher! A Nachmann Jew—in case anyone doesn't understand—is one who shits on the Germans' heads whenever he can while looking for a warm spot in their arses where he can live and be well looked after for the rest of his life. He takes German money and German silence, helps to celebrate the Week of Brotherhood, and pays in Jewish silence. But he keeps his own money and adds it to the German money he's just got, because the only function of Jewish money is to have more added to it: to other money, the money that people like Pucher make out of shit and the Germans' bad conscience, and we know these people would do just the same trade in false teeth, spectacle-frames, soap, and lampshades, ladies and gentlemen, if you take my meaning... '

It is hard to say how much truth or falsehood there was in this stream of consciousness that was yelled out. However, Salomon Pucher cannot be denied the right of self-defence. Pucher exerted it in an uncharacteristically uncontrolled manner by uttering another torrent of mainly offensive words, culminating in the sentence: 'You, Herr Aszkowicz, talk a lot and don't do much work. You're a first-class smart-arse, and you can go take a shit.' And once more Salomon Pucher pushed the microphone aside, but this time, instead of puffing and lip-smacking, there was heard a strange, inhuman, hundred-throated muttering from the crowd assembled before the podium. The Community tribe, previously rebellious and inflexible, were now completely unnerved by Salomon Pucher's outburst, for though he often came out with surprises, they hadn't expected the word 'shit'.

No, it wasn't Werner Nachmann, German and Jewish Holocaust hypocrisy, genuine neuroses and false accusations, that divided Salomon Pucher and Henry Aszkowicz. There was something else between them... Henry, who like me was born in Prague in 1960, had come to Germany with his parents during the Prague Spring. He came from a Russian Jewish family which (just like ours) had some time after the war found its way out of the Soviet Union and into Czechoslovakia. For over twenty years the Aszkowiczes had been great Jewish patriots with no link to religion or tradition, and as a young man Henry's father—who still kept his father's prayer-shawl and Sabbath goblet in some hidden corner—had performed many services in the cause of Communism. In his sixties, however, he dumped his last remaining Marxist ideas in the dustbin of history, though what disillusioned him was not the Thaw in the fifties but the way Khrushchev failed and fell.

Henceforth Henry's father looked towards Israel, and when the Six-Day War swept over the Middle East, he finally realized that the Jews were not an ethnic or religious minority but a nation. This idea linked father and son, but at the same time they were separated by a feeling: when documentaries about death-camps were shown on TV, the old man always left the room, his face pale, muttering pathetic-ally to himself: 'I can't look at it, I can't... '; but Henry would stare at the screen, oblivious to all else. A safe thrill of death suddenly stroked his stomach, he was in the camps with heart and soul (as another viewer might have been absorbed in an exciting football match or a particularly bloodthirsty chase), and he felt a similar shudder when he saw Hitler giving a speech or came across a stall with military mementos in the flea-market. Thus, in a warped fash-ion, Henry developed the same relation to the past as many of the Jews living in Germany. They worshipped the Shoah as a golden calf, explained, interpreted, and justified their entire lives by refer-ence to the great burning with its consequences and obligations, and anyone who objected to this strategy ran into the same problems as Spinoza* once did. Or Henry Aszkowicz. One day he roused the Frankfurt Community to fury with a report on a trip to Poland made by fifty young German Jews, entitled 'See Auschwitz and die'. In it he described how, on the one hand, Jewish teenagers still get a shock when they are taken into a gas-chamber in Maidanek, but on the other hand—Henry had witnessed it himself—half an hour later they're again laughing, flirting, or cracking disrespectful jokes. 'For pain at the slaughter of Jews', wrote Henry, 'is automatically coupled with the decipherment and demystification of these actions through

contempt and indifference, hence through spite and scorn and cold-
ness.' He went on: 'A trauma is no good to the living, only to the
dead or those who might easily have been.'

It was in the nature of the case that Henry, as the chronicler, was
called to account for what he had merely observed and recorded. In
the last resort the Frankfurt citizens shouldn't have been angry with
him but with their own children, who had more fun in Polish
restaurants and hotel beds than in German concentration camps.
Apart from the scandal over his report, the trip to Poland involved
Henry in personal complications. On the very first night, in the
Wroclaw Interhotel, he got off with Jael Pucher, the daughter of
Salomon Pucher. Ari and Danni, her elder brothers, had simply
failed to keep an eye on their sixteen-year-old sister. For most of the
trip they had themselves been preoccupied with the pursuit of love.
So Henry and Jael spent all their Polish nights together without
interference; by day they pitched their camp in the last row of seats
in the tour bus, or walked hand in hand through Lodz and Cracow,
Birkenau and Treblinka, as though under a spell. On the trip they
also took part in the 'March of the Living' put on by Israeli youth
organizations on Yom ha-Shoah.* This procession led from Auschwitz I to Birkenau, and on it they passed the spot where, forty-five
years earlier, little Saleczek had let himself drop, just before his
friend Jurek was killed a few yards further on. They might well have
kissed or embraced or perhaps just gazed into each other's eyes on
this very spot, but Salomon Pucher was never to find out. Instead,
his secretary told him two months later that his daughter had been
pregnant and had had an abortion a couple of days ago. The
secretary—a Russian Jew with whom Salomon slept in the office
now and again—had heard it from Frau Gurjewitsch, who had heard
it from Frau Lachs, who had heard it from her daughter, who had
been told by Rena Blum, who in turn was the best friend of Jael's
best friend.

So nothing could stop Salomon Pucher from calling on his daughter's violator (who had been getting on his nerves for a while with
clever-dick remarks, and whose report from Poland had proved once
and for all what a bad Jew he was) in the middle of the night,
slapping him twice in the face, and telling him three times to leave
Jael alone and never enter his house again. Henry, though at first
scared by Pucher's furious appearance, listened respectfully to the

reproaches of the enraged father. Henry made no attempt to justify himself, because Salomon Pucher would in any case never have believed that Henry would a thousand times sooner have inflicted the horror of abortion on his own body than on the desperate Jael, who wanted the child. Henry realized, humbly and submissively, that he had done wrong. He punished himself by ceasing to sleep with Jael after Pucher's midnight visit, and this temporarily lightened his bad conscience, while Jael suffered even more from sudden celibacy than from the after-effects of the operation. She couldn't understand Henry's behaviour, she was suddenly afraid she was too young for him, for his cares and troubles, and for that very reason she didn't even try to resist his decision.

Jael and Henry stayed together, despite the paternal prohibition. Although they hadn't slept together for over six months, they wanted to get married on Jael's eighteenth birthday. They often talked about children, apparently forgetting that these had somehow to be engendered. Only apparently: at night Jael dreamed about Henry, about erections like trees; while Henry in his sleep kept seeing a single dreadful image of himself in a white cubicle, having to masturbate into a test-tube. They would then tell each other their dreams, and this excited them, and so they talked more and more often about their wedding night, when they would not lose their innocence but regain it, the innocence of their wild Polish beginnings. Day after day they strolled through the Fressgasse, and when they were tired of talking about their future sexual adventures, they would stop and kiss. Their behaviour in public was talked about, and so it was soon part of the regular morning ritual in the Pucher estate agency at 27 Bockenheimer Landstrasse that Larissa, even before massaging her boss's testicles, would say: 'They've been seen at it again... The whole street is talking...' This went on for a couple of weeks, until Salomon Pucher lost patience for a second time and again showed up in Henry's flat in the middle of the night, but this time Henry was anything but quiet. His voice cracking with excitement, Henry declared that he wanted to marry Jael and absolutely nothing would make him change his mind. After he said this, Pucher looked at him in silence. Then his face went as white as the sky over Poland, his eyelids dropped, and Salomon Pucher lay down crosswise on the floor. His fainting-fit lasted for less than a minute. When Pucher regained consciousness, he knocked the glass of water that

Henry was going to give him out of his hand and said: 'Four hundred thousand.' Henry's eyebrows shot upwards. 'I'm going to marry Jael,' he said. 'Then you won't get a penny, not even for the wedding,' said Pucher. Henry sat down beside him on the floor. 'I'm marrying her,' he repeated. 'Five hundred thousand.' 'I won't be bought!' 'You're not getting more than five hundred thousand, you bastard.' Henry stood up. 'Herr Salomon Pucher,' he said, 'leave my house.' Pucher got up likewise and went slowly towards the door. 'Six hundred,' he said. 'Out!' cried Henry, with his nose touching Pucher's chin. 'Out!' Pucher opened the door, took a step outside, then turned round once more and whispered: 'Six hundred and fifty... ' Henry slammed the door behind him with the whole force of his young body, but then Pucher heard the journalist's hesitant voice saying somewhat indistinctly through the door: 'Million?' 'What?' 'A million!' Pucher thought it over quickly and said: 'Okay.' Then the light went out on the stairs.

Pucher and Henry both stood by their bargain. Henry broke with Jael, and of course she never found out why he had suddenly stopped loving her. Salomon Pucher had the agreed sum transferred to Henry—it first arrived in his savings account and was later increased many times over. So you might say that the two men had concluded a business deal which differed from other deals only in the kind of goods that were disposed of, and, as must always be the case, each gained and at the same time lost something... But there was no zealot dwelling in their breasts—only a dirty little inferiority complex.

Soon we'll all be dead for the second time. But then for real. Dead, dead, dead.

KATJA BEHRENS
Everything Normal

Katja Behrens was born in Berlin in 1942 and has spent most of her life in Germany apart from two years in Israel (1968–70) and extended visits to India and North and South America. She has translated American novels by William Burroughs and Henry Miller into German and has been a freelance writer since 1978, when she published her first collection of short stories, *The White Woman*. Her fiction deals especially with single women or relationships between mothers and daughters and with the persistence of patterns of thought and behaviour down the generations. She has won numerous literary prizes.

Behrens first wrote about Jewish experience in her only novel, *The Thirteenth Fairy* (1983), which focuses on three Jewish or half-Jewish women—a grandmother, her daughter, and her granddaughter—who survived the Third Reich by pretending to be Aryan Germans and are still haunted by the trauma of the past while living in post-war West Germany. The Jewish identity that Behrens expresses is largely negative. It consists, not in religious practice or cultural traditions, but in the indelible memory of the Holocaust. It makes Behrens's protagonists angry and uneasy in Germany among people who want to suppress the past, but it is not strong enough to make commitment to Israel a realistic alternative.

Behrens's story, 'Everything Normal', with a strong autobiographical tinge, exposes many facets of the problem of facing the past. The protagonist is ill at ease in Germany. Israel does not seem to be an alternative: her two years there are passed over hastily. She feels anti-Semitism lurking everywhere. She notes how insensitively people indicate exhaustion by the phrase 'bis zur Vergasung' (literally 'till I'm gassed'; figuratively 'till I'm burned out, till I'm blue in the face'). Revisiting her old teacher, an anti-Semite, she realizes that he comes from Silesia (now part of Poland), so probably resents the loss of German territory, and that his spell in the territorial militia (not even the regular army) has laid the foundations for a militaristic fantasy-life. Her story confronts two groups of people, the one traumatized by the past, the other fixated on it through their very attempts to ignore it.

I've been all over the world and yet never got rid of this feeling that I have to dive out of sight. No encouragement helps: 'I've nothing to hide, haven't had for ages, I can show my face.'

We could show our faces too when I was small. It was just that nobody must know *what* we were. Something really bad. I didn't know what the bad thing was, just that we weren't like the other people in the village where we survived. I could feel that we didn't belong even before I had learnt to speak, a charming, sing-song dialect with a heavily rolled *r*.

After my return to the country where we should have been gassed, I forgot the dialect. I kept the sense of not belonging.

Something still wasn't right about us. Despite prayer: 'I'm a child... keep my heart pure... no one but Jesus.' Despite badminton and friends, Heidi and Toxi, 'I'd so much like to go home, ai-ai-ai, I'd like to see my home again', despite *Winnetou** and dancing-class, petticoats and Harry Belafonte. Like all the others. But the others didn't have to fight with people I can't remember, I've forgotten their names, their faces, everything. Just that it was about the millions, whether it was six or not. I fought wildly, but my violence didn't help. They wouldn't be convinced.

It was a long time before I grasped that talking is no use. After all, I thought, they were human. They must feel. Feel compassion. Feel horror. But they didn't. It wasn't six million, they said, and I said, it doesn't matter, even if it was only four million—and they said: but that does make a difference; they talked like accountants.

It's part of my inheritance, like my freckles, my stubbornness, and my nose. I know that now. But at that time I thought I could somehow annul it, mother staying there and keeping her head down, taking off her glasses outside the door of some office with the Führer's picture above the desk, unable to see but taking off her glasses 'because they emphasize the Jewish element'. I thought I could make up for our lost emigration, standing in for those who stayed, as it were, standing in for them and with retroactive effect, because it wasn't necessary any longer, at least not a matter of survival, it was only at the dancing-class that they 'came for you', and mother got a reparation,* as they call it, even though she still kept her eyes on the ground, no question of walking upright. Head down till the end, lower and lower, whether from shame at her nose or shame at having survived, that was her secret.

To make up for our lost emigration and at last to be no longer surrounded by people who justified the past, people who kept quiet, turned the tables, had nothing to do with it, wanted to forget all about it, no longer in the place where people do things till they're 'burned out', buttering bread, counting, playing the flute 'till you're burned out', not just 'people', but also those who are honest, concerned, well-intentioned, friends, and even your own brain keep parroting these words, and only your mouth can be stopped from saying them out loud. Heard so often, since I was tiny, as long as I can think, already meaningless. Meaningless, but normal.

What do you expect, that's perfectly normal, said my friend. But got angry at the pictures of piles of corpses in a colour magazine. It was the fifties. Children might see that, said my friend. As if these naked, murdered people were something disgusting from which the child's soul had to be protected.

I sensed that my friend's mother, who was a perfectly normal woman, was speaking through her mouth.

It's time to leave the past in peace, agreed her husband.

That was perfectly normal then, most people thought that way.

We were the ones who weren't normal, in our normal town, in our normal street, inhabited by normal people.

For example, there was an ordinary, well-respected man, who never drew attention to himself, but in our house he was said to have 'a skeleton in his cupboard'. I was not sure how to imagine this 'skeleton in his cupboard'.

The man lived with his family in a handsome old villa on the hill.

Under a false name, said my mother. Everyone knows that.

His daughter's birthday parties were always something very special. Once I was invited. The man danced with me. It was the first time a man danced with me. I think he was a tailor. His suit was made of fine cloth. That made an impression on me. Nothing else. A normal man. The only thing special about him was that he was master in this handsome villa. I couldn't be afraid of him. And he probably thought nothing of holding a girl in his arms whom, as a baby, he might have smashed against the wall. Or thrown her alive into a pit to follow her dead mother. That was past, it was work, dirty work, but it had to be done.

A nice man. He showed me the steps, shuffle or foxtrot. I was clumsy, trod on his toes, felt ashamed. I was constantly ashamed about something in those days, in the fifties, when everybody was normal except me. Now I know that that too is normal: those who get kicked feel ashamed afterwards, not those who kick them.

Some time in the first few months after we moved in to the street of normal people, a strange woman rang our bell. Wanted to come up for a moment. Just like that. To see someone who'd been in a concentration camp. Normal curiosity. It was a rumour going round in the street. Would have been perfectly normal, if we had been in a camp. Mother denied it as if it were disgraceful. She ought to have realized by then that there was no chance of being a normal person. Yet she kept enthusing about a nose job. An operation that would bring the delights of normality. If not for her, then at least for me.

When she at last got her 'reparation pension', she wanted to use it to buy me a snub nose. I decided to do without the snub nose and emigrated to the land of noses.

I stayed for two years and came back.

Nothing had changed.

They're educated. They're progressive. They're terribly nice. We took part in a peace vigil and an Easter march.

And then suddenly you hear a sentence like—

'But they like business. You must admit it. It's in their blood.'

—or a silence. A word that recalls persecution, expulsion, and extermination, and at once an embarrassed silence spreads among people who have just been close to me, a silence that tells me: now you've put your foot in it. In the stillness the gap between us becomes apparent.

It keeps on showing. At a smart dinner in town or on a mild summer evening with wine and olives.

Chirping of cicadas, a conversation about music. The man was about my age. A German church musician, sensitive. Had had a bit to drink.

'To get anywhere in music,' he said, 'you've got to be either a Jew or a queer.'

I saw the blue veins throbbing under his temples and thought I had heard wrong.

'Oh yes, they're back wherever you look, occupying all the key positions. What? All gassed? Not at all. Help each other to get the best jobs. I'm telling you.'

I saw the blue veins under his alabaster skin.

Since emigration hadn't helped, I had a go at confronting the past.

'Let's leave the past in peace,' said my old form teacher when I called on him or rather sought him out.

He was still teaching at the same school. Grey-haired. Otherwise his old self. His hair combed smoothly back. His too small, upturned nose. His sardonic eyebrows.

I had rung up and been astonished that his voice sounded as if he were human, just human, a perfectly normal human being. What I remembered had left no trace in this voice.

The stairs smelt of cleaning fluid. I saw him at the door, which was open a crack, saw his outstretched hand, and for a moment things were just as in the past.

Then I noticed that something had changed.

There was no finger pointing scornfully at me. Only the question whether I had had a good journey, and no reference to my nose.

His invisible wife had laid the table for coffee. He was sitting opposite me in waistcoat and slippers.

I had never seen the coffee-cups on his table in anyone else's home. Except mine. For years I had drunk my breakfast coffee out of cups like these, eaten my bread from these plates. I couldn't accept the idea that I had something in common with that swine.

There was a piano in the room. The lid was down. There were no scores lying about on it. There was nothing lying about. No books, no newspapers, no knitting, no evidence of life. Everything was clean and tidy. The silent piano was polished till it shone.

I asked where he was born.

'In Silesia,' he said.

Had he been a soldier, I asked.

His waistcoat and slippers didn't match the dash with which he rattled off the number of his territorial battalion, as though he'd forgotten that it was me sitting opposite him, his former pupil, a left-over national pest* whom he had done his best to render harmless and who had now sought him out in the hope of liberation. It was a long number, it sounded like a pistol-shot, almost half a century since he had last stood to attention.

'Let's leave the past in peace,' he quoted his former teacher. 'We now have to look to the future.'

Did he still tell his pupils that Hitler built the autobahns, I asked.
He threatened to break off the conversation.

We were silent. I looked out of the window. There was washing hanging up on the balcony. My old teacher tapped his foot impatiently.

I didn't give up. But there was nothing to be done.

'... I'm afraid I must ask you to leave.'

I handed him the pencil he had lent me. After drinking coffee I had rummaged in my handbag and found nothing to write with. I had unpacked my handbag item by item and still not found a pencil. With my purse, lipstick, and powder-box on my lap, I had felt strangely naked.

He helped me into my coat and wished me a good journey home.

On the way back I felt I had been a long way away. I entered my flat and was surprised that I had a home. I recognized my furniture like something you've forgotten owning.

It was no liberation. He was stronger than I was. For him the past is at rest. He looked as though he slept soundly. They all sleep soundly. They have nothing to fear. That too seems to be normal.

EXPLANATORY NOTES

MENDELSSOHN

40 *opposed to it*: Mendelssohn was wrong in saying that Judaism never sought converts: it did under the Roman Empire and in the early Middle Ages; indeed, the anti-Jewish animus of some Christian preachers may well result from the Jews' success as competitors.

religion of the patriarchs: in a footnote Mendelssohn here refers to the Noahide laws which express the natural obligations binding on non-Jews: the avoidance of idolatry, blasphemy, bloodshed, incest, theft, injustice, and eating live animals.

41 *Confucius or a Solon*: 'Confucius' is the Latin form of the Chinese sage Kung Fu-tsu (551–479 BC); Solon was the ancient legislator of Athens (c.638–558 BC). Both are cited here as supreme examples of natural virtue unaided by revelation.

Marmontel: Jean-François Marmontel (1723–99) pleaded for the civil toleration of Protestants in Chapter 15 of *Bélisaire* (1767) and got into trouble with the French religious authorities.

44 *Essai de Psychologie*: an earlier work by Bonnet (1755).

MAIMON

47 *Quis desiderio . . . capitis*: Horace, *Odes*, i. 24: 'When somebody as dear as he is dead, Grief must be huge and uninhibited' (James Michie's translation).

48 *Wolff–Leibniz system:* Gottfried Wilhelm von Leibniz (1646–1716) advanced an optimistic and rationalist theory of the universe which was developed and popularized by Christian Wolff (1679–1754) and became the standard world-view of the early German Enlightenment.

49 *esprit de bagatelle*: frivolity.

50 *Maimonides*: or Rabbi Moses ben Maimon (1135–1204), born in Spain, left it in his boyhood, settled in Egypt, and presently became leader of the Jewish community there; he sought to show that the philosophy of Aristotle (transmitted through Arabic translations) was compatible with traditional Jewish teaching, both in his codification of the Law and in his *Guide for the Perplexed*, a treatise demonstrating the harmony between the Scriptures and reason.

51 *Menasse Ben Israel*: in 1782 Mendelssohn published a German translation of the pamphlet *Vindiciae Judaeorum* (*Vindication of the Jews*, 1656) by Menasse ben Israel, written originally to support the Jews' readmission to Britain; he added a preface in which he advocated civil rights for Jews in Germany.

51 *Jerusalem*: *Jerusalem, or On Religious Power and Judaism* (1783), a treatise in which Mendelssohn set forth his understanding of Judaism as being not a revealed religion (hence not a rival to Christianity) but a 'revealed legislation' in which God had disclosed laws that were eternally binding on Jews.

53 *malgré lui*: 'despite himself', 'unknown to himself'.

displayed to the public: the philosopher Friedrich Heinrich Jacobi (1743–1819) published in 1785 a series of letters entitled *On the Teaching of Spinoza* and addressed to Mendelssohn, in which he claimed that towards the end of his life Lessing had inclined to the pantheism of Spinoza. Since Baruch de Spinoza (1632–77) had been excommunicated by the Jews of Amsterdam for maintaining that God was identical with Nature, Mendelssohn was gravely embarrassed at being associated with these claims.

Jakob: Ludwig Heinrich Jakob, a follower of Kant, published in 1786 a reply to *Morning Hours* (1785), the treatise in which Mendelssohn attempted a systematic proof of the existence of God.

LEVIN AND VEIT

57 *female*: Rahel uses the disparaging word for a woman, *Frauenzimmer*.

raison: 'good sense'; Rahel breaks into French when polite behaviour is under discussion.

Mrs Veit: Henriette ('Jettchen') Mendelssohn and her sister Dorothea Veit, daughters of Moses Mendelssohn. Dorothea was at this time married to David Veit's uncle Simon, but was divorced from him in 1798, becoming the lover and then the wife of the Romantic critic Friedrich Schlegel.

58 *schlemiel*: person who suffers from bad luck.

'. . . *at my roots*': a quotation from Goethe's play *Egmont* (first published in 1788), implying that Rahel identifies with the hero who is imprisoned and facing execution for championing the cause of Dutch liberty against the Spanish oppressors.

59 *Markus and his wife*: Markus Levin, Rahel's brother, who ran the family firm after their father's death in 1790, and his wife Henriette (the sister-in-law mentioned on p. 56). Markus was a reluctant businessman whose frustrated literary talents are evinced by an unpublished comedy he wrote for private performance.

60 '. . . *talks nonsense*': another reference to *Egmont*, this time to the subordinate role allotted to the hero's lover Klärchen.

vous sentez bien: you understand.

'. . . *the earth-born giant*': yet another quotation from the prison scene in *Egmont*.

62 *encore un coup, mon cher ami*: 'once more, my dear friend'.

esprit de faction et de corps: factional and party spirit.

BÖRNE AND HEINE

69 *Hundt-Radowsky*: Hartwig Hundt-Radowsky, an early anti-Semitic author, published in 1820 a polemical account of the Jews entitled *The Jews' Mirror*.

70 *sole*: cf. *The Merchant of Venice*, IV. i. 123–4: 'Not on thy sole, but on thy soul, harsh Jew, | Thou mak'st thy knife keen.'

72 *roquelaures*: a man's knee-length coat with a cape collar, named after the Duc de Roquelaure (1656–1738).

Sultan Mahmud: Mahmud II, Emperor of Turkey 1808–39.

Austrian Observer: a notably conservative newspaper.

Greeks: the Greek struggle for independence from Turkish rule began with Prince Alexander Ypsilanti's unsuccessful rising in 1821, and attracted European attention when its supporter Byron died at Missolonghi in 1824; Britain, France, and Russia intervened against Turkey and defeated its fleet at the Battle of Navarino in 1827; an independent Greek state was established in 1830.

Cato's: Cato of Utica (95–46 BC), famous for his unbending principles, tried in vain to defend the liberty of the Roman Republic against Julius Caesar and committed suicide rather than submit.

73 *Drury Lane*: the famous London theatre which Heine visited during his four-month stay in England in the summer of 1827.

75 *Franz Horn*: critic and biographer (1781–1837), published an edition of Shakespeare's plays with a commentary in 1823–33. Heine criticizes him elsewhere in the essay for reading too much Christian morality into Shakespeare, and satirizes him in *Atta Troll* by including him in the pagan Wild Hunt, where, clinging to a donkey, he struggles to keep up with Shakespeare's horse.

79 *Cimbri . . . as their slaves*: the Teutons and Cimbri were German tribes defeated by the Roman general Marius at Aquae Sextiae in 102 BC. Heine took the story about their wives seeking refuge with the virginal priestesses of Vesta from the *Facta et dicta memorabilia* (*Memorable Deeds and Sayings*) by Valerius Maximus (first century AD).

spice-dealer: Heine's preface to his book begins as follows: 'I know a good Hamburg Christian who has never been able to accept that our Lord and Saviour was a Jew by birth. He feels a deep anger whenever he has to admit that that man, a pattern of perfection deserving the utmost reverence, nevertheless belonged to the same kindred as the people with long, runny noses whom he sees peddling goods in the street, whom he so utterly despises, and whom he detests even more when they, like him, start dealing in spices and dyes, and thus injure his own interests.

'I feel about William Shakespeare just as this worthy son of Hammonia feels about Jesus Christ. It depresses me to think that, after all, he was an Englishman and a member of the most repulsive nation that God created in His wrath.'

79 *Josephus*: Flavius Josephus (AD 37–*c*.100), Jewish statesman and historian whose works include the *History of the Jewish War*, culminating in the fall of Jerusalem to the Emperor Titus in AD 70.

80 *letter*: probably written by Heine himself.

San Domingo: Caribbean island (now divided between Haiti and the Dominican Republic) where in 1803, inspired by the French Revolution, the slaves under Jean-Jacques Dessalines and Toussaint l'Ouverture rose in revolt against the French colonists.

'. . . *les blancs*': 'the whites killed him, let's kill all the whites.'

HEINE

84 *. . . O Jerusalem*: from Psalm 137: 5–6.

Jehuda ben Halevy: Judah Halevi (*c*.1075–1141) was born in Tudela (not Toledo, as Heine says), and spent his early life as a physician in Toledo, the capital of Castile in the Christian part of Spain, but violence against Jews made him move to Cordoba in the Muslim part and thence to the Holy Land. He wrote over a thousand poems, with the longing for Zion his favourite theme.

85 *the Torah*: the first five books (the Pentateuch) of the Old Testament, seen as the repository of the Jewish Law.

Tropp: The melody used in reading the Torah aloud, following the accents with which some texts were provided.

Shalsheleth: Hebrew for 'chain'.

Onkelos's Targum: in the Diaspora, the Aramaic-speaking Jews of Palestine no longer understood Hebrew, so the Torah was translated by the scholar Onkelos into Aramaic. 'Targum' is Aramaic for 'translation'.

86 *Halacha*: the part of the Talmud (the body of commentary on the Torah) which consists of legal discussion.

Kuzari: Halevi wrote *The Book of Argument and Proof in Defence of the Despised Faith*, later known as *The Book of the Kuzari*, an imaginary dialogue between a Jewish scholar and the King of the Khazars, who had adopted Judaism in the eighth century.

Haggada: the part of the Talmud consisting of moral instruction illustrated by stories and fables.

Babylonia: Much of the Talmud was written in Babylon by Jews exiled there.

Semiramis' great garden: legendary queen of Assyria who was supposed to have founded Babylon and established its hanging gardens, which were among the seven wonders of the ancient world.

88 *Gaia scienza*: 'Gay science', the troubadour poetry of medieval Europe.

89 ... *weeping willow*: Psalm 137: 1–2.

boils: Job was smitten with boils (Job 2: 7), conflated with the Gospel story of the beggar Lazarus (Luke 16: 20–1).

90 ... *against the stones*: Psalm 137: 9.

Western–Eastern: allusion to Goethe's collection of poems, modelled on Persian poetry, the *West–Eastern Divan* (1819).

sirventes ... ghazels: *sirventes*: poems addressed to a feudal lord (Old Provençal); *madrigal*: an Italian lyric poem; *terzina*: a three-line verse; *canzonet*: a humorous poem or song, popular in Italian literature from the fifteenth to the eighteenth centuries; *ghazel* (from Arabic *ghazal*, love poem), a poem originating from Persian literature in which the same rhyme is used in the first two and then in all other even lines. By crediting Jehuda with Western and Eastern metres Heine makes him a 'west–eastern' figure, like himself and Goethe.

91 *Poitou ... Roussillon*: districts of southern France where medieval troubadour poetry flourished.

Laura: the beloved of the Italian poet Petrarch (1304–74), who first saw her in a church in Avignon on 6 April 1327 (widely but wrongly supposed to have been Good Friday).

92 *rejuvenation*: the beard turning black again identifies him as the Wandering Jew, who appears elsewhere in Heine (*The Town of Lucca*).

pilgrim: this pilgrim's white beard, turning black again at the tip, identifies him as the Wandering Jew, who for insulting Christ on His way to Golgotha was condemned to wander the earth until the Second Coming, and hence as an archetype of the Jewish destiny. Heine also introduces him into *The Town of Lucca*, chapter 13.

93 *Ab*: the ninth of Ab (late July, early August) is the anniversary of the destruction of Jerusalem in 586 BC by Nebuchadnezzar and in AD 70 by Titus, son and successor of the Roman Emperor Vespasian.

Rudel: the twelfth-century troubadour Jaufré Rudel, *vidame* (lord) of Blaye in southern France, was said in legend to have fallen in love with the Lady of Tripoli without seeing her, to have sailed to Tripoli, fallen ill aboard ship, and died in her arms. See Heine's poem 'Geoffrey Rudel and Melisande of Tripoli', also in *Romanzero*.

94 *battle of Arbela*: as Heine knew from reading Plutarch's *Life of Alexander*, Alexander the Great defeated King Darius of Persia in 331 BC at Arbela in what is now northern Iraq.

95 *Cyrus*: (d. 528 BC), founder of the Persian Empire which was defeated under Darius.

95 *Queen Atossa*: Herodotus tells in Book 3 of his *Histories* how Atossa, daughter of Cyrus, married her brother Cambyses, who murdered his own brother Smerdis as a potential rival; but while Cambyses was away campaigning, an impostor, the 'bogus Smerdis', took his place for several months.

Thaïs: A famous prostitute who accompanied Alexander on his campaign and persuaded him to burn the Persian palace in Persepolis as revenge for the Persians' destruction of Athens two centuries earlier.

96 *Memphis*: the ancient capital of Egypt.

... *Antony*: Cleopatra (69–31 BC) was said by ancient historians to have been so extravagant that once, to win a bet from her lover Mark Antony, she drank a pearl that had been melted in vinegar.

Omayyads: the dynasty of Caliphs who ruled the Muslim empire from 661 to 750.

Caliph in Cordova: Abd-er-Rahman III, the first Omayyad ruler of Spain, who assumed the title of Caliph in 929.

97 *auto-da-fés*: public burnings of heretics and Jews condemned by the Spanish Inquisition.

Mendizábal: Juan Alvares Mendizábal (1790–1853), Spanish liberal politician of Jewish extraction who became finance minister of Spain in 1836; 'son of Satan' is what anti-Semites would have called him.

Madame Solomon, the baroness: The wife of a Jewish banker who has been ennobled and is received at the French Court; not necessarily a specific person, but an illustration of Jewish finance dominating the modern world.

101 *'L'khah dodi likras kallah'*: 'Come, my soul, to meet the bride', a synagogue hymn for Sabbath evening, written not by Judah Halevi but by the sixteenth-century poet Solomon Halevi Alkabets.

102 *Marquis*: A famous Paris sweetshop.

Merovingian shadow-monarchs: The Merovingians were the kings of France from the fifth to the eighth centuries; they were increasingly overshadowed by the Mayors of the Palace.

103 *Solomon Gabirol*: (c.1021–55), poet born in Malaga who lived mainly in Saragossa; his work includes love poems, personal reflections, and a large-scale work in verse alternating with rhythmic prose, *The Kingly Crown*.

Moses ibn Ezra: (c.1055–1135), another poet of the Spanish school, born in Granada, famous for his sensual love poems and also for his treatise on poetics, *The Book of Conversations and Memories*.

Alcharisi: Judah Alcharisi (c.1170–1235) wrote epigrams and satires, the latter including the *Makamen* which rivalled the famous *Makamat* of the Arabic poet Abu Muhammad al Kasim ibn Ali al Hariri (1054–1122).

105 *Schlemihl*: see note to Levin–Veit Correspondence, p. 58.

Chamisso: Adalbert von Chamisso (1781–1838), a German poet and traveller of French extraction. His story *The Wondrous Tale of Peter Schlemihl* (1814) is about a man who sells his shadow to the Devil.

Hitzig: Julius Eduard Hitzig (1780–1849), a Berlin friend of Heine's, was a lawyer who mixed in literary circles; he wrote a biography of Chamisso and helped Heine to publish his first book. The family name was in fact changed in 1808 by his father, the factory owner and town councillor Elias David Hitzig.

106 ... *it is written*: an invention based on Numbers 25.

FRANZOS

111 *The Robbers*: Schiller's first play (published 1781) tells of strife between two brothers: the villainous Franz deceives their father into disinheriting the debauched but essentially noble Karl, who thereupon revolts against society and founds a band of robbers; while he tries to help the poor against the rich, his followers commit such atrocities as attacking a convent and raping the nuns.

112 *birth*: Schiller was born on 10 November 1759, and Franzos's story was first published on 10 November 1875.

Schiller loved Laura: Schiller's early love-poem 'Fantasy' is addressed to a fictitious 'Laura', inspired by Petrarch's beloved.

trente ou quarante: a card game in which thirty and forty are respectively winning and losing numbers.

Homburg: a spa town near Frankfurt, with a casino.

115 *Paul de Kock*: (1793–1871), immensely popular French author of sometimes sentimental, sometimes titillating novels.

goblet: in Goethe's song 'There was a King in Thule', the King treasures a goblet which was given him by his lover, and weeps whenever he drinks from it.

117 '... *stream of light!*': the last lines of Schiller's long philosophical poem 'The Artists' (1789), which celebrates artists, even if they are neglected in their own time, as 'the freest mother's freest sons', guardians of human dignity, and prophets of the future.

Greiner: a printing firm based in Stuttgart which specialized in pamphlets and cheap editions.

'*Sustine et abstine*': 'sustain and abstain'.

Lemberg: now Lviv in the Ukraine, then the capital of Galicia, the north-easternmost province of the Austrian Empire.

118 *Justinian's Institutions*: an elementary textbook of legal institutions compiled in AD 533 as part of the Code of Justinian, the collection of laws sponsored by the Byzantine Emperor Justinian I (483–565).

SAAR

123 *'. . . faded fronds'*: from no. 9 of the *Waldlieder* (Forest Songs) by Nikolaus Lenau (1802–50), a Hungarian aristocrat and late-Romantic poet and dramatist in German, famous for his expressions of *Weltschmerz* (cosmic pain).

124 *'the diphthong au as if it were o'*: a feature of the German spoken by Eastern European Jews. In his anti-Zionist pamphlet *A Crown for Zion*, Karl Kraus reports a Jew from Tarnopol in Galicia saying woefully: 'Sie brochen uns nicht!' ('They [i.e. the Gentiles] don't need us', where German requires 'brauchen'), and adds: 'I suspect the entire Jewish question depends on this vowel,' meaning that Jews' conspicuously non-standard German was the main obstacle to their assimilation.

collier grec: a short beard running round his face to meet his hair.

126 *Graz*: an important provincial town, the capital of Styria, in the south-east of present-day Austria.

127 *Norma*: opera (1831) by Vincenzo Bellini (1801–35), turning on doomed love between members of two hostile nations, Gauls and Romans; it was admired by Saar's mentor Schopenhauer and cited in *The World as Will and Representation* as an exemplary tragedy.

129 *tarock*: a card-game for three players, played with a mixed pack of fifty-four cards, comprising thirty-two standard cards (here called 'colours') and twenty-two tarot cards which count as permanent trumps.

134 *Astrakhan*: port at the mouth of the Volga on the Caspian Sea, where the sturgeon are caught whose roe is served as caviar.

Hasid: a devotee of Hasidism, the eighteenth-century revival movement within Galician and Ukrainian Judaism, which, by the nineteenth century, usually implied strict Orthodox practice.

135 *cut off . . . hair*: a married woman in an Orthodox community was obliged to have her hair cut off and wear a wig.

136 *'Recha or Gonovril'*: Hirsch's mistake for Shakespeare's Regan and Goneril; 'Recha', a familiar form of Rachel, is also the name of the Jewish heroine in Lessing's *Nathan the Wise* (1779). He goes on to confuse Ophelia (from *Hamlet*) with Cordelia.

1848: although the 1848 revolutions in Vienna, Prague, and Budapest were suppressed, the Austrian constitution of March 1849 made civil and political rights independent of religious denomination and gave Jews freedom to acquire landed property.

untam: clumsy lout (Viennese dialect, derived from Yiddish).

137 *schlemiel*: see note to Levin–Veit correspondence, p. 58.

puszta: the Hungarian plain.

140 *gulden*: the basic Austrian coin until its replacement by the krone (crown) in 1892 when Austria adopted the gold standard. It was divided into 100

kreuzer. Twelve gulden corresponded roughly to a pound sterling.

142 *Hietzing*: an elegant suburb on the western edge of Vienna.

145 *pofel*: inferior goods (Viennese dialect, from Yiddish).

146 *in nuce*: in a nutshell; on a smaller scale.

HERZL

148 *de Lesseps*: Ferdinand de Lesseps, the builder of the Suez Canal.

scandalous episode: the French Panama Canal Company, headed by de Lesseps, attracted thousands of small investors, but ran out of money in 1889; an investigation discovered that much of the money had been misappropriated, and many of the culprits, including de Lesseps, were imprisoned. Since some were Jews, the Panama scandal encouraged the anti-Semitism which found an outlet in the Dreyfus affair.

149 *Shivah*: the seven-day period of mourning, during which the mourners sit on low stools and do not bathe, shave, or work.

Verbindung: a student society with elaborate drinking and duelling rituals; membership was signified by wearing a distinctive cap.

Burgtheater: the main theatre in Vienna, founded in 1776.

150 *Tannhäuser*: opera by Wagner, first performed in 1845.

151 *Nordau*: Max Nordau (pseudonym of Simon Südfeld, 1849–1923), journalist, playwright, and cultural critic, best known for *Degeneration* (1892–3), who worked closely with Herzl in the Zionist movement.

MANN

156 *boiserie*: wood-panelling.

160 *Parsifal*: the hero of the medieval romance by Wolfram von Eschenbach, *Parzival* (c.1210), and of Wagner's opera *Parsifal* (1882). Brought up in the forest, he appears a simpleton or holy fool.

161 *'Here's Rhodes ... dance!'*: an ancient Greek anecdote, transmitted by Aesop, Erasmus, and Goethe, tells of a man who returned from a visit to Rhodes boasting how he had jumped across the harbour, and received the sceptical answer: 'This is Rhodes; show us how you can jump here.'

162 *belladonna powder*: a stimulant derived from deadly nightshade.

SCHOLEM

187 *'. . . generations'*: quoted from an article by Martin Buber in the *Jüdische Rundschau (Jewish Review)*, Jan. 1910.

188 *'. . . homeless down below'*: from David Friedrich Strauss, *The Old and the New Faith* (1872), a profession of Darwinian atheism by a theologian who had become famous with his sceptical *Life of Jesus* (1835–6).

189 *swallow them up*: cf. Revelations 6: 16; Numbers 16: 32.

190 *Tetragrammaton*: the name of God, composed of the four consonants YHWH (Yahweh, Jehovah).

'. . . *my rest?*': Isaiah 66: 1.

191 . . . *voice of God*: Genesis 3: 8.

Enoch: the Hebrew Apocalypse of Enoch says that Enoch (Genesis 5: 21–4) had 365,000 eyes and seventy-two wings.

192 *Moses*: tradition says that Moses died gently from God's kiss.

193 *Grenadierstrasse*: a street in the poor quarter of Berlin (the Scheunenviertel) inhabited by Jewish immigrants from Eastern Europe, like Whitechapel in London or the Lower East Side in New York.

Kishinev: now Chisinau in Moldova; scene of a notorious pogrom in 1903.

'. . . *holy ground*': Exodus 3: 5.

194 *(Heine)*: quotation from Heine's poem 'Jehuda ben Halevy': see p. 88 above.

Herzl: see the introduction to his 'Autobiography', p. 147.

Mizraim: (Hebrew) Egypt.

Moses da Leon: a Kabbalist (*c.*1240–1305), formerly thought to be the author of the *Zohar*.

Israel ben Eliezer: (*c.*1700–60), also known as the Baal Shem (Master of the Name), the founder of Hasidism.

Old–New Land: Altneuland (1902), Herzl's utopian novel about a future Jewish state.

BEER-HOFMANN

214 *Babel, Mizraim*: Babylon and Egypt.

LASKER- SCHÜLER

225 *month of Gam*: an invention, perhaps suggested by the summer months Tammuz and Av in the Jewish calendar; the ninth of Av commemorates the destruction of the Temple at Jerusalem in AD 70.

231 [*Hebrew*]: 'There is no understanding the ways of the Eternal One' (the usual version of this formula, common in the Talmud, speaks of 'the Lord'). I owe this information to David Groiser.

ZWEIG

237 *Alserstrasse*: this street, separating Vienna's eighth and ninth districts, runs westward from the centre, and is near the University and the medical school.

heder: traditional Jewish education began with the *heder*, where male and often also female children were taught the Hebrew alphabet and started on the study of the Torah and the Talmud.

238 *Mesmer*: Franz Anton Mesmer (1734–1815), Austrian physician, who practised hypnotism for curative purposes, a technique called 'mesmerism' after him.

239 *parch*: unpleasant person (Yiddish; literally 'baldhead').

Gassner . . . Blavatsky: Johann Joseph Gassner (1727–79) professed to cure sick people by exorcising devils; he gained a great following, and was made chaplain to the Bishop of Regensburg. His activities provoked scores of pamphlets for and against him. Helena Petrovna Blavatsky (1831–91) founded the Theosophical Society in 1875 in order to promote the study of spiritualism and Asian religions.

240 *sechel*: intelligence (Yiddish).

'amhorets': (Hebrew) literally, a countryman; hence an ignorant person who has not studied the Torah.

241 *Mezzofanti's . . . Busoni's for music*: Cardinal Giuseppe Mezzofanti (1774–1849), keeper of the Vatican Library, is said to have known over fifty languages and many of their dialects; Emanuel Lasker (1868–1941), chess grandmaster, son of a Jewish cantor; Ferruccio Busoni (1866–1924), pianist and composer, famous for his vast musical and literary erudition.

Buffon: Georges-Louis Leclerc, comte de Buffon (1707–88), classified animals, plants, and inorganic nature in the thirty-six volumes of his *Natural History* (1749–1804).

Neue Freie Presse and the Neues Wiener Tagblatt: two great liberal dailies in Vienna; their mention associates Mendel with the self-confidence of the Vienna liberal bourgeoisie before the First World War.

242 *an imperial*: a small beard just below the lower lip, as worn by Napoleon III.

Eusebius Mandyczewski: (1857 1929), director of the Archive of the Vienna Society of Music-Lovers, a friend of Brahms, editor of Brahms and Schubert, and responsible for the familiar numbering of the Haydn symphonies. I owe this information to Peter Branscombe.

Glossy: Karl Glossy (1848–1937), director of the Vienna City Library, a literary and theatrical historian, who edited many plays by Raimund, Grillparzer, and other Viennese authors.

244 *yingele*: 'lad': Zweig uses a Yiddish word.

Gluck: (1714–87), lived mainly in Vienna: he founded modern opera by his combination of music and drama, first in *Alceste* (1767) and in later works including *Iphigénie en Aulide* (1773) and *Iphigénie en Tauride* (1779).

245 *Joseph*: Exodus 1: 8: 'Now there arose a new king over Egypt, which knew not Joseph.'

247 *Gorlice*: after Russian troops had in autumn 1914 overrun Galicia, on 2 May 1915 German and Austrian troops began a counter-offensive which broke through the Russian lines between Gorlice and Tarnow, north of the Carpathian Mountains, and enabled the Austrians to reconquer Galicia and the Germans to occupy Russian Poland.

Przemysl: a great Austrian fortress in Galicia, near the Russian frontier. Its garrison of over 110,000 men surrendered to the Russians after a four-month siege in March 1915.

250 *Hötzendorf*: Franz Count Conrad von Hötzendorf (1852–1925), Austro-Hungarian Chief of Staff, 1906–11 and 1912–17. Warsaw was captured from the Russians by German and Austrian troops in August 1915.

Komorn: a town in western Hungary, on the Danube between Vienna and Budapest.

251 *Tungus*: Siberian tribesmen.

Araucanians: a warlike tribe in Chile.

252 *miraculum mundi*: wonder of the world.

253 *Pythian*: from Pytho, another name for Delphi, the seat of the famous Greek oracle.

256 *Bibliotheca Germanorum erotica et curiosa*: a nine-volume collection of erotic writing in German (1912–29), edited by Hugo Hayn (1843–1923).

habent sua fata libelli: *Pro captu lectoris habent sua fata libelli*, 'As the reader receives them, so books have their fate'; from the *Carmen heroicum* (Heroic Song) of Terentianus Maurus (3rd century AD).

KRAUS

258 *cyclists*: a standard joke ran: 'The Jews are to blame.' 'No, the cyclists.' 'Why the cyclists?' 'Why the Jews?'

battlefields: an allusion to the advertisement for luxury tours of First World War battlefields, headed 'Unforgettable Impressions' and published by the *Basler Nachrichten* in autumn 1921; Kraus's response can be found in *In These Great Times: A Karl Kraus Reader*, trans. Harry Zohn (Manchester, 1984), pp. 89–93. (Information from Edward Timms.)

259 *a much-travelled nation!*: a quotation from *Faust, Part II*, line 7118 (David Luke's translation).

Horst Wessel Song: the National Socialist anthem written by the early Nazi Horst Wessel (1907–30).

attention: the original has 'müllern', alluding to the gymnastics devised by the Dane J. P. Müller (1866–1938).

Schlageter . . . Johst: the Nazi dramatist Hanns Johst (1890–1978) wrote a play, *Schlageter* (1933), about Albert Leo Schlageter (1894–1923), who was shot resisting the French occupation of the Ruhr and was elevated to martyr status by the National Socialists. Jacques Offenbach (1819–80), the Germano-French composer of operettas, was among Kraus's favourites.

260 *Minister of Propaganda*: Joseph Goebbels (1897–1945), whose physical resemblance to stereotypes of the dark, hunchbacked Jew was the object of much sarcasm.

261 *Kube*: Wilhelm Kube (1887–1943), a German Nazi politician, also a dramatist.

Krems: Austrian town, where on 19 June 1933 Nazis threw hand-grenades at a group of unarmed volunteer policemen who were marching out for a gymnastic exercise. (Information from Edward Timms.)

262 '. . . *sicken*': *Macbeth*, IV. iii. 164–73. Emphasis added by Kraus.

'. . . *a hand accurs'd*': *Macbeth*, III. vi. 48–9.

'. . . *message!*': *Macbeth*, III. vi. 45–7.

263 '. . . *the blind*': *King Lear*, IV. i. 47.

ROTH

266 *versts*: a verst is a Russian measure of length equal to 3,500 feet.

269 *percale*: a light, fine cotton fabric.

271 *kvass*: Russian rye beer.

Saaz: town in northern Bohemia, now Zatec.

Judenburg: town near Graz in Styria.

272 *kasha*: gruel or porridge made from cooked buckwheat.

phylacteries: black leather boxes containing Hebrew texts, attached to straps which orthodox Jews wind round their arms during morning prayers.

275 *Tsarskoye Selo*: town near St Petersburg where Russian imperial palaces, built by Catherine II and Alexander I, are situated.

287 *poods*: Russian weight equivalent to 36 pounds.

CELAN

301 *Ya'akov*: Celan uses the Hebrew form of the name 'Jacob', perhaps taking it from the Bible translation by Martin Buber and Franz Rosenzweig which sought to convey the Hebrew character of the original.

Hetman: title of a Cossack military commander, associating the murder of Jews in Transnistria with the massacres of Ukrainian Jews in 1648 by Cossacks led by the Hetman Khmelnitsky.

Cedar: suggests the cedars of Lebanon (e.g. Ezekiel 27: 5) and also the anthem of the First Zionist Congress, beginning: 'Where the slender cedar kisses the skies.'

Margareta: probably an allusion to 'Margarete' (Gretchen), the heroine

of Goethe's *Faust*, while her 'golden hair' may suggest that of the Lorelei
in a famous early poem by Heine.

302 *Shulamith*: (German 'Sulamith'), the 'girl from Shulam' addressed in the
Song of Songs (6: 13) and described as 'black but comely', hence a
counterpart to the blonde Margareta.

303 *Ruth! Naomi! Miriam!*: not only biblical figures, but also women friends
whom Celan left behind in Romania; the only one of whom much is
known is the actress Ruth Lackner, who in 1942 helped him to hide from
the Germans and escape deportation.

Tenebrae: literally 'darkness'; the Roman Catholic service held in the last
three days of Holy Week, during which the lights in church are extinguished one by one in reference to Matthew 27: 45: 'there was darkness
over all the land.'

Near are we: an inversion of Hölderlin's hymn 'Patmos', which begins:
'Near is the God and hard to grasp.'

clawed into each other: Celan took this phrase (*ineinander verkrallt*) from a
passage in the German translation of Gerald Reitlinger's *The Final Solution* in which Jews suffocating in a gas chamber are so described.

304 *did not praise God*: cf. Psalm 115: 17: 'The dead praise not the Lord,
neither any that go down into silence.'

Stork: the hotel in Zurich, opposite the Minster, where Celan met Nelly
Sachs on 26 May 1960 (Ascension Day).

305 *thousand-word*: this coinage evokes the 'thousand-year Reich' of Nazism.

polygoddedness: *Vielgötterei*, literally 'polytheism', but the translator has
sought a less bland, more barbaric word.

Kaddish: a Jewish prayer for the dead, recited by the surviving child; set
against the polytheism which Nazis sought to revive as the Germanic
religion.

306 *Yizkor*: (Hebrew) 'may he remember'.

gonifs: thieves, from Yiddish; the German *Ganove*, used by Celan, has the
same origin.

Paris emprès Pontoise: François Villon (*c*.1431–after 1463) tells us in one
of his low-life ballads that he was 'born in Paris, near Pontoise'.

To Edom: an early poem by Heine, addressed to the Gentiles; the second
stanza runs in full: 'Now and then only, in dark times, you got into a
strange mood and dyed your pious, loving claws with my blood.'

Jew-patch: the yellow patch of cloth that Jews were obliged to wear in the
later Middle Ages and again from 1941 in Germany.

307 *straight*: cf. Isaiah 40: 4: 'and the crooked shall be made straight.'

Friuli: region in north-eastern Italy; the italicized parts, including '*the
Plague*', are taken from a sixteenth-century soldiers' song.

Envoi: the heading of the final quatrain of Villon's ballads.

rears up: Celan puns on *Baum* (tree) and *sich bäumen* (to rear, rise up, resist), thus introducing his favourite motif of defiance.

Radix, Matrix: (Latin) 'root, womb'.

308 *the field, alone*: cf. Ruth 2: 2–3.

Jesse: cf. the prophecy of the Messiah in Isaiah 11: 1: 'And there shall come forth a shoot out of the stock of Jesse.'

Mandorla: (Italian) 'almond'; also the almond-shaped glory of light with which Renaissance painters surround the figures of the risen Christ or the Virgin Mary.

309 *Löw*: Rabbi Judah Löw ben Bezalel of Prague (1520–1609).

evening door: Felstiner, noting that Celan finished this poem on Yom Kippur (the Day of Atonement) 1961, quotes the prayer for sunset on that day: 'Open the gates to us when the gates are being closed, for the day is about to set.'

BECKER

323 *meschugge*: (Yiddish) crazy.

BILLER

349 *Salek*: like Saleczek, a diminutive of Salomon.

350 *Joint*: the American Jewish Joint Distribution Committee, the largest American-Jewish charitable organization, which did much to help Jewish refugees from 1945 onwards.

351 *Zyklon B*: the gas used in Auschwitz and other extermination camps.

aliyah: 'going up', i.e. emigrating to Israel.

sabra: a Jew born in the territory of Israel.

352 *Fressgasse*: 'Guzzling Alley', the local nickname for the Grosse Bockenheimer Strasse, a Frankfurt street full of delicatessens and smart restaurants.

27 Bockenheimer . . . Hof: Bockenheimer Landstrasse: a street in the business district of Frankfurt, where Pucher's office is situated; *Café Schwille*: a traditional café on that street; *the Frankfurter Hof*: a luxury hotel in the Old Town of Frankfurt.

353 *reparation money*: this scandal occurred in 1988. Nachmann had been head of the Jewish Central Council for nineteen years; at his funeral the Chancellor, Helmut Kohl, delivered a eulogy on him; his embezzlement of reparation money came to light a few weeks later.

355 *Spinoza*: see note to Maimon, p. 53.

356 *Yom ha-Shoah*: Holocaust Remembrance Day, established by the Israeli Knesset in 1953.

BEHRENS

360 *Winnetou*: a novel set in the Wild West by Karl May (1842–1912), an extremely popular author of adventure stories for children.

reparation: *Wiedergutmachung*: Behrens alludes bitterly to the inadequacy of this term (literally 'making good again').

363 *pest*: *Volksschädling*, a barely translatable Nazi term for people regarded as harmful to the nation, equating them with vermin.

ACKNOWLEDGEMENTS

The publisher gratefully acknowledges permission to reproduce the following copyright material:

Jurek Becker: 'Die Mauer' from *Nach der ersten Zukunft: Erzählungen*, copyright © Suhrkamp Verlag, Frankfurt am Main, 1980, translated from the German as 'The Wall' by Ritchie Robertson, translation copyright © Ritchie Robertson 1999, by permission of Suhrkamp Verlag.

Richard Beer-Hofmann: final scene from *Jaákobs Traum* (1919), from *Grosse Richard Beer-Hofmann-Ausgabe* (6 volumes), edited by Günter Helmes, Michael M. Schardt, and Andreas Thomasberger, v: *Die Historie von König David und andere dramatische Entwürfe*, edited with an introduction by Norbert Otto Eke (Paderborn, 1996), translated as *Jacob's Dream* by Ritchie Robertson, translation copyright © Ritchie Robertson 1999, by permission of Dr Andreas Thomasberger.

Katja Behrens: 'Alles Normal' from *Salomo und die anderen: Jüdische Geschichten*, copyright © 1993 S. Fischer Verlag GmbH, Frankfurt am Main, translated from the German as 'Everything Normal' by Ritchie Robertson, translation copyright © Ritchie Robertson 1999, by permission of S. Fischer Verlag.

Maxim Biller: 'Roboter' from *Wenn ich einmal reich und tot bin* (Kiepenheuer & Witsch Verlag, 1990), translated from the German as 'Robots' by Ritchie Robertson, translation copyright © Ritchie Robertson 1999, by permission of the Tanja Howarth Literary Agency on behalf of Kiepenheuer & Witsch.

Paul Celan: selected poems translated by John Felstiner, reproduced by permission of John Felstiner.

Franz Fühmann: 'Das Judenauto' from *Das Judenauto. Kabelkran und Blauer Peter. Zweiundzwanzig Tage oder Die Hälfte des Lebens*, copyright © Hinstorff Verlag, Rostock, 1979, translated from the German as 'The Jews' Car' by Ritchie Robertson, translation copyright © Ritchie Robertson 1999, by permission of Hinstorff Verlag.

Heinrich Heine: 'Jehuda ben Halevy' from *The Complete Poems of Heinrich Heine: A Modern English Version* by Hal Draper (OUP, 1982).

Franz Kafka: 'Jackals and Arabs' ('Schakale und Araber', 1919) from *The Transformation and Other Stories*, translated by Malcolm Pasley (Penguin Classics, 1992). Copyright © Malcolm Pasley, 1992, by permission of Penguin Books Ltd.

Karl Kraus: extracts from *Dritte Walpurgisnacht*, from *Schriften, Band 12*, edited by Christian Wagenknecht, copyright © Suhrkamp Verlag, Frankfurt am Main, 1989, translated from the German as *The Third Walpurgis Night* by Ritchie Robertson, translation copyright © Ritchie Robertson 1999, by permission of Suhrkamp Verlag.

Else Lasker-Schüler: *Der Wunderrabbiner von Barcelona* (1921) from *Prosa und Schauspiele*, edited by Friedhelm Kemp (Kösel, 1962), translated by Ritchie Robertson as 'The Wonder-Working Rabbi of Barcelona', translation copyright © Ritchie Robertson 1999, by permission of Suhrkamp Verlag; 12 Hebrew ballads (*Hebraische Balladen*, 1913) from *Your Diamond Dreams Cut Open My Arteries: Poems by Else Lasker-Schüler*, translated by Robert Newton, published for the University of North Carolina Department of Germanic Languages and Literatures. Copyright © 1980 by the University of Carolina Press, reprinted by permission of the publisher.

Thomas Mann: 'The Blood of the Volsungs' translated from the German 'Wälsungenblut' (1905), translation copyright © Ritchie Robertson, 1999.

Joseph Roth: 'The Leviathan' (1940) from *Werke*, edited by Klaus Westermann and Fritz Hackert (6 volumes, Kiepenheuer & Witsch, 1989–91), translated from the German by Ritchie Robertson, translation copyright © Ritchie Robertson 1999, by permission of the Tanja Howarth Literary Agency on behalf of Kiepenheuer & Witsch.

Nelly Sachs: selected poems from *Fahrt ins Staublose. Die Gedichte der Nelly Sachs*, copyright © Suhrkamp Verlag, Frankfurt am Main 1961, in English translations by Michael Hamburger *et al.* from *O The Chimneys*, translation copyright © 1967 and copyright renewed © 1995 by Farrar, Straus & Giroux, Inc., reprinted by permission of Farrar Straus and of Suhrkamp Verlag.

Gerschom Scholem: extract from *Tagebücher 1. Halbband 1913–1917*, edited by Karlfried Gründer and Friedrich Niewöhner, copyright © 1995 by Jüdischer Verlag, translated from the German by Ritchie Robertson, translation copyright © Ritchie Robertson, 1999.

Stefan Zweig: *Buchmendel* (1929), copyright © Williams Verlag AG, Zurich 1976, translated by Ritchie Robertson as *Book-Mendel*, by arrangement with Williams Verlag.

Despite every effort to trace and contact copyright holders of translations prior to publication this has not been possible in every case. If notified the publisher will be pleased to rectify any errors or omissions at the earliest opportunity.

The Oxford World's Classics Website

www.worldsclassics.co.uk

- Information about new titles
- Explore the full range of Oxford World's Classics
- Links to other literary sites and the main OUP webpage
- Imaginative competitions, with bookish prizes
- Peruse *Compass*, the Oxford World's Classics magazine
- Articles by editors
- Extracts from Introductions
- A forum for discussion and feedback on the series
- Special information for teachers and lecturers

www.worldsclassics.co.uk

American Literature

British and Irish Literature

Children's Literature

Classics and Ancient Literature

Colonial Literature

Eastern Literature

European Literature

History

Medieval Literature

Oxford English Drama

Poetry

Philosophy

Politics

Religion

The Oxford Shakespeare

A complete list of Oxford Paperbacks, including Oxford World's Classics, OPUS, Past Masters, Oxford Authors, Oxford Shakespeare, Oxford Drama, and Oxford Paperback Reference, is available in the UK from the Academic Division Publicity Department, Oxford University Press, Great Clarendon Street, Oxford OX2 6DP.

In the USA, complete lists are available from the Paperbacks Marketing Manager, Oxford University Press, 198 Madison Avenue, New York, NY 10016.

Oxford Paperbacks are available from all good bookshops. In case of difficulty, customers in the UK can order direct from Oxford University Press Bookshop, Freepost, 116 High Street, Oxford OX1 4BR, enclosing full payment. Please add 10 per cent of published price for postage and packing.